Effective Strategies for Communicating Insights in Business

Ross Jackson
Wittenberg University, USA

Amanda Reboulet
Jacoulet, USA

A volume in the Advances in Human Resources Management and Organizational Development (AHRMOD) Book Series

IGI Global
PUBLISHER of TIMELY KNOWLEDGE

Published in the United States of America by
IGI Global
Business Science Reference (an imprint of IGI Global)
701 E. Chocolate Avenue
Hershey PA, USA 17033
Tel: 717-533-8845
Fax: 717-533-8661
E-mail: cust@igi-global.com
Web site: http://www.igi-global.com

Library of Congress Cataloging-in-Publication Data

Names: Jackson, Ross, 1974- editor. | Reboulet, Amanda, 1984- editor.
Title: Effective strategies for communicating insights in business / Ross Jackson and Amanda Reboulet, editors.
Description: Hershey : Business Science Reference, 2020. | Includes bibliographical references and index. | Summary: "This book provides relevant theoretical frameworks, critical and creative insights and the latest empirical research findings in communication approaches within organizations. It is written for professionals who aspire to improve their understanding of effective strategies for communicating insights within organizational contexts"-- Provided by publisher.
Identifiers: LCCN 2020019414 (print) | LCCN 2020019415 (ebook) | ISBN 9781799839644 (hardcover) | ISBN 9781799858546 (paperback) | ISBN 9781799839651 (ebook)
Subjects: LCSH: Communication in organizations.
Classification: LCC HD30.3 .E334 2020 (print) | LCC HD30.3 (ebook) | DDC 658.4/5--dc23
LC record available at https://lccn.loc.gov/2020019414
LC ebook record available at https://lccn.loc.gov/2020019415

This book is published in the IGI Global book series Advances in Human Resources Management and Organizational Development (AHRMOD) (ISSN: 2327-3372; eISSN: 2327-3380)

British Cataloguing in Publication Data
A Cataloguing in Publication record for this book is available from the British Library.

Advances in Human Resources Management and Organizational Development (AHRMOD) Book Series

Patricia Ordóñez de Pablos
Universidad de Oviedo, Spain

ISSN:2327-3372
EISSN:2327-3380

Mission

A solid foundation is essential to the development and success of any organization and can be accomplished through the effective and careful management of an organization's human capital. Research in human resources management and organizational development is necessary in providing business leaders with the tools and methodologies which will assist in the development and maintenance of their organizational structure.

The **Advances in Human Resources Management and Organizational Development (AHRMOD) Book Series** aims to publish the latest research on all aspects of human resources as well as the latest methodologies, tools, and theories regarding organizational development and sustainability. The **AHRMOD Book Series** intends to provide business professionals, managers, researchers, and students with the necessary resources to effectively develop and implement organizational strategies.

Coverage

- Personnel Policies
- Organizational Behavior
- Recruitment Process
- Employment and Labor Laws
- Collaborative Method
- Skills Management
- Corporate Governance
- Compliance
- Disputes Resolution
- Workplace Discrimination

IGI Global is currently accepting manuscripts for publication within this series. To submit a proposal for a volume in this series, please contact our Acquisition Editors at Acquisitions@igi-global.com or visit: http://www.igi-global.com/publish/.

The Advances in Human Resources Management and Organizational Development (AHRMOD) Book Series (ISSN 2327-3372) is published by IGI Global, 701 E. Chocolate Avenue, Hershey, PA 17033-1240, USA, www.igi-global.com. This series is composed of titles available for purchase individually; each title is edited to be contextually exclusive from any other title within the series. For pricing and ordering information please visit http://www.igi-global.com/book-series/advances-human-resources-management-organizational/73670. Postmaster: Send all address changes to above address.

Titles in this Series

For a list of additional titles in this series, please visit: www.igi-global.com/book-series

Handbook of Research on Remote Work and Worker Well-Being in the Post-COVID-19 Era
Daniel Wheatley (University of Birmingham, UK) Irene Hardill (Northumbria University, UK) and Sarah Buglass (Nottingham Trent University, UK)
Business Science Reference • © 2021 • 420pp • H/C (ISBN: 9781799867548) • US $265.00

Cases on Critical Practices for Modern and Future Human Resources Management
Devi Akella (Albany State University, USA) Niveen Eid (Birzeit University, Palestine) and Anton Sabella (Birzeit University, Palestine)
Business Science Reference • © 2021 • 322pp • H/C (ISBN: 9781799858201) • US $195.00

Asian Women in Corporate America Emerging Research and Opportunities
Sambhavi Lakshminarayanan (Medgar Evers College, City University of New York, USA)
Business Science Reference • © 2021 • 263pp • H/C (ISBN: 9781799843849) • US $185.00

Critical Issues on Changing Dynamics in Employee Relations and Workforce Diversity
Radha Yadav (Dayananda Sagar University, India) Priyanka Panday (Doon Business School, India) and Naman Sharma (Indian Institute of Foreign Trade, India)
Business Science Reference • © 2021 • 326pp • H/C (ISBN: 9781799835158) • US $215.00

Handbook of Research on Autopoiesis and Self-Sustaining Processes for Organizational Success
Małgorzata Pańkowska (University of Economics in Katowice, Poland)
Business Science Reference • © 2021 • 432pp • H/C (ISBN: 9781799867135) • US $275.00

Designing and Implementing HR Management Systems in Family Businesses
Luca Gnan (University of Rome "Tor Vergata", Italy) and Giulia Flamini (University of Rome "Tor Vergata", Italy)
Business Science Reference • © 2021 • 368pp • H/C (ISBN: 9781799848141) • US $195.00

Transforming Human Resource Functions With Automation
Anchal Pathak (Bule Hora University, Ethiopia) and Shikha Rana (IMS Unison University, India)
Business Science Reference • © 2021 • 192pp • H/C (ISBN: 9781799841807) • US $195.00

Examining the Career Development Practices and Experiences of Immigrants
Jared Keengwe (University of North Dakota, USA) and Kenneth Kungu (Clayton State University, USA)
Business Science Reference • © 2021 • 362pp • H/C (ISBN: 9781799858119) • US $215.00

IGI Global
PUBLISHER of TIMELY KNOWLEDGE

701 East Chocolate Avenue, Hershey, PA 17033, USA
Tel: 717-533-8845 x100 • Fax: 717-533-8661
E-Mail: cust@igi-global.com • www.igi-global.com

Table of Contents

Detailed Table of Contents

This chapter explores and develops a framework to more effectively develop and utilize data and analytics-driven insights within a business. The key components of the framework are first derived from how the business, the analyst, and the computer communicate with each other. This results in clear distinctions between the language of the business and the language of the computer that positions the analyst within a conceptual chiasm. This positioning means that the analyst must first and foremost play the role of translator. The implications of this positioning within the framework arguably creates a more consistent conceptual model with more explanatory power than is typically found in popular business blogs and articles on the topic. As a result, potential strategies are developed from the framework to enable more successful data and analytics efforts, hiring practices, and communication strategies.

Analysts ignore the context that shapes and constrains communication at their peril. The rhetorical context in which analytics is enacted influences the communicative approach. In this chapter, two dominate elements are considered: 1) analytic complexity and 2) rhetorical context. Along this analytic-rhetorical spectrum, a four-square matrix is developed using these elements to describe distinct environments in which analytics is enacted. While each of the four positions are addressed for inclusion in this chapter, the focus is narrowed to an exposition of strategies for effectively communicating insights within the realm of decision analytics. Marked by a more basic analytic framework, decision analytics aims to support successful consumption and utilization at senior levels of organizations. Decision analytics differ from other types of analytics since they support the process of making decisions versus providing information. This chapter focuses on how analysts can use decision analytics to effectively communicate analytic results and insights to senior leaders of organizations.

Neuroeconomics will help solve questions that constitute a good decision, the factors that influence decisions, and how they are made. The study will expose from the experts' opinion the tangible and intangible factors that influence decisions from the perspective of the neuroeconomics. A modified Dephi method that integrates neuroeconomics is used. Neuroeconomics has the potential to explain phenomena that are considered a deviation from the prediction or behavioral bias of decision-making models in economic theory. The study exposes the opinions that have a greater degree of relevance from the experts.

In the last decade, leadership researchers have demonstrated greater interest in the concept of shared leadership, perhaps due to increasing globalization and changes in organizational cultures. This leadership style, based on inclusivity, may replace traditional structures of hierarchical leadership, or exist as a complement. Despite potential benefits, unspoken power dynamics may prevent shared leadership from being completely inclusive. Guided by three research questions and explored via an online survey, this quasi-experimental study investigated significant racial differences in the levels of overall shared leadership among IT managers of different races, specifically White, Black, Asian, and other. Descriptive statistics and an analysis of variance (ANOVA) were used to examine the responses of 200 LinkedIn IT managers employed within the United States. Findings revealed that shared leadership did not differ across racial lines, and IT managers who engage in shared leadership may maintain their competitive edge in this ultracompetitive field.

This chapter presents an exploratory case study of how Mr. Zero, a pencil developed by the Ecologically Conscious Architectural Studio (ECAS) at Auroville, India integrates product micro-culture and the concept of conscious business in deriving sustainable practices with an aim of achieving a sustainable future. Through this chapter, the authors make an attempt at developing a deeper understanding of the concept of conscious business and its importance. Finally, the authors, through a qualitative analysis of a case study of Mr. Zero, map the practice of connecting conscious business movement through the adoption of product micro-culture at ECAS to evaluate its applicability in modern day business. At the end, the authors record findings on the interplay between product micro-culture and the conscious business movement for adoption by other businesses or even adaptation by others depending upon the context for viable sustainable solutions.

Companies have to communicate with their consumers and deliver value. This is achievable in areas where consumers are educated and have access to media – and these conditions exist in markets in the developed world and also in urban areas in developing countries. But communicating to distant, scattered villages, or areas where the majority of the population is poor—areas called media-dark—poses a great challenge for business. Further, the target audience may also have no access to education or media. Communicating in these markets physically is simply not economical or feasible. This chapter describes the challenges of reaching consumers in media dark environments. It explores how companies are getting over these obstacles. Drawing on case studies describing innovative use of communication methods, it explains how initiatives can succeed in BOP areas using innovative approaches. A media communication mix is proposed for successfully reaching out to consumers in BOP markets.

With the growing popularity of science, technology, engineering, and mathematics (STEM) degrees, it is important to understand the value of a business degree coupled with a liberal arts education. Business degrees provide one with a multitude of beneficial skills including analytical thinking, problem solving, decision making, critical thinking, and project management. When coupled with a liberal arts education, business degrees become even more powerful providing young professionals with a competitive advantage by creating a more well-rounded individual with a broader education base. In addition to the benefits of a business degree, the liberal arts education provides increased leadership skills, creativity and innovation, adaptability, and both richer native communication and foreign language skills. This chapter focuses on how a liberal arts education provides one with more pronounced, stronger communication skills both written and orally, which directly provides value to businesses.

The government of India has taken multiple economic reforms such as Jan Dhan Yojna, UPI, demonetization, and digitalization moving India towards a cashless economy. The financial landscape of India has undergone a radical change with the insurance sector bearing the torch on the road of exponential growth. The insurance penetration recorded was only 3.69% in 2017. The shockingly low participation of individuals indicated the existence of challenges that need to be addressed. The first section of the chapter explores the various factors creating a dilemma for investment in the insurance sector. The other sections of the chapter focus on the current scenario of Insurance investment and the paradigm shift in the perception of customers towards insurance products. The basic purpose is to implement systems thinking of looking at the whole and holistic picture with the highest inclusion towards nation-building and improving the penetration percentage and density of insurance in India.

Being able to transcend disciplinarity in the development of effective strategies for the communication of insights in business is pivotal to progressive development and dynamic processes of change management. The unique cultural and situational specificity of military life has a long recognised and multifactorial impact on lives lived in active service, and veteran retirement is the focus of this chapter. This is highlighted via a consideration of how understanding the nature of 'self' is epistemologically determined by human capacity to make meaning of experience, to reflect on the pre-existing of historical memories, and perhaps, most significantly of all, to formulate a reflexive and proactive response to the future. The situated nature of military service provides the chapter with a means of examining the fundamental nature of knowledge and ways of knowing, interpretation, and processes of meaning making transcend several fields of individual knowledge, such as philosophy, social science, medical science, psychology, and faith.

Business communication is comprised of standards designed for efficiency. Like commodities, official correspondences are often indistinguishable. Adherence to templates provides uniformity in arrangement if not also content. When this approach works well, it is both efficient and effective. However, the universal applicability of this paradigm is suspect. Such standardization stifles creativity. When one is responsible for communicating insights in business, a radical break with convention might be beneficial in terms of gaining attention and provoking thought. Deviating from established norms is risky. Further, while one learns key tenants of business communication at work and in college, one is seldom informed as to when to stop following the rules and forge a new communicative path forward. In this chapter, existential insights are combined with communication theory to illustrate how authentic organizational communication can assist in one becoming who one is while also communicating insights in a business in a way that the form and content are strategically aligned.

Foreword

Communicating effectively is essential to organizational success. Such communication is even better when executed with a degree of style. Across the spectrum from military operations to academia and from *Fortune 500* companies to business startups, I have experienced firsthand how rare effective communication is in practice. Too many times, late in the evening as everybody else in the office has left for the day, I have found myself reviewing documents which are utterly incoherent. Making sense of such jumbled prose is made all the more challenging by the fact that by the time these communications make it to the desk of senior leaders the deadline has been reached. There is precious little time for correction. More importantly, given that one is dealing with professionals, there shouldn't be a need for substantial rework in the first place. The complexity of business today, whether in terms of advanced analytics, artificial intelligence, business strategy or simply executing work in a globally integrated environment requires improved communication throughout organizations. *Effective Strategies for Communicating Insights in Business* addresses these concerns.

What new information can possibility be presented about business communication? At first, I was skeptical. Unique to this work, is its focus on the creative and critical aspects of communicating insights within organizations. Insights are essential for breakthrough advancements and success. But without a strategic approach to effectively communicate these insights they often go unacknowledged, misunderstood, or ignored. This book that Ross Jackson and Amanda Reboulet edited is global in scope and focused on effective communication strategies in organizations. Collectively, the chapters cover benefits of learning business communication approaches in college, case study applications in organizations, as well as theoretical extensions for communicating and achieving personal and organizational success at work.

Effective Strategies for Communicating Insights in Business is an important contribution to the fields of business and communication. It contains a pragmatic mix of theory and application. Importantly, it addresses central philosophical aspects of business communication without getting bogged down in esoteric minutia. Taken together, the chapters are thought-provoking and useful. The information presented in this book is broadly relevant to those operating in or concerned with business. Students will find this information useful for expanding their thinking about business communication and providing a context for understanding its role in organizations. Those currently engaged in work execution will benefit from an improved perspective on how their daily work activities fit within this framework. Executives will benefit from its strategic perspective.

It's never too early or too late to learn to improve one's business communication skills. This book provides an exciting path forward. I hope you enjoy exploring *Effective Strategies for Communicating Insights in Business*, and that you find its content enhances your ability to communicate effectively and contributes to your organizational success.

Paul Hartman
RGBSI Aerospace & Defense, USA

Preface

What are insights and how can one effectively communicate insights within organizational contexts? Insights can be viewed beneficially as fragments of knowledge which are achieved through experience or education. More commonly, insights occur at that special *aha moment* when one might say "eureka;" a sudden instant of awareness and understanding. Organizationally, insights hold the power to shatter previously conceived ideas, notions and ways of doing business. And although insights have the potential to be transformative, communicating these paradigm-shifting ideas to organizational leaders presents a challenge. Effectively communicating insights in organizational contexts requires an ability to draw upon various areas of studies. To be successful, organizational leaders and members must make use of different strategies to effectively communicate insights at various levels within organizations. Doing so benefits from both academic and practitioner perspectives as well as perspectives from around the globe. Synthesizing creative, critical and existential insights across analytics, communication and management provides a powerful point of intersection to address this current gap in understanding and praxis.

Effective Strategies for Communicating Insights in Business provides relevant theoretical frameworks, critical and creative insights and the latest empirical research findings in communication approaches within organizations and business. This work is polyvocal, incorporating perspectives from authors from around the globe, including chapters from authors from India, Mexico, Portugal, the United Kingdom and the United States of America. This timely collection reflects how business has become increasingly global and benefits from a variety of perspectives. While this book has broad application potential within businesses and organizations, it is useful to narrow the focus of this work to its target audience.

Who would benefit from reading this book? The target audience for *Effective Strategies for Communicating Insights in Business* is professionals and researchers working in the field of analytics, business, communication and knowledge management across various disciplines. While not exhaustive, those operating in the fields of decision science, organizational behavior, political science, communications, administrative sciences and management would benefit from reflecting on the chapters presented here. Moreover, this book provides insights and support to executives concerned with improving organizational performance through the improved utilization of insights in different types of communities, environments and contexts. Lastly, business students would benefit from an early exposure to the pitfalls and potentialities associated with communicating novel insights in organizations.

As with any work of this nature, *Effective Strategies for Communicating Insights in Business* is the collective result of independent efforts. With this in mind, it is important to provide context for each individual chapter. The following paragraphs include a description of the chapter title, author, author's country of residence and a brief overview of the chapter's content and contribution. To fully understand the work, one should read the chapter, but these summaries should provide one with a useful starting point of discovery.

In "The Communication and Translation of Data and Analysis Driven Insights" (Chapter 1), Brian Heath (Heath Analytics, USA) explores and develops a framework to more effectively utilize data and analytic-driven insights within businesses. In this chapter, Heath develops a framework for how businesses, analysts and computers communicate with each other. Through this framework, Heath highlights distinctions between the language of businesses and the language of computers, in which analysts find themselves within a conceptual chiasm. Through this positioning, Heath brings focus to how analysts must play the role of translator. Heath's work is important as it creates a more consistent conceptual communication model with more explanatory power than is typically found in popular business blogs and articles on the topic. Potential strategies are developed to enable more successful data and analytics efforts, hiring practices, and communication strategies.

Amanda Reboulet (Jacoulet, USA) and Ross Jackson's (Wittenberg University, USA) "Effective Communication Approaches for Decision Analytics: An Exploration of Strategies" (Chapter 2) explores the rhetorical contexts in which analytics is enacted and finds that context influences one's communicative approach. In this chapter, Reboulet and Jackson develop a four-square matrix in which analytic complexity and rhetorical context are accounted. Reboulet and Jackson focus specifically on strategies for effectively communicating insights within the area of decision analytics. Reboulet and Jackson's work is important as it brings attention to how analysts can use decision analytics to effectively communicate analytic results and insights to senior leaders of organizations.

In "From Management 1.0 to Management 3.0 and Beyond" (Chapter 3), Eduardo Espinheira (Porto Business School, Portugal) and Fernando Almeida (Polytechnic Institute of Gaya, Portugal) explore how traditional management models reveal issues with the introduction of unnecessary hierarchies, slow decision making that have left a large number of workers out of the process of seeking efficiency and growth. Faced with these concerns, Espinheira and Almeida present third generation of management models focused on agility and collaboration. Within Management 3.0, focus shifts from hierarchies and functions towards the way people behave and relate. The work of Espinheira and Almeida is important because through their analysis of this phenomenon, along with the various dimensions of Management 3.0, one is able to understand better the practices and challenges that are posed in its business implementation with special focus on the role of people and information and communication technologies.

Julio Silva (University of Algarve, Portugal), Silvia Fernandes (University of Algarve, Portugal) and Paula Ventura Martins' (University of Algarve, Portugal) "Process Improvement Through Visual Management: An Insight Management Tool?" (Chapter 4) explores how departments in enterprises can benefit from visual management (VM) methods. As developed by Silva, Fernandes and Martins, the VM framework is useful in terms of clarity, motivation, process review, real knowledge of results, and correction procedures. When used in conjunction with an insight management (IM) platform, Silva, Fernandes and Martins show that it is possible to integrate data in diverse ways to produce visual analytics. The work of Silva, Fernandes and Martins is relevant for exploring new strategies based on the indexes envisioned to replicate the positive results throughout organizations.

In "Neutralizing Maleficent Effects of COVID-19 Through Entrepreneurship: Peeping Through the Lens of Communication" (Chapter 5), Roshan Lal Sharma (Central University of Himachal Pradesh, India) and Manpreet Arora (Central University of Himachal Pradesh, India) explore how entrepreneurs are regarded as the leaders of socio-economic, industrial and business development, and are the employment generators contributing to economic growth. Sharma and Arora examine the current scenario caused by COVID-19 pandemic in which people across the world lost their jobs and has led to an inclination towards entrepreneurial activities in 2020. This chapter addresses the concept of entrepreneurship with special reference to communication. The work of Sharma and Arora is important as it highlights challenges and issues in the post-pandemic world as well as it examines the use of the term 'entrepreneurship' by the general public on social media such as Twitter in particular with a view to work out its implications.

Jovanna Nathalie Cervantes-Guzmán's (Centro Universitario de Ciencias Económico Administrativas Universidad de Guadalajara, Mexico) "Neuroeconomics as a Factor in the Decision-Making of Women Entrepreneurs in Developing Countries" (Chapter 6) explores how neuroeconomics will help solve questions that constitute a good decision, the factors that influence decisions and how they are made. Cervantes-Guzmán exposes tangible and intangible factors that influence decisions from the perspective of the neuroeconomics methodological approach. This work of Cervantes-Guzmán is important as the study finds that neuroeconomics has the potential to explain phenomena that are considered a deviation from the prediction or behavioral bias of decision-making models in economic theory and exposes the opinions that have a greater degree of relevance from the experts.

In "Racial Differences in Perceptions of Shared Leadership Among IT Managers" (Chapter 7), Eugene J. Petrie (University of Phoenix, USA), Auslyn G. Nieto (University of Phoenix, USA) and Kate Andrews (Walden University, USA) explore racial differences in the levels of overall shared leadership among IT managers. Petrie, Nieto and Andrews present that shared leadership is based on inclusivity, but that despite potential benefits, unspoken power dynamics may prevent shared leadership from being completely inclusive. Through an online survey, Petrie, Nieto and Andrews' quasi-experimental study investigated significant racial differences in the levels of overall shared leadership among IT managers of different races. Statistics and an analysis of variance (ANOVA) were used to examine the responses of 200 LinkedIn IT managers employed within the United States. The work of Petrie, Nieto and Andrews is important as their findings revealed that shared leadership did not differ across racial lines, and IT managers who engage in shared leadership may maintain their competitive edge in this ultracompetitive field.

Pinaki Nandan Pattnaik (NALSAR University of Law, India) and Mahendra Kumar Shukla's (NALSAR University of Law, India) "Communicating Conscious Business Practice at Ecologically Conscious Architectural Studio: A Case of Mr. Zero" (Chapter 8) presents an exploratory case study of how Mr. Zero, a pencil developed by the Ecologically Conscious Architectural Studio (ECAS) at Auroville, India integrates product micro-culture and the concept of conscious business in deriving sustainable practices with an aim of achieving a sustainable future. Through this chapter, Pattnaik and Shukla develop a deeper understanding of the concept of conscious business and its importance. Through their qualitative analysis of a case study of Mr. Zero, Pattnaik and Shukla map the practice of connecting Conscious Business Movement through the adoption of product micro-culture at ECAS to evaluate it applicability in modern day business. The work of Pattnaik and Shukla is important as it records findings on the interplay between product micro-culture and the conscious business movement for adoption by other businesses or even adaptation by others depending upon the context for viable sustainable solutions.

In "Communicating in Media Dark Areas" (Chapter 9), Dinesh Kumar (Jagran Lakecity University, India) and Punam Gupta (Career College, India) explore the necessity of companies communicating with their consumers to deliver value. Kumar and Gupta explain that this is achievable in areas where consumers are educated and have access to media and that these conditions exist in markets in the developed world and also in urban areas in developing countries. However, as Kumar and Gupta note, communicating to distant, scattered villages, or areas where the majority of the population is poor – areas called media-dark – poses a challenge for business. Further complicating this situation, Kumar and Gupta explain that the target audience may also have no access to education or media and that communicating in these markets physically is simply not economical or feasible. In this chapter, Kumar and Gupta describe the challenges of reaching consumers in media-dark environments and explore how companies are getting over these obstacles. The work of Kumar and Gupta is important as it draws on case studies describing innovative use of communication methods to propose a media communication mix is proposed for successfully reaching out to consumers in media dark areas.

Rachel Wilson (Wittenberg University, USA) and Amanda Reboulet's (Jacoulet, USA) "Benefits of a Liberal Arts Education on Effective Business Communication" (Chapter 10) explores the communicative benefits to be derived from obtaining a business degree as part of a liberal arts education. As explained by Wilson and Reboulet, business degrees provide one with a multitude of beneficial skills including: analytical thinking, problem solving, decision making, critical thinking and project management. The research of Wilson and Reboulet suggests that when coupled with a liberal arts education, business degrees become even more powerful providing young professionals with a competitive advantage by creating a more well-rounded individual with a broader education base. In addition to the benefits of a business degree, Wilson and Reboulet contend that a liberal arts education provides increased leadership skills, creativity and innovation, adaptability, and both richer native communication and foreign language skills. The work of Wilson and Reboulet is important as it brings focus on how a liberal arts education provides one with more pronounced, stronger communication skills both written and orally, which directly provides value to businesses.

In "Prelude of Investment: Freshman's Dilemma in the Insurance Sector Investments" (Chapter 11), Shilpi Gupta (Amity University Chhattisgarh, India) and Monica Shrivastava (SSTC-SSGI, India) explore the dilemma for investment in the Insurance sector in India. As explained by Gupta and Shrivastava, the government of India has taken multiple economic reforms to move India towards a cashless economy. Gupta and Shrivastava note that low participation indicates the existence of challenges that need to be addressed. To do this, Gupta and Shrivastava first examine various factors creating a dilemma for investment in the Insurance sector and then turn their attention towards the current scenario of Insurance investment and the paradigm shift in the perception of customers towards Insurance products. The work of Gupta and Shrivastava is important as it seeks to implement systems thinking to look at a holistic picture with the highest inclusion towards nation-building and improving the penetration percentage and density of Insurance in India.

Catherine Hayes (University of Sunderland, United Kingdom), Colonel Ian Corrie (University of Cumbria, United Kingdom), and Brigadier Toby Lloyd Rowland's (Defense Medical Service, United Kingdom) "Driving Insights via Processes of Socioemotional Being and Becoming" (Chapter 12) explores the multifactorial impact on lives lived in active service and veteran retirement. As explained by Hayes, Corrie and Rowland, being able to transcend disciplinarity in the development of effective strategies for the communication of insights in business is pivotal to progressive development and dynamic processes of change management. Hayes, Corrie and Rowland bring focus to the unique cultural and situational specificity of military life to bring focus on how understanding the nature of *self* is epistemologically determined by human capacity to make meaning of experience, to reflect on the pre-existing of historical memories, and to formulate a reflexive and proactive response to the future. The work of Hayes, Corrie and Rowland is important as it makes use of the situated nature of military service as a means to examine the fundamental nature of knowledge and ways of knowing, interpretation and processes of meaning making to transcend several fields of individual knowledge, such as philosophy, social science, medical science, psychology and faith.

In “Becoming Who You Are Through Authentic Organizational Communication” (Chapter 13), Ross Jackson (Wittenberg University, USA) explores aspects of authentic organizational communication along with the strategic alignment of the form and function of business communications. As described by Jackson, business communication is comprised of standards designed for efficiency. In this chapter, Jackson examines the tensions between the benefits achieved through adherence to organizational templates and those which can only be achieved through deviation. Specifically, Jackson notes that standardization stifles creativity and a radical break with convention might be beneficial for gaining attention and provoking thought. Along this path, Jackson explores the risks associated with deviating from conventional norms. The work of Jackson is important as it brings focus to business readers existential insights combined with communication theory to illustrate how authentic organizational communication can assist in self-awareness while also communicating insights in a business in a way that the form and content are strategically aligned.

Collectively, the chapters contained in *Effective Strategies for Communicating Insights in Business* make contributions to the fields of business and communication. As described, each chapter in this book has a unique focus and captures a perspective from around the globe. While each chapter is distinct, unity and coherence are achieved by the singular focus on understanding and overcoming the persistent challenges associated with communicating insights in business organizations. Across a spectrum of methodological approaches, to include theoretical speculation, quantitative analysis and case studies, and organizational goals, including efficiency, sustainability and existential authenticity, each chapter contributes something distinct and useful as one explores how to make meaningful contributions to organizational success through improved communication.

As one explores these chapters, we encourage active engagement with the text. Take notes, ask questions and bounce the perspectives presented in this book against your own experiences. While care was given to the sequence of chapters, one is always free to determine strategically the best path forward. We hope you find information of value in the book and that through your reading you are able to express your insights more effectively.

Ross Jackson
Wittenberg University, USA

Amanda Reboulet
Jacoulet, USA

Acknowledgment

Accomplishing anything of merit benefits from the support and encouragement from a myriad of people. We would like to acknowledge the hard work of the contributing authors. This book would not exist without their contributions. Additionally, we appreciate their willingness to review chapters and assist in making the chapters more rigorous, clear, and compelling. Special appreciation goes to Dr. Tim Bode (Wittenberg University), Dr. Linda Burrs (Step Up to Success!), Dr. Brian Heath (Heath Analytics), Dr. Jason Jackson (Jackson Research Institute), Dr. Edward Slover (Grand Canyon University) and Dr. Wendy Gradwohl Wells (West Shore Community College) for their gracious reviews and editorial advice. We are grateful to Dr. Paul Hartman (RGBSI Aerospace & Defense) for writing the forward to this book. To all those who contributed to this work, named and unnamed, thank you.

Chapter 1
The Communication and Translation of Data and Analytics-Driven Insights

Brian Heath
Heath Analytics, USA

ABSTRACT

This chapter explores and develops a framework to more effectively develop and utilize data and analytics-driven insights within a business. The key components of the framework are first derived from how the business, the analyst, and the computer communicate with each other. This results in clear distinctions between the language of the business and the language of the computer that positions the analyst within a conceptual chiasm. This positioning means that the analyst must first and foremost play the role of translator. The implications of this positioning within the framework arguably creates a more consistent conceptual model with more explanatory power than is typically found in popular business blogs and articles on the topic. As a result, potential strategies are developed from the framework to enable more successful data and analytics efforts, hiring practices, and communication strategies.

INTRODUCTION

Leveraging data and analytics within businesses is increasing important to maintain competitive advantage and to maximize the utility of the unprecedented amount of data being generate by not only customers but by competitors themselves. The emergence of data has largely created and proliferated an entirely new language from which to understand the world. While this new language is littered with potential ripe fruit for business picking, it is a very different way to think and speak. It is heavy in logic, mathematics, statistics, precision, and is much more akin to computer programming languages than anything spoken today in business settings. This implies that a person fluent in data and analytics must possess the training and aptitude of these highly technical disciplines that requires years of education and on-the-job training. Suffice to say, most of the workforce today does not have nor will likely possess this fluency. However, the expectation and current trajectory is that data and analytics will be as

DOI: 10.4018/978-1-7998-3964-4.ch001

pervasive in business as organizational charts, meetings, and coffee. This creates a critical point that is widely talked about in one form or another on "pop-business" articles and blogs: how do you build and utilize data and analytics in today's business climate.

Each of these blogs, books, and experts has a theory as to how to build and effectively utilize data and analytics, and many highlight the importance data and analytics communication strategies. The typical communication strategies proposed focuses on traditional methodologies utilized to describe complex topics from one person to another person with some emphasis placed on the importance of understanding the technical foundations of field (or at least the terminology). A prime example is the work of Davenport and Kim (2013). These strategies mimic approaches commonly used by journalists who simplify mathematical, scientific, and philosophical articles into headlines for the common public. However, a key missing component of these strategies is that the language of data and analytics doesn't live in the realm of person to person communication as data largely lives within computers. Thus, the truest communication channel in the language of data and analytics is between computer and person, not between people. The role of the analyst (i.e. person fluent in data and analytics and business speak) within the business is that of a translator: they listen to the language of the business, translate that message into the data and analytics language within a computer, receive a response, and translate that response back into the language of the business. This is fundamentally different than the standard strategies recommended in data and analytics communications. These strategies emphasize simplification of the message to meet understood business needs while this "analyst as translator" paradigm involves interpretations between languages that are primarily incompatible.

To understand how the data and analytics language is largely incompatible with business language, first consider that within the data and analytics language (or that of the computer) there is no emotion or feeling. However, by human necessity any language within business to communicate between people requires or, at the very least, implies emotion. While some may not want to believe the importance of emotion in human communication, consider the rare case studies when a person has suffered a brain injury or tumor that 'shuts off' the emotional part of their brain. These people are completely incapable of making any decision to the point that it will paralyze them (Damasio, 2005). This include even the most mundane tasks such as deciding what clothes to wear that day. The obvious implications of no emotions in business communication means that nothing will ever be decided and highlights a major challenge for the analyst as a translator.

Another consideration in understanding the incompatibility of these languages is that there are gaps in vocabulary simply because the data and analytics language in only concerned with a small space with respect to spoken languages. For example, there is no concept of "maximizing a business strategy" within data. The analyst must translate this into a query that entirely consists of 0's and 1's and statistically aggregate that result into a mathematical entity that might translate to a business strategy abstraction. This is equivalent to there being no word in Spanish for the English word "insight." In this case, an interpreter must figure out how to convey meanings from completely different paradigms of thought.

Ultimately, the incompatibility of business and data and analytics language may be more fully explained and realized by considering the concept of linguistic determinism. Linguistic determinism hypothesizes that languages themselves limit and determine human thought and knowledge. As Nietzsche wrote "We cease to think if we do not want to do it under linguistic constraints" (Deutscher, 2016). There are two studies that highlight the potential power that language has on limiting our thoughts. The first is a study of people who grew up speaking Hopi, a native North American language, and their inability to think about time because their language lack verb tenses (Whorf, 1956). The second is a study of those who spoke Pirahã, a native South American Amazonia language, and their struggle with mathematics because their language lacks quantities and numbers (Frank et al, 2008). If indeed the language of business and the language of data and analytics are different, then we can infer that there may be utterly incomprehensible concepts, thoughts, and knowledge that monolingual native speakers of either language will never understand about the other language. If you've ever been in a business meeting between monolingual business professionals and monolingual analysts, then you'll immediately recognize where the frustration and confusion came from as both parties complain that the other doesn't "get it." It's because they don't "get it" and their language may prevent them from ever "getting it" entirely.

When examining data and analytics as a language and the analyst as a translator, it should perhaps be no surprise that data and analytics within business has yet to reach its fully marketed potential. The technology, data, and desire are there, but the ability to communicate is a much more complex problem than is given credit for. From this perspective, first a framework will be proposed to more effectively deliver data and analytics driven insight. Next the framework will be used to provide insights into potentially effective communication strategies for data and analytics. This section will explore possible reasons that data and analytics strategies and initiatives fail, the potential attributes of successful analysts to support effective data driven communication, how the business can better communicate with the analyst, and how the analyst can better communicate with the business.

A DATA AND ANALYTICS COMMUNICATION FRAMEWORK

The previous section highlighted several key concepts that are important towards building a data and analytics communication framework. First, the language of the business is primarily a person to person communication channel and the language of data and analytics is primarily a person to computer communication channel. As a result, an analyst can be thought of as a translator between a person and a computer. They translate the message of the business into the computer and translate the results from to computer back to the business. This will require a more complex way of thinking about how to effectively utilize and communicate data and analytics within business. Second, the language of business and the language of data and analytics are incompatible in many ways that include but are not limited to emotional expressions, untranslatable vocabulary, and conceptualizations. This will require a communication framework that identifies the known gaps between languages so strategies can be developed to mitigate these incompatibilities.

To start, we must begin with a solid foundation and extend it. In 1948, Shannon identified what has been widely accepted as the eight steps present in all communications. These steps are:

1. Motivation
2. Composition
3. Encoding
4. Transmission
5. Noise
6. Reception
7. Decoding
8. Interpretation

Communication begins with some motivation or reason for communication. In our case, we will assume that the business has identified a pain point in the organization and would like that pain point to be resolved with the help of analytics. With this motivation, the communication process begins. The next step is composing the message that will be sent. Here the business will formulate the motivating pain point being felt into, ideally, a more precise expression of the situation and request of the analyst. Next the composed message must be encoded into the means by which that message will sent. In the business setting, the message is typically encoded into an email or verbal speech. After the message has been encoded, it is transmitted. In our example, the business decided to encode their message in a written-out email, and they transmitted it via the internet to the analyst. As the message is being transmitted, there is a chance that noise may interfere with the quality of the message. This noise could come in the form of the email becoming corrupted and unreadable or through human activities such as speaking too softly to be properly heard. The next communication step is the message being received. For our analyst, they now see the message from the business in their inbox. Now the analyst must decode the message. This involves opening the email and reading it. At this point the message is in the analyst's head, but they have yet to interpret it. The final step is then for the analyst to interpret and attempt to make sense of the message.

In an ideal case, the business has effectively constructed a message that the analyst received and understood. Unfortunately, this is not always the case, so the analyst may need to follow the exact same process to send a message to the business to ask a clarifying question. One could see how this process could go back and forth many times until a both parties agree on an action to take. This example highlighted the person to person communication steps, but as this is a general communication framework, we can also use it for the other side of the analyst's job of person to computer communication.

Keeping with our example, the analyst has had several rounds of person to person communication and feels that they are ready to begin communicating with the computer to accomplish the agreed to task. First, the analyst has conceived of a data query that might help them answer the business's question. Next the analyst composes a more well structure expression of what must be done. Then they begin to encode that data query into a series of computer instructions. Next the analyst hits "run" and transmits the instructions for a computer program to run. Luckily no noise occurred during the transmission. Now the computer program has to receive the instructions, decode them, and interpret them. From here, hopefully the analyst has formulated message well enough that the computer understands and can execute the instructions. Just as with our person to person example, the computer and analyst may go back and forth communicating with each other via this same framework until the analyst is satisfied.

So far, the business and analyst have gone through several rounds of communications and the analyst and computer have gone through several rounds of communications. Now, the analyst must go through several rounds of communications with the business to relay the outcomes of the analyst's work with the computer. When put together, this represents a more complete data and analytics communication framework. Business to analyst, analyst to computer, and analyst back to business. Figure 1 extends and visualizes Shannon's communication steps to serve as a preliminary operating framework for communicating data and analytics driven insights.

With the more complete framework of data and analytics communication, the incompatibility of the language of the business with the language of data and analytics can be addressed. This incompatibility comes in at least three forms. First, the language of business and business decision making depends upon emotional expressions while the language of the computer has no construct of emotional expression. Second, the language of the business and the language of the computer have untranslatable elements, the vocabulary overlap simple does not exist. Ask an analyst to find the best customers and they will have to completely define a statistical equation and label it "best customers" because the computer and data has no inherent term for best customer. This data and analytics version of "best customer" is a compiled interpretation of the original business term and often not completely representative of the business term meaning. In other words, the computer interpretation does not grok the business meaning. Third, the language of the business and the language of computer are each conceptually constrained by their own language, making some messages between the two parties completely uninterpretable.

Figure 1. Preliminary data and analytics communication framework

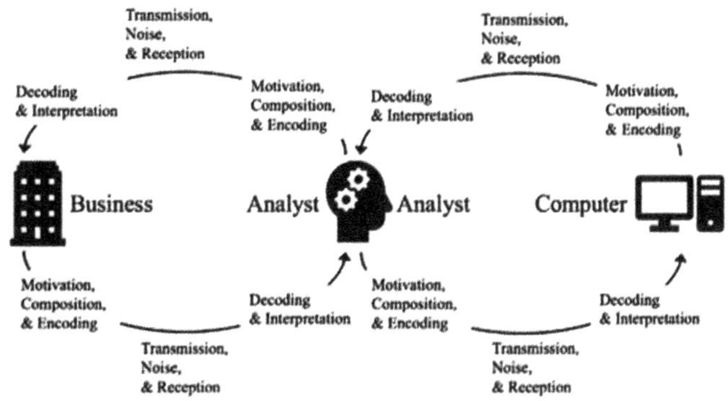

All three of these incompatibilities can be pinned to the Motivation and Interpretation steps of the communication model. Essentially, messages can easily pass between the parties, but the messages either seem unclear or not understood. The business asks for a report showing the "best customers" and the computer doesn't know what a "best customer" is. The analyst translates as best they can so the computer can understand and then sends a report back to the business. The business doesn't understand what all the numbers mean and why that was the response to their request. The business decides to send another message asking for clarity and repeating the need for a report about the "best customers." The cycle begins again.

To represent this incompatibility dynamic several elements must be added to the data and analytics communication framework. First, a dynamic must be added the shows the uniqueness of how the business and the computer handle the motivation and interpretation steps of communication. Here the business's motivation and interpretation steps are driven by emotional expressions while the computer's motivation and interpretation steps are driven purely by logical expressions. Second, the role of analyst as a translator between the business and the computer needs to be added as the primary driver of their motivation and interpretation communication steps. Finally, a conceptual misalignment needs to be added to represent the potential misalignment in thoughts and knowledge between the business and the computer. In the framework this is shown by having the two communication circles existing in separate conceptual frames of reference with the work of the analyst to cross the conceptual chiasm. Figure 2 displays the final data and analytics communication framework that will inform and guide the remainder of discussion towards achieving success in data and analytics driven insights.

Figure 2. Final data and analytics communication framework

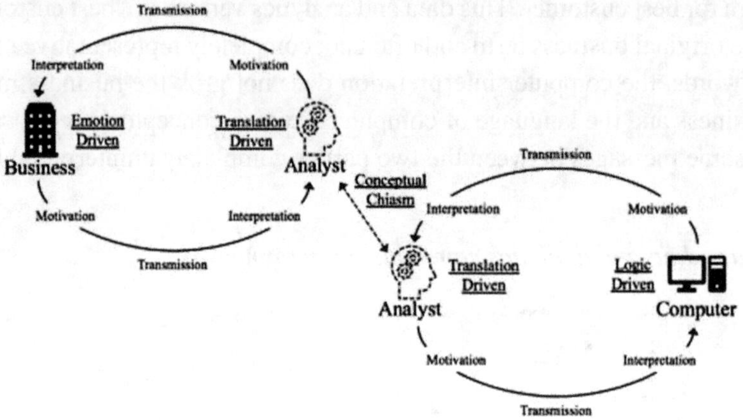

The developed data and analytics communication framework provides a more complete conceptual understanding of how the business, the analyst, and the computer work together. Thus, commonly accepted strategic business heuristics and perspectives about how to achieve success in making data and analytics driven decisions can not only be more well understood but also extended. Where the space before may have seemed cluttered with many anecdotes and rules-of-thumbs, the hope is that this conceptual grounding begins to organize them into a more coherent message. For this framework as a conceptual model to be valuable it must improve a person's understanding of the system, facilitate more effective communication between stakeholders, provide a reference point for exploration, and improve collaboration (Kung & Solvberg, 1986). The following section hopes to achieve this by utilizing the framework as a conceptual model to build and explain strategies for effective data and analytics communication.

TOWARDS EFFECTIVE DATA AND ANALYTICS COMMUNICATION STRATEGIES

Potentially effective data and analytics communication strategies can be developed and better understood based on the conceptual model displayed in the data and analytics communication framework. While this framework could constitute nearly endless observations, explorations, and areas to research, only a comparably few strategies and implications will be explored in this section. Readers and researchers are encouraged to extend, explore, and challenge the framework itself further.

WHY MANY DATA STRATEGIES FAIL

A quick internet search for business data and analytics strategies will show a plethora of articles and software vendors advocating that businesses need to be closer to their data. Getting closer to the data is thought to improve efficiency and quality by making it faster for decisions to be made and reducing the number of steps between the business and the data. From the data and analytics communication framework, one can immediately see where this line of thinking comes from. From a simplistic operations perspective, decreasing the number of communication steps between the business and the computer (where the data resides) should improve speed and quality. It improves speed because less steps means less time between messages. It improves quality because noise may be introduced in each communication step. Reducing the number of steps reduces the likelihood of noise being introduced into a message and potentially causing errors.

All of this seems logical, so how do consultants and software vendors propose to get businesses closer to the data? Most often their strategy is to make the data more accessible. Consultants and software vendors typically make the data more accessible for the business by either removing the analyst or minimize the role of the analyst via "smarter" software. This "smarter" software attempts to replicate the role of the analyst by making it easier for business users to query data and conduct analyses themselves, regardless of experience or with minimal training. Businesses have bought into the idea and it is estimated that by 2022 United States businesses will spend $260 billion per year on data and analytics (James, 2018). Yet, it seems that after many attempts that businesses are still largely failing in their efforts to get closer to their data and become data-driven (Bean & Davenport, 2019).

Reviewing the data and analytics communication framework quickly reveals the flaw in this strategy to get the business closer to the data. The main failure point is it assumes that the work of the analyst can mostly be replaced by "smarter" software. In other words, it assumes that the computer can be programmed well enough to perform the work of the analyst. But it has been demonstrated that the language of the computer (the "smarter" software) is not the language of the business. There are conceptual, vocabulary, and expression gaps between the business and the computer. Perhaps with enough time and effort the computer could be sufficiently programmed to interpret, anticipate, and express emotions as well as handle vague business terminologies, but this is not the current state and would likely represent a complete paradigm shift in computer science that seems some time off into the future. Fixing the computer side of this language barrier seems unlikely. Therefore, this seems like an ineffective approach and explains why businesses continue to fail to get closer to the data and become data driven.

So, how might the framework help in identifying a potentially more fruitful approach in reducing the distance between the business and their data? Since teaching the computer to speak business has failed, the most apparent alternative strategy is to teach the business to speak the language of the computer. This would achieve the same result of removing or minimize the analyst as the entity between the computer and the business to improve speed and quality. However, this is likely a much more expensive and time intensive solution. While it would enable the business to be data-driven and completely fluent in data and analytics, it would require teaching and training everyone within the business to the language of data, analytics, and the computer. Thus, a pure business-side strategy is likely not practical because it would take too long and cost too much.

At one extreme the strategic communication approach to the make computers smarter misses critical understanding of the language of data and analytics and the other extreme training everyone in the business to essentially become an analyst is costly and would take too long. The synthesis of these extremes is to not immediately eliminate the analyst, but to leverage them to bring the two languages together until the marginal costs and returns in the current paradigm are optimized. With this strategy, the analyst's central point is positioned as a necessary advantage and not a perceived non-value-added step. Here the role of analyst is to not only provide translation, but to work with the business to increase their technical language skills and to work with software engineers to improve the business lexicon of the computer. No one else is better positioned to perform this work than the analyst.

Initially this strategy will resemble business as usual. The business will communicate with the analyst, the analyst will communicate with the computer, and the analyst will communicate the results back to the business. How this eventually changes will be reflected by strategies that reorient the analyst to have additional roles within the organization. For example, a third of their time should be spent on training the business how to speak data and analytics, another third should be spent on the development of "smarter" software, and the final third should be spent as the translator. Over time the amount of analytical resources and the mixture of their time should shift as both the computer and business become "smarter" via the analysts. This shift may eventually result in a new equilibrium such that there are less analysts overall but that the remaining analysts are highly skilled in their translator role. These highly skilled translator analysts will at some point become more cost effective as a specialized resource than what it would take to completely cross the conceptual chiasm from the business or computer side.

THE ANALYSTS TO HIRE

A good strategy without the right person to implement it will fail. The previous section dove into a strategy that focused on how to revalue the analyst to achieve an effective data and analytics insight driven strategy. The analyst's role in this strategy continues with the theme of thinking of them as a translator. But what exactly are the attributes of these analysts to achieve this strategy? To answer this question let's consider further how the analysts fits into the framework.

The analyst is first and foremost a translator in the framework. The analyst exists within the conceptual chiasm between the business and the computer. They must be able to effectively interpret a message from the business, recompose that message into something that the computer can interpret, receive and interpret the return message from the computer, recompose the computer's message into something that the business can interpret, and then send that message to the business. All of this work requires that the analyst be not only an effective communicator but also fluent in multiple languages. In this case, the language of business and the language of the computer.

The ability to manage and understand the language of the business and language of the computer is especially non-trivial when considering what drives each entity and the conceptual chiasm that exists between the two. On one side, the business is driven to act by emotion, but the computer is incapable of receiving or sending emotional expressions. Thus, the analyst must capture and infer logical meaning of a request from the business and then must present a result to the business that will illicit an emotional response. As highlighted earlier, emotion is required by humans to make even mundane decisions. Here a successful analyst must be skilled in not only logic to work with the computer, but they must also possess high emotional intelligence to not only translate and understand emotion but to effectively work with businesspeople.

Together, some core skills of a successful analyst as a translator are:

- Effective communicator
- Fluent in multiple languages (human and computer)
- High emotional intelligence
- High logic skills

Typically, within any organization there are many more technical skills like Python or SQL listed as core analyst abilities. While there is a pragmatic reality to these, they often are not sufficient for an analyst to be successful as a translator for the business. They will do work, but both parties will be frustrated as they won't speak each other's language. Elevating the non-technical skills to be the primary sought after attributes for analysts has the potential to transform how the business communicates and utilizes data and analytics for decision making.

HOW TO BETTER COMMUNICATE TO THE ANALYST

The ability of the business and the analyst to effectively communicate with each other is critical to achieving successful data and analytics driven decisions. As shown in the framework, this communication is bidirectional with potential failure points on both the business and the analyst side. This section explores how the business might better communicate with the analyst given the position of the business and the analyst within the data and analytics communication framework.

For the business to better communicate with the analyst, the business must first recognize their role in the framework. First, the business is the primary driver of the communication. This is not to say that the analyst or the computer wouldn't ever begin a communication process. It is just much more likely that the business will be starting communications as they are charged with the responsibility of the entire organization. As the primary driver, the business is motivated to initiate communication. This communication propagates to the analyst and the computer. If the initial message is unclear or in error, then it will propagate and cause organizational confusion. Thus, the business must take care that any message they send will carry with it costs, benefits, efficiencies, and inefficiencies. It is crucial that the business strongly consider the weight of their messages.

After understanding the importance of their messages, the business should reflect on the motivation and composition of any message before transmitting it to the analyst. This reflection should come from two perspectives. The first is that they are motivated to communicate from an emotion frame of reference. For example, the business observed something, didn't like it, and it made them decide to send a message to the analyst. While a good analyst can understand emotion motivations, it is important for the business to recognize that the analyst must translate this message into a system devoid of the concept of emotion. Therefore, the business should reflect on and fully explain the motivation in the message to the analyst. This will ensure that the analyst has the full context and can do their best to translate the business's message into something computable. The second perspective that the business should reflect on is that they are composing a message in a language that is in many ways incompatible to the language that the analyst will be using with the computer. The business's language is highly imprecise and vague by comparison to any computer language. The more precise and clear the language of the business's message, then the more likely it will be that the analyst can correctly interpret and translate the message of the business. Therefore, the business should attempt to be as precise, logical, and clear in the composition of their message to the analyst as possible.

HOW TO BETTER COMMUNICATE TO THE BUSINESS

The other side of the effective communication coin is how the analyst can better communicate to the business. This is where the vast majority of "pop-business" and "pop-analytics" blogs and books spend their time. They convey many ideas, theories, and strategies for the analyst to employ that allows them to better communicate to the business. From the data and analytics communication framework, several key foundational elements are exposed for the analyst to consider when communicating with the business.

Similar to how to better communicate with the analyst, it is important for the analyst to understand their role and the role of the business. The analyst should view themselves as a translator first. They are to interpret the message from the business, translate that into a message for the computer, receive the results, and then translate that back to the business. To be an effective translator, the analyst must not only know the language of the computer but, more importantly, also the language of the business. From the framework many of the features of the business language can be understood. First, they are emotion driven. Second, their language has conceptual incompatibilities with the computer. So, as a translator the analyst should respond in the same language as which they were communicated with by the business. For example, the analyst shouldn't reply to a message from the business with a message that are essentially lines of computer code. This is not a translation. Instead, the analyst should respond with a message that is conceptually understood by the business and contains emotion elements for the business to respond to. However, this is often easier said than done because of the pure quantitative, cold, and precise nature of the messages that come from the computer.

It could be said that the role of the analyst in the framework is part art and part science. The science side comes primarily in working with the computer, but art side comes primarily in working with the business. The artwork of analyst is particularly clear when considering how they must transform logical and systematic results into something that evokes the emotion needed for a decision to occur. As the analyst is most often dealing with data, one of the most common techniques to evoke emotion and effectively communicate data from a computer is via data visualizations. Visualization are particularly good means of communications to the business because they can compress large amounts of quantitative data and attract and stimulate the attention of the viewer to support decision making (Tufte, 1983). Furthermore, data visualizations may be considered a piece of art themselves and art is well known for evoking emotional responses.

While data visualizations are an effective method for communicating to the business, they are often not sufficient by themselves. They must be combined and correctly positioned with an understanding of what the business is looking for and feeling. This positioning is one of the primary challenges that the analyst faces and defines the emotion context of the message that the business will receive. It should be made clear that there is largely no scientific consensus on the definition of emotion, but we know that it is needed to make a decision. This does not mean that the message should be positioned to invoke what typically may be thought of as strong emotions like extreme fear, anger, or joy. Instead, more subtle approaches may be more than sufficient as long as that message is positioned with relation to the business's circumstances, mood, or relationships. To contrast this, consider that the computer and the data has no concept or requirement to decide what to do based on their equivalent circumstances, mood, or relationships.

CONCLUSION

Data and analytics have been positioned as a critical element in any business's strategy. However, unlocking the value has proven to be a challenge. This chapter has created a data and analytics communication framework as a conceptual model for how to better develop, communicate, and operationalize the insights that come from the data and analytics function. The primary conclusion from the framework was identifying the language barriers between the business and the computer which positioned the analyst within a conceptual chiasm as a translator. The analyst must both effectively communicate to an emotion driven business and to a logic driven computer. As a result of this relationship, several implications were derived and explored. A better strategy to spread data and analytics insight driven decisions within a business was developed, the attributes of a successful analyst as translator were identified to improve hiring, and better communication methods were identified for the business and the analyst. This is certainly only some of the insights that can be derived from the data and analytics communication framework. One could further extend or challenge this conceptual model based on other strategic communication models and strategies highlighted in Plowman & Wilson (2018), Raupp & Hoffjann (2012), and Heide et al. (2018). However, the proposed conceptual model shows the power and value of the framework in developing more cohesive and fruitful outcomes when communicating data and analytics insights within the business setting. Future research should focus on validating or invalidating this conceptual model in a pragmatic effort to deliver value to business and management.

REFERENCES

Bean, R., & Davenport, T. H. (2019). *Companies Are Failing in Their Efforts to Become Data-Driven.* https://hbr.org/2019/02/companies-are-failing-in-their-efforts-to-become-data-driven

Damasio, A. R. (1994). *Descartes' Error.* G.P. Putnam's Sons.

Davenport, T. H., & Kim, J. (2013). *Keeping Up with the Quants: Your Guide to Understanding and Using Analytics.* Harvard Business School Publishing Corporation.

Deutscher, G. (2016). *Through the Language Glass: Why the World Looks Different in Other Languages.* Cornerstone Digital.

Frank, M. C., Everett, D. L., Fedorenko, E., & Gibson, E. (2008). Number as a cognitive technology: Evidence from Pirahã language and cognition. *Cognition, 108*(3), 819–824. doi:10.1016/j.cognition.2008.04.007 PMID:18547557

Heide, M., von Platen, S., Simonsson, C., & Falkheimer, J. (2018). Expanding the Scope of Strategic Communication: Towards a Holistic Understanding of Organizational Complexity. *International Journal of Strategic Communication, 12*(4), 452–468. doi:10.1080/1553118X.2018.1456434

James, L. (2018). *Big data and business analytics spend to reach US$260 billion in 2022.* https://www.technologyrecord.com/Article/big-data-and-business-analytics-spend-to-reach-us260-billion-in-2022-72124

Kung, C. H., & Solvberg, A. (1986). Activity Modeling and Behavior Modeling. In *Proceedings of the IFIP WG 8.1 Working Conference on Comparative Review of Information Systems Design Methodologies: Improving the Practice*, (145-171). North-Holland.

Plowman, K. D., & Willson, C. (2018). Strategy and Tactics in Strategic Communication: Examining their Intersection with Social Media Use. *International Journal of Strategic Communication, 12*(2), 125–144. doi:10.1080/1553118X.2018.1428979

Raupp, J., & Hoffjann, O. (2012). Understanding strategy in communication management. *Journal of Communication Management (London), 16*(2), 146–161. doi:10.1108/13632541211217579

Shannon, C. E. (1948). A Mathematical Theory of Communication. *The Bell System Technical Journal, 27*(3), 379–423. doi:10.1002/j.1538-7305.1948.tb01338.x

Tufte, E. R. (1983). *The Visual Display of Quantitative Information*. Graphics.

Whorf, B. L. (1956). Science and Linguistics. In J. B. Carrol (Ed.), *Language Thought, and Reality: Selected Writings of Benjamin Lee Whorf.* MIT Press.

Chapter 2
Effective Communication Approaches for Decision Analytics:
An Exploration of Strategies

Amanda Reboulet
Jacoulet, USA

Ross A. Jackson
https://orcid.org/0000-0002-5358-966X
Wittenberg University, USA

ABSTRACT

Analysts ignore the context that shapes and constrains communication at their peril. The rhetorical context in which analytics is enacted influences the communicative approach. In this chapter, two dominate elements are considered: 1) analytic complexity and 2) rhetorical context. Along this analytic-rhetorical spectrum, a four-square matrix is developed using these elements to describe distinct environments in which analytics is enacted. While each of the four positions are addressed for inclusion in this chapter, the focus is narrowed to an exposition of strategies for effectively communicating insights within the realm of decision analytics. Marked by a more basic analytic framework, decision analytics aims to support successful consumption and utilization at senior levels of organizations. Decision analytics differ from other types of analytics since they support the process of making decisions versus providing information. This chapter focuses on how analysts can use decision analytics to effectively communicate analytic results and insights to senior leaders of organizations.

DOI: 10.4018/978-1-7998-3964-4.ch002

INTRODUCTION

Communicating effectively and strategically benefits from an examination of context and intent. While generally accurate, this assessment is perhaps even more pressing when one is communicating analytic results in an organizational setting. When analysts focus exclusively on the techniques of their craft, important considerations such as the best way to convey results are minimized or ignored. Without an adequate appreciation for the rhetorical context in which analytics is enacted organizationally and aligned appropriately to a communication approach, analysts implicitly assume the weight of the results will be compelling enough for managers to accept and act. Analysts' actions suggest a belief in this even if the results and methodology are not fully understood by those in power. Such an approach, even if successful, is ultimately a disservice to analysts, managers and the organization as it rests on ignorant acceptance rather than deep understanding. Consequently, the rhetorical context ought to influence the communicative approach adopted to convey the results. This communicative approach benefits from an awareness of how analytics is often integrated into business decision making.

Businesses are making increased use of analytics (Bose, 2009; Kohavi, Rothleder & Simoudis, 2002; Năstase & Stoica, 2011). In fact, analytics and analytic insights increasingly reside at the core of leaders' attempts to make sense (Weick, 1979 & 1995) of what is going on (Bois, 1975) within organizations. As Năstase and Stoica explained, "data analysis is at the heart of decision making in all business applications" (p. 604). How is the integration of analysis into business decisions actually enacted? It is worth noting that analytics is a complex and emerging field of study. In fact, "the science of advanced analytics is not an easy concept or technology for users to understand or know how to use" (Bose, p. 166). As a result of its inherent complexity, there is a potential asymmetry of knowledge between those creating analysis and those consuming it. Kohavi, Rothleder and Simoudis noted that, "business users, while expert in their particular areas, are still unlikely to be expert in data analysis and statistics" (p. 45). This knowledge gap highlights the need for analysts to be able to communicate effectively. Năstase and Stoica admonished that "analysis results must be distributed to a wide audience" and that much of what analysts produce are not designed "for the broader base of business users who need the output to be translated into language and visualizations that are appropriate for the business needs" (p. 610). More succinctly, analysts need to "produce results that are actionable" (Kohavi, Rothleder & Simoudis, p. 48). In order for analysts to communicate effectively and transform analytic results into something which is organizationally actionable, it is advantageous to assess the rhetorical context in which analysis is consumed.

Rhetorical context can be defined as the elements comprising a specific communication act to include the nexus of purpose, audience, structure and style (Lamm & Everett, 2009). The concept of rhetorical context is particularly important for delimiting the parameters of effective communication approaches for decision analytics as it has application potential in both business (Randazzo, 2012) and scientific research methodologies (Herrera, 2009). From a general perspective, Cho and Choi (2018) assessed that "contextual factors influence the way we speak and write" and further, "an audience is central to the rhetorical context and helps identify the parameters of a writing task" (p. 25). Narrowing the focus to the highly specialized, rhetorical context of technological endeavors, Ornatowski (1998) described that "technology and technical artifacts," like analysis, "appear to be largely products of interaction and communication, not mere embodiments of scientific principles, laws of mechanics, and specialized, esoteric knowledge" and that therefor analysis might be beneficially understood as "a rhetorical enterprise," one in which, "the margin of indeterminacy surrounding technical artifacts constitutes a rhetorical space" (p. 317). Business analysis is consumed within such a rhetorical space. Jackson and Reboulet's (2019) work illustrates how such a rhetorical space is increasingly problematic when dealing with both the inherent and translation-induced semantic ambiguity associated with conducting business internationally. With this in mind, this chapter attempts to bridge the gap between the praxis of analysis and communication through the development of effective communication approaches for decision analytics. This chapter is comprised of a survey of literature, methodology review, results & concept development and conclusion. In order to establish context for the methodology and results & concept development, the survey of literature is presented in the following section.

SURVEY OF LITERATURE

Research benefits from context. A robust survey of literature is useful for constructing a milieu of understanding. In fact, Trochim (2001) considers the literature review "one of the most important early steps in a research project;" the step that sets a given research project "within a conceptual and theoretical context" (p. 27). This traditional view of the survey of literature is not above critique as any selection is also, by extension, an act of exclusion. Alvesson and Deetz (2000) explained that there is a "systematic privileging of certain discourses and meanings associated with forms of power," and that addressing these is "a crucial element in critical research" (p. 142). The selection protocol for this survey of literature was to identify relevant early works and recent applications within each major research section. Such an approach provides a mix of both foundational conceptualizations and subsequent developments. Collectively, while the selection certainly privileges certain dialogues, they provide a point of reflection for informing action. Such active contemplation holds potential for increased autonomy. As Waring (2009) explained, it is through a focus on the "evaluation of, and reflection on, the different strands of research" that one might come to realize "how they collectively contribute to an understanding of emancipatory practice" (p. 57). To this end, it is worth explicating the different research strands for this chapter.

Three overarching areas of research comprise the major foci of this survey of literature: a) business management, b) applied analytics and c) communication theory. Reducing these areas to their essential, functional elements, business management represents both the *where* and the *to whom* of this research, applied analytics is the *what* that transpires organizationally, and communication is the *how* it is executed. Each of these sections contain a mix of early research associated with concept development and later applications. While any selection privileges some insights and perspectives at the expense of others, this process provides a basis for understanding subsequent sections of this chapter (e.g., methodological review, results and concept development). Since the literature associated with business management provides the *telos* for effective communication strategies for decision analytics, it is presented first.

Business Management

In order to begin discussing business management, it is important to define it. Business management can be understood as a "specific process of planning, co-ordinating, motivating, direction and controlling the efforts of people manning the different business activities with an aim to attain the predetermined objectives of the business" (Kumar & Sharma, 2000, p. 3). Business management encompasses many professional disciplines and concepts such as traditional management, finance, marketing, human resources, to list only a few. Among these disciplines, there are qualitative and quantitative aspects, which help CEOs and leaders understand the decision space (Burrow & Kleindl, 2013). In order to sustain effectiveness across these disparate functions, developing managerial skills is a career-long activity (Heney, 2008). Collectively, all of these complementary disciplines make up generic business management, which aims to influence better decisions for companies and organizations.

Part of successful business management is the creation of competitive advantage over other companies to include "technology, product development, innovations, but also adopting and mastering managerial practices" (Sokolic, Mrak & Vretenar, 2017, p. 139). Being able to capture such competitive advantage requires a degree of flexibility and agility in management approaches. For Bârgău (2015), "the most important key to successfully leadership is to know how, when and how much of what leadership style is needed in a particular situation" (p. 565). Along with management flexibility, in developing this competitive advantage, it is important to focus on the benefits of data and analysis to help inform decisions across the company within these areas. Additionally, communicating analytical results to stakeholders is imperative to the decision-making process (Sokolic, Mrak & Vretenar). This focus on business management through analytics is critical for firms to make data-driven decisions and optimize their strategies.

Linkages among business management, applied analytics and communication are abundant. While business analytics represents the more quantitative side of business management, it is important to develop the qualitative side that includes effective communication. Without effective communication skills, it is difficult for organizations to succeed or evolve to meet new challenges. According to Markovic and Salamzadeh (2018), "communication, as a management function is the process of creating, communicating and interpreting ideas, facts, opinions and feelings about work performance, organisational effectiveness and efficiency as well as goals attainment in organisation" (p. 11). While Markovic and Salamzadeh lay out the implications of poor communication from a management perspective, the same pitfalls and challenges exist for analysts and other personnel within organizations. The communicative implications of applied analytics are developed more explicitly in the following section.

Generically, organizations and companies partake in business management, which includes many aspects of doing business. In order to understand better the decision space in which these organizations and companies conduct business, it is important to study the qualitative and quantitative aspects of business management (Burrow & Kleindl, 2013). Within this context, the qualitative aspect is broadly represented by effective communication while the quantitative aspect is characterized by analytics. In the following sections, both analytics and communication will be explored further as imperative aspects of business management.

Applied Analytics

As a fast-growing profession, business analytics emerges as a force multiplier for organizations and companies alike. According to Bayrak, "by implementing Business Analytics initiatives in their organizations, decision makers can integrate disparate data sources, predict trends, improve performance, see key performance indicators, identify business opportunities, and make better and more informed decisions" (2015, p. 230). Maximizing the organizational effect of applied analytics requires correct positioning. Determining where the analysis department should reside within an organization, and to whom it should report is a longstanding question. Folsom (1924) concluded, "in order that the statistical department may develop to the fullest extent and cover all phases of the business, it is very important that the head of this department report directly to the president or the general manager" (p. 178). Once situated, it is imperative to determine what functions applied analytics will be applied. Under the business analytics umbrella, there are three main types of analytics organizations utilize for decision purposes: descriptive, predictive, and prescriptive (Bayrak).

Descriptive analytics depict trends for past or current performance data utilizing various software tools and statistics. Predictive analytics "uses a variety of models and techniques to predicts future outcomes based on historical and current data" (Bayrak, 2015, p. 233). Finally, prescriptive analytics utilize mathematical modeling to determine courses of actions based on various "objectives, requirements, and constraints" to inform business operations (Bayrak, p. 234). With these three forms of applied analytics in mind, what type of qualities enables an individual to successfully execute these tasks organizationally? Again, this isn't a new concern for businesses. Folsom (1924) explained, "the analysis and correlation of reports requires a person with a keen analytical mind, who can see the purpose of the analysis and can visualize a statement from the point of view of the executive" (p. 179). "A major part" of analysts' task is to provide executives such information "quickly, clearly, and concisely" ("X", 1926, p. 21). The three types of analytics described here work in concert to assist decision maker's understanding of the present and future states of their organization. In order for organizations and companies to fully benefit from analytics, it is necessary to employ all three types and for analysts to be able to communicate results effectively to executives.

Business analytics provides many potential benefits to organizations and business to include increased competitive advantage, improved business processes, increased growth and developed innovation. Implementing business analytics within an organization becomes an important strategic decision, but it's important to consider how to operationalize it to ensure maximum benefit and value. When considering the business impact, there are four main themes: building actionable analytics, tracking performance improvement, creating competitive advantage, and complying with regulatory guidance (Parks & Thambusamy, 2017). As described, business analytics aren't effective at supporting business decisions without organizations operationalizing the results and findings.

While conducting analytics may have a profound effect on the operation of organizations and businesses, effectively communicating findings maximizes the benefit. According to Isson and Harriott (2013), "communication is the biggest challenge some analysts face. It is sometimes their pitfall, simply because analysts primarily care about doing analytics…to communicate analytics effectively, analysts need to really spark their audience's interest and attention" (p. 315). Often, analysts are not known for being great communicators; however, to get the most out of their analytics and findings, they need to embrace and evolve to communicate better. The purpose of effective communication at the hands of an analyst is to encourage decision makers to accept and utilize analytics in their decision-making process. Effectively communicating analytics is important at every level within an organization or business.

Communication Theory

Executing applied analytics within a business management context can be viewed as specific manifestation of a *communicative act* (Smith, 1950; Speroff, 1953 & 1955). Given the focus of this chapter is on the exploration of strategies for effective communication approaches for decision analytics, it is essential to develop a framework which is grounded in communication theory. This section of the survey of literature contains an overview of the early development and application of communicative acts, followed by a presentation of more recent applications within business environments. Collectively, these early and recent applications hold implications for how decision analytics might be effectively communicated within organizations. Since they are foundational, the early theory development and applications are presented first.

Smith (1950), described that a communicative act "must begin in a situation where two or more organisms are in a state of readiness for interstimulation and interresponse…it is necessary to add as an element of the communicative act the utilization of some element that has the capacity of being used for purposes of reference" (p. 276). In the narrower case of oral interpretation, Brooks (1978) defined communicative acts as "the process by which a reader, communicating from the manuscript through vocal and physical suggestions, stimulates a listener response that is favorable to the reader's judgments of the intent" (p. 167). Consistent with Smith's and Brook's construction, one can envision an analyst and a manager being interlocutors engaged in a communicative act during the presentation of analytic results with the results being considered the referent element around which the communicative act occurs. In such a case, the analyst (i.e., the reader) would be attempting to get the manager (i.e., the listener) to respond favorably to the analyst's judgment. In fact, the analysis and subsequent writing of analytic reports can form the basis one uses "to claim and maintain authority" within an organization (Hansen, 1995, p. 105). Such a dynamic calls into question the notion of authority, as the subordinate (i.e., analyst) has superior knowledge to the manager in this context.

McGuire (1977) explored the relationship between speech acts and the paradox of authority, noting that the paradox emerges "because man exists in social organizations" (p. 34). More essentially, McGuire defined language as "a universal medium within which the social life of the human species unfolds" (p. 34). Being able to effectively communicate, using the universal medium of language, perhaps rests on trust between the interlocutors. Haas (1981) explained that "the problem of creating and maintaining trust may be seen as a problem in the presentation of one's self as a trustworthy person," and that "in any communicative activity, this must be accomplished largely through the use of a conventional language" (pp. 4-5). Understanding that the use of conventional language (i.e., terms with which both members are familiar) can be useful in establishing and maintaining the trust which facilitates communicative acts is important; however, it is also beneficial to understand when in the interlocution miscommunication is likely to occur. This suggests that the very point at which communicative acts transpire are essential moments for clarity and effect. Speroff (1953) explained that "the crux of most misunderstanding arises while the communicate acts are unfolding" (p. 118). The work of Speroff is useful here for two reasons, first it is helpful for identifying the "crux" of misunderstanding in communicative acts. Second, Speroff provides an early point of reference for examining communicative acts within a business context.

Speroff (1955) asserted, that it was "self-evident that failure in spoken communication, written communication, and other types of communicative acts is as prevalent among the leaders of industry and labor as it is among office personnel" (p. 163). As previously mentioned, the work of Speroff is useful in situating communicative acts within a business context. Once situated, it is imperative to appreciate that the pragmatic considerations of business (e.g., the bottom line) influence the type of communication acts as well as the appropriate and effective language to be used. As Al Sharoufi (2014) explained, "negotiating pragmatics is thus situated at the centre of institutional language, which necessitates a high awareness of cultural repertoires" (p. 104). In negotiating these cultural repertoires, one benefits from understanding that in addition to the verbal elements, communication includes nonverbal elements and an important time component (Bolotova, 2012). Both verbal and nonverbal elements of communicative acts are embedded within a framework of interrelated power dynamics which inform the execution of organizational tasks. For Wright (2019), prior research "neglects to consider how power is exercised in the day-to-day unfolding of routines" and that by addressing the shortfall one becomes "better able to integrate the fundamental role of power" into the "descriptions and explanations of the embodied, communicative accomplishment of routines (p. 156). This is consequential as one could reasonably consider applied analytics as an organizational routine executed through communicative actions.

Applied analytics are executed within existing organizational power structures of business management. Within this environment both the potential basis for analysts' authority (Hansen, 1995) and that of managers is called into question (McGuire, 1977). Through the dynamic tension of this struggle, one benefits from viewing applied analytics as a routinized function (Wright, 2019), which includes both verbal and nonverbal elements (Bolotova, 2012). More directly, one is able to see applied analytics as a specific form of communicative act (Brooks, 1978; Smith, 1950; Speroff, 1953 & 1955). One in which trust (Haas, 1981) between analyst and manager is essential. Collectively, these insights point to important implications for strategies for effectively communicating decision analytics in organizations. With this understanding established, it is possible to now summarize the key findings from the survey of literature.

Selection and interpretation are acts open to critique. The works presented in this survey of literature, along with the proposed meanings, are not definitive but are potentially informative. One benefits from staking a weak ontological stance in relation to the grounding developed here. As developed by White (2000) a weak ontology "cannot claim a validity completely divorced from its context of cultural meanings. And yet, the way in which it interprets those meanings should be capable of generating a critical edge that cuts, potentially at least, against the existing status quo" (p. 38). As developed originally, and synthesized in the survey of literature, these works reflect a given regime of power (Foucault, 1980). However, a regime that is as generative as it is contestable. Summarizing the key insights is useful for highlighting points of contestation.

Business management was defined here as being focused on the classic functions of planning, coordinating, motivating, directing and controlling the people and resources within an organization (Kumar & Sharma, 2000). Under the umbrella term *business management* are disparate disciplines like management, finance, marketing, human resources, along with the qualitative and quantitative analytic activities, which inform CEOs' constructions of the decision space (Burrow & Kleindl, 2013). Three main types of applied analytics organizations were presented: a) descriptive, b) predictive, and c) prescriptive (Bayrak, 2015). From both a business management and applied analytic perspective the centrality of communication to success was established. Leveraging communication theory, applied analytics was defined here as a specific form of communicative act (Brooks, 1978; Smith, 1950; Speroff, 1953 & 1955).

To summarize, the major foci for this survey of literature were: a) business management, b) applied analytics and c) communication theory. Collectively these elements were useful for constructing a milieu of understanding. This understanding is both essential for establishing the conceptual and theoretical context of the study (Trochim, 2001), and open to critique (Alvesson &Deetz, 2000). A weak ontological stance allows one to balance these conflicting demands and move forward productively. With this background sufficiently developed it is possible to turn attention now to the section of this chapter focused on the methodological review, which is presented next.

METHODOLOGICAL REVIEW

Business research benefited from applications of both descriptive (McAdam, Leonard, Henderson, & Hazlett, 2008; Salamzadeh, Bidaki & Vahidi, 2018) and normative (Cepani & Lamani, 2013) methodologies. Each of these two research methodologies offers something unique and potentially useful for understanding business phenomena. While addressing a research methodology, it is important to position it within a particular and delimited context. Cepani and Lamani explained that one should not only address the research methodology, but also "consider the logic behind the methods" (p. 34). Ultimately, by defining its logic one provides the rationale for the study. The logic behind the methodological selection for this study is that previously published research will provide insight and benefit into strategies analysts can adopt to more effectively communicate their findings. As such, the empirical material used in the concept development section of this study was generated by synthesizing key insights from an intentional, systematic review of previously published research. From a descriptive research methodological perspective, an accumulation and interpretation of previously published evidence is an acceptable research approach (Nisha & Khan, 2016). As indicated by Salamzadeh, Bidaki and Vahidi, applied-descriptive research can make use of an interpretative paradigm in which results are produced by putting "accepted realities together" (p. 5); however, once these findings are assembled, it remains to be determined what (if anything) one should do. Answering that question requires a normative assessment.

Normative research is essential for establishing coherence. While normative assessments lack objectivity, they are nonetheless imperative for moving from an accumulation of facts to the determined meanings which legitimate action. Cepani and Lamani (2013) explained that normative research attempts to address, "how the world should be" (p. 33). The importance of such a determination cannot be overstated. Making an assertion is precarious since there is a persistent gap between positivist and normative claims. Salloch, Wäscher, Vollmann and Schildmann (2015) explained, "the question of how to determine, justify and make the normative framework explicit for empirical-ethical research is a crucial one because direct inferences from descriptive data to normative conclusions are problematic for theoretical, methodological and pragmatic reasons" (p. 2). It is useful to note that simply accumulating more data does not, and can never, substantiate a normative claim. Rather, the strength of one's logic resides in the coherent unification of the two distinct approaches. Salloch, Wäscher, Vollmann and Schildmann explained "the interrelation between descriptive and normative aspects and theories applied is of central interest" (p. 3). As such, it is useful to assess research in which a descriptive-normative research methodology was used.

As suggested, there is potential power to be derived through a descriptive-normative research approach. Integrating the *is* of positive research with the *should* of normative claims allows those responsible for decision-making to move forward with greater clarity. Doing so effectively requires acknowledging and overcoming the fissure between the two approaches. Keller (1989) described the gap "between the descriptive observation that people are sometimes intransitive and the normative principle that people ought to be transitive," finding that "a prescriptive purpose is designed to bridge the gap" between the descriptive and normative approaches (p. 485). Since these paradigms are incommensurable (Kuhn, 1996), the gap between them has persisted, along with the identified need to bridge it. Kloosterhuis (2000) identified "the need for an integration of descriptive and normative research" (p. 186). More recently, Yeoh (2009) indicated that, "determining what the situation in business 'is' and then being able to assess how it 'should be' are imperative to advance the field," and explained the benefits of "greater normative/descriptive integration" (pp. 115-116). As indicated, the descriptive-normative research approach adopted for this study was based on a synthesis of key insights from an intentional, systematic review of previously published research. With this in mind, it is useful to provide context for systematic reviews in general.

What is a systematic review and why might one want to use the approach in business research? Colbran, Ramsden, Stagnitti and Toumbourou (2019), asserted that systematic reviews are "widely accepted as a gold standard in evidence synthesis" (p. 3). As such, one might use a systematic review to understand business phenomena since it holds a recognized, privileged position in methodological approaches for synthesizing across studies. This explains why one might want to use the approach but provides little insight as to what the approach entails. Moher, Liberati, Tetzlaff and Altman (2009) described a systematic review as consisting of "clearly formulated question that uses systematic and explicit methods to identify, select, and critically appraise relevant research, and to collect and analyze data from the studies that are included in the review" (p. 1). As described, the identification and selection of relevant research is an essential component of systematic reviews. Khademi (2020) explained how one's "initial pool of articles to be reviewed" could be identified through a "synthesis of keywords" (p. 17). EBSCOhost was used as the search site for academic articles. The keywords *applied analytics*, *communication* and *business management* were used to identify relevant, full-text, scholarly (i.e., peer-reviewed) journal articles for this study.

As presented, the methodology of this study is descriptive-normative research based on an intentional, systematic review of previously published articles containing the keywords *applied analytics*, *communication* and *business management*. With this defined methodology, it is feasible to present the results & concept development, which were based on the critical assessment of the collected empirical material. These insights are presented in the following section.

RESULTS AND CONCEPT DEVOLOPMENT

As indicated in the methodological review, an intentional, systematic review of previously published articles containing the keywords *applied analytics*, *communication* and *business management* formed the basis of this descriptive-normative study. This section is comprised of two parts: a) results and b) concept development. The results are presented first as they provide the basis for the development of the concept.

Results

Keywords of *applied analytics*, *communication* and *business management* were used in EBSCOhost on 7 April 2020 to identify full-text, scholarly (i.e., peer-reviewed) journal articles. Through this search, a population of ten articles was identified. A close reading of each article was used to identify emergent themes within and between these ten articles. The themes which emerged (along with percentage density in the population) were: a) utilizing skills (100%), b) analytic rigor (40%), c) communication strategy (30%), d) decision influence (30%), e) skill development (20%), and f) professional contribution (10%). A summary of these findings is presented in Table 1.

While the theme of utilizing skills is the most prevalent (100%), this theme is not considered overly interesting since articles discussing applied analytics naturally have a pronounced focus on skill utilization. Given the obviousness of this theme, it will not be presented in any further detail. However, the themes of analytic rigor (40%), communication strategy (30%) and decision influence (30%) are prominent enough to warrant elaboration. The themes of skill development (20%) and professional contribution (10%) are mentioned for completeness but are not subsequently expounded.

Table 1. Summary Assessment of Article Thematic Content

Author Last Name(s)	Publication Year	Utilizing Skills	Analytic Rigor	Communication Strategy	Decision Influence	Skill Development	Professional Contribution
Fritz & Canavari	2008	X		X	X		
Liao, & Chang	2009	X			X		
Chen & Wu	2010	X		X		X	
Liao, Chang & Tseng	2010	X					
Wachowicz	2010	X	X		X		
Kimbrough, Chou, Chen & Lin	2014	X	X				
Kheirbek et al.	2015	X					
Nguyen et al.	2018	X	X			X	
Martinez-Millana et al.	2019	X	X	X			X
Zhou & Yang	2020	X					

The theme of analytic rigor draws attention to the increasing complexity of both the technique and praxis of applied analytics. Depending on who is consuming the analysis, rigor can increase the overall level of gratification associated with the analytic product. According to Wachowicz (2010) a consumer's "satisfaction…is significantly different if the system helps only to present or organize the data or if it offers advanced analytic mechanisms that allow him to act as an advisor or facilitator" (p. 580). This helps to bring attention to the interrelationship between *who* is consuming the analysis, *what* they want to accomplish through its consumption, and *how* much analytic rigor is desired. Beyond allowing individuals to potentially act as advisors, advanced analytic techniques can be used to improve organizational operations. Martinez-Millana et al. (2019) focused on "the advantage of grounding advanced data analysis techniques to improve…processes" (p. 1). While potentially powerful as a basis for organizational improvement and process efficiency, such advancements in rigor fail to mitigate all of the complications or the need for knowledgeable analysts (Kimbrough, Chou, Chen & Lin, 2014). Nguyen et al. (2018) discussed a lack of research as to "*how*…advanced analytic techniques" can be used "to support…decision-making" (p. 255). Making analysis relevant requires analysts to be able to effectively communicate results so that decision makers can act.

Communication strategy, as an identified theme, focuses upon aspects associated with the rhetorical context(s) of analysis. Two important aspects of any communication strategy for analytics is to determine what is to be explained and how to explain it. As Fritz and Canavari (2008) explained, "the essential question…is how to communicate which information" (p. 356). Such a determination is consequential because the absence of a strategically aligned, rhetorical approach could reasonably limit the effectiveness of one's analysis. Chen and Wu (2010) described that a "lack of effective communication could impede the learning capability and effectiveness of a partnership" (p. 689). How might one overcome such impediments? Technology holds potential for improving both analysis and its communication. Martinez-Millana et al. (2019) explained how "information and communications technology (ICT) can provide tools and systems to support both the programming and assessment of operations" (p. 2). While potentially beneficial as a tool, one should avoid conflating communication strategies with adoption of ICT. Essentially, any communication strategy is focused upon influencing the actions of others in the context of making business decisions. As such, one might reasonably expect linkages between the theme of communication strategy and that of decision influence.

Since the work of Fritz and Canavari's (2008) is identified in both the communication strategy and decision influence themes, their work provides an effective transition between the two. They observed that "business transactions are realized in an interaction and communication process between two partners…and their decision upon the continuation of the transaction process" (p. 356). While analysis is frequently conceived as an objective matter, it is beneficial to acknowledge it is often enacted in a decision environment which blends subjective and objective aspects. Wachowicz (2010) explained how key inputs to the analytic model "are defined subjectively by the decision maker" and that "the process of the objectives elimination is repeated until the decision maker is able to find the best decision" (p. 585). The work of Wachowicz highlights the dynamic interplay between analyst and decision-maker. Such influence can extend to the selection of the research methodology used in a given study. Liao and Chang (2009) focused on how one's research approach might be informed by leadership, noting that, "the decision makers would react well to the method" (p. 15). Ultimately, analysis is only as effective as the degree to which it influences organizational decisions and actions.

As presented in Table 1, the themes which emerged from an intentional, systematic review of previously published articles were: a) utilizing skills (100%), b) analytic rigor (40%), c) communication strategy (30%), d) decision influence (30%), e) skill development (20%), and f) professional contribution (10%). Given the unique mix of novelty, interrelation and density, the themes of analytic rigor, communication strategy, and decision influence were developed in more detail. Collectively, these themes and corresponding insights were used as the basis for the development of an analytic taxonomy that is referred to here as the analytic-rhetorical spectrum. This is presented in the following section.

Concept Development

While one should be careful not to read too much into the insights gained from a population of ten articles, it is still nonetheless possible to develop structure around common themes and insights. Based on these results, a taxonomy was developed for understanding different rhetorical approaches based on distinct analytic forms. The analytic-rhetorical spectrum is presented as Figure 1.

Figure 1. Analytic-Rhetorical Spectrum

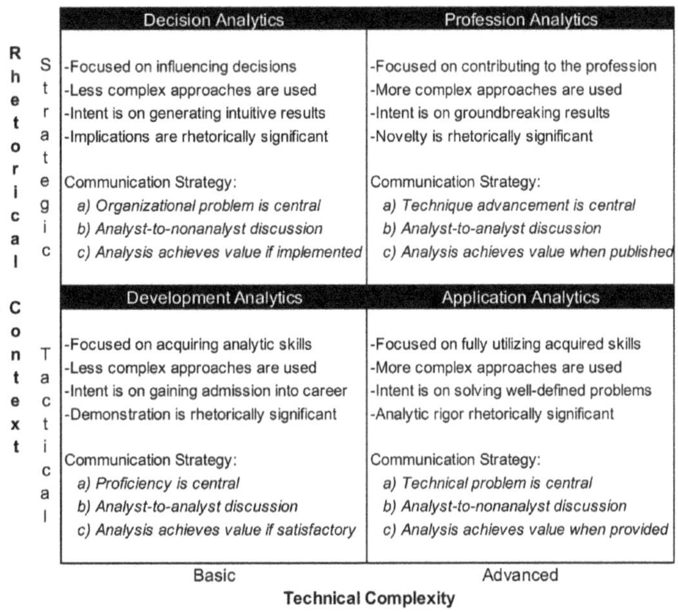

For this initial assessment, the focus of this review will be centered on decision analytics. To do so, it is beneficial to discuss where decision analytics fit into this analytics taxonomy. The analytic-rhetorical spectrum consists of two axes of focus: analytic complexity and rhetorical context. From these two axes, four quadrants are formed using basic to advanced analytic complexity and tactical to strategic rhetorical context (see Figure 1). Starting at the top left of the figure, the first quadrant is decision analytics and corresponds to strategic rhetorical context and basic analytic complexity. The focus for this quadrant is to influence decisions across an organization at the CEO or senior leader level. When developing these types of visuals, simplistic approaches are used to generate relatively intuitive results with impactful implications for the organization. Understanding the organizational challenge is imperative to successfully providing value as well as the ability to communicate between analysts and non-analysts. For the purpose of this chapter, decision analytics are the primary focus.

Rotating clockwise from the decision analytics position, profession analytics composes the second quadrant and represents the intersection of advanced analytic complexity as well as strategic rhetorical context. Unlike the first quadrant, the focus of this quadrant is more academic with more analyst-to-analyst discussions. Additionally, these types of visualizations and analytics emphasize the contribution to the profession with the intent of revolutionary results with advancement in praxis as central to success. Analysts working in this quadrant tend to communicate results through academic papers and conferences with minimal consideration given to implementation or practical application.

The quadrant located in the lower-right hand corner focuses on application analytics. The corresponding juncture for this type of analytics is tactical rhetorical context and advanced analytic complexity. Typically, application analytics take place between an analyst and a non-analyst with full consideration given that the method of analysis chosen accurately and appropriately tackles the challenge. The focus for analysts in this quadrant is to fully utilize their acquired skills and utilize more complex approaches, with an intent to solve well-defined organizational challenges with analytic rigor. Communication in this quadrant focuses on achieving tactical value by utilizing complex analytic methods to solve technical challenges across the entire organization. Within this quadrant, it is imperative that analysts have the ability to communicate complex approaches concisely and simplistically so relevant stakeholders understand the decision.

Finally, the fourth quadrant is composed of development analytics, which have tactical rhetorical context and basic analytic complexity. With this mix, the focus is on acquiring analytic skills where less-complex approaches are used. Discussions for this area typically take place between two analysts, one senior and the other junior, where the junior analyst acquires and demonstrates proficiency in the field to the senior analyst. Additionally, analytics within this quadrant are successful if they provide educational value to the overall company with consumption at a more senior analyst level.

Distinctions among these quadrants are crucial given that the communication strategies and the types of people consuming the data for decision making are different. Over the last sixty years, analysts have inundated organizations with rigorous praxis without a sufficiently clear distinction of the appropriate research methodology (Bertrand & Fransoo, 2002), or corresponding rhetorical approach. Lacking clarity in strategic intent, analytic results quickly become garbled, meaningless and add to the mindless chatter within a business. The ability to effectively communicate across these different analytic types becomes critical to organizational decision making. Since the focus of decision analytics is on providing decision support to CEOs and senior leaders, this form is likely to be considered the most influential and important. Decision analytics direct and inform some of the most complex decisions and strategy across companies. As such, the rhetorical approach adopted here is exceedingly consequential to success.

An important aspect to discuss within the communication strategy is the failure to persuade or inform a decision. If the form of rhetoric adopted by an analyst operating within decision analytics is not strategically developed and aligned with purpose, it is often difficult for CEOs and senior leaders to act upon the information provided. Along with the decision analytic, it is important that a well-developed communication strategy is established to maximize the influence and effectiveness of the overarching message. Failure to persuade a leader to make a decision suggests that this type of analytics may not be influential enough for businesses to have confidence in analysis, thus questioning the need for analysts altogether. Effective communication can assist with publicizing the key benefits and effectively support the overall strategy of a business.

A well-rounded analyst brings objectivity, independence and flexibility in rhetorical approach to powerful organizational effect. Ironically, analysts tend to focus on the positives analytics brings, while decision makers focus on the negatives. For an analyst, a completely successful communication strategy will inform decision makers how to harmonize the positives and negatives of organizational reality as revealed through analysis. Often, it is difficult for analysts to propose a course of action, but arguably, they are the most equipped to objectively and independently provide a recommendation. Unfortunately for most CEOs and senior leaders, they do not have the time or capacity to contemplate and consider different aspects of a detailed analysis, which is why decision analytics are critical for them to make quick, well-informed decisions.

Based on the insights gained from the intentional, systematic review of previously published articles containing the keywords *applied analytics*, *communication* and *business management*, the descriptive-normative results, summarized in Table 1, enabled the development of an analytic taxonomy. As indicated in Figure 1, across the analytic-rhetorical spectrum four types of analytics emerge: a) decision, b) profession, c) application and d) development. Each form of analytics calls for a unique rhetorical focus in order to effectively communicate results. Since decision analytics is the form which has the greatest potential for influencing strategic, organizational outcomes, it received the most exposition here. While rudiments of the other three forms were presented, collectively these types of analytics are better addressed within the narrower confines of professional analytic organizations. This along with other implications and extensions to this study are presented in the following section.

IMPLICATIONS AND EXTENSIONS

Selectivity is required for any successful project. The focus of this initial research effort was on the development of the analytic-rhetorical spectrum and the explication of decision analytics as a distinct form of analysis requiring its own communication strategy. Given its focus on informing CEOs and leaders of organizations, decision analytics is especially consequential for establishing business strategy and informing project execution. However, to make decision analytics organizationally effective, two implications associated with how analysts are trained and developed warrant examination. First, analytic programs would likely benefit from increased focus on the enhancement of communication skills along with the praxis of analysis. If analysis is concerned not only with technique but also with the ability to make results organizationally useful, enhancing the communication skills of analysts is essential. Second, operating across the analytic-rhetorical spectrum requires discernment and flexibility. Analysts would benefit if programs were established to cultivate critical and creative thinking skills. Along with these two implications there are few extensions to this study which are worth considering.

The first extension is focused on conducting case study research to explore further the application and consequence of decision analytics. Such use cases are important for establishing the pragmatic utility of this conceptualization. Rowley explained, "case studies are one approach that supports deeper and more detailed investigation" (p. 17). Furthermore, as noted by Guenther (2003), "use cases form the necessary foundation for a project" and can also "serve as a reality check" (p. 66). Detailing rich descriptions of pitfalls and successes of analytics at the most strategic levels within organizations will provide a basis of understanding. Such insight would be helpful in the further refinement of both the concept of decision analytics and its subsequent application.

As indicated in the concept development section of this chapter, the other three forms of analytics: a) profession, b) application and c) development, would benefit from further elaboration. Since these three forms of analytics are focused on the rhetoric of praxis, the development and refinement for these might be undertaken most beneficially by professional, analytic organizations. This is especially the case for profession analytics. Since both development and application analytics have organizational connections, the following is offered for consideration. Both forms of analytics are highly personal. Development analytics is based on the personal relationship between a senior and junior analyst, whereas application analytics is executed based on the personal connection between colleagues across departments to address a tactical concern at the working level (i.e., at the discretion of those doing the work and not requiring additional coordination and approval). While it is possible to execute these in a purely perfunctory manner, it seems that both would benefit from authenticity and care. If professional, analytic organizations take up the development and refinement of these forms of analytics, it might be useful to address how subjective, human investment is to be balanced effectively with the objective praxis of analysis.

Article selection plays an important part in understanding. In fact, one might say it is determinative. As such, it would be beneficial to conduct a comparative study to this one making use of different search terms. With its focus on organizational decision making, this study searched for articles using the terms *applied analytics* and *business management* (along with the term *communication*). This resulted in a much narrower focus than what would be generated using the terms *analytics* and *management*. Broadening the search could provide sufficient material for increased granularity and nuance; however, the number of articles would likely require a change in approach. While this study examined the full population of identified articles, broadening the search along the lines indicated would benefit from the adoption of a sampling technique, the use of corpus linguistic techniques, or a combination of those two approaches.

As indicated, there are two implications presented for this study. The first deals with incorporating communication skills development and the second with the development of critical and creative thinking skills as part of analytic programs. Additionally, there were three broad extensions proposed: a) develop case studies for decision analytics, b) elaborate on profession, application and development analytics, and c) conduct a comparative study to this one based on articles selected using different search terms. While certainly far from exhaustive, these implications and extensions point to concrete ways to build upon this research and extend our collective understandings of executing analysis across the analytic-rhetorical spectrum. With these in mind, it is possible to summarize the key aspects of this chapter.

CONCLUSION

Ineffective analysts become organizationally marginalized. Disconnects between the required level of rigor and the rhetorical context hold the potential to sideline otherwise useful analysis. Through the process, analysts can become alienated from the institutions they seek to improve. As John Mayer (2006) stated in, *Waiting on the World to Change*, "it's hard to beat the system when we're standing at a distance" (track 1). If analysts are going to make a difference organizationally, they must be integrated into the decision-making processes and be able to communicate effectively with decision makers. This chapter highlighted how flexibility across the analytic-rhetorical spectrum is important for such integration.

Methodologically, this descriptive-normative study used an intentional, systematic review of ten previously published articles, obtained through EBSCOhost and identified using a keyword search on the terms *applied analytics*, *communication* and *business management*. An analytic taxonomy was developed by means of a critical assessment of the ten research articles (Table 1). Across the analytic-rhetorical spectrum four types of analytics emerge: a) decision, b) profession, c) application and d) development (Figure 1), each benefiting from its own unique rhetorical approach and focus. Decision analytics, as the type with the greatest potential for influencing strategic, organizational outcomes, received the preponderance of exposition. Two implications of this study were presented for improving analytics programs: a) incorporating development of communication skills and b) developing critical and creative thinking skills. Lastly, three broad extensions were proposed: a) develop case studies for decision analytics, b) further elaborate on profession, application and development analytics, and c) conduct a comparative study based on articles selected using different search terms.

Analysts ignore the context that shapes and constrains communication at their peril. Effectively communicating analytic results benefits from an assessment of, and a response to, the rhetorical context of its representation. This chapter contains an initial exploration of strategies associated with effective communication within the realm of decision analytics. Through this exposition, key propositions were presented. Among these were the notions that within decision analytics, an analyst should make use of less complex techniques and praxis and communicate intuitive results which enable leaders to understand and act. In so doing, analysts can avoid the marginalization that keeps them "standing at a distance," and allows them to inform effectively the decisions which propel organizations forward.

REFERENCES

Al Sharoufi, H. (2014). The role of pragmatics in understanding human communication in an institutional setting. *Journal of Defense Resources Management*, *4*(2), 95–108.

Alvesson, M., & Deetz, S. (2000). *Doing critical management research.* SAGE publications. doi:10.4135/9781849208918

Bârgău, M. A. (2015). Types of leader in Organisation. *EIRP Proceedings, 10*(1), 559-565.

Bayrak, T. (2015). A review of business analytics: A business enabler or another passing fad. *Procedia: Social and Behavioral Sciences*, *195*, 230–239. doi:10.1016/j.sbspro.2015.06.354

Bertrand, J. W. M., & Fransoo, J. C. (2002). Operations management research methodologies using quantitative modeling. *International Journal of Operations & Production Management*, *22*(2), 241–264. doi:10.1108/01443570210414338

Bois, J. S. (1975). *The art of awareness* (2nd ed.). William C. Brown Publisher.

Bolotova, A. K. (2012). Time parameters of nonverbal communication and personal communicative competence. *Psychology in Russia. State of the Art*, 289-300.

Bose, R. (2009). Advanced analytics: Opportunities and challenges. *Industrial Management & Data Systems*, *109*(2), 155–172. doi:10.1108/02635570910930073

Brooks, K. (1978). Evaluating the communicative act of oral interpretation. *Communication*, *7*(1), 167–180.

Burrow, J., & Kleindl, B. (2013). *Business Management* (13th ed.). South-Western, Cengage Learning.

Cepani, L., & Lamani, D. (2013). Development of the accounting research methods in Albania. *Studies in Business & Economics*, *8*(3), 32–40.

Chen, S.-P., & Wu, W.-Y. (2010). A systematic procedure to evaluate an automobile manufacturer-distributor partnership. *European Journal of Operational Research*, *205*(3), 687–698. doi:10.1016/j.ejor.2010.01.036

Cho, Y., & Choi, I. (2018). Writing from sources: Does audience matter? *Assessing Writing*, *37*, 25–38. doi:10.1016/j.asw.2018.03.004

Colbran, R., Ramsden, R., Stagnitti, K., & Toumbourou, J. W. (2019). Advancing towards contemporary practice: A systematic review of organisational performance measures for non-acute health charities. *BMC Health Services Research*, *19*(132), 1–12. doi:10.118612913-019-3952-1 PMID:30795742

Folsom, M. B. (1924). The organization of a statistical department. *Harvard Business Review*, *2*(2), 178–193.

Foucault, M. (1980). *Power/Knowledge: Selected interviews & other writings 1972-1977*. Pantheon Books.

Fritz, M., & Canavari, M. (2008). Management of perceived e-business risks in food-supply networks: E-trust as prerequisite for supply-chain system innovation. *Agribusiness*, *24*(3), 355–368. doi:10.1002/agr.20163

Guenther, K. (2003). Assessing Web Site Usability. *Online (Bergheim)*, *27*(2), 65–69.

Haas, D. F., & Deseran, F. A. (1981). Trust and symbolic exchange. *Social Psychology Quarterly*, *44*(1), 3–13. doi:10.2307/3033857

Hansen, C. J. (1995). Writing the project team: Authority and intertextuality in a corporate setting. *Journal of Business Communication*, *32*(2), 103–122. doi:10.1177/002194369503200201

Heney, P. (2008). Managing employees takes a sense of style. *Hotel & Motel Management*, *223*(13), 6.

Herrera, C. (2010). Commentary: Ethics and the rhetorical context of human research. *International Journal of Epidemiology*, *39*(1), 12–16. doi:10.1093/ije/dyp400 PMID:20100822

Isson, J. P., & Harriott, J. (2013). Effective analytics communication strategies. In Win with Advanced Business Analytics: Creating Business Value from Your Data (pp. 301-319). John Wiley & Sons.

Jackson, R. A., & Reboulet, A. M. (2019). Parlant de business: An application of combined probability theory to inherent and translation-induced semantic ambiguity. *International Journal of Trade, Economics and Finance*, *10*(6), 162–170.

Keller, L. R. (1989). Decision research with descriptive, normative, and prescriptive purposes – some comments. *Annals of Operations Research, 19*(1-4), 485–487. doi:10.1007/BF02283536

Khademi, B. (2020). Ecosystem value creation and capture: A systematic review of literature and potential research opportunities. *Technology Innovation Management Review, 10*(1), 16–34. doi:10.22215/timreview/1311

Kheirbek, R. E., Beygi, S., Zargoush, M., Alemi, F., Smith, A. W., Fletcher, R. D., Seton, P. N., & Hawkins, B. A. (2015). Causal analysis of emergency department delays. *Quality Management in Health Care, 24*(3), 162–166. doi:10.1097/QMH.0000000000000067 PMID:26115064

Kimbrough, S., Chou, C., Chen, Y.-T., & Lin, H. (2014). On developing indicators with text analytics: Exploring concept vectors applied to English and Chinese texts. *Information Systems and e-Business Management, 12*(3), 385–415. doi:10.100710257-013-0228-x

Kloosterhuis, H. (2000). Analogy argumentation in law: A dialectical perspective. *Artificial Intelligence and Law, 8*(2/3), 173–187. doi:10.1023/A:1008385531494

Kohavi, R., Rothleder, N. J., & Simoudis, E. (2002). Emerging trends in business analytics. *Communications of the ACM, 45*(8), 45–48. doi:10.1145/545151.545177

Kuhn, T. S. (1996). *The structure of scientific revolutions* (3rd ed.). The University of Chicago Press. doi:10.7208/chicago/9780226458106.001.0001

Kumar, A., & Sharma, R. (2000). *Principles of Business Management*. Atlantic Publishers and Distributors.

Lamm, R. L., & Everett, J. (2009). *Dynamic argument* (2nd ed.). Cengage Learning.

Liao, S.-K., & Chang, K.-L. (2009). Select televised sportscasters for Olympic Games by analytic network process. *Management Decision, 47*(1), 14–23. doi:10.1108/00251740910929678

Liao, S.-K., Chang, K.-L., & Tseng, T.-W. (2010). Optimal selection of program suppliers for TV companies using an analytic network process (ANP) approach. *Asia-Pacific Journal of Operational Research, 27*(6), 753–767. doi:10.1142/S0217595910002983

Markovic, M. R., & Salamzadeh, A. (2018). The importance of communication in business management. In *The 7th International Scientific Conference on Employment, Education and Entrepreneurship* (pp. 11-28). Belgrade, Serbia: Academic Press.

Martinez-Millana, A., Lizondo, A., Gatta, R., Vera, S., Salcedo, V. T., & Fernandez-Llatas, C. (2019). Process mining dashboard in operating rooms: Analysis of staff expectations with analytic hierarchy process. *International Journal of Environmental Research and Public Health, 16*(2), 1–14. doi:10.3390/ijerph16020199 PMID:30642000

Mayer, J. (2006). *Waiting on the world to change. On Continuum*. Columbia Records.

McAdam, R., Leonard, D., Henderson, J., & Hazlett, S.-A. (2008). A grounded theory research approach to building and testing TQM theory in operations management. *Omega, 36*(5), 825–837. doi:10.1016/j.omega.2006.04.005

McGuire, R. R. (1977). Speech acts, communicative competence and the paradox of authority. *Philosophy & Rhetoric*, *10*(1), 30–45.

Moher, D., Liberati, A., Tetzlaff, J., & Altman, D. G. (2009). Preferred reporting items for systematic reviews and meta-analyses: The PRISMA statement. *PLoS Medicine*, *6*(7), 1–6. doi:10.1371/journal.pmed.1000097 PMID:19621072

Năstase, P., & Stoica, D. (2011). A new business dimension – Business analytics. *Accounting & Management Information Systems*, *9*(4), 603–618.

Nguyen, T., Zhou, L., Spiegler, V., Ieromonachou, P., & Lin, Y. (2018). Big data analytics in supply chain management: A state-of-the-art literature review. *Computers & Operations Research*, *98*, 254–264. doi:10.1016/j.cor.2017.07.004

Nisha, K. M., & Khan, M. A. (2016). Leveraging economy through MSMEs: Recent trends and challenges of women's entrepreneurship in south India. *Journal of Entrepreneurship. Management & Innovation*, *12*(4), 127–149.

Ornatowski, C. M. (1998). 2+2=5 if 2 is large enough. *Journal of Business and Technical Communication*, *12*(3), 316–342. doi:10.1177/1050651998012003003

Parks, R., & Thambusamy, R. (2017). Understanding Business Analytics Success and Impact: A Qualitative Study. *Information Systems Education Journal*, *15*(6), 43–55.

Randazzo, C. (2012). Positioning resumes and cover letters as reflective-reflexive process. *Business Communication Quarterly*, *75*(4), 377–391. doi:10.1177/1080569912459267

Rowley, J. (2002). Using case studies in research. *Management Research News*, *25*(1), 16–27. doi:10.1108/01409170210782990

Salamzadeh, Y., Bidaki, V. Z., & Vahidi, T. (2018). Strategic thinking and organizational success: Perceptions from management graduates and students. *Global Business and Management Research*, *10*(4), 1–19.

Salloch, S., Wäscher, S., Vollmann, J., & Schildmann, J. (2015). The normative background of empirical-ethical research: First steps towards a transparent and reasoned approach in the selection of an ethical theory. *BMC Medical Ethics*, *16*(20), 1–9. doi:10.118612910-015-0016-x PMID:25889221

Smith, M. (1950). The communicative act. *The Journal of Social Psychology*, *31*(2), 271–281. doi:10.1080/00224545.1950.9919012

Sokolic, D., Mrak, M. K., & Vretenar, N. (2017). Business management tools and firm performance. In *4th International Multidisciplinary Scientific Conference on Social Sciences and Arts – SGEM* (pp. 139-146). Sofia, Bulgaria: Academic Press.

Speroff, B. J. (1953). Empathy and role-reversal as factors in industrial harmony. *The Journal of Social Psychology*, *37*(1), 117–120. doi:10.1080/00224545.1953.9921876

Speroff, B. J. (1955). Empathy and role-reversal as factors in communication. *The Journal of Social Psychology*, *41*(1), 163–165. doi:10.1080/00224545.1955.9714259

Trochim, W. M. K. (2001). *The research methods knowledge base*. Atomic Dog Publishing.

Wachowicz, T. (2010). Decision support in software supported negotiations. *Journal of Business Economics & Management, 11*(4), 576–597.

Waring, T. (2009). Emancipatory practice and information systems implementation: An action research project in an NHS acute trust. In J. W. Cox, T. G. LeTrent-Jones, M. Voronov, & D. Weir (Eds.), *Critical management studies at work: Negotiating tensions between theory and practice* (pp. 40–63). Edward Elgar Publishing. doi:10.4337/9781848449497.00010

Weick, K. E. (1979). *The social psychology of organizing* (2nd ed.). Addison-Wesley Publishers.

Weick, K. E. (1995). *Sensemaking in organizations.* Sage Publications, Inc.

White, S. K. (2000). *Sustaining affirmations: The strengths of weak ontology in political theory*. Princeton University Press.

Wright, A. (2019). Embodied organizational routines: Explicating a practice understanding. *Journal of Management Inquiry*, *28*(2), 153–165. doi:10.1177/1056492617713717

X. (1926). The management aspect of the comptroller's work. *Harvard Business Review, 5*(1), 21-26.

Yeoh, P.-L. (2009). Earning the doctoral degree: An example of relationship marketing. *Advances in International Marketing*, *8*(19), 109–117.

Zhou, S., & Yang, P. (2020). Risk management in distributed wind energy implementing Analytic Hierarchy Process. *Renewable Energy: An International Journal, 150*, 616–623.

Chapter 3
From Management 1.0 to Management 3.0 and Beyond

Eduardo Espinheira
Porto Business School, Portugal

Fernando Almeida
https://orcid.org/0000-0002-6758-4843
Polytechnic Institute of Gaya, Portugal

ABSTRACT

Traditional management models reveal issues with the introduction of unnecessary hierarchies, slow decision making, among other obstacles, which left a large number of workers out of the process of seeking efficiency and growth. In this sense, the third generation of management models focused on agility and collaboration emerged. Instead of focusing on hierarchies and functions, there is a priority on the way people behave and relate. In this sense, this study aims to analyze this phenomenon and to understand the various dimensions of Management 3.0. Furthermore, it intends to explore and understand the practices and challenges that are posed in its business implementation, focusing on the role of people and information and communication technologies.

INTRODUCTION

There are different ways to manage the processes of an organization. These different approaches are perceived as organizational management models and explain how managers lead their teams and get results. One of the key factors in business success is people management. This component is essential for the company to achieve its global and specific objectives, regardless of its area of expertise or organizational structure (Griffin et al., 2016; O'Malley & Baker, 2019). The way people behave, work in teams, and interact with clients differs from multiple perspectives. This variability, according to Leroy et al. (2018), depends largely on the policies and guidelines of organizations on how to deal with people in their activities.

DOI: 10.4018/978-1-7998-3964-4.ch003

Organizational management models have evolved. At the beginning of the 20th century, at a time when there was a focus on efficiency and when companies were under pressure to have high levels of productivity, workers were guided to perform repetitive tasks and evaluated solely by their productivity. Tasks were well delimited, and workers were confined to a simple routine of activities. According to Hlupic (2014), there was a clear separation between the leadership and the workers. The workers followed only the guidance obtained by the decision-makers that decided what to do and how to do it. Consequently, no space was given to the creativity and autonomy of decisions by workers. The concept of Management 1.0 is associated with this model.

This management model has become obsolete essentially due to the rapid evolution of society and to the growth of the multiplicity of fields of industrial evolution. The previous model focused essentially on the industrial sector proved to be gradually inefficient in activities outside this scope (Hougaard, 2018). As a result, new organizational forms of work have emerged that also look at work processes and also enable managers to increase efficiency. The focus became the optimization of processes and the quality of the goods produced gained relevance. Salah et al. (2009) report that new and more effective management methodologies like Total Quality Management (TQM) or Six Sigma emerged during this period. In parallel, this management model proposes decentralization and sharing of ideas among the hierarchy edges. However, the decision structure was still based on a vertical and not very flexible organizational structure. According to Van Gaans (2018), decisions were still slow in decision-making and left operational workers out of the process of seeking efficiency and growth. This model was coupled with the concept of Management 2.0.

In the early 2000s, a new model called Management 3.0 emerged. This model is based on the basic principles of complexity and people management. Management 3.0 considers the concept that people management is a complex adaptive system where iterations enable improvement and continuous learning. According to Appelo (2011), self-organized teams should emerge naturally through their evolution and not be created or directed by the manager. The role of the manager is thus altered. The manager is now responsible for providing an ideal environment and conditions for the workers so that they can feel happy at work and, consequently, become more productive. Therefore, the manager should focus on finding ways to encourage the team to work autonomously, respecting some restrictions, to achieve an established result. Management 3.0 encourages companies to rethink their own structure and turns processes more productive. This concept brings more humanized management to organizations, where people should be the most important asset of the companies (Van Roosmalen, 2017).

Initially, Management 3.0 was widely used in the IT industry, and subsequently attracted interest from other business areas. Based on agile management models, it is possible to accelerate and improve the product development process (Stare, 2013). According to Pollack (2017), this paradigm also leads to changes in the way teams organize themselves and perform their tasks. Management 3.0 also offers a diverse set of techniques in team empowerment, competence development, employee energization, and other important missions for a manager. However, the consequences of the Management 3.0 paradigm are not limited to the context of organizations and teams, but also support the development of other paradigms of professional skills development. The Management 3.0 paradigm also makes important contributions to the model proposed by Appleby & Pilkington (2014), which highlights the importance of learning in business contexts that are developed and learned through reflective practice. This learning process does not come out of anywhere and needs time and support as it is also advocated in the Management 3.0 skills development model. Management 3.0 emerges as a valuable tool for companies to re-evaluate their organizational structure and products to become more productive and innovative. Its impact is in both corporate and personal development dimensions.

The principles of agile methodologies and Management 3.0 are the same and address issues such as autonomy, self-management, and continuous improvement. However, there is a difference in the objectives of each model. While agile methodologies focus on the delivery of the product under development, Management 3.0 aims to grow the business and its professionals. The Management 3.0 concept is organized in six visions as suggested by Appelo (2011): (i) align constraints; (ii) develop competence; (iii) grow structure; (iv) energize people; (v) empowers teams; and (vi) improve everything. Each pillar of this vision represents a sector or a value of the company that needs attention. Furthermore, it becomes evident that the hierarchical taxonomy of leadership behaviors proposed by Yukl (2012) is interlinked with the dimensions and values advocated by Management 3.0 in key areas such as task-oriented, relations-oriented, change-oriented, and external. In both models, the role of empowerment, continuous support and recognizing, and monitoring operations are promoted as key elements for the success of organizations.

The fundamental objective of Management 3.0 is to assist leaders in developing an environment that enables employees to feel continuously motivated. In this way, it seeks to propose approaches to how teams can work together to find the best way to produce and/or achieve their goals. At the same time, this objective must be reconciled with the personal satisfaction of the employees. Brace (2016) states this approach stimulates creativity and emotional intelligence. Consequently, the company can offer its employees an engaging and relaxed atmosphere, in which there are no hierarchies and communication failures that impair the fluidity of routines.

The implementation of Management 3.0 is a challenge in an organizational context. It is not a fixed model that dictates a way to deploy Management 3.0 in a company. The concept itself allows and even favors flexibility. Consequently, it is necessary to understand the practices that make sense and that add value in daily life. At the same time, communication is a key element in the implementation of management 3.0. The high autonomy that is given to the teams can only be implemented if there is a strong emphasis on communication so that the teams feel motivated and are able to develop skills. The development of competence should not be limited only to technical aspects, but also to soft skills that prove decisive in the success of organizations, as is recognized in those carried out by Araújo & Pedron (2016) and Marques (2013). Furthermore, communication also assumes a key role in aligning constraints. Appelo (2011) refers that restrictions are important to guide and align the interest of all involved. However, if the focus is not unique, even actions taken by engaged people may not meet the proposed objective.

This study aims to analyze the phenomenon of the evolution of organizational management models and intends to identify convergent and divergent points between them. The study also seeks to explore the various ways in which the Management 3.0 model can be implemented since there is no fixed model or linear rules to be adopted for its implementation. The Management 3.0 concept favors flexibility and its adaptation according to the company's characteristics. Furthermore, it is intended to explore the role of people, communication, and new information and communication technologies in Management 3.0. Furthermore, it is also intended to envisage the future evolution of organizational management models by understanding how they can evolve in light of new social and technological developments. This study pretends to be a relevant reference for top managers and team managers that intend to implement and stimulate their management models supported by the Management 3.0 paradigm.

BACKGROUND

Organizations systematically invest in material and human resources to achieve their goals. This approach is relevant in an extremely competitive organizational world. However, there is not always an awareness on the part of organizational managers of the role that communication can play.

For a long time, the companies' communication was essentially market-oriented, in which it was a tool at the service of the purely commercial strategy. In the current paradigm, in which it becomes increasingly difficult to have distinctive elements in an organization, communication has become a fundamental and strategic element in management. Through it, the company can increase awareness and transmit attributes and values that are difficult to impute to products or services (Markovic & Salamzadeh, 2018).

Communication has four basic functions within an organization or group (Cheney et al., 2011): (i) control, in the sense that communication determines people's behavior, namely who communicates a piece of information or event in the first place; (ii) motivation, in which communication is an element that facilitates the understanding of the actions that should be taken by employees to improve their performance; (iii) emotional expression, considering that it is a means for employees to express their feelings (e.g., satisfaction, frustration, etc.); and (iv) information, by allowing decisions to be more informed, complete and rigorous. Communication therefore appears as an essential tool for the performance of an organization. Through investment in communication, it is possible to improve organizational management from multiple perspectives, such as relationships among employees, clients, and top management (Florea & Duica, 2017; Mihai, 2017; Vercic & Vokic, 2017).

The organizational communication of a company can be divided into its external and internal dimensions. Each of them serves a different audience, so that companies can inform and engage people inside and outside the institution. The external aspect focuses on communication for customers, suppliers, partners, and public agencies; while the internal communication focuses on employees. These two dimensions should not go in opposite directions, but rather complement each other (Locker & Kaczmarek, 2013).

For a long time, the focus of organizational communication was essentially on external communication channels. Investment in internal communication was low and this area was seen as an expense. However, internal communication is gradually being recognized by organizations as a key factor for profitability. According to Yeomans (2007), internal communication should be able to create a climate of commitment and integration of all employees, increasing motivation and productivity. Sebastião et al. (2017) state internal communication helps in fundamental aspects of business competitiveness because it transmits its mission, culture, and organizational value. Furthermore, as Dolphin (2005) points out, organizations should pay special attention to internal communication, because before making the organization known to the external public, it is important to start communicating internally and involving employees in this process.

However, internal communication cannot be reduced to a set of channels through which information flows. Rather, it should be understood as a system of interactions, in which there is feedback between the sender and receiver to understand and exceed the needs and goals of all parties. Sarka (2014) advocate internal communication should foster the circulation of information and knowledge, through which employees identify with organizational objectives. To turn this possible, it is necessary to offer a facilitating environment that makes everyone aware of the reality of the organization and explains the objectives to be achieved.

Before establishing an internal communication plan, the company should seek to understand the social state of the organization from multiple perspectives (Mazzei, 2010): (i) recognize the expectations of employees; (ii) consistency of internal policy with their culture; and (iii) adequacy of the internal media that has been adopted. This internal diagnosis can be carried out through qualitative approaches to each employee or, in larger organizations, using quantitative models based on sufficiently representative surveys.

Table 1 explores different types of internal communication. For each of them, their main advantages and limitations are presented. Despite the diversity of tools available, the digitalization of this area has occurred at a slower pace than what happens in the field outside organizations. According to Linke & Zerfass (2011), this innovation is slower because when changing the way communication occurs within companies, several factors like culture and employee profile must be considered.

Table 1. Internal communication media

Media	Advantages	Limitations
Apps	- High dynamism and interactivity - Possibility to segment the information - Reaches all employees, even those who are not physically in the company	- Not all employees have a smartphone - Can have a high deployment and maintenance cost - Possible resistance to the technology which obstructs its dissemination to all employees
Corporate email	- Ease of access - Low cost of operation and maintenance - Possibility to create custom lists	- Low attractiveness - Can decrease employee productivity due to excess incoming emails - It's typically read-only once
Corporate social network	- High interactivity and attractiveness - Possibility to segment content distribution - Metrics can be applied to measure the tool usage	- High cost of implementation and maintenance - Needs high employee proactivity - Difficulties in controlling the relevance of publications
Corporate tv	- High interactivity - Remote content update - Possibility to segment the message	- High implementation cost - Needs constant content updating to remain attractive
Intranet	- Allows to centralize information - Enables you to measure usage rates - Keeps information organized and updated	- High cost of implementation and maintenance - Dependence on internet access
Meetings	- Without implementation costs - High interactivity with easy sharing of opinions	- Reduced range - Low attractiveness - Decreases productivity
Murals	- Implementation cost is very low - Ease of use - Reaches employees without internet access	- Supports only static content, except for virtual murals - High operational maintenance cost - Low scalability
Newsletter	- Attractive and dynamic channel - Simplified content production - Low cost of production, maintenance, and distribution of content	- Depends on the employee's action to open and read their content - It is usually seen only once
Suggestion box	- Low implementation cost - Allows sharing of ideas - Allows anonymity	- Low interactivity - Limited scope - Feedback process can be long

Source: authors

MAIN FOCUS OF THE CHAPTER

The main focus of this study is to explore the impact of the evolution of management organizational models, from Management 1.0 to Management, on the internal communication of a business. It seeks to characterize the role of information technologies in the revolution of how people organize and communicate. Furthermore, this study also aims to find effective strategies that can be used in environments that implement the Management 3.0 paradigm.

The Management 3.0 concept favors flexibility and its adaptation according to the company's characteristics. There isn't a fixed model or linear rules to be adopted for its implementation, but it can be identified several best practices. Moreover, it is also intended to envisage the future evolution of organizational management models by understanding how they can evolve in light of new social and technological developments. This study pretends to be a relevant reference for top managers and team managers that intend to implement and stimulate their management models supported by the Management 3.0 paradigm.

The study uses a qualitative methodology in which the field research methods are complemented by ethnography as a data collection process. The use of field research is particularly advisable in a scenario where the behaviors and attitudes of stakeholders are better understood within their organizational context (Queirós et al., 2017). Furthermore, this method can be applied in ongoing processes, without the need for changes in context (Bailey, 2017). Jamshed (2014) states that two types of methods can be used to obtain data, namely through direct field observation and complementing this information through interviews.

Ethnography, on the other hand, is a research method that was originally applied by anthropologists to describe the customs and traditions of a human group. According to Fetterman (2019), this method helps to know the identity of a human community that develops in a concrete socio-cultural field. This approach has been progressively used in other contexts such as the social sciences, educational sciences, or engineering (Monahan & Fisher, 2010; Sharp et al., 2016; Yanik, 2017). According to Rashid et al. (2015) and Van Dooremalen (2017), several advantages are associated to this process: (i) the behavior of people is studied in their usual context, and no artificial conditions imposed by the researcher are created; (ii) data is collected from multiple sources; (iii) data collection is unstructured, although the analysis process can be systematized; (iv) the focus of the study is traditionally a large group of individuals, and it is therefore useful in organizational contexts of some scale; and (v) data analysis is carried out according to a descriptive and interpretative model.

Depending on the techniques of data collection and analysis, the research may acquire a greater emphasis on the qualitative or quantitative dimension (Jamshed, 2104). Considering the emerging area of management 3.0, and the lack of quantitative information on how this phenomenon is implemented in organizations, the qualitative approach is the advisable methodological process. The planning and execution process initiated with the definition of the work theme and the research problem supported in three fundamental areas: (i) identifying the characteristics of the management 3.0 paradigm; (ii) exploring the relevance of communication in the context of management 3.0; and (iii) exploring the role of information and communication technologies in the implementation of management 3.0 and as a facilitator of communication within this paradigm. The collection of information was based on the consulting activities performed by the authors in the last two years in this field and that involved organizations in the national and international markets. It is in this area that ethnography has played a key role because the analysis process of each business consultancy aims to record not only the technical success rate of the solutions proposed to each organization, but also to capture the culture and behavior of the various groups in the organization. Indeed, it is precisely in this last point that it becomes possible to perceive the communication dynamics existing within the 3.0 management paradigm. In order to synthesize this process and enable its conceptual and practical analysis, the six principles of management 3.0 advocated by Appelo (2011) were followed. Each consulting activity gives rise to a dossier. These individual qualitative notes were then organized and discussed in two sessions lasting 60 minutes to identify convergent points between them. Afterward, each of the identified themes was compared with the literature in the area and are later explored in the discussion section.

The adoption of the proposed methodology allows us to explore and understand the organizational context of each company. However, the conditions of the environment in which the study takes place are maintained, as there is no contact of researchers about the environment. The replication model for various contexts allows exploring the way Management 3.0 is implemented by each organization. This approach is important because it is known that the challenges of communication and collaborative work posed to each company will necessarily be distinct. The cultural and organizational context is also a distinctive element that makes the consulting activity challenging and unique. It is necessarily a learning process, but also an evolutionary adaptation process.

This study is structured into three stages as shown in Figure 1. In the first stage, a contextual analysis of the Management 3.0 concept is carried out and several strategies to promote communication within companies are explored. The aim is to find an analysis framework that allows us framing the relevance of the findings identified. In phase II, the first step is to establish a chain of evidence to explore the application of various Management 3.0 practices in several contexts. The intention is that the evidence resulting from this process can be properly generalized and not be conditioned by the specific context of each organization. Finally, in phase III, the data obtained are analyzed and synthesized. With this, it is intended to conduct a discussion of the results obtained and compare them with those already identified in the literature. In the analysis of the results, information was organized according to the six main characteristics of Management 3.0 proposed by Appelo (2011). The last step is to extract the conclusions of this study. The conclusions intend to show the conceptual and practical relevance of this study and to highlight its implications for practitioners.

Figure 1. Phases of the adopted methodology

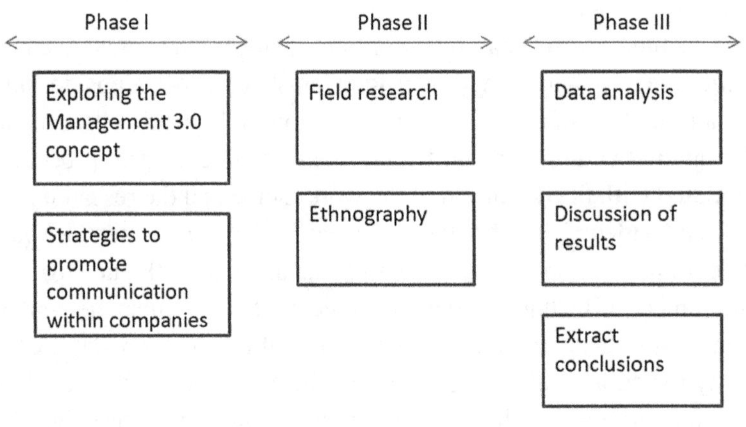

SOLUTIONS AND RECOMMENDATIONS

Align Constraints

Align constraints supports the view that organizations need to have a common goal that is known and shared by their employees. Several companies face challenges in this dimension. Because not all individuals and groups are effectively engaged in shaping the objectives of the organization as a whole, it is very common for the various groups to react negatively to the decisions taken. Consequently, many of these decisions will be ignored or rejected, which will make it impossible to implement these same objectives. According to Hatch (2018), the organizations that manifest these difficulties become monolithic, which over the years become instruments of difficult action. By assuming that the objectives established by the segments with the greatest institutional power coincide with the objectives of the other levels, the organization becomes excessively bureaucratic. Moreover, these constant impositions could be interpreted as abuses and lead to situations of internal opposition.

Defining organizational goals is a necessity and should not be seen as an imposition. Appeal (2011) indicates that setting goals has a dual purpose: (i) to express guidelines and define the direction of the company; and (ii) to improve morale among team members. Consequently, having a common goal will increase team cohesion and motivation. This objective should be shared and achievable (Bang & Midelfart, 2017). Furthermore, Sheridan & Williams (2011) state that common objectives should overlap with individual objectives. Table 1 provides an overview of the various goals considering various sectors of activity in the engineering field.

Table 2. Examples of shared goals in the engineering field

Field	Shared Goal
Chemical	To be the chemical supplier with the lowest delivery times while maintaining high standards of product quality and service.
Electronics	Reach 10% of export share in the electronic equipment sales market segment until the end of 2020.
Information Technology	To create the first mobile augmented virtual reality solution for the tourism sector in Portugal.
Manufacturing	Obtain ISO 9001:2015 certification by the end of this semester.
Mechanic	Start producing electric power cars at a lower cost than other competitors.

One question that emerges in this field is whether the company should define a single goal or whether, on the contrary, multiple goals should be established. The answer to this question is not unanimous. The existence of a single goal can be too generic and not relevant for a group of employees; while the existence of multiple goals can disperse the attention of those who are really important. A hybrid approach that Berkun (2008) presents is the inclusion of multiple goals, but in which an ordered list of their priorities is defined. In any case, the number of goals on that list should be reduced. Appelo (2011) argues that these shared goals should have some properties: simple, concise, measurable, realistic, and ambitious.

Develop Competence

Competence can be seen as the ability to mobilize a set of knowledge, skills, and action capabilities to enhance performance. Eraut (2003, p. 117) defines competence as: "the ability to perform the tasks and roles required to the expected standards". According to this definition, competence includes both technical knowledge and generic and transversal abilities, typically associated with soft skills. From an employability perspective, Suleman (2007, p. 12) defines competence as "the set of knowledge and skills that must be held by any individual to enter and/or remain in the labor market, and to successfully face a professional situation". Competence can be revealed at two levels: as a personal characteristic associated with the skills and knowledge of the individual; as a structuring part of the individual's personality and conditioning his/her behavior.

The management of competences in an organization can be seen as the implementation of a systematized program that allows the development of professional profiles. It involves the planning, development, and evaluation, at different levels of the organization, of the organizational competencies critical to organizational success (Naquim & Holton, 2006). Its purpose is to minimize potential differences that may exist between the current competencies of employees and the competencies required for the function. It is pertinent to emphasize that these necessary competencies can be highly dynamic since the external context of the organization is quite uncertain and it is necessary to define a process of competencies evolution.

The organization has to offer effective mechanisms for motivating employees by establishing a system for continuous improvement in the performance of individuals and organizations. Through this model, employees know, in a precise and evolutionary way, the competences they need to develop. Competence management predicts the future behavior of employees based on the appropriate behavior for which they are trained. Furthermore, the analysis of concrete behaviors to be performed in a given job facilitates the identification of the required competencies and allows the prediction of training needs (Boyatzis, 2011).

One of the basic principles of Lean software development that is followed in Management 3.0 is optimization of the whole (Poppendieck, 2007). According to this principle, measurement is a key aspect of competence development. This measurement must still be comprehensive. Due to the importance of performance measurement, metrics can be considered as the center of perception of an organization. These metrics can focus on several areas of an organization's performance, such as finance, marketing, or innovation (Almeida et al., 2019). However, the use of performance measurement as a strategic element is relatively recent.

In the business environment, many companies focus on efficiency, productivity, or quality of their products and services in an isolated way, seeking only to maximize their individual performance. Traditional performance indicators are criticized for focusing too much on short-term results, encouraging local optimizations (e.g., maximizing a machine's profitability), and encouraging little innovation (Looy & Shafagatova, 2016). In this sense, performance monitoring systems should function as the integration tools of a company. Consequently, several problems in their implementation, like the lack of shared or outdated information by departments should be avoided.

According to Sahlin & Angelis (2019), performance monitoring systems must take into account several factors of the company such as the strategic plan, key business processes, and accounting measures. When implementing a performance monitoring system, the various processes related to cross-functional integration, customer-supplier partnerships, global scale, continuous improvement, and team responsibility must be analyzed. Other key factors are communication and employee involvement (Motyka, 2018).

The combination of these metrics will help managers to understand many interconnections within companies. This comprehension contributes to the crossing of traditional functional barriers and provides conditions for improved decision making.

It is recognized that organizational strategies should reach all actors in the company. Therefore, strategies should be designed to achieve results, and direct the actions of people regardless of their positions within the organizations. For this to happen, feedback on the results of activities is essential. Through this process, it is possible to compare with the plans and goals defined by the organization, and it also becomes feasible to carry out the necessary readjustments. This view is confirmed by Henri (2010) who advocates the periodic review and updating of metrics and the development of new indicators when necessary.

Grow Structure

The growth of companies brings unequivocal challenges at the organization of work and knowledge sharing level. One of the main risks is that the company grows according to organizational silos that make them less responsive to changes in context and market needs. Another pertinent question is to explore how teams should organize themselves. This issue is one of the central themes of debate in the education field since it concerns the levels of generalization or specialization that should be given in education. The paradigm in this area has changed. 20 years ago having higher education was enough condition for a graduate to act in his or her area of education. However, gradually, professionals have been migrating to specialization, due to the high demand to know in depth the area of knowledge of their work. However, the employee is now having problems in getting a comprehensive organizational vision, since after all he/she was more concerned with his/her area of expertise.

The 3.0 management paradigm takes an interesting approach to this problem. It considers that both models are compatible. First of all, an individual must be an expert in his/her field of knowledge. This should be his/her main expertise. However, it must be complemented with generalist knowledge that allows him/her to act in other areas. Consequently, the concept of "generalizing specialist" emerges, which according to Appelo (2011) is an individual who has the following characteristics: (i) has one or more technical areas of expertise; (ii) has general knowledge about software development; (iii) has knowledge about the business domain in which he works; and (iv) actively seeks to "develop knowledge in other areas. The second point is clearly the most debatable in many companies. Its relevance in the context of software engineering companies seems clear, but its relevance to other sectors of activity is widely questionable. However, this does not detract from the importance of knowledge in the IT field. Indeed, the recent impact of Covid-19 has shown the importance of IT knowledge, especially with the need for many companies to implement the teleworking regime and to start using synchronous and asynchronous communication tools, which were not widely known by those people.

The organizational model is another element that should be considered. Traditionally companies use a model of division of teams by area of training and performance. However, this is not the only way of organizing teams, as it becomes possible to create cross-functional teams. Cross-functional teams involving multidisciplinary skills are increasingly present in organizations. They differentiate themselves through innovative products, services and care (Troy et al., 2008). This type of organization is less hierarchical and vertical than more traditional structures. The idea is to form several teams that contain a wide variety of expertise. These teams can end at the conclusion of each project or continue for future projects. Table 3 lists the main advantages of organization using cross-functional teams.

Table 3. Advantages of cross-functional teams

Advantage	Description
Team integration	The model provides an approximation between people that possibly would not happen in the division of sectors.
Follow-up of the process	Working in smaller teams turns easier to follow the progress of the project.
Reducing bureaucracy	Cross-functional teams have autonomy, which allows them to eliminate impediments.
Greater autonomy	The manager empowers people so they can have the autonomy to deliberate on strategic issues.
Fosters creativity	Multifunctional teams promote thinking outside the box. With this, innovation and creativity can be stimulated.
Build team spirit	Cross-functional teams have more openness to take on big challenges. Overcoming these barriers develops team spirit and increases their cohesion.

One of the criticisms leveled at this model is the management of team autonomies, since this model enables its members to define their priorities (Wishart, 2020). Consequently, it is necessary to ensure that everyone aligns their goals with those of the company in an assertive manner. The importance of aligning the model with the first practice of Management 3.0 ("Align Constraints") is stressed here. Furthermore, depending on the organizational culture, deploying a cross-functional team can be a difficult task. This process will require a redefinition of roles within the teams and a division of power that leads to the horizontalization of the organization. Another challenge of this model is the communication that becomes essential for the model to work properly. This model requires much more dedication, as people of different roles and backgrounds need to interact and make themselves understood. Besides having a global vision of the project and the company, those involved need to be in constant conversation and interaction. As Bushe & Marshak (2015) propose in its organization development model dialogue, the reality is not unique and objective and must be socially constructed. Therefore, and as it is also advocated in Management 3.0, the reality results from a process of negotiation between teams and the organization, in which changes are encouraged in the context of self-managed teams.

Energize People

In order to promote good functioning within organizations, their members need to be motivated. Motivation arises as a crucial factor, since it leads to certain behaviors and performance of employees (Zeglat, 2017). Therefore, the motivational levels of individuals in an organization impact on organizational performance. This individual performance will generate organizational performance. The latter will necessarily result from other factors such as organizational culture, strategy, human resources, and technology (Gochhayat et al., 2017).

The relevance of the effective emotional aspect in motivating individuals is addressed by Pink (2011), in which it is stated that there has been a great development of technology and organizational models, but motivation models tend to be much more static and rigid. In this sense is advocated a motivational model applied to Management 3.0 in which managers need to understand that people want to help build better results for the company but as autonomy. However, and also as Pink (2011) points out, giving more autonomy to people requires greater emotional and professional maturity. Moreover, this model does not work in the same way with all people. It is important to consider that each individual responds differently to stimuli and benefits, hence standard models based on the theory of reward and punishment do not prove adequate.

Motivation assumes two components: intrinsic and extrinsic. Intrinsic or internal motivation is related to the inner strength of each individual in the face of adversity. Intrinsic motivation is usually associated with goals, objectives, and personal projects that stimulate the individual in his/her daily life. This is a kind of feeling that is present in most people. Extrinsic or external motivation is related to the environment and external factors. The awards obtained and organizational promotions are two examples of external motivations. A more complete vision of intrinsic and extrinsic factors of motivation is given in Figure 2. In the corporate environment, the organizational climate, diversified activities, improvement training, and other benefits stand out as efficient forms of external stimulation. These elements appear as transversal to several sectors of activity. They help to keep employees committed and productive. This type of incentive is seen as a way to help people stay engaged.

Figure 2. Intrinsic and extrinsic factors of motivation

These two components of motivation must be properly balanced. A widely adopted paradigm in the industry is that a rewards system is in itself a sufficient condition to motivate employees. According to this model, to increase productivity and engagement, it is enough to reward good actions and punish bad ones. However, an important part forgotten in the previous model is that the intrinsic motivation for an individual to make a creative lake, to contribute, to help, to have fun, and to learn. Pink (2011) reveals that people tend to be more likely to find a high level of achievement at work, rather than at leisure. This conclusion is very interesting and allows us to consider simultaneously the development of both components. Alone, extrinsic rewards can weaken intrinsic motivation, decrease performance, and impair good behavior. It is enough that the reward is fair and from that, we can develop a healthy intrinsic motivation. The fundamental point is that the organization has a clear mission and a higher purpose that is accepted by each individual.

Empowers Teams

In a highly dynamic and volatile market, characterized by fierce competition, autonomy is one of the most fundamental skills for productivity and to achieve organizational results. By giving employees more autonomy, allowing them to make agile decisions, the company will be more receptive to market demands.

Several approaches can be used to stimulate autonomy in teams. Wide and seamless communication helps to increase team performance, giving more autonomy to operational decisions. In this way, teams will be able to exchange information more easily and, conversely, will be more agile in responding to the various processes and challenges. Equally important is the clarification of individual and collective goals. Therefore, organizations should disclose individual (i.e. what is expected of each employee) and collective (i.e. what the team as a whole should deliver) goals. Clarifying business goals is fundamental to fostering autonomy, and to each individual knows his/her part in achieving the goals.

However, the concept of empowerment is often confused with the delegation of activities. There are necessarily differences to be noted. Delegation is only the act of giving activities and responsibilities to another individual. Empowerment is more than just the act of delegating. Empowerment also includes the support of risk, fosters a change in the cultural paradigm of the organization, and contributes to personal growth (Zhang et al., 2017). In the context of Management 3.0, it becomes very relevant to understand the level of delegation maturity followed by the teams. Seven levels of delegation can be identified as shown in Figure 3. There is not exactly one ideal level of maturity. It should emerge in the context of each team and in the context of each task. One way to know the delegation maturity of each team is through the delegation poker game as suggested by Appelo (2011).

Figure 3. Delegation levels

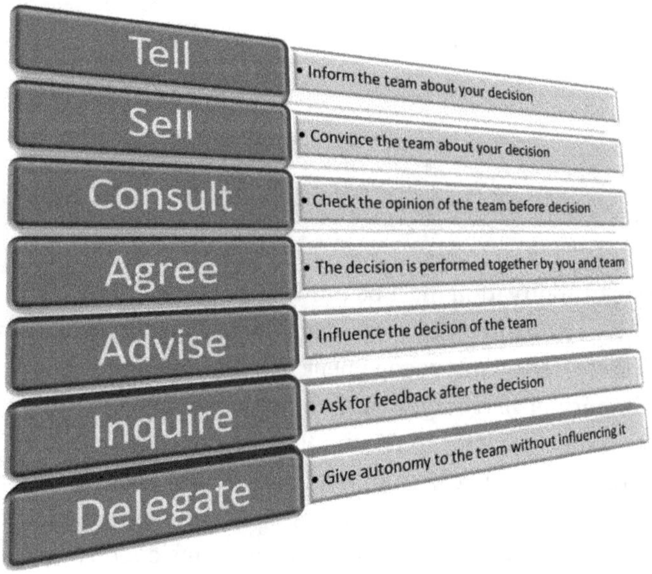

Several advantages associated with empowerment can be realized. Empowerment seeks to obtain the commitment of employees to the organization, through their participation in management processes. An organization, in which employees feel more valued and work more motivated, will have better conditions to achieve results of excellence. Rothman et al. (2019) report that empowerment offers an increase in the responsiveness of the organization to meet the demands of customers, technologies, competitors, among others. Therefore, in the era of a globalized society, where decentralization of powers is sought and decisions made in less time, empowerment can become a factor of competitive differentiation.

Improve Everything

Organizations and teams need to be constantly in a process of continuous improvement. Several business process methodologies (e.g. Six Sigma, Lean, etc.) can be adopted to improve processes and increase productivity while helping to solve quality problems and reduce waste. Each improvement opportunity is also an opportunity for employees to develop their leadership skills. Many improvement opportunities will require cross-functional collaboration. In this sense, having people with different profiles and motivations observing the same problem can produce better results.

Most continuous improvement processes tend to be linear. However, there are areas (e.g. software engineering projects) where evolution processes are not necessarily linear (Kasyoka, 2017). Significant advances can be achieved by questioning previous advances, which can leverage the identification of new solutions to problems. Therefore, the two processes of continuous and radical improvement must coexist.

The 3.0 management model is not based on the "first-mover advantage" principle, but on the "faster-learner advantage" principle. The organization best prepared for the challenges of the market will be the one with the most learning capacity. For this purpose, Appelo (2011) argues that an organizational environment should: (i) promotes the safe-to-fail environment, in which risk is shared; (ii) development of experiments, which may contribute to the creation of new paradigms; and (iii) continuous realization of faster and cheaper experiments. It is argued that only through experimentation will it be possible to know and measure the success of the introduction of a new product, service, or process.

Appelo (2011) considers that there are fundamentally three approaches to achieving optimal performance: (i) experimentation through changes in individual practices; (ii) identification of best organizational practices in the sector; and (iii) learning from others throughout development processes. The first approach essentially results in highly collaborative environments where broad communication and knowledge is sharing to ensure that the developed practices are not merely individual. It is an approach that necessarily takes a long time to produce results. The 2nd alternative applies essentially in more vertical organizations and in which leadership plays a key role in defining and sharing organizational practices. The 3rd approach also implies a high level of communication and collaboration, which can be complemented by the adoption of wikis, synchronous tools, and corporate social networks (Almeida & Rocha, 2011). The monitoring of several 3.0 management organizational projects allows us to conclude that often several of these practices can be applied together, without any of them assuming predominance over the others. Likewise, it cannot be concluded that one of these practices is better than the others. A model that results in one organization may not result in another, and the organizational culture, the way work is organized, the specificities of each organization should be taken into account in defining the established model.

FUTURE RESEARCH DIRECTIONS

Motivation is a key factor for the performance of Management 3.0 in an organization. In this area, two relevant sub-themes can be explored. Firstly, it is pertinent to explore how an individual can enhance his/her intrinsic motivation and also to understand which models the organization can help to introduce elements of extrinsic motivations. The balance between these two components of motivation is a key factor in applying Management 3.0 practices. Another area of great relevance is to explore the ideal level of balance of the intrinsic and extrinsic component. It is expected that a proposed model in this area will be able to take into account the specificities of each company and its employees.

Another future research topic associated with Management 3.0 is the role intrapreneurship can play. Empowerment is also a key factor in applying this paradigm and therefore it is also important to complement this vision with the concept of intrapreneurship. In increasingly dynamic environments, companies need to be concerned with the internal growth and development of their employees. One of the key competences in highly technological companies is the ability of the employee to have an entrepreneurial attitude, being able to assume leadership and responsibility. In this sense, one of the topics to investigate is how Management 3.0 can instill intrapreneurship phenomena.

Finally, another relevant future research topic is to explore the tools that can be used to develop the six components of Management 3.0. Appelo (2014) suggests several tools, such as: kudo cards, personal maps, delegation boards, problem time, moving motivators, among others. However, it is relevant to explore the role of each of these tools in the development of strategies for communication insights in business.

CONCLUSION

Management 3.0 is a movement in the management, innovation, and leadership fields that seeks to redefine business management models based on the concept of group responsibility. This model brings the paradigm of agility to management and considers that not only technology companies can benefit from this technology. This paradigm brings a more humanized management to companies, where people should be the most important asset of the organization. The fundamental objective of this paradigm is to engage employees and thus leverage business growth. Consequently, all employees must be focused on a common goal. The focus is to create an environment where everyone is responsible for the success of the business and it is up to the teams how the tasks are performed, taking away the verticality of the management system.

The Management 3.0 model is based on the implementation of six visions for a business. Firstly, it becomes essential to motivate people to always keep them creative and motivated to do their best. This motivation is achieved by looking at both the intrinsic and extrinsic aspects of each individual's motivation. Next, teams must be self-organized and therefore need management authorization and trust. At the same time as encouraging team autonomy, it is important to put in place a set of rules and boundaries so that this freedom is aligned with the fundamental objectives of the organization. To this end, the organizational objectives must be formally defined and known. The idea is to ensure that the organizational goals overlap the individual objectives. Fourthly, the importance of developing competencies through the existence of multidisciplinary teams is assumed. A model based on cross-functional teams is advocated that promotes the management of skills in the organization. After that, sustainable growth in the business must be encouraged with a focus on communication and collaboration between the teams.

Finally, continuous process improvements are sought, and mistakes should be seen as opportunities for improvement. In this dimension, the existence of a system to continuously measure the performance of each individual and the organization is defended. This is intended to reduce the risk of organizational silos and encourage the harmonious growth of the various areas of the organization.

This study offers essentially practical contributions by exploring and understanding the practices and challenges posed by the implementation of Management 3.0 in each of its 6 dimensions. Some limitations can be pointed out in this work. First of all, the difficulties that may arise in replicating Management 3.0 practices to other organizations. Typically, as addressed throughout this work, replicating these practices to another organizational context that does not follow the lean and agile paradigm can lead to catastrophic results. Therefore, it is critical that organizations are willing to change their organizational model and that the adoption of this model is done gradually. Another limitation of this study is that the impact of distributed teams on the functioning of Management 3.0 was not addressed. Building cross-functional teams involving geographically distinct employees can be a challenge. In this sense, and as future work, it is important to analyze how Management 3.0 can be gradually adopted by organizations, and also to explore models of integration of geographically distributed teams in highly dynamic and agile environments.

REFERENCES

Almeida, F., Kennedy, A. J., Lin, B., & Nowak, I. (2019). Measuring innovation through a crowd source initiative. *International Journal of Innovation Science*, *11*(3), 471–488. doi:10.1108/IJIS-04-2019-0046

Almeida, F., & Rocha, R. (2011). Introduction of a WIKI in an enterprise: Motives and challenges. *Journal of Systems Integration*, *2*(4), 46–53. doi:10.20470/jsi.v2i4.101

Appelo, J. (2011). *Management 3.0: Leading Agile Developers, Developing Agile Leaders*. Addison-Wesley Professional.

Appelo, J. (2014). *Management 3.0 Workout*. Happy Melly Express.

Appleby, Y., & Pikington, R. (2014). *Developing Critical Professional Practice in Education*. NIACE.

Araújo, C., & Pedron, C. D. (2016). The Importance of Soft Skills and it Project Managers' Personality Type. *International Journal of Professional Business Review*, *1*(1), 40–59. doi:10.26668/businessreview/2016.v1i1.8

Bailey, C. (2017). *A Guide to Qualitative Field Research*. SAGE Publications.

Bang, H., & Midelfart, T. N. (2017). What characterizes effective management teams? A research-based approach. *Consulting Psychology Journal*, *69*(4), 334–359. doi:10.1037/cpb0000098

Berkun, S. (2008). *Making Things Happen: Mastering Project Management*. O'Reilly Media.

Boyatzis, R. E. (2011). Managerial and Leadership Competencies A Behavioral Approach to Emotional, Social and Cognitive Intelligence. *Vision – The Journal of Business Perspective, 15*(2), 91-100.

Brace, L. (2016). *The Seven Principles of Managing for Creativity*. Retrieved from https://management30.com/blog/the-seven-principles-of-managing-for-creativity/

Bushe, G. R., & Marshak, R. J. (2015). *Dialogic Organization Development: The Theory and Practice of Transformational Change*. Berrett-Koehler Publishers.

Cheney, G., Christensen, L. T., Zorn, T. E., & Ganesh, S. (2011). *Organizational Communication in an Age of Globalization: Issues, Reflections, Practices*. Waveland Pr Inc.

Dolphin, R. (2005). Internal Communications: Today's Strategic Imperative. *Journal of Marketing Communications*, *11*(3), 171–190. doi:10.1080/1352726042000315414

Eraut, M. (2003). *Developing Professional Knowledge And Competence*. Routledge.

Fetterman, D. (2019). *Ethnography: Step-by-Step*. SAGE Publications.

Florea, N. V., & Duica, A. (2017). Improving Communication and Relationship with Customers using Models to Measure their Value. *Valahian Journal of Economic Studies*, *8*(1), 47–56. doi:10.1515/vjes-2017-0006

Gochhayat, J., Giri, V. N., & Suar, D. (2017). Influence of Organizational Culture on Organizational Effectiveness: The Mediating Role of Organizational Communication. *Global Business Review*, *18*(3), 691–702. doi:10.1177/0972150917692185

Griffin, R. W., Phillips, J. M., & Gully, S. M. (2016). *Organizational Behavior: Managing People and Organizations*. Cengage Learning.

Hatch, M. J. (2018). *Organization Theory: Modern, Symbolic, and Postmodern Perspectives*. Oxford University Press.

Henri, J. F. (2010). The Periodic Review of Performance Indicators: An Empirical Investigation of the Dynamism of Performance Measurement Systems. *European Accounting Review*, *19*(1), 73–96. doi:10.1080/09638180902863795

Hlupic, V. (2014). *The Management Shift: How to Harness the Power of People and Transform Your Organization For Sustainable Success*. Palgrave Macmillan. doi:10.1057/9781137352958

Hougaard, R. (2018). *The Real Crisis In Leadership*. Retrieved from https://www.forbes.com/sites/rasmushougaard/2018/09/09/the-real-crisis-in-leadership/#62e6fd173ee4

Jamshed, S. (2014). Qualitative research method-interviewing and observation. *Journal of Basic and Clinical Pharmacy*, *5*(4), 87–88. doi:10.4103/0976-0105.141942 PMID:25316987

Kasyoka, M. (2017). *The Non-Linear Nature Of Software Development*. Retrieved from https://www.otbafrica.com/index.php/otb/item/192-the-non-linear-nature-of-software-development

Leroy, H., Segers, J., Van Dierendonck, D., & Den Hartog, D. (2018). Managing people in organizations: Integrating the study of HRM and leadership. *Human Resource Management Review*, *28*(3), 249–257. doi:10.1016/j.hrmr.2018.02.002

Linke, A., & Zerfass, A. (2011). Internal communication and innovation culture: Developing a change framework. *Journal of Communication Management (London)*, *15*(4), 332–348. doi:10.1108/13632541111183361

Locker, K., & Kaczmarek, S. (2013). *Business Communication: Building Critical Skills*. McGraw-Hill Education.

Looy, A., & Shafagatova, A. (2016). Business process performance measurement: a structured literature review of indicators, measures and metrics. *SpringerPlus, 5*(1797), 1-24.

Markovic, M. R., & Salamzadeh, A. (2018). The Importance of Communication in Business Management. *Proceedings of the 7th International Scientific Conference on Employment, Education and Entrepreneurship*, 11-28.

Marques, J. (2013). Understanding the Strength of Gentleness: Soft-Skilled Leadership on the Rise. *Journal of Business Ethics, 116*(1), 163–171. doi:10.100710551-012-1471-7

Mazzei, A. (2010). Promoting active communication behaviours through internal communication. *Corporate Communications, 15*(3), 221–234. doi:10.1108/13563281011068096

Mihai, R. L. (2017). Corporate Communication Management: A Management Approach. *Valahian Journal of Economic Studies, 8*(2), 103–110. doi:10.1515/vjes-2017-0023

Monahan, T., & Fisher, J. A. (2010). Benefits of "Observer Effects": Lessons from the Field. *Qualitative Research, 10*(3), 357–376. doi:10.1177/1468794110362874 PMID:21297880

Motyka, B. (2018). Employee engagement and performance: A systematic literature review. *International Journal of Management and Economics, 54*(3), 227–244. doi:10.2478/ijme-2018-0018

Naquin, S., & Holton, E. III. (2006). Leadership and Managerial Competency Models: A Simplified Process and Resulting Model. *Advances in Developing Human Resources, 8*(2), 144–165. doi:10.1177/1523422305286152

O'Malley, M., & Baker, W. F. (2019). *Organizations for People: Caring Cultures, Basic Needs, and Better Lives*. Stanford Business Books. doi:10.1515/9781503611054

Pink, D. H. (2011). *Drive: The Surprising Truth About What Motivates Us*. Riverhead Books.

Pollack, J. (2007). The changing paradigms of project management. *International Journal of Project Management, 25*(3), 266–274. doi:10.1016/j.ijproman.2006.08.002

Poppendieck, M. (2007). *Implementing Lean Software Development*. Addison-Wesley.

Queirós, A., Faria, D., & Almeida, F. (2017). Strengths and Limitations of Qualitative and Quantitative Research Methods. *European Journal of Education Studies, 3*(9), 369–387.

Rashid, M., Caine, V., & Goez, H. (2015). The Encounters and Challenges of Ethnography as a Methodology in Health Research. *International Journal of Qualitative Methods, 14*(5), 1–16. doi:10.1177/1609406915621421

Rothman, L., De Vijlder, F., Schalk, R., & Van Regenmortel, M. (2019). A systematic review on organizational empowerment. *The International Journal of Organizational Analysis, 27*(5), 1336–1361. doi:10.1108/IJOA-02-2019-1657

Sahlin, J., & Angelis, J. (2019). Performance management systems: Reviewing the rise of dynamics and digitalization. *Cogent Business & Management*, *6*(1), 1–21. doi:10.1080/23311975.2019.1642293

Salah, S., Carretero, J. A., & Rahim, A. (2009). Six Sigma and Total Quality Management (TQM): Similarities, differences and relationship. *International Journal of Six Sigma and Competitive Advantage*, *5*(3), 237–250. doi:10.1504/IJSSCA.2009.028095

Sarka, H. (2014). Tools of Internal Communication from Knowledge Transfer Perspective. *Journal of Competitiveness*, *6*(4), 50–62. doi:10.7441/joc.2014.04.04

Sebastião, S. P., Zulato, G., & Trindade, A. D. (2017). Internal communication and organisational culture: The management interplay in the view of the Portuguese communication consultant. *Public Relations Review*, *43*(4), 863–871. doi:10.1016/j.pubrev.2017.05.006

Sharp, H., Dittrich, Y., & de Souza, C. (2016). The Role of Ethnographic Studies in Empirical Software Engineering. *IEEE Transactions on Software Engineering*, *42*(8), 786–804. doi:10.1109/TSE.2016.2519887

Sheridan, S., & Williams, P. (2011). Developing Individual Goals, Shared Goals, and the Goals of Others: Dimensions of Constructive Competition in Learning Contexts. *Scandinavian Journal of Educational Research*, *55*(2), 145–164. doi:10.1080/00313831.2011.554694

Stare, A. (2013). Agile project management – a future approach to the management of projects? *Dynamic Relationship Management Journal*, *1*(2), 43–53. doi:10.17708/DRMJ.2013.v02n01a04

Suleman, F. (2007). *O valor das competências: um estudo aplicado ao sector bancário*. Horizonte.

Troy, L. C., Hirunyawipada, T., & Paswan, A. K. (2008). Cross-Functional Integration and New Product Success: An Empirical Investigation of the Findings. *Journal of Marketing*, *72*(6), 132–146. doi:10.1509/jmkg.72.6.132

Van Dooremalen, T. (2017). The pros and cons of researching events ethnographically. *Ethnography*, *18*(3), 415–424. doi:10.1177/1466138117709293 PMID:29081715

Van Gaans, M. (2018). *What is Management 3.0?* Retrieved from https://wuwei-inst.org/management-3-0-what-is-it-all-about/

Van Roosmalen, R. (2017). Doing It! AL Nuland, The Netherlands: Agile Strides.

Vercic, A. T., & Vokic, N. P. (2017). Engaging employees through internal communication. *Public Relations Review*, *43*(5), 885–893. doi:10.1016/j.pubrev.2017.04.005

Wishart, J. (2020). *How to Manage and Coordinate Successful Cross-Functional Teams*. Retrieved from https://www.rhythmsystems.com/blog/dos-and-donts-of-coordinating-cross-functional-teams

Yanik, B. (2017). An Ethnographic Approach to Education: What Are You Doing in This Village? *Journal of Education and Practice*, *8*(26), 113–118.

Yeomans, L. (2007). Effective Internal Communication. *Journal of Communication Management (London)*, *11*(1), 90–91. doi:10.1108/13632540710726012

Yukl, G. (2012). Effective Leadership Behavior: What We Know and What Questions Need More Attention. *The Academy of Management Perspectives*, *26*(4), 66–85. doi:10.5465/amp.2012.0088

Zeglat, D. (2017). The Impact of Employee Motivation on Organizational Commitment. *European Journal of International Management*, *9*(15), 134–145.

Zhang, X., Qian, J., Wang, B., Jin, Z., Wang, J., & Wang, Y. (2017). Leaders' Behaviors Matter: The Role of Delegation in Promoting Employees' Feedback-Seeking Behavior. *Frontiers in Psychology*, *8*, 1–10. doi:10.3389/fpsyg.2017.00920 PMID:28638357

ADDITIONAL READING

Abdallah, S. (2020). Social Interactions in Electronic Networks of Practice: A Model for Effective Knowledge Construction, Problem Solving, and Learning. *International Journal of e-Collaboration*, *16*(2), 27–44. doi:10.4018/IJeC.2020040103

Bond-Barnard, T., Fletcher, L., & Steyn, H. (2018). Linking trust and collaboration in project teams to project management success. *International Journal of Managing Projects in Business*, *11*(2), 432–457. doi:10.1108/IJMPB-06-2017-0068

Chen, H., & Bishop, I. D. (2013). Collaborative Environmental Knowledge Management. *International Journal of E-Planning Research*, *2*(1), 58–81. doi:10.4018/ijepr.2013010104

DeWitt, P. M. (2016). *Collaborative Leadership: Six Influences That Matter Most*. Corwin.

Fuchs-Kittowski, F., & Siegeris, E. (2012). An Integrated Collaboration Environment for Various Types of Collaborative Knowledge Work. In N. Kock (Ed.), *Advancing Collaborative Knowledge Environments: New Trends in E-Collaboration* (pp. 102–113). IGI Global. doi:10.4018/978-1-61350-459-8.ch007

Hsieh, J. Y., & Liou, K. T. (2018). Collaborative Leadership and Organizational Performance: Assessing the Structural Relation in a Public Service Agency. *Review of Public Personnel Administration*, *38*(1), 83–109. doi:10.1177/0734371X15623619

Joy, S. P., & Chandran, P. (2019). Towards a Secure Development Environment for Collaborative Applications. *International Journal of e-Collaboration*, *15*(1), 1–20. doi:10.4018/IJeC.2019010101

Markova, D., & McArthur, A. (2015). *Collaborative Intelligence: Thinking with People Who Think Differently*. Spiegel & Grau.

Masud, M. (2015). Knowledge Update in Collaborative Knowledge Sharing Systems. *International Journal of Knowledge Society Research*, *6*(3), 19–31. doi:10.4018/IJKSR.2015070102

Prinz, W., Martínez-Carreras, M. A., & Pallot, M. (2012). From Collaborative Tools to Collaborative Working Environments. In N. Kock (Ed.), *Advancing Collaborative Knowledge Environments: New Trends in E-Collaboration* (pp. 1–10). IGI Global. doi:10.4018/978-1-61350-459-8.ch001

Schmitt, R., & Almeida, F. (2020). Building a Culture of Continuous Innovation: How Pixar and Google Address This Challenge? *Journal of Management, Economics, and Industrial Organization*, *4*(1), 22–39. doi:10.31039/jomeino.2020.4.1.2

KEY TERMS AND DEFINITIONS

Empowerment: Strategic management action aimed at improving the use of human capital in organizations through the delegation of power.

Intrapreneurship: An entrepreneurial mode that consists in the practice of employees having the ability to act as business founders, helping above all to stimulate the creation of ideas within organizations, even if indirectly.

Lean: Management methodology based on three fundamental ideas: delivering value to the customer, eliminating waste, and continuous improvement.

Six Sigma: A set of practices developed to maximize the performance of processes within the company, eliminating their defects and non-conformities according to the manufacturer's specifications.

Teleworking: A form of work carried out in a place far from the office and/or production center, allowing physical separation and involving the use of a new technology facilitating communication.

Wiki: Concept used to refer to web pages whose contents can be edited by multiple users through any browser.

Chapter 4
Process Improvement Through Visual Management:
An Insight Management Tool?

Julio Silva
Faculty of Economics, University of Algarve, Portugal

Silvia Fernandes
https://orcid.org/0000-0002-1699-5415
FE, Cinturs, University of Algarve, Portugal

Paula Ventura Martins
https://orcid.org/0000-0002-3199-4517
FCT, Cinturs, University of Algarve, Portugal

ABSTRACT

Departments in enterprises can benefit from visual management (VM) methods. This involves observing a framework of planning activities on a desktop. The information should be clearly visible and easy to understand to all involved. The VM framework used in this case really proved to be a great option in terms of clarity, motivation, process review, real knowledge of results, and correction procedures. The implementation of VM methods will bring to companies a cultural change. There will be some points of resistance to be worked; however, through the income statement, these will be overcame. Then, if we use an insight management (IM) platform, it is possible to cross all those data in diverse ways to produce several scenarios, which can be considered as visual analytics. This is relevant for the case in study, especially in order to explore new strategies based on the indexes envisioned to replicate the positive results throughout the entire restaurant group.

DOI: 10.4018/978-1-7998-3964-4.ch004

INTRODUCTION

While operations management has been studied on its benefits and functions, the technique of visual management (VM) has not been systematically investigated (Kurpjuweit et al., 2019). Nevertheless, the best practices observed provide insights of its advantages and how to implement it (Yik & Chin, 2019).

Either strategic, tactical, or operational departments may derive benefits from a VM framework for planning their activities. One contributing factor is that it stimulates information sharing and dissemination. There are great advantages from getting all items involved in the same level of practice. For example, at a restaurant, if the manager visualizes the waiter's work, he also captures the real preparation and confection conditions, timings, etc. Everyone can have the same knowledge from the visual framework. This way, every employee can have a holistic view of his work, and the way it integrates in the whole process.

The information should be clearly visible, easy to follow and understandable (Tonkin, 1998; Kurpjuweit et al., 2019). Also, the framework should have characteristics such as:

- informative – that transfers useful and motivating information to those who consult it
- beneficial – that enables an easy, fast, safe and satisfying service
- attractive - interesting and enjoyable for the viewers.

Moreover, the information can be displayed in various formats (figures 1, 2): tables, charts, panel data, banners, posters, electronic media (if using computer networks), etc.

Figure 1. Example of VM panel

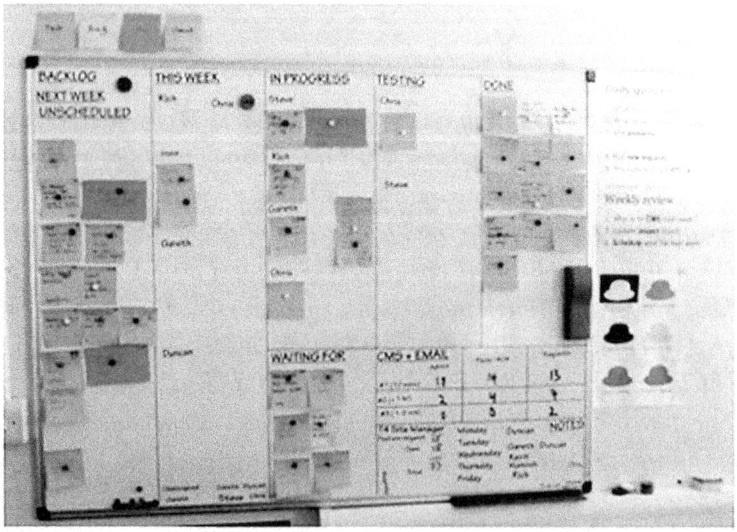

Problem Formulation

Today, having quick access to information and answering time have become crucial issues for competitive advantage. From comparing practical studies (Costa et al., 2015; Ward & Dagger, 2017; Yik &

Chin, 2019) that discuss VM, the present work aims at applying VM to the management of a modern restaurant. Thus, it is oriented to answer the following research questions:

1. Q1. *What are the difficulties from lacking information about the restaurant's activities?*
2. Q2. *What are the benefits of implementing the VM methods in the restaurant?*

These questions will be answered through a case-study conducted at a restaurant group (named *Chelsea Pizza & Pasta*). It is located at Faro, capital in the region of Algarve in Portugal. This region is relevant to consider, due to the type of customers, either residents or tourists. Europe often receives international tourists, due to a number of countries with focus on tourism growth. Portugal is a good example, with a growth of over 11% in 2017 (WTO, 2018).

According to the Algarve Cook and Oenological Report (Turismo Algarve, 2018) which addresses sustainability aspects in Algarve's gastronomy, the travel and tourism sector contributed with about 10.2% to global economy and 6.6% to total exports (World Economic Forum, 2017). This sector has generated 292 million jobs and has exceeded 1.3 billion international arrivals in 2017 (Turismo Algarve, 2018). Regarding these data, companies need to be prepared to have an excellent service, delivering higher quality products and services.

Objectives of the Work

Managers around the world must develop the feeling, state of mind, passion/desire to be effective, creating high quality services (Maister, 2013; Ivancevich et al., 2006). Managing human resources in hospitality has changed in recent years, due to market dynamics of new needs and use of technological innovations in service delivery (Murata, 2019). Even working relationships have changed because of supporting technologies such as wireless devices.

In business, practice should guide the company to produce more and spend less (lean management). Also, many organizations have encouraged their employees to be *intrapreneurs*. Following these footsteps, *Chelsea Pizza & Pasta* restaurant is experimenting methods such as: QCDSM (Quality, Cost, Delivery, Safety, Morale); 5W2H (What? Who? Where? When? Why? How? How much?); flowcharts; and PDCA (Plan, Do, Check, Action). These are holistic VM methods with advantages such as: sharing, disseminating and timely monitoring the management information of processes and teams.

This research aims to discuss and implement the VM approach, as a model for displaying and verifying monthly, quarterly, or annual results by area, at the restaurant under study. As well as integrating the staff in their perception and understanding, to aid their interpretation and monitoring on time.

LITERATURE REVIEW

The search for theoretical grounding is essential to identify main concepts related to this theme. Concepts will be presented in this section, especially within the QCDSM and 5W2H methods, as well as crucial indicators of performance in the analyzes and actions derived throughout a VM panel (or dashboard).

Visual Management Approach

VM is a subject that has been discussed in the last decade by experts in the field and organizational leaders facing environmental, management and operational uncertainties (Torghabehi et al., 2016). Organizational environment has quickly changed, challenging managers to seek for new strategies to remain competitive (Rangel et al., 2010). Also, consumers are demanding higher product/service quality.

VM is an important method of disseminating information within departments. Its function is mainly to transmit content easily to everyone involved. In VM, charts and other visual resources are spread across the various areas of an organization. It is curious that, as humans, we process visual information faster than any other form (about 60000 times faster than text). Visual information is also stored in a unique way: 83% of what we learn is visual, and the data remain more than if we simply read it (Packer & Suski, 2013).

VM can turn important control items available to entire teams (Araújo, 2009). These items include charts, data, and management information that can be easily interpreted by all participants. This can be performed in various ways, from a break-room whiteboard to a departmental video projection. It allows that any information submitted is not only quickly understood, but also effectively retained. Thus, VM can be a relevant management tool to save time and work effort (Yik & Chin, 2019). In addition, teams feel more involved. Such visual communication ensures that everyone can easily see how their performance impacts or is aligned with company's goals (Lins & Holanda, 2011).

Silva & Loos (2017) reinforced VM as a tool capable of improving productivity, quality, internal communication, information flow, and decision-making support. For Souza et al. (2014), the main goal of VM is to provide accessible information that facilitates daily work. People can register the productivity achieved, the stops (due to external/internal influences), defective parts, and then spread the information. Weekly meetings occur in front of the VM framework for knowledge exchange, evaluation of achieved results, and validation by team members.

As everyone has opportunity to participate in decision making and problem solving, the degree of assertiveness is high, facilitating communication between people and work shifts (Neese & Kong, 2007). Everyone has the same responsibility to fill in the VM board with information on cell productivity, quality, number of defects, downtime due to internal/external problems, and consumable expense. Before presenting some examples of VM, some cautions are necessary, such as:

- defining the indicators to establish the visual standards to be adopted. Limiting the choices to relevant metrics is crucial, to avoid unnecessary data. It is also important to create a team responsible for collecting and updating standards continuously (Lins & Holanda, 2011)
- preparing managers to use this tool efficiently, so they can spread the approach among other collaborators (Mello, 1998).

Figure 2 presents another example of VM, illustrating the variety that can exist depending on the focus, process structure and technological support used:

It is important that the dashboard is regularly updated to prevent outdated data and diminishing value added. Next sections stress methods that help in this continuous updating and monitoring.

Figure 2. Another example of VM panel (automatized)

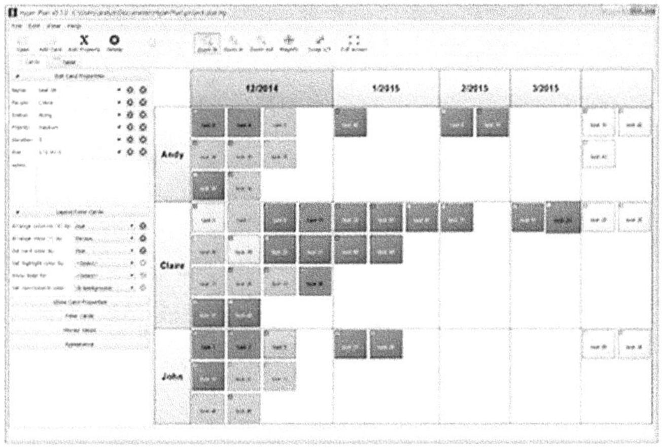

The QCDSM Method

QCDSM (Quality, Cost, Delivery, Safety, Morale) is a process measurement method, applicable to simple or complex business processes. This method aims at reaching full customer satisfaction. It focuses on people from various departments and establishes a methodology for measuring their performance in their procedures. Another function is the ability to measure customer/supplier relationships, in the supply chain, for suggesting new ideas to continually improve it. The main feature is the use of detailed and graphically registered data (facts, figures) to make logical decisions.

It is designed to process potentially large problems and break them into smaller ones. These minor problems can be prioritized, and the necessary resources can be allocated to ensure the desired operation. When referring the QCDSM method, it is important to know the meaning of each acronym:

- Quality - the quality of products must be high, and consistently good
- Cost - the cost of goods must be competitive. No matter how high the quality of a product, its price is important. Cost efficiency can be attained by reducing waste and defects
- Delivery - customers want products delivered on time, otherwise they can look for another company that meets their needs. Proper planning of orders will ensure on-time delivery
- Safety - with an internal focus, safety will benefit everyone. Identifying risks (and eliminating them) should be a priority at any product/service
- Morale – keeping the employees' morale high has a positive impact on many business areas. Companies with a high morale usually outperform.

Another advantage of this method is related with employees' engagement, where they become promoters or guardians of their work managing the results. The management structure should facilitate people's involvement and use of the same principles in managing their functions (figure 3).

In today's competitive world, companies are looking for ways to reach their customers, improve their market share, and expand their business. Ultimately, they are concerned with involving their employees. Enabling employees to, not only share their goals but also actively promote them, is a major challenge.

Figure 3. Example of a meeting with collaborators

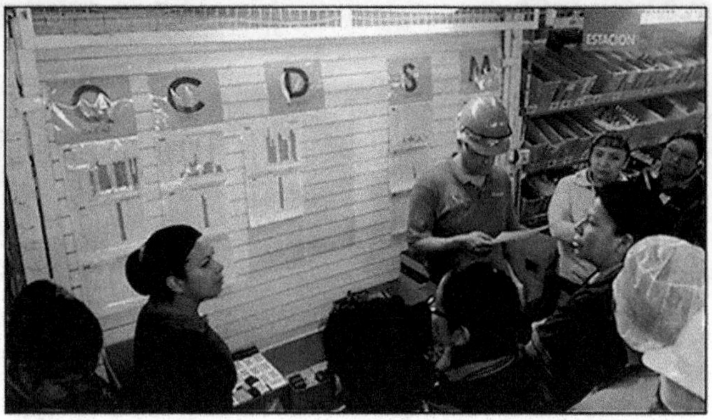

The 5W2H Method

Persistent problems indicate that the firm has rooted issues and needs to discover their cause and eliminate it. It is convenient to resolve slight problems immediately (as they require less time). However, solutions are not permanent and changes can lead to a waste of time and resources.

The 5W2H method (What? Who? Where? When? Why? / How? How much?) is known as the *subordinate's dream* or *manager's hope* because the employee 'dreams' about receiving 5W2H orders and the boss 'hopes' his subordinates present problems in a 5W2H format (Polacinski, 2012). This tool is considered one of the most effective quality management tools, due to its clarity and simplicity (Marshall Junior et al., 2008).

Today, both organizational activities and communications need to be agile. Many problems can arise from misinformation. The focus of this method is to make information safe and error-free (Silva et al., 2013). It can be a tool designed to prepare ideas operationally through a list (figure 4):

Figure 4. Dimensions of the 5W2H method

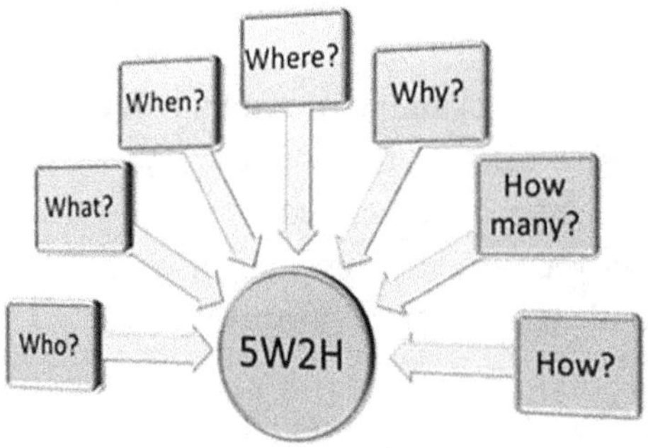

In problem solving, a main goal is to clarify complex situations through proper techniques and documentation. This method is a complete analysis of how a specific problem arises (Polacinski, 2012). Its queries are very useful when brainstorming is required for any action plan. A problem is segmented into different parts, making it easier to solve. Firstly, it requires answers to the following questions:

- What is needed to be done?
- Why should it be done?
- When to do it?
- Where should it be done?
- Who is going to do it?
- How to do it?
- How many resources are needed?

Alves (2010) describes the meaning of those open questions:

1. Why? - understands all possible reasons for the specific situation
2. When? - analyzes frequency of the problem and incidence time, to define precautions
3. Where? - helps to understand fault location, and examines geographic distribution of customer complaints
4. Who? - identifies the causes of the situation, which can be personal or processual. For example, buyers who complain and operators experiencing difficulties
5. How? - investigates the type of scenario and its difficulties. Examines the procedures applied to problem solving
6. How much? - determines the resources/budget available or needed for problem solving.

Silva et al. (2013) refer that the 5W2H method is very important in process management and improvement since:

- it is a simpler and more efficient problem-solving technique than other quality management tools
- several problems, associated with the main problem, can be discovered
- generally, no statistical data is required to perform the method.

CASE STUDY

In the company under study, during the execution of activities, we noticed there are problems related to: lack of control, tables' complaints, non-standard dishes, delays in delivering orders, etc. With this in mind, we decided to apply the referred tools in the process and assess the level of control and standardization in accomplishing tasks. Then, the research questions were considered for assessing the impacts of those visual management tools.

Considering Research Questions

Regarding the first question - Q1. *What are the difficulties from lacking information about the restaurant's activities?* - the first step was to observe the restaurant in a macro way, to verify which departments sell the most and which ones sell less. Based on this first objective, we used the QCDSM method.

Within each topic, a monthly tracking was used to evaluate restaurant performance. It was accomplished through an excel file, organized to include all items sold in the restaurant and then a daily input (from June 2018 to January 2019):

Q (Quality) - in this topic we checked the restaurant's rating by customers, collecting information from websites (Google, Facebook, Trip Advisor) considering the total rating in all months and the ratio 'total rating /total complaints' (%). The main complaint is the delay in service delivery. As the volume increased, the waiting time also increased. This results in the delay of pizzas' delivery and so an analysis was made to understand the reasons. It showed that the delay was due to the oven, which is not able to meet the demands per hour.

C (Cost) - the survey used was divided into two topics, one for installation costs and one for input costs (dividing the latter by department). There was no robust action for this topic. A goal was to clearly show the owner which department consumed the most.

D (Delivery) – this category is linked to the issues of Q topic (quality). There are no specific actions for this topic since, at the time, the evaluation from customers and consequent reduction of waiting times would improve delivery.

S (Safety) - in this topic we chose to evaluate items related to the building safety. Issues were observed on the building's structure, where the restaurant is located, to identify possible irregularities. Also, to verify possible equipment failures, checklists were implemented to ensure all appliances were checked daily to prevent potential accidents. As these imply time lost, the idea is to register possible occurrences related to accidents/ incidents.

M (Morale) - at this topic, an organizational chart was prepared to follow the evolution of each employee in the restaurant. A perceived issue is, when presenting the menu at a table, customers ask deeper questions and waiters usually do not know details (such as dish preparation). To solve this, worksheets of the dishes were created to inform them, contributing to a more effective service.

After all the evaluations, we decided to work on the indicator of most concern: customers' complaint about delays. The focus is to reduce the waiting time, proposing the owner to install an oven with a larger capacity. A suggestion is to bring a larger oven from another restaurant of the group. It was also observed that the physical space supports more customers than can be served. This turns lead time higher due to the lack of ovens to fulfill orders.

While many delays are caused by inefficiencies in the service delivery process, other seem almost inevitable. For example, consumers usually do not come to the restaurant at equal intervals. Then, some services may overlap with those to other customers, causing waiting problems.

Managers may have difficulties in coordinating all these situations. However, a service provider may mitigate the impacts of such delays if he has knowledge about the factors that influence consumer reactions (Q1). By discovering those factors, and the contexts in which they occur, managers can boost customer satisfaction.

Maister (2013) studied several situational effects on consumers' perception of waiting. He suggested the following four propositions: (1) unoccupied time seems longer than busy time; (2) preprocessing waits seem longer than in-process waits; (3) uncertain waits are longer than expected waits; and (4) unexplained waits are longer than explained ones.

Regarding the second research question - Q2. *What are the benefits of implementing VM methods in the restaurant?* - an individual's visit to a restaurant can be divided into three distinct phases: (1) a preprocess phase, from the arrival at the restaurant until the meal's request; (2) a process that includes the order and consuming the meal; and (3) a post-payment process until the customer leaves the place. During each of these phases, there is an 'interval' that customers expect. However, what happens if this interval extends beyond customer expectations?

Following Lewin's (2010) theory, we consider that delays at different stages of the stay have different effects on customer's behavior. In addition, the uncertainty level of a delay's duration and the need of an individual would influence his perceived delay and evaluation of the service. All this information is dynamic, whose data if visually gathered and shared, can be a relevant source of coordination and control (Q2). For example, figure 5 illustrates a report on waiting times.

Figure 5. Report with the analysis on the high waiting time

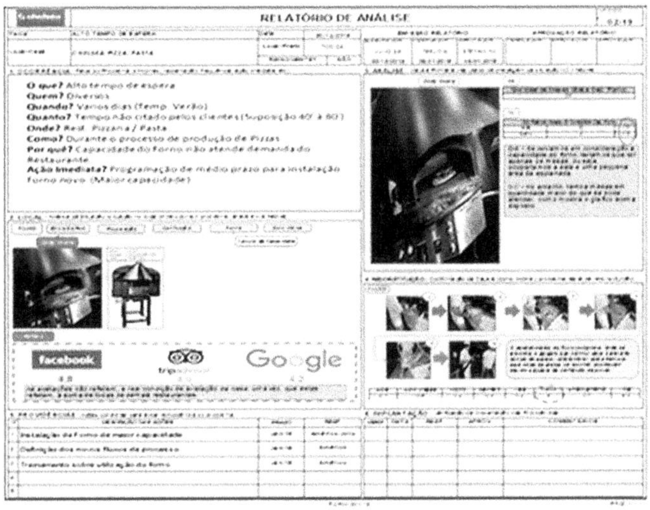

Another issue refers to accidents: although customers associate restaurants with comfort and pleasure, these places have real risks (Albuquerque et al., 2012). Managers should also remember that expenses can include hiring substitute workers, paying overtime work and retraining.

The 5W2H method (What? Who? Where? When? Why?/ How? How much?) is an interesting tool for mapping processes, elaborating action plans, and establishing procedures and their indicators. This questioning method is very useful as the problem is segmented into different parts, turning it easier to solve.

Resuming to the case-study, the installation of an oven with larger capacity, the training on its use, and definition of new process flows are the main steps to take during the application of the proposed approach to avoid recurring problems.

From Visual Management (VM) to Insight Management (IM)

Events gathered in the VM approach can refer to patterns, relationships, anomalies, etc. As direct products of visual exploration, they can give business insights. The facts discovered from visual data are predictable and application independent. Then, if we use 'insight management' platforms (such as Power BI) it is possible to cross all those data in diverse ways, to produce several scenarios. These can be considered as visual analytics (figure 6). This can answer more effectively to the queries of the 5W2H method.

Figure 6. Example of an IM panel

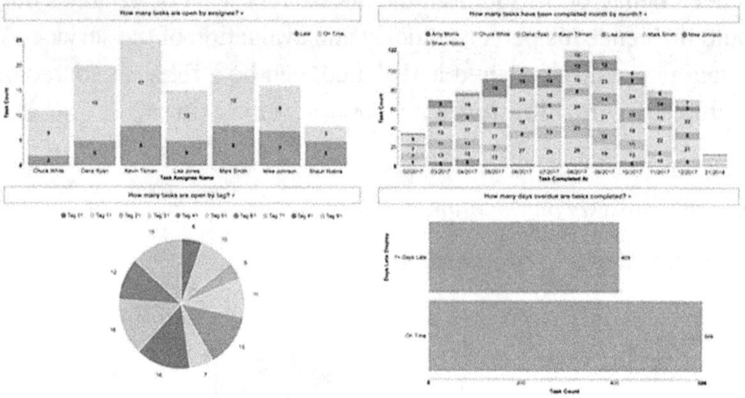

Insight exchange, in collaborative visual analytics, should be a practice to discuss. It can be easily developed a mobile app for this kind of shared work, either among workers or with clients. Further, a 'fact taxonomy' would be useful to categorize various facts and capture their essential attributes. This taxonomy would serve as a conceptual framework of fact management.

DISCUSSION

When information about processes is disseminating well, the tendency is doing tasks more efficiently what enhances a team's agility and productivity. VM can bring that to all employees in a standard way. Everyone will know how to develop their own activities toward the required results. Thus, they can take actions to strengthen that path or to improve it.

When using the SQCDM methodology, we become more specific and direct in the aspects we will measure: how is firm's security? how is this evaluation viewed by its customers? which is its service delivery time? is the work staff properly prepared for executing their activities?

In the company under study, 58% of the evaluations from social networks (Facebook/ Tripadvisor/ Google) reflect that people did not like the time they waited for their requests. This delay was due to the required capacity of the existent oven. With it, the ideal number of tables attained is 24. But in summer time, they were 52, what means that summer demand can become unattainable.

After the proposed changes, such as exchanging current oven by one of greater capacity (from 480 pizzas/day to 1080 pizzas/day), the waiting time decreased significantly (from 60'/80' to 15'). For installing the larger oven, the restaurant has to change its layout to host it.

Considering VM methods will turn the company more analytical about its processes. Undoubtably, everyone will work more accurately. Using VM approaches is important as it becomes easy to know who contributes (or not) to the firm's performance. VM implementation will also bring a cultural change to the group. Any changing situation, to produce effective results, requires the participation of all levels. There can be some points of resistance to overcome.

This case-study shows that proper use of VM approaches can raise the level of productivity, promote greater communication among people, disseminate most relevant indicators, reduce costs, and guide decision making. A VM management system can really be a great option in terms of clarity, motivation, process review, real and immediate knowledge of results, and correction focus.

In today's scenario, process management enthusiasts often alert managers to continually evaluate and improve processes at all levels. This is increasingly important because it can improve the right activities and 'ignore' those that matter less. And the transition from VM to IM, i.e., to a higher level of visual analytics, can help to assess results in terms of key performance indicators (KPI). Most common targets that decision-makers need to hit are financial. VM and especially IM approaches will easily show them the financial value of recommendations and how much it will cost if they do not act.

These holistic approaches to management are increasingly relevant as they boost transparency, discipline, shared resources, team involvement, and open mindset (Torghabehi et al., 2016). They assist the achievement of significant and concrete process improvements.

CONCLUSION

Several companies that compete to provide customers with consistent, reliable and cost-effective products/services need to continually improve a range of supporting processes.

Strategic priorities, and consequent definition of most important processes, may change over time. Leadership changes, business cycles, mergers/acquisitions, shareholder pressures, and incentive systems can influence those priorities.

Given all these factors, process improvement should help managers determine where to focus their attention. Process managers must clearly show where and why change is crucial. They need to translate company's competitive strategy (i.e., why customers buy its offers over its competitors) into a process improvement strategy. This can mean a difference of hundreds, or even thousands, in revenue and profit.

Service quality is a vital ingredient of the company's ability to maintain profit and continue business success. It creates not only loyalty, to both company and product/ service, but also guarantees firm's viability in today's competitive market.

Limitations and Implications

This ongoing research has contributed to improve operational issues in the firm under study, especially the referred delays. Practical and agile solutions were proposed, as the company is in the market for a long time. Its reputation includes the brand and service offered.

Main limitations are related to manager's influence on process improvement tools and subsequent implementation. There is still a need for managers to understand more about benefits of visual management (VM). There is some resistance, but the demonstration of results and related agility is attracting firm's managers to this kind of approaches (which can complement other methods).

VM emphasizes that optimal competencies require that associated efforts are continuous and able to follow the analysis of all areas of improvement. Such efforts can involve modifying, supplementing, or eliminating certain processes. Process improvement skills, if effectively used within an organization, can result in higher delivery efficiency, creativity, quality, and customer satisfaction. This leads to higher productivity and ultimately higher return on the investment made.

Future Research

Even though the suggested framework for VM is applicable to other business environments, further research is required. The interconnection between VM, continuous improvement and performance based on a case-study was investigated. But more quantitative researches, on bigger scales, are required to enhance knowledge of these tools.

However, the focus remains in restaurants (and related sectors such as hospitality), to outline sustainable tourism strategies for the region, as gastronomy highly influences the influx, choices and satisfaction of tourists and residents.

ACKNOWLEDGMENT

This paper is financed by National Funds provided by FCT- Foundation for Science and Technology through project UID/SOC/04020/2013.

REFERENCES

Albuquerque, E., Seabra, L., Rolim, P., & Gomes, L. (2012). Riscos físicos em uma unidade de alimentação e nutrição: Implicações na saúde do trabalhador. *Revista da Associação Brasileira de Nutrição*, *4*(1), 40–47.

Alves, T. P. (2010). *Melhoria contínua: Importância e aplicação no processo produtivo de uma indústria metalúrgica*. Manole.

Araújo, L. E. (2009). *Nivelamento de capacidade de produção utilizando quadros Heijunka em sistemas híbridos de coordenação de ordens de produção* (Dissertação de Mestrado). Pós-Graduação em Engenharia de Produção, São Paulo, Brazil.

Chen, Y., Yang, J., & Ribarsky, W. (2009). Toward effective insight management in visual analytics systems. *IEEE Pacific Visualization Symposium*, 49-56.

Costa, A. S., Santana, L. C., & Trigo, A. C. (2015). Qualidade do atendimento ao cliente: Um grande diferencial competitivo para as organizações. *Revista de Iniciação Científica*, *2*(2), 155–172.

Ivancevich, J., Konopaske, R., Donelly, J., & Gibson, J. (2006). *Organizações: Comportamento, estrutura e processos*. McGraw Hill.

Kurpjuweit, S., Reinerth, D., Schmidt, C., & Wagner, S. (2019). Implementing visual management for continuous improvement: Barriers, success factors and best practices. *International Journal of Production Research*, *57*(17), 5574–5588. doi:10.1080/00207543.2018.1553315

Lewin, K. (2010). Defining the field at a given time. *Psychological Review*, *50*(3), 292–310. doi:10.1037/h0062738

Lins, N. V., & Holanda, M. S. (2011). *Proposta de gestão visual da produção naval em estaleiros*. XXII COPINAVAL - Congresso Panamericano de Engenharia Naval, Transporte Marítmo e Portuária, Buenos Aires, Argentina.

Maister, D. H. (2013). The psychology of waiting lines. Managing employee/customer interaction in service businesses. In J. A. Czepiel, M. R. Solomon, & C. F. Surprenant (Eds.), (pp. 113–123). Lexington Books.

Marshall, I. Jr. (2008). *Gestão da qualidade* (6th ed.). Editora FGV.

Mello, C. H. (1998). *Auditoria contínua: Estudo de implementação de uma ferramenta de monitoramento para sistema de garantia da qualidade com base nas normas NBR ISO9000* (Dissertação de Mestrado). EFEI, Minas Gerais, Brazil.

Murata, K. (2019). On the role of Visual Management in the era of digital innovation. *Procedia Manufacturing*, *39*, 117–122. doi:10.1016/j.promfg.2020.01.246

Neese, M., & Kong, S. M. (2007). Driving lean through the visual factory: Visual instructions offer the simplicity employees need. *Circuits Assembly*.

Packer, C. L., & Suski, C. (2013). *Gestão à vista na produção como ferramenta de trabalho*. Inova.

Polacinski, E. (2012). *Implantação dos 5Ss e proposição de um SGQ para uma indústria de erva-mate. Gestão Estratégica: Empreendedorismo e Sustentabilidade*. Congresso Internacional de Administração.

Rangel, A. S., Silva, M. M., & Costa, B. K. (2010). Competitividade da indústria têxtil Brasileira. *Revista de Administração e Inovação*, *7*(1), 151–174.

Silva, A., Roratto, L., Servat, M. E., Dorneles, L., & Polacinski, E. (2013). *Gestão da qualidade: Aplicação da ferramenta 5W2H como plano de ação para projeto de abertura de uma empresa*. Horizontina.

Silva, J. N., & Loos, M. J. (2017). Proposta de implementação da gestão à vista no auxílio à produtividade. *Revista Espacios*, *38*(27), 34–46.

Souza, R. P., Hékis, H. R., Ribeiro, R. M., & Valentim, R. A. (2014). Avaliação e monitoramento de processos de produção utilizando recurso da gestão à vista em uma grande indústria do setor têxtil no estado do Rio Grande do Norte. *Revista de Administração e Inovação*, *11*(1), 162–180. doi:10.5773/rai.v11i1.1142

Tonkin, L. (1998). *Effective visual management: Bring excellence into sharper focus*. LTC.

Torghabehi, Y., Maki, A., Kurczewski, K., & Abdekhodaee, A. (2016). Visual management, performance management and continuous improvement: A lean manufacturing approach. *International Journal of Lean Six Sigma*, *7*(2), 187–210. doi:10.1108/IJLSS-09-2014-0028

Turismo Algarve. (2018). *Balanço turístico do ano 2018*. https://www.turismodoalgarve.pt/pt/noticias/7512/algarve-consolida-resultados-turisticos-em-2018.aspx#prettyPhoto

Ward, T., & Dagger, T. (2017). The complexity of relationship marketing for service customers. *Journal of Services Marketing*, *21*(4), 281–290. doi:10.1108/08876040710758586

Wills, S. (2013). *Insight management: A new profession*. Insight Management Academy.

World Economic Forum. (2017). *Annual Meeting 2017*. http://www3.weforum.org/docs/WEF_AM17_Overview.pdf

WTO. (2018). *World trade report 2018*. https://www.wto.org/english/res_e/publications_e/world_trade_report18_e.pdf

Yik, L., & Chin, J. F. (2019). Application of 5S and Visual Management to improve shipment preparation of finished goods. *IOP Conference Series. Materials Science and Engineering*, *530*, 012039. Advance online publication. doi:10.1088/1757-899X/530/1/012039

Chapter 5
Neutralizing Maleficent Effects of COVID-19 Through Entrepreneurship:
Peeping Through the Lens of Communication

Manpreet Arora
Central University of Himachal Pradesh, Dharamshala, India

Roshan Lal Sharma
Central University of Himachal Pradesh, Dharamshala, India

ABSTRACT

Entrepreneurs are regarded as the leaders of socio-economic, industrial, and business development. They are important pillars of any economy. They are the employment generators and contribute to economic growth. In the current scenario caused by the COVID-19 pandemic, we witnessed people across the world losing their jobs. An inclination towards entrepreneurial activities has been observed in 2020. People have started communicating how entrepreneurial activities are the only solution for economies in crises. The role of social media platforms cannot be under-emphasized, and therefore, an entrepreneur today has to be a master of various media of communication. This chapter aims at exploring the concept of entrepreneurship with special reference to communication. It highlights challenges and issues in the post-pandemic world with reference to entrepreneurship and the role effective communication can play in handling them. It also attempts to examine the use of the term 'entrepreneurship' by general public on social media such as Twitter in particular with a view to work out its implications.

DOI: 10.4018/978-1-7998-3964-4.ch005

INTRODUCTION

In today's fast changing business environment, key developmental strategies and planning done by the policy makers require a combination of vision, mission, value creation, resource organization and sustainable development of various businesses. Such businesses/ business ventures are initiated based on the risk-taking abilities of entrepreneurs. According to Joseph Alios Schumpter, it is the entrepreneur who shackles and disturbs the equilibrium in business cycles and contributes toward economic development. Schumpter (2000) further observes that the entrepreneurial spirit of entrepreneurs contributes directly towards creativity and innovation. All the technological changes which are brought in the economy are the result of innovation only which leads to prosperity and welfare of the state (Audretsch, 2007). Entrepreneurs are regarded as the leaders of industrial development (Davis, 1968). They are important pillars of any economy. They are basically the employment generators and primarily contribute to the economic growth (Mitra, 2019). Entrepreneurship is often explained as the process of starting and running one's own business. Entrepreneurs are the key drivers of fostering production process in the economy by setting up small, medium or large-scale enterprises (Vogel et al., 2014).

Entrepreneurship also contributes toward structural changes in the society (Gries & Naudé 2010). The structural transformation of the society helps in moving towards equitable distribution of income and greater opportunities leading to prosperity. Entrepreneurial activities foster the development of new projects and ventures by encouraging creativity and innovation (Autio et al., 2014). When new capital is invested in the economy it helps create additional capacities in existing and new product lines. This creates new demand and helps in the growth of the economy due to contribution of consumers who ultimately spend and buy these products. Entrepreneurs take risks and try to grab opportunities (Brockhaus 1980). They help discover new ideas, create knowledge by thinking creatively, innovate and solve various problems pertaining to capital formation, resource utilization, and resource allocation for starting new ventures. Entrepreneurs are often visionary (Allen 1997). They basically carry the trait of "having the ability to see the unseen". Quite often it has been seen that they dream big. Most of the entrepreneurs carry the intrinsic ability of visualizing the unseen things. They spend a lot of time in interpersonal communication with various stakeholders.

Various dimensions of communication play crucial part in the successful realization of entrepreneurial vision. Entrepreneurs can undoubtedly be charismatic but most of the things that they do and envision can be learnt through experience. Considerable degree of persistence towards working in a single direction to actualize a dream/vision is their passion. We all dream and most of the times visualize several ventures/ endeavors, but we lack that risk-taking ability to make our dreams come true. This trait of converting dreams into reality is inherent in entrepreneurs and they have the capacity to work passionately and with sincerity (Murmann & Sardana). The ability of an entrepreneur and his inner drive to chase his passion, to achieve something unseen is what makes him/her stand apart from the rest. Existing literature suggests that entrepreneurs often are excellent social networkers also (Dashtiet al., 2011). They build relations with people in no time and keep in mind as to who can act as a resource for him at the opportune time. Fast changing and complex business environments which are driven by social, political or economic factors require high quality networking skills.

To grow a business, it becomes imperative to seek and find right people for help. Entrepreneurs build and maintain their networks/ contacts that matter immensely in their businesses (Johannisson & Nilsson 1989). They need to be quite reflective and charismatic in their decisions and implementation to win the hearts of their followers and teammates. True entrepreneurs maintain strong relationships at intra- and inter-organizational levels (Kelley et al., 2009). This is a skill which helps them strengthen their team for accomplishing the assigned tasks/ jobs in time. Businesses survive due to mutual dependency. For the supplies of raw materials, labour, and machinery networking is required, and therefore an entrepreneur should be good at building and nurturing relationships for the sustainability of the business. Engaging and channelizing the energies of many minds for the accomplishment of a job is not an easy task. It is very easily and sophisticatedly done by a successful entrepreneur. Networking helps in building long lasting relations with stakeholders who matter most in the growth of a business (Elg, Ghauri, & Tarnovskaya, 2008; Lechner, Dowling, & Welpe, 2006; Saxena 2005; Thorelli 1986). This chapter tries to analyze the importance of communication in entrepreneurial activities alongside ascertaining how important it is in the current scenario where the world is facing economic crises at various levels due to the COVID 19 pandemic.

Looking at the current scenario where lakhs of people in every country lost their jobs, an inclination towards entrepreneurial activities has been observed during the last year. People have started communicating in one form or the other that entrepreneurial activities are the only solution for the economies in crises. The role of social media platforms cannot be under-emphasized in such a scenario. During lockdowns across various countries, the social media platforms like Twitter, Facebook and Instagram have become voices to share not only ideas or business solutions, but also platforms to share their sentiments and emotions. Analyses of these things besides being interesting have also drawn the attention of researchers across the world to share as well as explore the research problems involved therein. Communicating the social concerns and use of effective communication for the upliftment of economy can prove to be an important tool if used wisely. We live in an age wherein communication plays a critical role in all businesses and entrepreneurial pursuits (Morreale et al., 2000; Azmi, et al., 2012).

Right from the moment any business plan is devised/envisioned, communication occupies a place of centrality right up to a point where a business or an enterprise reaches its culmination. In other words, planning of business along with strategizing its implementation involves diverse but crucial dimensions of entrepreneurial communication. It is interesting to know that entrepreneurial communication which includes written as well as verbal exchange of information is never a casual or flawed activity. In fact, a lot of effort goes into it by way of serious research and careful study of various stakeholders and their behaviors. Entrepreneurial communication cannot afford to be erroneous when it comes to passing on information in the form of written and verbal instructions. Here it would be pertinent to underscore the importance of written communication that takes place in a business organization. No entrepreneur can ignore the fundamentals of business communication simply because entrepreneurial success by and large depends on how effective and successful you are as a communicator (Darling & Beebe, 2007).

In today's complex scenario where businesses are highly dependent on accuracy of information, understanding of gaps/deficiencies in business communication paves way for a more productive, harmonious entrepreneurship. Since people communicate in diverse ways, it becomes difficult for an entrepreneur to create an environment which is conducive for effective communication. In fact, an entrepreneur remains ethically duty-bound to share his ideas, vision and mission to his managers and employees effectively so that they are able to create an understanding of the vision of the entrepreneur. An effective communication can only occur because of the ability of an entrepreneur to make his followers understand his vision, mission and goals (Filion, 1988). These goals can be short-/long-term, and to achieve them, strategies need to be devised after arriving at a consensus with the teammates. Therefore, effective communication is a must for an entrepreneurial leader. Sharing the vision also has communicative dimensions, on which the success of the venture is totally dependent (Witt 2007). Most of the oral communication which is done by an entrepreneur depicts his level of confidence in his team. He must be sincere enough to communicate his goals by thoroughly explaining each aspect of the task. His approachability, mindset, body language, gestures, facial expressions, and empathetic demeanor play an important role in winning the confidence of his team. It is very important for him to win their trust if he wants the desired results in a stipulated timeframe. Needless to mention, that an entrepreneur must communicate effectively with all the stakeholders namely the employees, customers and others in diverse market scenarios. One may view entrepreneurial communication from the perspective of diverse business activities such as designing the vision, mission, objectives, plans and devising various strategies to achieve business goals.

OBJECTIVES OF THE STUDY

The objectives of this chapter are:

1. To analyze the concept of entrepreneurship with special reference to communication
2. To analyze the challenges and issues in the post-pandemic world with reference to the role entrepreneurship and effective communication can play in handling them
3. To examine the use of the term 'entrepreneurship' by general public on social media such as Twitter in particular and carry out sentiment analysis of its use

RESEARCH METHODOLOGY

This chapter is conceptual and qualitative and aims at using data from secondary sources like websites and publication reports of international repute for substantiating theoretical perspectives/ opinions. The survey of literature will strengthen the theoretical dimensions of the chapter and help develop conceptual understanding of the core concepts of entrepreneurship and communication. To understand the sentiments of public and their views in the form of written communication, tweets on entrepreneurship have been extracted with the help of NVivo software and a sentiment analysis has been done. With the help of word cloud, the usage of various terms in their tweets on entrepreneurship has been represented and analyzed. The first part of the paper focuses on entrepreneurial communication and its role, the second assesses challenges facedby economies during and post-COVID-19 pandemic world, and the third examines public sentiments concerning the use of the term 'entrepreneurship' on social media platforms like Twitter.

I. ENTREPRENEURIAL COMMUNICATION AND ELEMENTS OF LEADERSHIP

In the modern age, entrepreneurial leadership cannot be imagined without taking recourse to authentic, trustworthy and genuine communication. The concept of communicative leadership is used in those organizations which have thrust on analyzing as well as developing the communication competence of the people. Communicative leadership is a concept which basically focuses on employee engagement as well as better communication for the business (Fairhurs & Connaughton 2014). When the world is in the middle of crises and economies are trying to bounce back the only solution is initiating entrepreneurial activities, which have become indispensable in the current scenario. All over the world the supply chain management has been affected negatively and the trade at international level has come to a standstill. Now again when the world is grappling with second wave of COVID-19 pandemic and when trade, business and commerce have suffered a severe jolt, entrepreneurial activities hold the key to offer a counter discourse via creating business opportunities where they scarcely exist. Entrepreneurial spirit in fact serves as an antidote to stasis and despair caused by crashing economies and unprecedented job losses and sudden harm caused to livelihoods due to the pandemic. Entrepreneurship also opens up the possibilities of revival of businesses, trade and commerce, and thus paves way to refresh and rejuvenate varied sectors in financial and commercial arenas with a view to revive the sagging spirits of countries across the world. In all the above activities entrepreneurial communication plays a vital role.

An efficient entrepreneur has to be an effective and persuasive communicator. He has to prove his capability as successful mediator among a whole range of employees and various stakeholders s/he deals with. To mediate, one has to be powerful communicator as it is only then that he can be successful in group dynamics. An effective communicative entrepreneur must know the art of evolving consensus via democratically negotiating various issues and taking all stakeholders on board (Ray 1993). It is generally said as well as accepted that better the communication, better the negotiation will be. One should have excellent communication skills for exchanging ideas, thoughts and opinions with each other (Loué& Baronet 2012). The excellent communication skills for healthy and effective discussion are vital (Lunenburg 2010).

It is important for an entrepreneur that in business situations he is cautious in selecting right and apt words for converting his ideas and thoughts into reality. The power of speech is a tool which can help an entrepreneur in entering successful business negotiations that are carried out at various levels of the organization. It can be done with employees, other staff members and suppliers. Varied situations could crop up anytime/ anywhere, wherein negotiations are required. Various kinds of conflicts arise in the internal environment of a business. Conflicts after a point of time become dysfunctional (Rahim & Bonoma 1979). No organization at this point can gain from conflicts which lead to stress, anxiety and unrest in a business organization. Another aspect of communication in entrepreneurial activities is conversing well in the form of dialogues and debates that are discussed below.

DEBATING AND DIALOGUING AS FORMS OF COMMUNICATION

An effective entrepreneurial communicator should know how to debate and dialogue well (Arora & Sharma 2017). As a communicative leader, an entrepreneur should successfully instill the spirit of mutual trust and confidence and also team spirit to be able to come together and work together as a team (Johansson 2015). The quality of the communication is the core of communicative leadership (Mastrangelo et.al 2017). Communicative leaders follow problem-solving approach which they are able to effect with the help of the employees' feedback which they keep taking from time to time (Normore 2016). They lead from the front and thus pave the way of their co-workers even via assisting them, if the need be, in achieving their goals. In particular, communicative leaders actively engage in framing of messages as they understand how vital language of communication is and how critical is the sense that needs to be conveyed through language use (Johansson et.al 2014). The pitch and tone are of the utmost importance in debating and dialoguing. But the challenge which one faces while dialoguing in this digital world wherein social media has had maleficent effects on us is, that the entrepreneur has to deal with the world of fake news, propaganda, bullshit, fabricated truths and information-distortion in the outer world, which can be identified as post-truth scenario.

NOTION OF POST-TRUTH IN RELATION TO BUSINESS

Post-truth phenomenon impedes genuine communication which is characterized by candor, honesty and accountability and how it undermines critical thinking and accountability in public discourse. Word of the year 2016, 'post-truth' signifies a set of circumstances wherein objective facts are not at all influential in shaping the public opinion than appeal to emotions and personal beliefs (Arora2020). Post-truth phenomenon has arguably affected every phase of our life. Post- truth is prevalent to such an extent that it gives rise to parallel alternative facts with the help of playing with vague and unclear language (Arora2020). Language play has become so prevalent in our society that it hides the truth in such a way that we are unable to figure out what is true and what is not. And that is the reason language has become so crucial. In such a situation dealing with external stakeholders can be very challenging for an entrepreneur. Post-truth scenario has distorted authentic communication and its relevance especially in the age of digitalization. To deal with post-truth situations, entrepreneurs need to stay updated, and should have the foresight to deal with untrue, fake and deceptive information prevalent in the business environment. Oxford Dictionaries define the word 'post-truth' as "relating or denoting circumstances in which objective facts are less influential in shaping public opinion than appeals to emotion and personal belief". Collins Dictionary describes the post-truth scenario as "describing debate that is based on passion and emotion rather than reason and evidence".

According to Cambridge Dictionary, post-truth scenario "relates to a situation in which people are more likely to accept an argument based on their emotions and beliefs, rather than one based on facts". The empathy, the connect or the position of the receiver has lost its relevance. This is age of forwarding messages, making things viral, viewing and watching the stuff that is circulated on social media in a naïve manner, but it cannot be viewed as communicating. And that is where the problem lies. Nowadays communication has become so complex that we are not able to decide what exactly is factual as our life is totally dependent upon what we are made to see, visualize, receive/ perceive, and what is manipulatively offered to us as truth. Effective communicative entrepreneurs have their fact-checking mechanism intact with them. He knows about the devastating impact post-truth can have on entrepreneurial activities, and also knows when/how to press into service creative/ critical communicative strategies to chart out a course to be followed by the business organization s/he leads.

IMPORTANCE OF LISTENING IN ENTREPRENEURIAL ACTIVITIES

Besides paying attention to written or oral communication and what is being conveyed, an entrepreneur must know how to listen attentively to be able to respond critically. If an entrepreneur is sharp-minded, and attentive in his listening, he has tremendous ability and potential to understand what is being, intended, said, or left unsaid. He exactly knows what is required to deal with a particular situation successfully. Moreover, he can serve his employees better, benefit his clients, enhance sales, and manage various organizational situations effectively. He can also listen to the urgent demands of his employees and stakeholders and have the ability to take necessary actions to address them successfully.

An entrepreneur must understand that careful listening and keen observation are the steppingstones for the success of the entrepreneurial decisions. Listening, in fact, is regarded as very important communication tool for budding entrepreneurs who are in quest of seeking new information, and trying to find support for their new and innovative business ideas (Ray 1993). The first priority of the entrepreneur should be to understand the business market, the philosophies of the competitors and the current market trends. Plenty of modes of communication play role in that. Listening to business channels, their critical observations about the companies, the way experts of the market perceive certain situations or trends, the type of words and messages the competitors are using in their advertisement campaigns, require good listening skills on the part of the entrepreneurs (Abbasi et al., 2011). If the entrepreneur is working in rural or urban areas, attentive listening becomes very important here in knowing the customers directly. Small ventures are always built on relationship with the community. The direct intervention of the entrepreneur in the community is an important aspect of understanding the value addition which an entrepreneur can always make in business.

FOCUS ON DELIVERY-CENTERED COMMUNICATION

A successful entrepreneur should not only promise things but after assimilating all the concerns of the employees and various stakeholders, he should also have the capacity to deliver as his entire delivery mechanism is regulated by careful and well-thought over verbal and written communication. He can meet the basic challenge of fulfilling the expectations of various stakeholders in every business organization. Every single employee expects to grow while working within an organization and it is very natural to expect growth. In such a situation which is characterized by employees' expectations, communicative leadership of an entrepreneur becomes very crucial. Now the question that demands answer is: "Does an entrepreneur indulge in fear, hollow verbiage, or s/he has the capacity to rise up to the expectations of whole range of stakeholders"? Only that entrepreneur will be successful who is grounded well in his understanding of the fundamentals of effective and persuasive business communication. Another crucial aspect of entrepreneurial communication is how concise and precise is the flow of official information at intra-/ inter- organizational levels. The flow of communication should be transparent, uninterrupted and goal-oriented so that genuine measurement of the objectives becomes possible (Sharma & Arora 2015).

ROLE OF REPORTING IN ENTREPRENEURSHIP

This aspect, in fact, enables us to not only save time but ensure effective results owing to the fact that the whole information and technology networks are conducive to such type of communication. Moreover, when it comes to transmit official information, written communication is better than the verbal form of communication and it is arguably more effective also if it is prepared and delivered with an active focus. Unnecessary expressions/words should always be done away with and the language should be pruned and spruced up in such a manner that the recipient of the message gets immediately to the crux of the delivered message. There are various stakeholders who are dependent on the formal information shared by the entrepreneurs in the form of various reports to be published from time to time as per the mandatory law requirements. These stakeholders can be shareholders, directors, employees, bankers, financial institutions or even public at large. Another important aspect of any business venture is a transparent system of reporting. Reporting shows us as to what has happened so far and what the present status of things is. As business conditions change every entrepreneur should understand that the level and format of reporting should be such that helps remove the barriers of communication in the organization and evolve a support system within the organization.

IMPORTANCE OF CONTENT AND SUBJECT MATTER OF MESSAGE

Another aspect of entrepreneurial communication is concerned with the content or subject matter of the message. As stated above, it is always worthwhile to understand the 'why' and 'how' of what is being said. Each communiqué has to be focused at achieving a particular result. If the result is achieved, the 'why' of entrepreneurial communication stands 'vindicated'. To be able to work out 'whys' and 'hows' of effective entrepreneurial communication, it is always better to consult one's colleagues/co-workers, and as many as stakeholders as possible. Nevertheless, it does not imply that such large-scale consultation is required to make day to day entrepreneurial decisions as well. As a matter of fact, the communicative ability of the entrepreneur is tested several times a day depending on the number of the critical situations that arise in the course of doing business. Another important dimension that forms the basis of successful entrepreneurial communicative behavior is the level of soft and interpersonal skills. It can be undoubtedly claimed that an entrepreneur cannot afford to be deficient in/ indifferent towards acquiring such skills (Sharma & Arora 2015).

Successful entrepreneurs always ensure a strong research and development (R&D) support to the business vision and also the strategies of converting such a vision into reality. In that sense, it may not be the entrepreneurs who engage with hardcore academic research. However, they keep a sharp eye on what all goes on in their R&D department and the latest thrust areas of business research that reflects in their day-to-day conversations while engaging with various stakeholders in different business scenarios and diverse socio-cultural and political situations. They make sure that fundamental values that their organizations are known for are publicized far and wide. This is done very carefully to ensure not just visibility of their businesses but also their success. Unless an entrepreneur commands communicative leadership, the hardcore business research which involves heavy expenditure, may go haywire.

FREQUENT COMMUNICATION WITH EMPLOYEES AS A STRATEGY TO BUILD MUTUAL TRUST

Employees are the key stakeholders of a business firm's internal environment. An effective entrepreneurial communicator must frequently communicate with all employees to build mutual trust and healthy organizational climate (Berns, 1987). Also, they must be involved in participative decision-making. Success of every business venture depends on the channels of communication and the level of trust between the followers and the leader. Frequent, transparent, objective, timely communication increases the level of trust between entrepreneur and his employees/ followers. An effective communication bridges the gap between where we are and where we want to go.

AFFABLE NON-VERBAL COMMUNICATION AND FRIENDLY BODY LANGUAGE

Non-verbal communication plays an important role in expressing emotions like trust, happiness, a shared sense of feeling, empathy, and hope. We tend to unconsciously communicate non-verbally most of the times. It is necessary for every entrepreneur to properly use non-verbal communication as a tool to support for verbal communication. Friendly body language is an important aspect of positively influencing the followers. An effective communicative entrepreneur must have a friendly body language.

USING SOCIAL MEDIA PLATFORMS FOR CREATING BUSINESS VISIBILITY AND REPUTATION

It is a must for an effective communicative entrepreneur to be active on various social media platforms because that can be effectively used to communicate various types of business information. These days social media platforms offer various kinds of benefits to the business owners. It helps them reach out to the customers easily and in a relatively shorter period of time. It has now become easy to gain attention of more people at a negligible cost through these platforms. A considerable section of society uses social media sites regularly. High growth rate in the use of social media sites helps entrepreneurs make their business successful by creating visibility and reputation of their businesses (Taneja & Toombs 2014). More and more businesses are experimenting with digital modes of advertising and promotion. Brand awareness is significant for every enterprise. Social media platforms can prove to be powerful tools when the case of brand awareness comes forth (Monica &Balaş2014). An entrepreneur should wisely choose various platforms that can be used to publicize the product (Nakara et al., 2012). A wise, right as well as timely decision of showcasing the product can prove to be a boon to the business.

II. CHALLENGES OF/ OPPORTUNITIES FOR ENTREPRENEURSHIP IN THE POST-COVID-19 PANDEMIC WORLD

COVID-19 caused a lot of distress all over the world and there is a great need to find out as to how it has impacted various sectors of economies across the globe. The challenges in today's world are intricate and thus require path-breaking effort to find out workable and implementable solutions to rejuvenate and rebuild economies. It is a largely believed that entrepreneurship serves as the foundation of every economy. In the post-pandemic scenario, the small-scale businesses suffered immensely because typically they have less resources compared to the larger firms (Fabeil, Pazim, & Langgat, 2020; Kalogiannidis, 2020; Ogar, Okuta, Okon, & Odama, 2021). Since supply chain activities were grievously disrupted, the entrepreneurs had to grapple with situations wherein they had to cancel/ postpone business orders as they faced problems making payments to suppliers with a view to cover their operational costs. In the process they had to lay off their employees as well. The major challenges faced by entrepreneurs have been as follows:

1. Low mobility of factors of production (Mofijur, Fatta, Alam, Islam, Ong, Rahman & Mahlia, 2020)
2. Disrupted supply chains (Bonadio, Huo, Levchenko, & Pandalai-Nayar, 2020; Sharma, Luthra, Joshi, & Kumar, 2021)

3. Higher labor cost (Althaf, & Babbitt, 2020; Queiroz, Ivanov, Dolgui, & Wamba, 2020)
4. Difficulties in the access of raw material (Lakuma, Sunday, Sserunjogi, Kahunde, & Munyambonera, 2020)
5. Liquidity crises due to low sales (Schivardi & Guido, 2020)
6. Financial crises (Barua, 2020)
7. Difficulties in production activities (Kimura, Thangavelu, Narjoko, & Findlay, 2020)
8. Entry barriers from one region to the other due to lockdowns (Narayanan & Saha, 2020)
9. Higher cost of living (Qiu, Rutherford, Mao, & Chu, 2017)
10. Continuous stress (Barzilay, Moore, Greenberg, DiDomenico, Brown, White & Gur, 2020; Lahav, 2020).
11. Employee turnover as well as conditions of laying off (Barzilay, Moore, Greenberg, DiDomenico, Brown, White, &Gur, 2020; Dwomoh, Luguterah, & Duah, 2020; Godinic, Obrenovic, & Khudaykulov, 2020; Hernández, 2020; Hernández-Murillo, & Krolikowski, 2020; Lee, Xu, & Yang, 2021; Sunarsi, Suryani, & Jati, 2020).
12. Lower level of life satisfaction among people (Bidzan-Bluma, Bidzan, Jurek, Bidzan, Knietzsch, Stueck, & Bidzan, 2020; Eek, Larsson, Wisén, & Ekvall Hansson, 2021; Rogowska, Kuśnierz & Bokszczanin, 2020; Zheng, Miao, & Gan, 2020),).
13. Lesser spending of people on leisure items (Belk, 2020).
14. Shift of consumer spending towards basic necessities only (Loxton, Truskett, Scarf, Sindone, Baldry, & Zhao, 2020).

In many parts of the world, the pandemic impacted entrepreneurs' mental wellbeing negatively (Cameron, Joyce, Delaquis, Reynolds, Protudjer, & Roos, 2020; McCracken, Badinlou, Buhrman, & Brocki, 2020). Due to negative situations all over it ultimately changed the personal situations of entrepreneurs by increasing their responsibilities toward their families, elderly, childcare, etc. and many were forced to work from home (Achdut & Refaeli 2020; Tuzovic & Kabadayi 2020).

In a report published by IMF (https://www.imf.org/en/ Publications/ WEO/ Issues/ 2020/06/24/ WEOUpdateJune2020), it is clearly mentioned that the COVID-19 pandemic has left a very negative impact on economies all over the world. The report projects that recovery is going to be more gradual than anticipated. GDP in many countries is going to be lower than projected. It has eventually resulted in more poverty the world over.

The world economic update released in June 2020 shows a high downfall in many countries in terms of GDP. The projections for the coming years are also not very motivating and encouraging asshown in the table 1.

Thus, we may observe that countries like Argentina, Australia, Brazil, Canada, France, Germany, India, Iran, Italy, Japan Netherlands, Mexico, Poland, United Kingdom, and United States have shown a lot of variation in GDP projections. The situation is not very positive in terms of these projections, however, still encouraging is the situation that entrepreneurs all over the world have proven that agility as their characteristic is going to make the situation more normal in times to come. Startups came up with various kinds of innovative business solutions even after lockdown which focused on the development of new products and services harnessing the local resources in the most efficient manner. Another dimension of entrepreneurship could be seen when people started working from home and they came up with innovative business solutions to meet up the demands of people who were locked down in their houses. Social media emerged to be an important source of communication where the balance between demand and supply was created taking care of lockdown rules and regulations in many countries.

Table 1. World Economic Outlook, June 2020 Update. Selected Economies Real GDP Growth (Percent Change)

	Projections				**Difference From April 2020 WEO Projections 1/**	
	2018	**2019**	**2020**	**2021**	**2020**	**2021**
Argentina	–2.5	–2.2	–9.9	3.9	–4.2	–0.5
Australia	2.8	1.8	–4.5	4.0	2.2	-2.1
Brazil	1.3	1.1	-9.1	3.6	–3.8	0.7
Canada	2.0	1.7	–8.4	4.9	–2.2	0.7
China	6.7	6.1	1.0	8.2	–0.2	-1.0
Egypt 2/	5.3	5.6	2.0	2.0	0.0	–0.8
France	1.8	1.5	–12.5	7.3	–5.3	2.8
Germany	1.5	0.6	–7.8	5.4	–0.8	0.2
India 2/	6.1	4.2	–4.5	6.0	–6.4	–1.4
Indonesia	5.2	5.0	–0.3	6.1	–0.8	-2.1
Iran 2/	–5.4	-7.6	–6.0	3.1	0.0	0.0
Italy	0.8	0.3	–12.8	6.3	–3.7	1.5
Japan	0.3	0.7	–5.8	2.4	–0.6	–0.6
Kazakhstan	4.1	4.5	–2.7	3.0	–0.2	-1.1
Korea	2.9	2.0	–2.1	3.0	–0.9	–0.4
Malaysia	4.7	4.3	–3.8	6.3	–2.1	-2.7
Mexico	2.2	–0.3	–10.5	3.3	–3.9	0.3
Netherlands	2.6	1.8	–7.7	5.0	–0.2	2.0
Nigeria	1.9	2.2	–5.4	2.6	–2.0	0.2
Pakistan 2/	5.5	1.9	–0.4	1.0	1.1	-1.0
Philippines	6.3	6.0	–3.6	6.8	–4.2	–0.8
Poland	5.3	4.1	–4.6	4.2	0.0	0.0
Russia	2.5	1.3	–6.6	4.1	–1.1	0.6
Saudi Arabia	2.4	0.3	–6.8	3.1	–4.5	0.2
South Africa	0.8	0.2	–8.0	3.5	–2.2	–0.5
Spain	2.4	2.0	–12.8	6.3	–4.8	2.0
Thailand	4.2	2.4	–7.7	5.0	–1.0	-1.1
Turkey	2.8	0.9	–5.0	5.0	0.0	0.0
United Kingdom	1.3	1.4	–10.2	6.3	–3.7	2.3
United States	2.9	2.3	–8.0	4.5	–2.1	–0.2

Source: International Monetary Fund, World Economic Outlook, June 2020 *Update*.
Note: The selected economies account for approximately 83 percent of world output.
1/ Difference based on rounded figures for the current and April 2020 WEO forecasts.
2/ Data and forecasts are presented on a fiscal year basis.

No doubt economic disruptions caused by COVID-19 devastated the world and it is going to have a long-term effect on employment and innovation, but these things can be mitigated if entrepreneurs come up with various kinds of innovative and creative solutions to the problems, as they can help to foster employment and can lead the economies to get back into the tracks by taking steps to support existing startups and the creation of new firms. The restructuring of the entrepreneurial models is going to happen, and the shift is going to bring a gradual but positive change in the market. People have devised ways to live their life in best possible manner according to their limited resources. Small business solutions are quite overwhelming where the resilience and coping strategies are based in induced persistent changes in societies, consumer shifted preferences and focused on harnessing the business opportunities available in the market. E-Commerce, education and Health Services are the sectors which have proven to the word that nothing is impossible. These all sectors were able to perform well due to a shift on improved focus, towards the means of communication. Global value chains are surely going to transform in the coming years and proper interventions after brainstorming can help entrepreneurs improve their awareness of various kinds of opportunities available in the market. The policy makers should aim at providing proper conditions and incentives for innovative startups as well as potential entrepreneurs so that their potential gets a boost and they come up with better business solutions.

III. SENTIMENT ANALYSIS OF TWEETS ON 'ENTREPRENEURSHIP'

To understand the public sentiments regarding entrepreneurship, Tweets on the key term 'entrepreneurship' were extracted by using and NVivo software which is used to perform qualitative analysis. The software with the help of Ncapture extracted 16,779 tweets on 'entrepreneurship'. It clearly indicates that in this situation where the world economies have become standstill, people are expressing their sentiments on public platforms like Twitter and are talking about entrepreneurship and related aspects. If a word cloud analysis of these Tweets is done, it highlights various terms associated with the notion of entrepreneurship having deeper implications. Shown in the word cloud below in addition to the word 'entrepreneurship', the key terms used by people are *rojgar*, 'business', 'innovation', 'education', 'marketing', 'small business', 'digital marketing', 'opportunities', 'learn', and 'youth'.

To refine the search further, data mining was done, and few words were added to the stop word list. The results obtained thus highlighted the words like 'motivation', 'opportunities', 'government', and 'women'. The cloud chart clearly highlights the fact that whenever people are tweeting about entrepreneurship, they associate the term with motivation, women entrepreneurs, opportunities in the field of business and marketing. Another association of the term 'entrepreneurship' found is with the terms like 'innovation' and 'creativity'. One of the important highlighted word in the word cloud is *rozgar*, which in Hindi means employment. It is clear indication that people associate entrepreneurship with employment opportunities. In this post-COVID-19 pandemic, where people are homeless and jobless and are striving hard to fight with the situation that has arisen, entrepreneurship is the most important activity which can bring the economy back on the track. The use of words such as 'startups', 'creativity', 'people', 'work', 'learn', and 'today' also indicates that it is influencing the minds of the youth, and it can thus be perceived, that entrepreneurial activity is associated with learning quickly which is the need of the hour. Indubitably, the youth is going to play an important role in rebuilding of every devastated economy during the post-pandemic situation. When the sentiment analyses of these Tweets were done, the results highlighted the fact that more than 50% of the tweets on 'entrepreneurship' are inclined towards moderately positive and very positive statements about entrepreneurship. It also highlights the fact that the public sentiment is positive towards entrepreneurship, and therefore, it is evident how it is the key to solve the current issues faced by economies wherein to move ahead towards the entrepreneurial activities has become inevitable.

Figure 1. Word cloud 1 on entrepreneurship: result of NVivo

Figure 2. Word cloud 2 on entrepreneurship: result of NVivo

Figure 3.

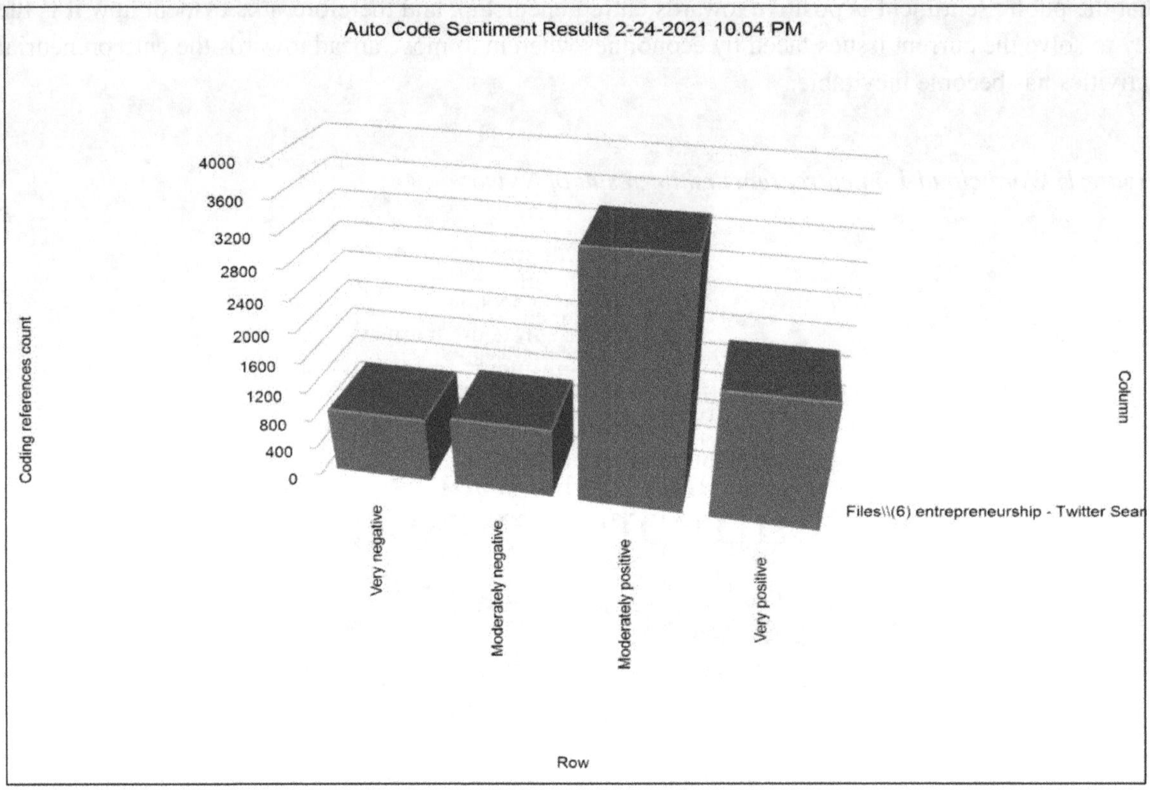

DISCUSSION AND CONCLUSION

To develop and create a business organization is a complex and never-ending process. It requires a lot of efforts on the part of entrepreneur at various stages. It involves coalescing of various concepts, principles and techniques that are oriented towards achievement of vision and mission of an organization. The present and future goals of business organizations require continuous decision making, which remains dependent on effective communication. An established fact is that no decision can be taken if the issue in hand is not communicated well to various stakeholders in the organization. Therefore, the success of any business depends on the way the communication channels are activated in an organization. Entrepreneurship is the process which involves envisioning, designing, launching, establishing, and running a business. It requires a great deal of willingness, capacity, and strength to taking risks, and ability to manage a business venture. All these things are totally dependent on effective communication. Another important aspect of entrepreneurial success is creativity and innovation. An entrepreneur should be proactive in bridging the gap between innovative ideas and putting them into reality. The advent of globalization and the interventions of governments in various sectors of economy the world over have fostered the process of entrepreneurship and innovation. Entrepreneurship, creativity and innovation are vital for economic growth. These involve intra- as well as inter-organizational communication of various stakeholders. To commercialize the knowledge, the entrepreneurial activity is a must, and it requires effective and transparent communication at every level of the business organization. An entrepreneur requires a right vision and foresight to achieve the organizational goals. A lot of risks and rewards are involved in this process. The one who is able to create a balance between risks and rewards achieves long-term sustainability in business. The success or failure of an enterprise is to a great extent determined by its credibility in the market. The perceived credibility of a business is directly associated with the credibility of the entrepreneur. The ability to create social networks, using media vehicles effectively, creating brand awareness, etc. are all the important facets involving communication in every entrepreneurial venture. The overall goal of business communication in every organization is to ensure effective and efficient functioning of the business system. Information is a vital source of strength for business sustainability, and a successful entrepreneur ever remains mindful of it.

REFERENCES

Abbasi, M. H., Siddiqi, A., & Azim, R. U. A. (2011). Role of effective communications for enhancing leadership and entrepreneurial skills in university students. *International Journal of Business and Social Science, 2*(10).

Achdut, N., & Refaeli, T. (2020). Unemployment and psychological distress among young people during the COVID-19 pandemic: Psychological resources and risk factors. *International Journal of Environmental Research and Public Health, 17*(19), 7163. doi:10.3390/ijerph17197163 PMID:33007892

Allen, M. (1997). *Visionary business: an entrepreneur's guide to success.* New World Library.

Althaf, S., & Babbitt, C. W. (2020). Disruption risks to material supply chains in the electronics sector. *Resources, Conservation and Recycling*, 105248.

Arora, M. (2020). Post-Truth and Marketing Communication in Technological Age. In *Handbook of Research on Innovations in Technology and Marketing for the Connected Consumer* (pp. 94–108). IGI Global. doi:10.4018/978-1-7998-0131-3.ch005

Arora, M., & Sharma, R. L. (2017). Decoding diverse dimensions of entrepreneurial leadership with special emphasis on persuasive communication. *Management Dynamics, 17*(1).

Audretsch, D. B. (2007). Entrepreneurship capital and economic growth. *Oxford Review of Economic Policy, 23*(1), 63–78. doi:10.1093/oxrep/grm001

Autio, E., Kenney, M., Mustar, P., Siegel, D., & Wright, M. (2014). Entrepreneurial innovation: The importance of context. *Research Policy, 43*(7), 1097–1108. doi:10.1016/j.respol.2014.01.015

Azmi, A. M., Hairi, O. N., Lee, K. Y., & Fauziah, I. (2012). Entreprenuers success in business: Some critical factors. *International Business Management, 6*(3), 369–373. doi:10.3923/ibm.2012.369.373

Barua, S. (2020). *Understanding Coronanomics: The economic implications of the coronavirus (COVID-19) pandemic*. Academic Press.

Barzilay, R., Moore, T. M., Greenberg, D. M., DiDomenico, G. E., Brown, L. A., White, L. K., Gur, R. C., & Gur, R. E. (2020). Resilience, COVID-19-related stress, anxiety and depression during the pandemic in a large population enriched for healthcare providers. *Translational Psychiatry, 10*(1), 1–8. doi:10.103841398-020-00982-4 PMID:32820171

Belk, R. W. (2020). Post-pandemic consumption: Portal to a new world? *Cadernos EBAPE.BR*, *18*(3), 639–647. doi:10.1590/1679-395120200175x

Berns, M. J. (1987). *Communication variables and female entrepreneurs: exploratory case studies of six former corporate executive women*. Academic Press.

Bidzan-Bluma, I., Bidzan, M., Jurek, P., Bidzan, L., Knietzsch, J., Stueck, M., & Bidzan, M. (2020). A Polish and German Population Study of Quality of Life, Well-Being, and Life Satisfaction in Older Adults During the COVID-19 Pandemic. *Frontiers in Psychiatry*, 11. PMID:33281646

Bonadio, B., Huo, Z., Levchenko, A. A., & Pandalai-Nayar, N. (2020). Global supply chains in the pandemic (No. w27224). National Bureau of Economic Research.

Brockhaus, R. H. Sr. (1980). Risk taking propensity of entrepreneurs. *Academy of Management Journal*, *23*(3), 509–520.

Cameron, E. E., Joyce, K. M., Delaquis, C. P., Reynolds, K., Protudjer, J. L., & Roos, L. E. (2020). Maternal psychological distress & mental health service use during the COVID-19 pandemic. *Journal of Affective Disorders*, *276*, 765–774. doi:10.1016/j.jad.2020.07.081 PMID:32736186

Cunningham, J. B., & Lischeron, J. (1991). Defining entrepreneurship. *Journal of Small Business Management*, *29*(1), 45–61.

Dali, M., Shah, N. R., Abdullah, M., Azman, A. R., Nordin, S. N., Muhammad, I., ... Nilai, B. B. (n.d.). *The Entrepreneurship Model Development Based on Truthfulness, Trustworthiness, Wisdom, and Communication Characteristics*. Academic Press.

Darling, J. R., & Beebe, S. A. (2007). Effective entrepreneurial communication in organization development: Achieving excellence based on leadership strategies and values. *Organization Development Journal*, *25*(1), 76.

Dashti, Y., Schwartz, D., & Pines, A. M. (2011). High technology entrepreneurs, their social networks and success in global markets: The case of Israelis in the US market. *Current Topics in Management: Global Perspectives on Strategy, Behavior, and Performance*, *1*, 131.

Davis, S. M. (1968). Entrepreneurial succession. *Administrative Science Quarterly*, *13*(3), 402–416. doi:10.2307/2391050

Dwomoh, G., Luguterah, A. W., & Duah, S. B. (2020). Hoteliers' human resource strategies for business sustainability during COVID-19 pandemic in Ghana. *The Journal of Business and Retail Management Research*, *14*(3). Advance online publication. doi:10.24052/JBRMR/V14IS03/ART-04

Eek, F., Larsson, C., Wisén, A., & Ekvall Hansson, E. (2021). Self-Perceived Changes in Physical Activity and the Relation to Life Satisfaction and Rated Physical Capacity in Swedish Adults during the COVID-19 Pandemic—A Cross Sectional Study. *International Journal of Environmental Research and Public Health*, *18*(2), 671. doi:10.3390/ijerph18020671 PMID:33466860

Elg, U., Ghauri, P. N., & Tarnovskaya, V. (2008). The role of networks and matching in market entry to emerging retail markets. *International Marketing Review*, *25*(6), 674–699. doi:10.1108/02651330810915583

Fabeil, N. F., Pazim, K. H., & Langgat, J. (2020). The impact of COVID-19 pandemic crisis on micro-enterprises: Entrepreneurs' perspective on business continuity and recovery strategy. *Journal of Economics and Business*, *3*(2). Advance online publication. doi:10.31014/aior.1992.03.02.241

Fairhurst, G. T., & Connaughton, S. L. (2014). Leadership: A communicative perspective. *Leadership*, *10*(1), 7–35. doi:10.1177/1742715013509396

Fernald, L. W., Solomon, G. T., & Tarabishy, A. (2005). A new paradigm: Entrepreneurial leadership. *Southern Business Review*, *30*(2), 1–10.

Filion, L. J. (1988). *The strategy of successful entrepreneurs in small business: vision, relationships and anticipatory learning* (Doctoral dissertation). University of Lancaster.

Gartner, W. (1985). A Conceptual Framework for Describing the Phenomenon of New Venture Creation. *Academy of Management Review*, *10*(4), 696–706. doi:10.5465/amr.1985.4279094

Godinic, D., Obrenovic, B., & Khudaykulov, A. (2020). Effects of economic uncertainty on mental health in the COVID-19 pandemic context: Social identity disturbance, job uncertainty and psychological well-being model. *Int. J. Innov. Econ. Dev*, *6*(1), 61–74. doi:10.18775/ijied.1849-7551-7020.2015.61.2005

Gries, T., & Naudé, W. (2010). Entrepreneurship and structural economic transformation. *Small Business Economics*, *34*(1), 13–29. doi:10.100711187-009-9192-8

Hernández, R. (2020). *Layoffs during the COVID-19 Pandemic: Four Findings from WARN Act Data*. Academic Press.

Hernández-Murillo, R., &Krolikowski, P. (2020). Assessing Layoffs in Four Midwestern States during the Pandemic Recession. *Economic Commentary*.

Johannisson, B., & Nilsson, A. (1989). Community entrepreneurs: Networking for local development. *Entrepreneurship and Regional Development*, *1*(1), 3–19. doi:10.1080/08985628900000002

Johansson, C. (2015). *Empowering employees through communicative leadership*. Academic Press.

Johansson, C., Miller, V. D., & Hamrin, S. (2014). Conceptualizing communicative leadership. *Corporate Communications*. Advance online publication. doi:10.1108/CCIJ-02-2013-0007

Kalogiannidis, S. (2020). COVID Impact on Small Business. *International Journal of Social Science and Economics Invention*, *6*(12), 387. doi:10.23958/ijssei/vol06-i12/257

Kelley, D. J., Peters, L., & O'Connor, G. C. (2009). Intra-organizational networking for innovation-based corporate entrepreneurship. *Journal of Business Venturing*, *24*(3), 221–235. doi:10.1016/j.jbusvent.2008.05.010

Kimura, F., Thangavelu, S. M., Narjoko, D., & Findlay, C. (2020). Pandemic (COVID-19) policy, regional cooperation and the emerging global production network. *Asian Economic Journal*, *34*(1), 3–27. doi:10.1111/asej.12198

Lahav, Y. (2020). Psychological distress related to COVID-19–the contribution of continuous traumatic stress. *Journal of Affective Disorders*, *277*, 129–137. doi:10.1016/j.jad.2020.07.141 PMID:32818776

Lakuma, P. C., Sunday, N., Sserunjogi, B., Kahunde, R., &Munyambonera, E. F. (2020). *How has the COVID-19 Pandemic impacted Ugandan businesses? Results from a business climate survey*. Academic Press.

Lechner, C., Dowling, M., & Welpe, I. (2006). Firm networks and firm development: The role of the relational mix. *Journal of Business Venturing*, *21*(4), 514–540. doi:10.1016/j.jbusvent.2005.02.004

Lee, P. C., Xu, S. T., & Yang, W. (2021). Is career adaptability a double-edged sword? The impact of work social support and career adaptability on turnover intentions during the COVID-19 pandemic. *International Journal of Hospitality Management*, *94*, 102875. doi:10.1016/j.ijhm.2021.102875

Loué, C., & Baronet, J. (2012). Toward a new entrepreneurial skills and competencies framework: A qualitative and quantitative study. *International Journal of Entrepreneurship and Small Business*, *17*(4), 455–477. doi:10.1504/IJESB.2012.050164

Loxton, M., Truskett, R., Scarf, B., Sindone, L., Baldry, G., & Zhao, Y. (2020). Consumer behaviour during crises: Preliminary research on how coronavirus has manifested consumer panic buying, herd mentality, changing discretionary spending and the role of the media in influencing behaviour. *Journal of Risk and Financial Management*, *13*(8), 166. doi:10.3390/jrfm13080166

Lunenburg, F. C. (2010). Communication: The process, barriers, and improving effectiveness. *Schooling*, *1*(1), 1–10.

Mastrangelo, L. M., Benitez, D. G., & Cruz-Ros, S. (2017). How social entrepreneurs can influence their employees' commitment. *Journal of Promotion Management*, *23*(3), 437–448. doi:10.1080/10496491.2017.1294878

McCracken, L. M., Badinlou, F., Buhrman, M., & Brocki, K. C. (2020). Psychological impact of COVID-19 in the Swedish population: Depression, anxiety, and insomnia and their associations to risk and vulnerability factors. *European Psychiatry*, *63*(1), e81. doi:10.1192/j.eurpsy.2020.81 PMID:32843115

Mofijur, M., Fattah, I. R., Alam, M. A., Islam, A. S., Ong, H. C., Rahman, S. A., ... Mahlia, T. M. I. (2020). Impact of COVID-19 on the social, economic, environmental and energy domains: Lessons learnt from a global pandemic. *Sustainable Production and Consumption*.

Monica, B., & Balaş, R. (2014). Social media marketing to increase brand awareness. *Journal of Economic and Business Research*, *20*(2), 155–164.

Morreale, S. P., Osborn, M. M., & Pearson, J. C. (2000). Why communication is important: A rationale for the centrality of the study of communication. *JACA-ANNANDALE*, *1*, 1–25.

Murmann, J. P., & Sardana, D. (2013). Successful entrepreneurs minimize risk. *Australian Journal of Management*, *38*(1), 191–215. doi:10.1177/0312896212444114

Nakara, W. A., Benmoussa, F. Z., & Jaouen, A. (2012). Entrepreneurship and social media marketing: Evidence from French small business. *International Journal of Entrepreneurship and Small Business*, *16*(4), 386–405. doi:10.1504/IJESB.2012.047608

NarayananS.SahaS. (2020). Urban food markets and the lockdown in India. SSRN 3599102.

Normore, A. H. (Ed.). (2016). *Handbook of research on effective communication, leadership, and conflict resolution*. IGI Global. doi:10.4018/978-1-4666-9970-0

Ogar, E. C. V., Okuta, A. J., Okon, E. E., & Odama, A. J. (2021). Assessment of the Socioeconomic Impact of COVID-19 Pandemic on Small and Medium Scale Business Enterprises: Nigerian Youths in Perspective. *Journal of World Economic Research, 10*(1), 18–27.

Qiu, W., Rutherford, S., Mao, A., & Chu, C. (2017). The pandemic and its impacts. *Health, Culture and Society (Pittsburgh, Pa.), 9*, 1–11. doi:10.5195/HCS.2017.221

Queiroz, M. M., Ivanov, D., Dolgui, A., & Wamba, S. F. (2020). Impacts of epidemic outbreaks on supply chains: Mapping a research agenda amid the COVID-19 pandemic through a structured literature review. *Annals of Operations Research*, 1–38. PMID:32836615

Rahim, A., & Bonoma, T. V. (1979). Managing organizational conflict: A model for diagnosis and intervention. *Psychological Reports*, *44*(3, suppl), 1323–1344. doi:10.2466/pr0.1979.44.3c.1323

Ray, D. M. (1993). Understanding the entrepreneur: Entrepreneurial attributes, experience and skills. *Entrepreneurship and Regional Development*, *5*(4), 345–358. doi:10.1080/08985629300000022

Ray, D. M. (1993). Understanding the entrepreneur: Entrepreneurial attributes, experience and skills. *Entrepreneurship and Regional Development*, *5*(4), 345–358. doi:10.1080/08985629300000022

Rogowska, A. M., Kuśnierz, C., & Bokszczanin, A. (2020). Examining anxiety, life satisfaction, general health, stress and coping styles during COVID-19 pandemic in Polish sample of university students. *Psychology Research and Behavior Management*, *13*, 797–811. doi:10.2147/PRBM.S266511 PMID:33061695

Saxena, G. (2005). Relationships, networks and the learning regions: Case evidence from the Peak District National Park. *Tourism Management*, *26*(2), 277–289. doi:10.1016/j.tourman.2003.11.013

Schivardi, F., & Guido, R. (2020). *A simple method to estimate firms' liquidity needs during the COVID-19 crisis with an application to Italy*. Academic Press.

Schumpeter, J. A. (2000). Entrepreneurship as innovation. *Entrepreneurship: The Social Science View*, 51-75.

Sharma, M., Luthra, S., Joshi, S., & Kumar, A. (2021). Accelerating retail supply chain performance against pandemic disruption: Adopting resilient strategies to mitigate the long-term effects. *Journal of Enterprise Information Management*. Advance online publication. doi:10.1108/JEIM-07-2020-0286

Sharma, R. L., & Arora, M. (2015). Communication as the mainstay of entrepreneurial leadership: A conceptual framework. *Management Dynamics, 15*(2).

Sunarsi, D., Suryani, N. L., & Jati, W. (2020). COVID-19 Pandemic Analysis Toward Productivity Giving Layoffs Effect in The Company of Industrial Sector around South Tangerang. *ProsidingICoISSE, 1*(1), 472–481.

Taneja, S., & Toombs, L. (2014). Putting a face on small businesses: Visibility, viability, and sustainability the impact of social media on small business marketing. *Academy of Marketing Studies Journal, 18*(1), 249.

Thorelli, H. B. (1986). Networks: Between markets and hierarchies. *Strategic Management Journal*, *7*(1), 37–51. doi:10.1002mj.4250070105

Tuzovic, S., & Kabadayi, S. (2020). The influence of social distancing on employee well-being: A conceptual framework and research agenda. *Journal of Service Management*. Advance online publication. doi:10.1108/JOSM-05-2020-0140

Vogel, P., & Fischler-Strasak, U. (2014). Fostering sustainable innovation within organizations. In *Sustainable entrepreneurship* (pp. 191–205). Springer. doi:10.1007/978-3-642-38753-1_13

Witt, U. (2007). Firms as realizations of entrepreneurial visions. *Journal of Management Studies*, *44*(7), 1125–1140. doi:10.1111/j.1467-6486.2007.00731.x

Zheng, L., Miao, M., & Gan, Y. (2020). Perceived control buffers the effects of the COVID-19 pandemic on general health and life satisfaction: The mediating role of psychological distance. *Applied Psychology. Health and Well-Being*, *12*(4), 1095–1114. doi:10.1111/aphw.12232 PMID:32955170

Chapter 6
Neuroeconomics as a Factor in the Decision-Making of Women Entrepreneurs in Developing Countries

Jovanna Nathalie Cervantes-Guzmán
Centro Universitario de Ciencias Económico Administrativas, Universidad de Guadalajara, Mexico

ABSTRACT

Neuroeconomics will help solve questions that constitute a good decision, the factors that influence decisions, and how they are made. The study will expose from the experts' opinion the tangible and intangible factors that influence decisions from the perspective of the neuroeconomics. A modified Dephi method that integrates neuroeconomics is used. Neuroeconomics has the potential to explain phenomena that are considered a deviation from the prediction or behavioral bias of decision-making models in economic theory. The study exposes the opinions that have a greater degree of relevance from the experts.

INTRODUCTION

The issue of gender equality in the business world is a vital issue for the economic development of countries, but inequality in legal regimes at a global level still exists, although women have a higher level schooling and occupy key roles in the process of economic development and even the creation and development of a company has a higher level of difficulty for females than male and they tend to be mostly SMEs (AEC, 2012)

The need to implement innovations for the growth of SMEs lies in the need to create favorable conditions and the conducive environment for women entrepreneurs to develop the potential of their businesses.

Artisanal SMEs are a great engine of the economy where 47% are directed by the female gender, contributing 37% of GDP, they also allocate 70% of their income to the community and the family, unlike the men who contribute only between 30% and 40% (González, 2016).

DOI: 10.4018/978-1-7998-3964-4.ch006

According to the United Nations Educational, Scientific and Cultural Organization (UNESCO, 2001), it states that the artisanal sector has a predominant role in economic development and the fight against poverty, but they lack a long way to go to achieve maximum potential in generating employment and income to achieve greater economic growth in developing countries.

Throughout history, researchers have searched for the way in which neuroeconomics is related to consumer decision-making, on the one hand by modifying rational choice models and on the other hand towards a critique of economic theory by difficulties experienced by people in evaluating their personal preferences and achieving their well-being (Rabin, 1998).

In the various investigations that have been carried out so far, no investigation has been carried out that relates neuroeconomics with decision-making, and the literature gap is yet to be investigated.

BACKGROUND

Problem Statement

SMEs in Mexico constitute 95% of established companies and contribute 23% to GDP, but they have a series of problems that cause 75% to close their operations after 2 years in the market (INEGI, 2009), and their chance of success is on average from 25% to 30% below the world average that is 40% (Fernández, 2014). At the international level, the percentage of survival and the half-life of SMEs is similar in countries such as Spain, where more than 70% does not exceed 4 years of life and 80% of SMEs fail within the first 5 years, in The United States of America 30% of SMEs do not reach the third year and have an average life of 6 years and in the underdeveloped countries only the first 3 years of life survive between 50% and 75%.

The population that was analyzed in the research were exponential SMEs, being these companies that employ and adapt the new technologies for their development, modifying their development and distribution model to reduce their growth constraints, the digital transformation being their axis. Integrating to new digital trends to sell their products (Ismail, et al, 2014).

These SMEs are within the artisanal industry that has a predominant role in economic development and the fight against poverty, since it is part of the global creative economy that produces the world's largest workforce and generates income of $ 34 thousand million a year according to the Inter-American Development Bank (IDB).

They are run by women entrepreneurs in developing countries, since this industry is mostly made up of women who perform traditional crafts to obtain economic resources that allocate 70% to the community and the family (González, 2016). As women are the key economic agents that produce prosperity, employment, innovation and increased economic development (UN Women, 2016),

These companies are certified by the Artisan Alliance, being one of the main NGOs recognized worldwide, in addition to their work with internationally recognized organizations. They focus on increasing the economic value and sustainable growth of the artisan sector to break down the barriers that businesses face for their integration into global trade. This certification being a formal guarantee that companies meet the universal standards of the criteria by being actively involved in the artisanal sector according to the requirements established by UNESCO (United Nations Educational, Scientific, and Cultural Organizations) and ITC (Technological Institute of the Canary Islands), (Artisan Alliance Enterprise, 2016).

Justification

The main decision makers in companies is the administrative hierarchy; sometimes the decision process adopted can cause errors of judgment and erroneous communication, so tangible and intangible factors must be taken into account (Hodgkinson & Starbuck, 2008).

The factors that influence decision making are qualitative that explain the decision behavior in the elections, these are integrated by neuroscience, psychology and rationality (Kutschera & Ryan, 2009); the latter can be transformed into delimited rationality which is defined by Simon (1957) as the capacity of the human mind to solve a complex problem that is reduced compared to the size of the problems whose solution requires objective rational behavior focused on the world real.

Sometimes the decisions made are predictably irrational, that is, inherent behaviors are repeated, but once you understand how wrong decisions are made, individuals are forced to think differently and / or use external resources such as technology to reduce inherent deficiencies (Ariely, 2009).

The different sciences that study decision making, according to Sanfey, Loewenstein, McClure & Cohen, (2006) are composed of:

- The economic theory that assumes that individuals choose between different courses of action based on a rational evaluation of the consequences.
- Psychological research on judgment and decision making has shown that in practice they do not provide a complete description of human behavior.
- Neuroscience states that human behavior is the result of the interaction of different specialized subsystems.

Neuroeconomics, which is made up of economics, psychology and neuroscience, focuses on providing a general theory of human behavior to reveal the mechanisms by which they are taken. the decisions (Glimcher & Rustichini, 2004), the integration of these approaches and the theoretical methodologies offer a potential to improve the understanding of the justification behind these decisions (Sanfey, et al, 2006).

According to Sadler & Shefy (2004), neuroeconomics will help solve questions such as: what constitutes a good decision, the tangible and intangible factors that influence decisions from the perspective of neuroeconomics, and how decisions are made.

In the following investigation, the opinion of experts on how they make this decision making process from the neuroeconomy will be presented by the directors and founders of SMEs of the artisan industry that are internationally certified.

MAIN APPROACH

Varible Operationalization Matrix

See Table 1.

Table 1. Varible operationalization matrix

General objective	**1.** Analyze from a qualitative perspective using a modified Delphy method that integrates neuroeconomics, the opinion of experts from founders and CEOs that are made up of women entrepreneurs who They run exponential SMEs in the artisanal industry in developing countries that are internationally certified.
Specific objectives	1. Analyze the impact that tangible factors have on the entrepreneur's decision making. 2. Analyze the impact that intangible factors have on the entrepreneur's decision making
General question	How is it from a qualitative perspective using the modified Delphy method that integrates the neuroeconomy, the opinion of experts from founders and CEOs who are made up of female entrepreneurs who run exponential SMEs in the craft industry in developing countries that are internationally certified?
Specific questions	1. What is the impact that tangible factors have on the entrepreneur's decision making? 2. What is the impact that intangible factors have on the entrepreneur's decision making?
Hypothesis	**H1:** Tangible factors have a direct effect on the entrepreneur's decision making. **H2:** Intangible factors have a direct effect on the entrepreneur's decision making.
Variables	Dependent: Decision making of the entrepreneur. Independent: Tangible and Intangible Factors.
Methodology	Qualitative (Modified Dephi Method that integrates neuroeconomics)

Source: Own elaboration.

LITERATURE REVIEW

Neuroeconomy

In recent decades' economists have integrated in their decision models the knowledge of various behavioural sciences, representing a significant advance in decision-making theory, evolved into the development of neuroeconomics.

Neuroeconomics is an emerging discipline that combines the findings and modelling tools of neuroscience, psychology and economics to explain the behaviour of human choice. Neuroscience provides tools to answer questions about economic models that cannot be explained; and economics provides neuroscience with decision models to examine the mechanisms of communication between brain circuits (Glimcher, 2003).

Neuroeconomics focuses on understanding the behaviour of choice; on the other hand, behavioural economics and cognitive psychology exposes conceptual and mathematical frameworks, and experimental designs; in contrast neuroscience explains the focus on economic behavior using neural data (Robert, 2007).

Neuroeconomics is divided into two approaches: in the neural substrate of the choice of behavior by the algorithms that are implemented in human neural architecture (Glimcher, et al, 2005, p. 215); and the phenomena explained by the neural-physiological evidence for the explanation of the decisions observed through a more accurate knowledge of neural humans (McCabe, 2003).

Classical economists would become neuroeconomists if they investigated the biological mechanisms that influence rational decision-making. (Camerer, et al, 2013) Neuroeconomics offers a promise to change the way we think of research into brain functions, decisions and socialization, providing a new perspective to examine economic questions that without innovation are beyond the traditional economy (Glimcher, et al, 2009).

Neuroeconomics is composed of theoretical modelling and empirical measurement, although at the moment it is focused on measurement can be modified for the increase of empirical knowledge for the catechization of integration theory (Camerer, et al, 2013).

According to Camerer, Cohen, Fehr, Glimcher & Laibson, (2013) there are five main reasons for the search for information on the topic of neuroeconomics:

1. Communities of researchers are willing to study neuroeconomics in their own interest.
2. Provides a basis for measuring human well-being, which according to studies conducted by Davidson, et al, (2000) and Urri, et al, (2004) neural activity is correlated with anticipation and receipt of reward.
3. Neuroeconomy will be a partaguas for the development of new models such as those developed by Loewenstein (1996), Laibson (2001), Bernheim & Rangel (2004), Loewenstein and O'Donoghue (2005), Fudenberg & Levine (2006), Caplin & Dean (2008), Krajbich & Rangel (2011).
4. Neuroeconomy allows to develop a new form for economic models through decisions that depend on observation, allowing to make specific neural predictions.
5. Neuroeconomy increases the ability to predict consumer behaviour (Smith, et al, 2013, Rietveld, et al, 2013)

Decision-Making Process

The analysis of decision-making depends not only on the evaluation of the consequences of each alternative but also on the preferences of individuals for these consequences (Buchanan & O´Connell, 2006). Taking into account not only the probabilities of choosing each alternative, but also, the judgments and values of the individuals who made the decision. The decision-making process is made up of the areas of cognitive psychology, social psychology, and management science.

The evolution in his studies takes into account the perception of human rationality, emphasized by the "utility model" that is exposed based on the expected results, the decision is made, but does not take into account the computational capabilities and the availability of information that employs the decision maker set forth in Simon's theory (1957) where the limitations they possess on complexity in circumstances and insufficient computational power are reduced in a state of limited rationality, where the individual simplifies the decision problem by the difficulty of evaluating the available alternatives and processing the information (Buchanan & O´Conell, 2006).

Currently researchers focused on investigating information processing to study decision-making are opposed to rationality theory, because behavior is formed through the interaction in information processing and the context in which information is carried out. homework (Simon, 1990)

Decision Making in Neuroeconomics

Throughout history, researchers have looked for ways in which neuroeconomics is related to consumer decision making, starting with an investigation conducted where economist Rabin (1998) distinguishes two ways in which the findings of psychology influence the economy for decision-making, on the one hand by modifying models of rational choice and on the other hand towards a critique of economic theory by the difficulties experienced by people in the evaluation of your personal preferences and the achievement of your well-being. In addition, Camerer, Loewenstein & Prelec (2005) propose how neuroscientific discoveries can contribute to economic decision-making and how these could be different if the findings in neuroscience had been taken into account from the beginning.

There are 3 independent ways in which the brain is ordered for decision-making:

1. Internal order of the mind, the "forte" from the inception of neuroscience
2. External order of socio-economic exchange that constitute the shared norms that characterize society.
3. Extended order of cooperation through market and technology institutions (Glimcher, et al, 2009).

The short-term goals for behavioral models of decision-making in neuroeconomics are to develop a neural model of specific behavioral patterns, and long-term is to provide a theoretical framework that unifies the disciplines of economics, psychology and neuroscience.

METHODOLOGY

The gathering of information for the company's purchase intention model included data collection through surveys using the modified Delphi method that integrates neuroeconomics to analyze the perception of the participants in a series of questioning, being used for the development of causal relationships in complex social and economic phenomena.

The Delphi method is a technique that combines the quantitative and qualitative method for its application. Its methodology focuses on obtaining information from experts based on knowledge in the industry and the ability to analyze the items appropriate to their area of knowledge (García & Lena, 2018) This was considered pertinent as there was the opportunity to access to a relevant number of experts in the professional and social environment of the object of study.

This was carried out by means of a literature review of the previous work carried out on the subject, using as a base the research of the doctoral thesis of Nada (2013) with the topic "Project approval decisions: exploring success factors"; the research analyzes the interaction of decision makers, taking into account executives and project managers through surveys using the modified Delphi method that integrates neuroeconomics.

This was executed through self-administered online surveys using the "Google Surveys" program. The method is integrated by a qualitative questionnaire of open questions, applied to experts who have knowledge and experience of the problem to be investigated and are composed of CEOs and founders who are made up of women entrepreneurs who run exponential SMEs of the artisanal industry in developing countries certified by Artisan Alliance.

Technical Sheet

See Table 2.

Table 2. Technical sheet

Methodology	
Study scope	Exploratory - descriptive research
Design	Cross-Sectional
Universe	35 exponential SMEs in the artisanal industry of female entrepreneurs
Geographical scope	Developing countries
Sample type	Probability for convenience
Sample size	28 questionnaires
Level of confidence and sample error	99%, +/- 12%
Data collection	Method Delphi modified method that integrates neuroeconomics
Period of field work	March- September 2019

Source: Own elaboration based on the methodology used in this research.

RESEARCH ANALYSIS AND RESULTS

Qualitative Analysis Results

1. Intuition in projects

Intuition, knowledge, learning and experience for decision making in a changing environment are crucial to survive, consolidate and grow. Because business decisions are nothing but a set of human decisions.

The theory exposes a series of processes to make a decision in an effective way such as obtaining information, analyzing it, proposing alternatives and deciding objectively. In reality, companies in developing countries use intuition as a fundamental element to decide on crucial strategic aspects, this is caused by accelerated dynamics and global competencies that influence how business decisions are made. Although intuition is a rational process that does not allow the use of knowledge, learning and experience, in business reality a balance must be taken to complement them and thus succeed in an environment of high competition. (Hernández, et al, 2010).

The quotes below present the most relevant information presented by the businesswomen of the subject:

"I went against my intuition because of the needs imposed by the market". Finatur Designs CEO.

"In general, if something doesn't beat, I won't go in." Founder of Amano Artisans

a. Repentance of the decision later

The importance of knowledge and experience in organizational decision making. In the new business management that faces an unpredictable and changing market, where basic resources are not made up of traditional aspects such as manufacturing labor, but rather information and innovation technologies. People are placed as the guiding axis in companies and they have as their main asset the knowledge and experience that increase their competitive capabilities and the improvement of their results, achieving a competitive advantage over a period of time (Pérez & Coutín, 2005).

The decision maker considers the internal aspect as the perception of the situation, the treatment of the information and its reality what determines its decision, being a process of continuous learning, feedback and evolution (Coronado, et al, 2007)

The appointments to They present the most relevant information presented by the businesswomen of the subject:

"Yes, but I learned a lot from the experience." Founder and CEO of Mofit.

"Normally I don't regret my decisions as they are always a way to learn and improve." Founder and CEO of Merkao.

"No, the organization learns as it overcomes obstacles." Manager of ESNET LLC for Village Artisan.

"No, because it was the lack of knowledge." CEO of Abury Collection GmBH

b. What was done about it

In the decision-making process, the person has control over the decision but not over the result, because a good decision is not a guarantee of a good result but does reduce the possibility of obtaining an unfavorable result (Abarca, 1979).

Learning regarding experience in decision-making in companies can be applied in future planning and in the solution of problems that may arise to achieve increased productivity in all areas and motivation in employees and with it achieve company well-being and a competitive advantage over the competition. Companies must learn from their past experience to be modern, agile, effective and face the challenges by seeing them not as problems but as opportunities that allow growth and continuous improvement (Salinas, 2001).

The quotes below present the most relevant information presented by businesswomen on the subject:

"The buyer and the director divided the company, the worst part was facing our disappointed artisans." Founder and CEO of Mortif.

"Use the opportunity as a moment of teaching and training." Sproud Entreprise CEO

"In making a decision that I regret later, I have to keep going because you can't turn back time." Founder and CEO of Merkao.

"Admit that it was a mistake, but I learned from it." Founder and CEO of DIOSA designs inc.

"I continue to pay attention to intuition, being the intelligence of the subconscious, I don't think it's something magical, I try to be updated, open up to new ideas, understand the disruption, what is generating artificial intelligence, the bigdata, etc." Tanya Moss CEO

c. The impact it had on future decisions on similar projects

Decisions are never repetitive due to the constant evolution of the environment and the experience gained, this learning being a way to evaluate previous results and consider new elements for the analysis of new situations, being considered a cluster of useful knowledge for management (Evans, 2006).

Improvements in decision-making in companies in the 21st century are influenced by information technologies (ICTs), these allow reducing human error in factors such as time and cost savings, improvements in handling, volume and treatment information which allows a deeper knowledge that favors optimal decision making (Sánchez, 2017).

The quotes below present the most relevant information presented by businesswomen on the subject:

"I make decisions with greater analysis and use secondary sources such as the internet." Founder of Amano Artisans

"I take more time before making hasty decisions". Founder and CEO of Nanay SRL.

"I now consider projects when they are closed and signed, and I no longer anticipate having the resources and infrastructure to deal with them ahead of time." Founder and CEO of DIOSA designs inc.

"Yes, I learned to research and inform myself using information technologies." Sproud Entreprise CEO

"Yes, because they are lived experiences and leave learning." CEO of Ibu Movement

2. Use of personal approach for personal decision making and business decisions

Decision making linking personal experience in business. According to Shneider (2010) in his study of irrationality of decisions, when analyzing psychological factors in decision-making, he states that personal and business human behavior does not always follow a logical order and are affected by the emotional process and unconscious, exposing:

- The actions of people are oriented by risk aversion
- Human preferences are not stable
- The positive impact of a profit is less than the negative impact of a loss
- People do not always maximize their profits
- People so frequently they act in an altruistic way.

The quotations below present the most relevant information presented by the businesswomen of the subject:

"Yes, in this trade you cannot separate the personal from the business ... it is only one thing, a lifestyle." Finatur Designs CEO.

"I use a personal approach first in my life for personal and business matters. My business is about women and I look at it personally, solving and helping women, but doing it through a business. Founder and CEO of DIOSA designs inc.

"Intestinal sensation is important, however, processes have priority." Founder and CEO of Merkao.

"I can be pragmatic in personal and business decisions." Founder and CEO of Mortif.

a. The focus on decision-making is the same or different.

The feelings in the decision-making of entrepreneurs are conditioned by the values, beliefs and perception of the individual. Although this can be analytical, but the emotional part that qualifies the previous experiences can provoke a visceral response. Between the rational and emotional there must be a synergy to generate a balance (Lonardi, 2007)

The entrepreneur when deciding to start a company has a combination between the conscious, analytical and emotional, the latter generates a visceral response to the decision to be taken (Aguirre, 2005)

The quotes below present the most relevant information presented by businesswomen on the subject:

"Equally important, but in different categories". CEO of Atellier.

"Likewise, I take feelings into consideration when making decisions." Founder and CEO of DIOSA designs inc.

"Equal, only if it is a financial decision is it more calculated." CEO of Abury Collection GmbH.

b. Similarities and differences in the decision-making approach

Differences in decision-making between the female and male gender from the scientific side is caused by the contrasts in the cognitive process between both genders that are integrated in the biological part by the neural bases of mental processes, anatomical configuration and functional structure of the brain (Londoño, 2011).

External factors in decision-making between men and women, according to Maniviesa (2019) are:

- Women: Innovative, creative, recognize skills in the group of people who make up their team and use them to achieve the objectives, pay attention to details and decisions take personal factors into account.
- Men: Ease in the delegation of tasks, greater focus and structuring.

The quotes below present the most relevant information presented by the businesswomen of the subject:

"Our company has a small operation; it is like a family business. This means that many business decisions are influenced by personal factors. " Founder and CEO of Mortif.

"Intuition and sensitivity are very important. I trust my instinct, I know the style I like and I use that same judgment in my personal life and in business. " CEO of Ibu Movement

"Being the owner of my company and this being a small business, the personal seal is inevitable. I manage the company with the values with which I live, it is likely that this limits some opportunities, but also enhances others ". Founder of Hello Crisp

"She evaluated the decisions, but also how they affect my family. Less focused on profit, more focused on relationships and reputation building. " Founder and CEO of Nanay SRL.

Results

See Table 3.

Table 3. Results of the entrepreneur's decision making in the online business

	Tangible Factors	No Tangible Factors
Intuition, knowledge, experience, and learning	Market needs	Training
	Administration of a company	Evolution
	Disruption of new technologies	Subconscious intelligence
		Research
		Analysis
Corporate approach: personal vs business	Strategic processes	Lifestyle
	Evaluation of decisions	Helping and supporting
		Intestinal sensation
		Pragmatism
		Feelings
		Values
		Interpersonal relationship
		Reputation building
		Rationality

Source: Own elaboration

CONCLUSION

The factors that affect decision making are different, may be affected by some particular characteristics such as gender, environmental factors and age. Gender in decision-making women have a greater risk aversion due to the high cortisol index, while men have a greater propensity to trust due to the high testosterone index. The environmental factors in the decision making that cause the decrease in sales and price reduction are influenced by various aspects such as lunar cycles, light intensity and geomagnetic storms (BBVA, 2011). Age influences decision-making since the reduction in the production of dopamine and serotonin decreases when a person is aging, having less effect on the appreciation and reception of the reward, in addition to the assumed risk (Mohr, et al, 2010).

Neuroeconomics has the potential to explain the phenomena that are considered as a deviation from the prediction or behavioral bias of decision-making models in economic theory

In relation to the overall objective aimed at analyzing from a quantitative perspective using modified Delphi method that integrates neuroeconomics, the opinion of experts of founders and CEOs who are made up of women entrepreneurs of exponential SMEs in the artisanal sector in developing countries that are certified.

The variable that has the greatest explanatory weight in the model is: consumer satisfaction. Exposing the importance to entrepreneurs of creating a bond of trust, commitment and loyalty in customer service.

Customer service is essential for companies because they are developed based on customers and sales, the lack of this can lead to low sales, low competitiveness and the possible failure of business projects (Loera, 2012).

The perceived quality of a service is the result of an evaluation process where customers compare their perceptions and results according to their expectations (Lovelock & Wirtz, 2009).

Quality elements in service are related to quality and attitude attributes. The quality attribute shows the opportunity indicator which implies that the service must be executed within the time limit requested by the customer, and the reliability indicator mentions that the service must be accurate, accurate, safe and truthful; the attribute of attitude is represented by kindness in which service should be pleasant and gentle; and the agility in which service must be fast, early and timely (Prieto, 2005).

REFERENCES

Abarca, A. (1979). La toma de decisiones: un proceso de aprendizaje. *Revista educación, 3*(1). Recovered from https://revistas.ucr.ac.cr/index.php/educacion/article/view/18667

Aguirre, M. (2005). El impacto de la emoción en la toma de decisiones. *La Gaceta de Económicas.*

Ariely, D. (2009). *Predictably Irrational: The Hidden Forces That Shape Our Decisions.* Harper Collins Books.

Artisan Alliance Enterprise. (2016). *Impact Report.* Alliance for Artisan Enterprise.

BBVA Innovation Center. (2011). *Neuroeconomía: Mecanismos cerebrales implicados en la toma de decisiones financieras.* KnowSquare: red de conocimiento.

Buchanan & O'Connell. (2006). A brief history of decision making. *Harvard Business Review, 84*(1), 32–41.

Camerer, C. F., Loewenstein, G., & Prelec, D. (2005). Neuroeconomics: How neuroscience can inform economics. *Journal of Economic Literature, 43*(1), 9–64. doi:10.1257/0022051053737843

Coronado, G., Cañan, F., & Herrera, B. (2007). *La Gestión del Conocimiento para la toma de decisiones. Serie Técnica No 5: Apoyando los esfuerzos en el manejo y protección de la biodiversidad tropical.* The Nature Conservancy.

Evans, M. (2006). El proceso de toma de decisiones como un espacio para el aprendizaje en las organizaciones. Revista Ciencias Estratégicas, 14(16), 153-169.

Fernández, L. (2014). *El comportamiento online del consumidor: factores que aumentan la actividad de búsqueda de ewom en el sector turístico* (Master's thesis). Universidad de Oviedo, Oviedo, España.

García, M., & Lena, F. (2018). Aplicación del método Delphi en el diseño de una investigación cuantitativa sobre el fenómeno FABLAB. *EMPIRIA. Revista de Metodología de Ciencias Sociales*, 129-166.

Glimcher, P., Camerer, C., Fehr, R., & Polorack, R. (2009). Neuroeconomics: Decision making and the brain. Academic Press Publications.

Glimcher, P. W., & Rustichini, A. (2004). Neuroeconomics: The Consilience of Brain and Decision. *Science*, *306*(5695), 447–452. doi:10.1126cience.1102566 PMID:15486291

González, C. (2011). *Pymes mexicanas, incubadoras del desarrollo y crecimiento económico del México actual* (Unpublished bachelor's thesis). Universidad Autónoma de San Luis Potosí, San Luis Potosí, RP.

González, M. (2016). 31% del PIB nacional es aportado por mujeres empresarias. *Informa BTL*. Recovered from https://www.informabtl.com/31-del-pib-nacional-es-aportado-por-mujeres-empresarias/

Hernández, M., Feijo, M., & Zarza, A. (2010). *Razón e intuición: prácticas en la toma de decisiones de las empresas de economías emergentes*. Tecnológico de Monterrey. Recovered from http://acacia.org.mx/busqueda/pdf/04_PF304_Toma_de_Decisiones.pdf

Hodgkinson, G., & Starbuck, W. (2008). *The Oxford Handbook of Organizational Decision Making*. Oxford University Press. doi:10.1093/oxfordhb/9780199290468.001.0001

INEGI. (2009). *Censo Económico. Micro, pequeña, mediana y gran empresa*. Recovered from https://www.inegi.org.mx/est/contenidos/espanol/proyectos/censos/ce2009/default.asp?s=est&c=14220

Insmail, S., Malone, M., & Van, Y. (2014). *Organizaciones Exponenciales: Por qué existen nuevas organizaciones diez veces más escalables y rentables que la tuya (y qué puedes hacer al respecto)*. Singularity University Book.

Kutschera, I., & Ryan, M. (2009). Implications of intuition for strategic thinking: Practical recommendations for gut thinkers. *S.A.M. Advanced Management Journal*, *74*(3), 12–20.

Sheang Lee, K., Hua Lim, G., Jiuan Tan, S., & Hou Wee, C. (2001). Generic marketing strategies for small and medium-sized enterprises- conceptual framework. *Journal of Strategies Marketing*, *9*.

Lonardi, E. (2017). *Como afecta las emociones en la toma de decisiones en las empresas Pymes, estudio de caso: Heladerías Persicco* (Master's thesis). Universidad de Buenos Aires. Recovered from ybibliotecadigital.econ.uba.ar/download/tpos/1502-0226_LonardiE.pdf

Londoño, C., Herrera, E., & Peláez, L. (2011). Diferencias de género en la toma de decisiones. *Cultura, Educación y Sociedad*. Recovered from https://revistascientificas.cuc.edu.co/culturaeducacionysociedad/article/view/930

Maniviesa, P. (2019). Diferencias entre la dirección empresarial femenina y masculina. *Pymerang*. Recovered from https://www.pymerang.com/direccion-de-negocios/funciones-del-director-general/liderazgo/505-diferencias-entre-la-direccion-empresarial-femenina-y-masculina

Mohr, P., Biele, G., & Heekeren, H. (2010). Neural Processing of Risk. *Journal of Neuroscience. Vol*, *30*(19), 6613–6619. doi:10.1523/JNEUROSCI.0003-10.2010 PMID:20463224

Nada, D. (2013). *Project approval decisions: exploring success factors* (PhD thesis). University of Calgary, Canada.

Pérez, Y., & Coutín, A. (2005). La gestión del conocimiento: un nuevo enfoque en la gestión empresarial. *ACIMED, 13*(6). Recovered from http://scielo.sld.cu/scielo.php?script=sci_arttext&pid=S1024-94352005000600004&lng=es&tlng=es

Rabin, M. (1998). Psychology and Economics. *Revista de Economic Literature*, *36*(1), 11–46.

Sadler, E., & Shefy, E. (2004). The intuitive executive: Understanding and applying 'gut feel' in decision-making. *The Academy of Management Executive*, *18*(4), 76–91. doi:10.5465/ame.2004.15268692

Salinas, O. (2001). *La experiencia como conocimiento de la empresa*. Gestiopolis. Recovered from https://www.gestiopolis.com/experiencia-como-conocimiento-empresa/

Sánchez, R. (2017). *Utilización de las TICs en la toma de decisiones de modo colaborativo* (Tesis de ingenería). Universidad de Valladolid. Recovered from https://uvadoc.uva.es/bitstream/handle/10324/23051/TFG-G2347.pdf;jsessionid=CCDC5F2838507A48AC7F932505CCCC4F?sequence=1

Sanfey, A. G., Loewenstein, G., McClure, S. M., & Cohen, J. D. (2006). Neuroeconomics: Cross-Currents in Research on Decision-Making. *Trends in Cognitive Sciences*, *10*(3), 108–116. doi:10.1016/j.tics.2006.01.009 PMID:16469524

Simon, H. (1957). *Administrative behavior*. Cambridge Univ Press.

Simon, H. (1990). Invariants of human behavior. *Annual Review of Psychology*, *41*(1), 1-20.

UNESCO. (2001). *Artesanías creadoras*. París: UNESCO, Sección de Artesanías y Diseño.

Chapter 7
Racial Differences in Perceptions of Shared Leadership Among IT Managers

Eugene J. Petrie
Universty of Phoenix, USA

Auslyn G. Nieto
University of Phoenix, USA

Kate Andrews
https://orcid.org/0000-0002-1337-4824
Walden University, USA

ABSTRACT

In the last decade, leadership researchers have demonstrated greater interest in the concept of shared leadership, perhaps due to increasing globalization and changes in organizational cultures. This leadership style, based on inclusivity, may replace traditional structures of hierarchical leadership, or exist as a complement. Despite potential benefits, unspoken power dynamics may prevent shared leadership from being completely inclusive. Guided by three research questions and explored via an online survey, this quasi-experimental study investigated significant racial differences in the levels of overall shared leadership among IT managers of different races, specifically White, Black, Asian, and other. Descriptive statistics and an analysis of variance (ANOVA) were used to examine the responses of 200 LinkedIn IT managers employed within the United States. Findings revealed that shared leadership did not differ across racial lines, and IT managers who engage in shared leadership may maintain their competitive edge in this ultracompetitive field.

DOI: 10.4018/978-1-7998-3964-4.ch007

INTRODUCTION

In the last decade, leadership researchers have demonstrated greater interest in the concept of shared leadership, perhaps due to increasing globalization and changes in organizational cultures. This leadership style, based on inclusivity, may replace or be complimentary to traditional structures of hierarchical leadership.

Shared leadership refers to a dynamic behavioral process depicted by team member influence, collaboration, and group exhibition of leadership (Stagnaro & Piotrowski, 2014). In animated work environments such as IT where the talents and skills of a variety of different workers are crucial to project success, shared leadership may be of particular benefit in increasing organizational performance (Erkutlu, 2012; Fausing et al., 2015; Hoch & Kozlowski, 2014; Hui-Ying & Jian-Peng, 2013; Stagnaro & Piotrowski, 2014; Wang et al., 2014), and, in most cases, drives its utilization.

Although a significant body of research indicates that shared leadership creates increases in organizational performance, little is known about the antecedents of successful shared leadership (Fausing et al., 2015). Such knowledge is critical to understanding how to implement effective shared leadership. In response to this gap in the research, Fausing et al. (2015) conducted a study of 81 knowledge and manufacturing teams employed by a green technology manufacturing company in Denmark. The company's annual performance rating system was used to measure team performance. The performance score represented team leaders' assessments of their employees' and teams' achievement and the processes they employed to achieve goals.

Involved in organizational performance is team performance to which shared leadership has been found to enhance team effectiveness (Perry et al., 1999). Katz and Kahn (1978) found shared leadership to influence the competitive advantage of organizations because of increased commitment and shared resources. In the generation of funding for non-profit organizations, shared leadership is part of the institutionalization of honesty and integrity that in turn generates stakeholder interest (Brown, 2017). Having a culture of shared leadership affects the resiliency and sustainability of organizations (Anwashe, 2020; Routhieaux, 2015).

However, socially engrained power dynamics may prevent shared leadership from being completely inclusive (Lumby & Morrison, 2010). Opponents argued that shared leadership encourages maintaining the status quo for those in power and acts as a tool for forcing increased worker productivity (Coleman, 2012; Harris, 2013; Lumby & Morrison, 2010). Hargreaves and Fink (2008) posited that it may be little more than another way to enforce hierarchical leadership. Still, other scholars opined that within shared leadership, the potential exists for racial, gender, and ethnic biases to prevent inclusiveness across teams (Mendez & Busenbark, 2015; Trenery & Paradies, 2012). Indeed, the silence within the body of literature on shared leadership regarding challenges to inclusion on issues such as race and ethnicity is notable. Within a society still plagued by racial and ethnic inequities, the dialog of power distribution in shared leadership settings is inevitably colored by race.

Notwithstanding the failure to acknowledge fundamental power dynamics related to race, the literature on shared leadership does indicate undeniable organizational benefits for the field of IT (Stagnaro & Piotrowski, 2014). Truly inclusive shared leadership has the potential to improve IT project efficiency. However, due to underlying power and race narratives, understanding the perceptions of shared leadership among racially diverse IT managers is imperative. Racial differences in levels of overall shared leadership may question the inclusiveness of shared leadership in IT and indicate the need for improvements to equality and power distribution within organizations.

This quasi-experimental survey study was conducted to explore racial differences in the levels of overall shared leadership among managers in the dynamic field of IT, and utilized Pearce et al.'s (2007) theory of shared leadership as a dynamic behavioral process depicted by team member influence, collaboration, and the exhibition of leadership.

BACKGROUND

To support new organizational directions influenced by the global marketplace, information technology (IT) departments are expected to solve problems quickly, to achieve and maintain competitive advantage through flexible processes, and to possess the abilities to acclimate to new business practices (Chickowski, 2009; de Ron, 1998; Jarvenpaa & Ives, 1994; Kayworth & Leidner, 2002). In an attempt to nurture collaboration and communication that promote timely response within globally dispersed teams, many IT departments have adopted more flattened hierarchical structures with the intention of meeting the needs of globalization and ever-changing work environments (Ramthun & Matkin, 2012).

Traditionally, leadership research is focused on followers and their interactions with leaders, with specific concentration on hierarchical leadership (Pearce et al., 2010). More recently, the concept of leadership has been recently broadened to include non-leaders, such as peers and followers (Avolio et al., 2009).

One form of developing leadership that has garnered growing attention is shared leadership that Pearce and Conger (2003) defined as "a dynamic, interactive influence process among individuals in groups for which the objective is to lead one another to the achievement of group or organizational goals or both" (p. 1). Another rendition of shared leadership was put forth by Stagnaro and Piotrowski (2014): a dynamic behavioral process depicted by team member influence, collaboration, and the exhibition of leadership by a group. Also referred to as *collective*, *distributed*, or *collaborative leadership*, shared leadership is a method which is collectively enacted, shared, and taught (Pearce & Conger, 2003).

When leadership is shared across organizational boundaries and structures, it becomes shared leadership, which can positively influence organizational goals (D'Innocenzo et al., 2014; Wang et al., 2014). As Pearce et al. (2014) explained, "Shared leadership moves beyond the moribund myth of leadership being a solely top-down hierarchical affair into the idea that leadership can be systematically fluid and simultaneously multi-versional based on a dynamic give-and-take relationship" (p. 277).

LITERATURE REVIEW

Definition of Shared Leadership

Shared leadership is a meta-theory of leadership which entails the ongoing mutual influence, information sharing, and coordination between official and unofficial leaders (Pearce et al., 2014; Yukl, 2010). Pearce et al. (2010) suggested that shared leadership is a practice in which team members purposefully transfer leadership roles to one another, as required by group needs or organizational goals. The premise of shared leadership is that all members of a group are capable of sharing leadership burdens and responsibilities to some extent, in any organizational situation (Pearce et al., 2014).

Even in traditional, hierarchical settings, leadership is inherently shared to some degree. After all, most leaders do not singularly possess all the skills and knowledge to lead every project in every situation (Pearce et al., 2014; Stagnaro & Piotrowski, 2014). Rather, leaders usually rely on the assistance and guidance of a cabinet of advisors. Accordingly, as Pearce et al. (2014) explained, "All leadership is shared leadership; it is simply a matter of degree – sometimes it is shared completely while at other times it is not shared at all" (p. 276).

Under shared leadership, members follow the subject matter expert or individual who possesses the most knowledge and skill in a given situation. Consequently, organizational objectives are met more effectively (Ramthun & Matkin, 2012). While traditional hierarchal leadership structures designate certain responsibilities to those in formal leadership positions, shared leadership is an inclusive structure that delegates leadership responsibilities based on individuals' strengths and expertise, making it supportive of effective teamwork (Stagnaro & Piotrowski, 2014). Thus, shared leadership may be critical to project and organizational efficacy in IT departments where the skills and knowledge of a variety of individuals are essential to project success.

Types of Leadership

Many prominent hierarchical styles of individual leadership, such as transactional, transformational, and laissez-faire, have gained considerable consideration in the leadership literature (Avolio, 1994; Bass, 1990a; Bass & Avolio, 1991; Beyer, 1999; Burns, 1978; Dai et al., 2013; Hinkin & Schriesheim, 2008; McClesky, 2014; Yukl, 2010). In discussing the emerging leadership style of shared leadership, it is helpful to review these main leadership styles, which have a hierarchical nature, in conceptualizing the differences in the approaches of individuals and organizations that employ shared leadership. The hierarchical status of these leadership theories give way to an individual and less collaborative leadership paradigm that shows less effectiveness in team performance (Gockel & Worth, 2010).

Transformational Leadership

Transformational leadership is a dominant leadership model (Bass & Avolio, 1991; Burns, 1978; Kendrick, 2011; Tracey & Hinkin, 1998; Tucker & Russell, 2004). Kendrick (2011) described transformational leadership as that which promotes positive changes across individuals and organizations. Transformational leaders inspire their followers to change by motivating them to improve their own performance while developing leadership skills among themselves. In this way, transformational leaders encourage followers to work together toward common goals that prompt changes throughout entire organizations. They lead by example, question assumptions, promote unconventional thinking, and provide positive feedback (Tracey & Hinkin, 1998; Tucker & Russell, 2004).

According to Avolio (1994), transformational leaders can connect their past experiences with their own transformational behaviors where a result is an internal connection, which can create external behaviors that prompt changes throughout entire organizations (Tucker & Russell, 2004). One of the most prominent characteristics of transformational leaders is their level of excitement and ability to excite followers to institute change. The energy formed in groups of followers can create dynamic work cultures and organizational changes that improve goal attainment (Tucker & Russell, 2004).

Transactional Leadership

Despite the benefits of transformational leadership, many organizational cultures still utilize transactional leadership to assist followers to achieve performance objectives, complete tasks, and direct followers. Its greatest drawback is that it encourages preserving the status quo instead of creating dynamic organizational climates that can change quickly and efficiently in response to evolving market demands (Bass, 1990a). Another common critique against transactional leadership is its failure to epitomize factors that may be unique to organizations or situations (Yukl & Mahsud, 2010). There is the possibility of discrimination when organizations use transactional leadership (Sitthiwarongchai et al., 2020). Transactional leaders have less inclination with protecting employee rights and dignities than with maximizing utility (Groves & LaRocca, 2010), and they favor procedural justice over social justice (Brown et al., 2019), thus leading to a pathway conducive to discrimination.

Laissez-Faire Leadership

Laissez-faire is the most passive, ineffective, and destructive form of leadership (Judge & Piccolo, 2004) or *leadership without leading* (Hinkin & Schriesheim, 2008). Laissez-faire leaders maintain social distance from their followers, are avoidant of all interactions with the latter, often fail to meet their needs (Bass & Avolio, 1991), and can cause significant organizational harm (Judge & Piccolo, 2004). A negative and weak relationship was found between Laissez-faire leadership and diversity management (Okcu, 2014).

Shared Leadership

Shared leadership represents a significant departure from the well-known styles of transformational, transactional, and laissez-faire leadership. Instead of leadership falling into the hands of one person, shared leadership is a collaborative and dynamic construct that focuses on most efficiently meeting group or organizational goals. Ramthum and Matkin (2012) explained that instead of counting on the top-down influence of one person, members of shared leadership groups collaboratively influence each other in a multi- directional (lateral, downward, and upward) fashion, through decentralized and distributed leadership. The conceptual basis of shared leadership includes self-management teams, leadership substitutes, and participative decision-making (Gockel & Werth, 2010).

In the discussion of understanding what shared leadership *is,* it is also essential to understand what it is *not.* While shared leadership does entail the active distribution of leadership responsibilities, it does not mean that everyone in a group is a leader (Harris, 2013). In groups governed by shared leadership, a manager is typically still present, but that main leader delegates leadership to others in the group, as appropriate, according to the needs of a project and the skills and expertise of group members. According to Leithwood et al. (2009), shared leadership describes an alternative model of organizational development that shifts away from traditional bureaucratic structures to those that are interconnected and provide innovative approaches to change.

Pearce et al. (2010) acknowledged that shared leadership may not be appropriate in all circumstances, and that in order for it to work, group members must be receptive to it. For example, the concept of shared leadership can encounter cultural resistance among individuals from cultures with low power distance (Hofstede, 1980), and can be influenced by a variety of factors, such as team member characteristics, task, technology, or organizational setting. In turn, it can be expected to influence very different factors that include affective, cognitive, and behavioral phenomena and team performance (Gockel & Werth, 2010).

Thus, organizations and managers must carefully consider shared leadership before enacting and must thoughtfully plan execution methods in order for teams to experience its benefits. As interest in the potential of shared leadership in a variety of fields and disciplines has increased, so too has the corresponding body of literature. An analysis and synthesis of several current articles on shared leadership follows in order to conceptualize it for the investigation, and covers shared leadership's relationship with organizational performance, cultural diversity, virtual teams, and information technology.

Shared Leadership and Organizational Performance

In most cases, the driving motivation behind the utilization of shared leadership is improved organizational performance. Although a significant body of research indicates that shared leadership engenders upsurges in organizational performance, little is known about the antecedents of successful shared leadership (Fausing et al., 2015). Such knowledge is critical to understanding how to implement effective shared leadership. In response to this research gap, Fausing et al. (2015) conducted a study of 81 knowledge and manufacturing teams - 562 team members - employed by a green tech manufacturing company in Denmark, utilizing the Short Version of the Shared and Vertical Leadership Questionnaire (Pearce & Sims, 2002), and a four-item measure of interdependence (Campion et al., 1993).

Results from Fausing's et al. (2015) study demonstrated that vertically empowering leadership and interdependence were positively related to the use of shared leadership in teams. Team use of shared leadership, in turn, was related to improved team performance. An important factor in successful shared leadership among teams was an empowering team leader who worked externally to encourage team members to provide and accept leadership as a team. These researchers concluded that empowering vertical leadership combined with task and goal interdependence could nurture shared leadership and foster improvements in team performance.

Further research indicates that shared leadership improves team efficiency (Avolio et al., 1996; Cox et al., 2003; Pearce & Sims, 2002) through increased information sharing (Small & Rentsch, 2010), and can serve as a valuable, intangible resource among teams (Day et al., 2004). Shared leadership can also improve team performance by providing individuals with feelings of self-efficacy and increased opportunities to contribute (Zhou et al., 2015). Consequently, team members may demonstrate greater organizational commitment and higher levels of performance. As Zhou et al. (2015) explained, "In complex team environments, a formal leader is often less likely than the team as a whole to have the knowledge and skills required to effectively guide the team" (p. 43).

A meta-analysis performed by Wang et al. (2014) substantiated a relationship between organizational performance and shared leadership. Interestingly, their investigation revealed that shared *new-genre* leadership – leadership emphasizing change and development - was more strongly correlated with team effectiveness than shared traditional leadership. Wang et al. posited that this may have been because sharing leadership functions oriented to change may be particularly salient to team effectiveness and concluded that shared leadership was more connected to attitudes and behaviors than team performance. Shared leadership fostered cooperative behaviors and connectedness among team members. These cooperative behaviors and connectedness resulted in improved team performance.

Shared Leadership and Communication Strategies

Effective communication is essential in providing effective feedback to each other in teams within both large and small IT organizations (Agnihotri & Agnihotri, 2020). High levels of communication skills become a business strategy necessary for high performing teams (Agnihotri & Agnihotri, 2020). Communication skills such as clarity, familiarity, and credibility are predictors of the level of shared leadership so that development of interpersonal communication skills is a strategy that can be used to create shared leadership (Nedzinskaite-Maciuniene & Merkyte, 2019). As a foundation for these findings, Slater (2008) found that communication strategies, such as problem solving, consensus in decision-making, and conflict resolution that increase trust in relationships, build shared leadership.

Shared Leadership in Information Technology

As with other industries, organizational performance is critical to the competitiveness of IT companies. A variety of factors increase the importance of performance in the field of IT, including economic globalization, rapid technological developments, fast changing markets and increases in knowledge economy (Hui-Ying & Jian-Peng, 2013). Shared leadership has also been shown to improve organizational performance in IT via *innovative performance*, which describes an organization's efficiency and the effects of technical, innovative activities and knowledge applications (Hui-Ying & Jian-Peng, 2013).

As demonstrated by Hui-Ying and Jian-Peng (2013), the relationship between innovative performance and shared leadership is partly facilitated by knowledge sharing and task complexity. The mediating effects of task complexity may be due to the constantly evolving nature of IT, which draws on the varied skillsets of team members, managers who often lead individuals with varied forms of expertise, and leadership roles within IT teams that are based on what is required to achieve project objectives (Stagnaro & Piotrowski, 2013).

Thus, shared leadership is a critical success benefiting IT teams because it coordinates individuals across multiple functions of a project (Stagnaro & Piotrowski, 2013).

As far as research on shared leadership in IT, Stagnaro and Piotrowski's (2013) study barely scrapes the surface but provides a valuable baseline from which other researchers could branch out. While the study did explore the influence of gender on shared leadership, it failed to acknowledge other important demographic variables such as race and age. As discussed in later sections of this chapter, diversity, race, implicit racism, and the distribution of power are critical factors to explore when investigating the effectiveness of shared leadership on IT team effectiveness.

Multicultural Shared Leadership

A potential challenge to shared leadership may exist in multicultural teams (Pearce & Conger, 2003). For shared leadership to work in any setting, members must extend and accept lateral influences; without this condition, shared leadership is difficult to achieve (Ramthun & Matkin, 2012). Although there are many benefits to teams through increased informational diversity, cultural diversity can significantly influence a team's cohesion, agreeableness, and collectivism (Ramthun & Matkin, 2012). Furthermore, cultural differences between team members have the potential to create conflicts and reduce cohesion and communication. Thus, cultural diversity can create relational obstacles to shared leadership (Cox et al., 2003).

Despite the potential barriers that cultural diversity can create for shared leadership, cultural differences can be powerful assets to teams (Adler, 2002). In a conceptual article by Ramthun and Matkin (2012), the authors posited that teams can enjoy the benefits of diversity in shared leadership environments so long as team members demonstrate high levels of intercultural competence or the ability to traverse cultural differences through interaction, awareness, and communication (Ramthun & Matkin, 2012). Individuals who are interculturally competent are able to manage interactions with people from other backgrounds or orientations while maintaining effective communication and focus on goals (Spitzberg & Changnon, 2009).

Ramthun and Matkin (2012) suggested that the key to maintaining effective shared leadership in diverse teams is team members who demonstrate high levels of multicultural competency. Such individuals may be able to overcome social challenges in order to facilitate creative thinking and equal distribution of control over projects. Although Ramthun and Matkin's conceptual model of multicultural shared leadership may be most beneficial to organizations and teams working in multinational contexts, it could also prove beneficial to individuals working in domestic teams such as those who comprised the sample of the current study.

In vibrant fields such as information technology (IT), shared leadership may be of particular benefit due to its inherent utilization of informational diversity, which refers to individual differences in perspectives and knowledge that workers bring to a team setting or project (Zhou et al., 2015). Informational diversity is an asset that can result from cultural diversity among team members.

Shared leadership may improve informational diversity especially among members of dissimilar teams that collectively possess a variety of backgrounds, knowledge, skills, and experiences (Ramthun & Matkin, 2012). However, as Zhou et al. (2015) cautioned, the mere existence of cultural diversity does not promise diversity among team members' ideas and perspectives. Second, when informational diversity is present, team members must be open to the concept of shared leadership to capitalize on the benefits of diverse teams.

Leadership Considerations in Multicultural Teams

The potential exists for racial, gender, and ethnic biases – which remain deeply engrained in society (Wiecek & Hamilton, 2014) – to prevent equality and inclusiveness across teams that practice shared leadership. The effects that demographic characteristics such as race and ethnicity may have on shared leadership have not been explored in the leadership literature (Lumby, 2013), and have created a necessity for research to investigate any differences that may exist in the levels of overall shared leadership among individuals of different races.

A small group of scholars has challenged the equality of shared leadership in multicultural teams. Whether the members of an IT team are working together in one geographic location or dispersed throughout the world, all leaders (regardless of leadership style) should be sensitive to cultural, racial, and ethnic differences present in diverse teams. Niederman and Tan (2011) recommended that IT leaders of diverse teams consider cultural differences in reward structures, be more explicit in considering the communicative contexts of different cultures and backgrounds when providing direction and feedback to teams and empowering team members to take initiative and self-facilitate through increased autonomy so they require less direction from managers.

Though not explicitly recommending shared leadership, Niederman and Tran's (2011)'s statement is particularly relevant to the current research:

It may be that global IT team leaders working with large numbers of people from such cultures need to extend their range of controlling strategies to successfully run such distributed teams. A transition period of moving from highly directive to more self-governing teams will be required. (p. 25).

While Niederman and Tran (2011) made recommendations analogous to shared leadership through increased team member autonomy and self-initiative, they also cautioned about the potential for self-facilitation to be destructive. Without some form of managerial oversight, teams have the potential to move in diverse directions and produce results that are harmful to organizations. Thus, even in shared leadership structures, it is important that some form of oversight and accountability is instituted.

Virtual Teams

Because of advances in communication technology, IT team members are no longer required to share the same office. Virtual teams can collaborate over time and space through electronic media (Bell & Kozlowski, 2002). Muganda and Pillay (2013) defined virtual teams as those that use communication technology over a virtual space to communicate, brainstorm, share information, and negotiate projects.

Researchers agree that a strong central leadership is difficult to establish among virtual teams; thus, success is more likely among virtual teams with shared leadership (Chen et al., 2008; Muganda & Pillay, 2013; Purvanova & Bono, 2009). As Hoch and Kozlowski (2014) explained, some of the advantages of virtual teams include the ability to create teams of experts distributed around the world, improve staffing flexibility, and reduce travel costs.

Research indicates that team leadership is crucial to improving team motivation and coordination (Bell & Kozlowski; Kirkman et al., 2012; O'Leary & Mortensen, 2010). However, geographic separation coupled with the lack of in-person contact can make it difficult for leaders to operate in traditional, hierarchical roles (Hoch & Kozlowski, 2014). Because of these factors, understanding the most effective forms of leadership is particularly important for the IT industry, thereby compelling consideration of shared leadership as a useful leadership alternative.

In exploring shared leadership on virtual IT teams, Hoch and Kozlowski (2014) conducted a study of its effects on the performance of virtually dispersed teams. The researchers found that hierarchical leadership was less strongly associated with team performance as levels of team virtuality increased. While the researchers expected that shared leadership would have the opposite effect –that shared leadership would be increasingly associated with team performance as virtuality increased – results from data analysis were unexpected. While shared leadership was positively associated with team virtuality, the relationship was stable in that it did not change as levels of team virtuality increased. Thus, the benefits of shared leadership may transcend team dispersion. Hoch and Kozlowski concluded that because shared leadership influence was not affected by the virtuality of teams, it appeared to have the potential to be a powerful approach to leadership among dispersed and centrally located teams alike.

Muganda and Pillay (2013) also explored leadership among virtual teams, with an additional focus on power and politics. Importantly, the researcher investigated seven leadership styles including transformational, transactional, participative, situational, virtual, charismatic, and shared. These researchers found that participative and shared leadership styles were linked with trust and networking, explaining that the common denominator to both was the importance of improving team ethos. Thus, shared leadership and diversity positively affected team performance despite team members being physically co-located or not.

Although Muganda and Pillay's (2013) findings that team ethos was significantly related to leadership style, the study failed to acknowledge inherent power dynamics or implicit racial discrimination that may be present in demographically diverse teams. The researchers did not explore how information was distributed among team members, or if shared leadership was *truly* shared. A largely unacknowledged problem with most of the studies that report positive associations between group performance and shared leadership is the balance of how much leadership and power is shared among team members who are not part of the dominant demographic groups. These non-dominant members include women (in many industries, including IT) or racial minorities.

Inequality

A fundamental issue with shared leadership that is largely ignored in the literature is inequality. Because the foundation of shared leadership, on the surface, seems to transcend inequality through the distribution of power among group members, researchers seem to have overlooked issues of inequity. As Harris (2013) explained, issues of power inevitably affect the practice of shared leadership. Few researchers have acknowledged the undertones of racial, ethnic, and gender inequities present in shared leadership (Coleman, 2012; Lumby, 2013; Lumby & Morrison, 2010).

Other researchers have questioned the motivations behind organizations that promote shared leadership (Coleman, 2012; Fitzgerald & Gunter, 2006; Hartley, 2009; & Lumby, 2013). Coleman (2012) suggested that a criticism of shared leadership is that it can appear to seek consensus over celebrating diversity and inclusion. Issues that must be taken into account when considering diversity and leadership include discrimination, inclusion, social justice, equality, equity, and equal opportunities.

Because social justice posits that equality must transcend demographic barriers such as gender, race, ethnicity, and religion (Coleman, 2012), conversations on equality and leadership must acknowledge these issues. As Coleman (2012) explained, it is important to differentiate between equal opportunities and equal outcomes. Equal opportunities refer to those that do consider demographic barriers in the selection of candidates, while equal outcomes mean that when making decisions regarding candidate selection and promotion, attention is given to the barriers that different groups may face.

Lumby (2013) provided a strong argument for caution in the employment of shared leadership, which this scholar posits is related to the inherent inequalities that pepper all forms of leadership. Lumby's concerns with shared leadership echoed many of those posed by a group of scholars who also acknowledged potential issues with the leadership style (Coleman, 2012; Fitzgerald & Gunter, 2006; Hargreaves & Fink, 2008; Harris, 2013; Hartley, 2009; Lumby & Morrison, 2010), and have argued that shared leadership creates issues of exclusion and disempowerment among team members who are excluded from the leadership script. As the premise behind shared leadership is the enabling of all group members to participate in leadership on the basis of their skills and expertise regardless of demographic barriers (such as race, gender, and religion) that often prevent them from accessing leadership roles in traditional hierarchical structures, those demographic factors may actually be barriers – even in situations of shared leadership – that are buried under social norms.

Lumby's (2013) concern with shared leadership hinged on the underlying power narrative woven throughout all social constructs. According to Lumby, power inequities are not mentioned in reference to the kinds of structural barriers such as race and gender, which might beg questions about the greater inclusiveness of shared leadership. The lack of acknowledgement of such barriers and unequal distribution of power does not mean these issues do not exist. Instead, tensions underlying social and cultural narratives influence the relationships between power and equalities. Because employees work within complex social structures of power, the opportunities to lead may be constrained for some. Ultimately, the web of power that disadvantages minority groups have been so long-established and normalized that unequal power distribution may appear normal – both to those in the dominant group as well as those in the minority. Thus, individuals may not even be aware of the inequalities that should be contested (Lumby, 2013). In this way, shared leadership has the potential to place veils over discriminatory employment practices by making group members believe that equality is inherent.

Disparaging perceptions of shared leadership in the field of IT can be particularly problematic because shared leadership is so integral to efficient operations (Stagnaro & Piotrowski, 2014). This is a result of the reality that often, the individual in a shared leadership culture who leads a particular project is not the overall department manager; rather, he or she is likely to be the worker who possesses the highest level of expertise and experience related to that project (Stagnaro & Piotrowski, 2014). Thus, shared leadership is an asset that leaders in the field of IT must recognize. If differences in perceptions of shared leadership are detected amongst managers of diverse races, it will be important for organizations to address those differences to maximize operational efficacy. Organizations may need to assist managers in better realizing the value of inclusion, equality, and shared leadership. In addition, stakeholders may need to make it clear that shared leadership does not endanger a manager's security in a position; rather, is an indicator of the ability to delegate.

While the body of research on racial inequalities in shared leadership is small, the body on gender equality is even smaller. Both, however, demonstrate inequities. As a result, Mendez and Busenbark (2015) conducted a study to investigate the effect of shared leadership on the influence possessed by men and women in groups. Although previous researchers predicted that shared leadership would foster gender equality and provide women with more opportunities to lead and contribute visibly to groups (Neubert & Taggar, 2004; Pearce & Conger, 2003), this assumption had not been empirically examined. Mendez and Busenbark's findings indicate that shared leadership had no significant effect on the relationship between leadership and gender, as men were likely to demonstrate greater levels of leadership influence in groups than women. Thus, just as inequalities were demonstrated in studies on race and shared leadership, gender seems to be another demographic factor for which shared leadership does not level the playing field.

Racism

Racism is a large factor in the documented concerns about shared leadership (Coleman, 2012; Fitzgerald & Gunter, 2006; Hargreaves & Fink, 2008; Harris, 2013; Hartley, 2009; Lumby & Morrison, 2010). Racism describes any unfair treatment based on demographic factors such as race, ethnicity, gender, or culture, and results in unequal access to power, opportunities, or resources (Paradies et al., 2009). In this study, racism refers to unfair treatment based upon race or gender. It is critical to address unintentional inequalities that may be inherent to shared leadership because discrimination and racism have significant negative outcomes for organizations. Such outcomes include reduced productivity (Berman, 2008), psychological distress (Kriger et al., 2011), diminished organizational commitment (Buttner et al., 2010), increased absenteeism, rapid turnover (Buttner et al., 2010), and poor health (De Castro et al., 2010).

According to Wiecek and Hamilton (2014), institutionalized racial segregation in the United States, which was dismantled during the Second Reconstruction, was replaced by structural racism. This form of racism is a subtle system of preference that is "maintained by *implicit* racism –covertly arising from nominally impartial structural arrangements in society assisted by unconscious biases – which assures racial disparate outcomes without the need to rely on overt discrimination" (Wiecek & Hamilton, 2014, p. 1100).

Implicit racism and discrimination are covert, but persistent effects can be observed in social institutions and structures that result in reduced opportunities for minorities. While workplace policies and procedures may appear to promote equality, they continue to result in disparate outcomes due to the implicit racism that permeates social institutions, including the workplace (Wiecek & Hamilton, 2014).

Trenery and Paradies' (2012) conducted a comprehensive review of existing research on organizational assessment tools related to workplace diversity and cultural competence and found that existing approaches to organizational assessment related to cultural competency and diversity management did not focus on addressing systemic racism. Because diversity, equality, and inclusion are often assumed to be inherent to shared leadership, this study is significant in that it assessed how participants' perceptions of shared leadership vary according to their racial backgrounds.

The problem with existing research on workplace inequality is that assessments focus on overt racism – yet it is the impartial structural racism that fuels the power narrative and maintains the status quo. By investigating employees' levels of overall perceptions of shared leadership against their racial background, the current study may unearth any impartial racial discrimination that exists among IT departments that employ shared leadership.

MEASURES OF SHARED LEADERSHIP

Shared Leadership Perception Survey

Multiple researchers have developed different measures of shared leadership. In the current study, levels of overall shared leadership were assessed using Wood's (2005) Shared Leadership Perception Survey. This 19-item instrument measures participants' responses to statements regarding shared leadership perceptions along a four-point Likert-like scale (*definitely not true, generally not true, generally true,* and *definitely true*). Factors assessed include joint task completion, mutual skill development, decentralized interaction, and emotional support.

Wood adapted instrument items from Hiller's (2002) leadership questionnaire which was designed to assess shared leadership along a 7-point scale ranging from never to always and was intended to be answered by respondents to indicate the frequency with which they perform managerial behaviors such as organizing, planning, mentoring, participating in development, providing support and consideration, and problem solving.

In developing the scale, Wood employed instrument items from Hiller's (2002) leadership questionnaire and used theoretical frameworks from Porter-O'Grady and Wilson (1995). According to Wood (2005), the reliability of the Shared Leadership Perception Survey exceeded a .70 standard. While other instruments are available to assess the perceptions of shared leadership, Wood's instrument was selected because it is designed to measure levels of overall perceptions of shared leadership from leaders' viewpoints.

RESEARCH QUESTIONS

The following research questions and hypotheses were examined:

RQ1: What are the levels of overall shared leadership among IT management?
RQ2: What are the levels of overall shared leadership among IT managers of different races?
RQ3: What significant differences exist in levels of overall shared leadership amongst IT managers of different races (White, Black, Asian, Hispanic, and Other)?

$H_0 3$: Significant differences do not exist in levels of overall shared leadership amongst IT managers of different races.
$H_A 3$: Significant differences do exist in levels of overall shared leadership amongst IT managers of different races.

A convenience sample was used to collect data gathered from prospective participants via an online survey. Participants in this study included experienced IT managers of all potential ages, races, and educational backgrounds who were LinkedIn members working within the United States. By only using participants within the United States, the data had a less likely chance of being skewed to include bias embedded within different global cultures and geographical regions. Participants who did not meet the two inclusion criteria – current IT manager and location within the United States - were not permitted to continue with the data collection process.

To target the participants who met for the study, the researcher joined the following professional groups:

1. Global Information Technology Professionals Association (36,417 members)
2. Information Security Careers Network (ISCN; 61,856 members)
3. Information Technology Professionals (191,159 members)
4. Information Technology: Jobs, Job Postings & Job Recruiters (315,590 members)
5. IT, Computer Software & Hardware, Softwarc & Technology (51,615 members)
6. Software & Technology Professionals (1,799,753 members)
7. Software as a Service – SaaS (103,315 members)
8. Technology Leadership (115,815 members)
9. Women in Technology International – WITI (11,383 members)

The total combined global membership for the nine (9) groups as of January 3, 2018 was 2,686,903. It is possible that some individuals are members in multiple groups. For this reason, this author chose to join and solicit participation from all nine (9) groups instead of relying on just the membership of one group. Because participation in this research study was strictly voluntary and no compensation was offered, it was unlikely that a member would partake in the questionnaire multiple times.

Sampling

In 2016, the number of IT managers in the United States was reported to be approximately 367,600 (Bureau of Labor Statistics, 2018). A power analysis was conducted to identify the minimum sample size requirement. Based on the power analysis calculation, a sample of at least 200 participants was deemed sufficient (Faul et al., 2014). The number of participants required to satisfy the sample was obtained by the posting of the Recruitment Announcement in all nine LinkedIn groups.

Survey responses were collected from a total of 214 participants. Twelve participants were removed for not responding to any portion so the questionnaire. The final sample consisted of 202 participants. Through calculation of a power analysis, it was determined that a minimum of 200 participants would be sufficient for an ANOVA with five ethnic groups (Faul et al., 2014).

The majority of participants were of White ethnicity (n = 131, 64.9%). The other three ethnicities examined were equally represented Black (n = 22, 10.9%), Hispanic (n = 20, 9.9%), and Asian (n = 18, 8.9%). The group who identified as "Other" comprised the smallest minority (n = 8, 4.0%). Table 1 presents the distribution of demographics.

Table 1. Frequency table for demographic variables

Variable	*n*	%
Ethnicity		
White	131	64.9
Black	22	10.9
Asian	18	8.9
Hispanic	20	9.9
Other	8	4.0
No response	3	1.5

Methodology

A quasi-experimental design with an online survey approach was utilized for this study and focused on how the levels of overall perceptions of shared leadership vary between races (White, Black, Asian, Hispanic, and Other). Survey Monkey was used to host the demographic questionnaire and Shared Leadership Perception Survey. To explore the first two research questions, the researcher utilized exploratory data analysis to examine for trends in survey responses. The third research question was assessed via an ANOVA to examine mean differences in levels of overall perceptions of shared leadership between individuals of different races (White, Black, Asian, Hispanic, and Other). RQ 3 was ranked on a Likert Scale, using interval coding. Wood's (2005) Shared Leadership Perception Survey was used to assess IT managers' perceptions of shared leadership.

The independent variable, race, was separated into five groups corresponding to White, Black, Asian, Hispanic, and Other. The researcher expected to discover a medium effect size of f = .15 (Cohen, 1988). A generally accepted alpha level (α) of .05 and a power of .80 were applied. With an alpha level of .05, the researcher was 95% confident that significant findings were not explained by pure chance (Tabachnick & Fidell, 2013). G*Power 3.1.9 was used to input the above parameters and calculate an appropriate sample size for the data collection process.

The total response was 0.00744% (200 / 2,686,903 = 0.0000744351396) of the total population of the nine combined groups. With this percentage in mind the following responses were needed per group, based on membership size.

1. Global Information Technology Professionals Association (2.70 ≈ 3 responses)
2. Information Security Careers Network (ISCN) (4.60 ≈ 5 responses)
3. Information Technology Professionals (14.23 ≈ 14 responses)
4. Information Technology: Jobs, Job Postings & Job Recruiters (3.49 ≈ 3 responses)
5. IT, Computer Software & Hardware, Software & Technology (3.84 ≈ 4 responses)
6. Software & Technology Professionals (133.96 ≈ 134 responses)

*Figure 1. G*Power output for ANOVA*

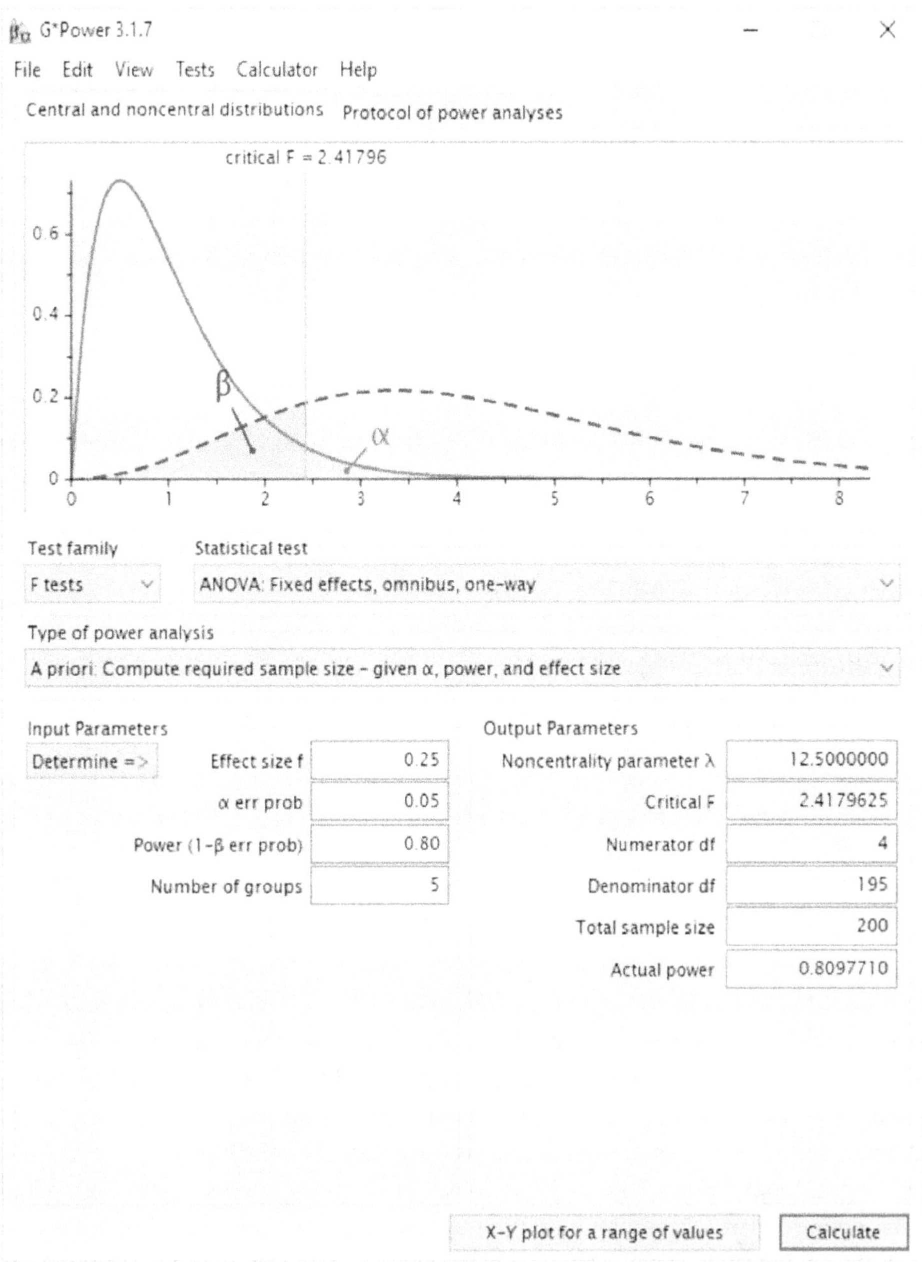

7. Software as a Service – SaaS (7.69 ≈ 8 responses)
8. Technology Leadership (8.62 ≈ 9 responses)
9. Women in Technology International – WITI (0.85 ≈ 1 response

DATA ANALYSIS

The data collected from Survey Monkey was compiled into SPSS version 22.0 for Windows. To examine the first two research questions, an exploratory data analysis was conducted to examine the levels of overall perceptions of shared leadership among IT management of different races. Descriptive statistics were used to examine the nominal and interval level variables and consequently the average scores of overall perceptions of shared leadership among IT management. Frequencies and percentages were used to describe the low, medium, and high cutoffs for the mean scores or the trends of the demographic variables. Means and standard deviations were used to describe the continuous variables of interest or trends of the overall sample, and to provide further breakdowns of statistics by the demographic factors. Data values falling closer to the arithmetic mean have standard deviations closer to zero. Graphical representations such as bar charts were provided for visual interpretation of the descriptive statistics trends (Howell, 2013).

Reliability

Cronbach's alpha test of reliability was evaluated for the perception of shared leadership scale. Brace et al. (2012) identified Cronbach's alpha as an evaluation of the mean correlations between each pair of survey items and the number of items that form scale. The alpha values were interpreted using the incremental cutoffs, in which $\alpha > .9$ excellent, $> .8$ good, $> .7$ acceptable, $> .6$ questionable, $> .5$ poor, and $\leq .5$ unacceptable (George & Mallery, 2016).

Analysis of Variance (ANOVA)

To examine research question three, a between-groups analysis of variance (ANOVA) was conducted to examine for significant differences in levels of overall perception of shared leadership between IT managers of different races. The independent grouping variable corresponded to race (White, Black, Asian, Hispanic, and Other).

Prior to analysis, the assumptions of normality and homogeneity of variance were assessed. Normality compared the research data to a theoretical bell-shaped distribution. The Kolmogorov-Smirnov (KS) test was used to test the normality assumption. Homogeneity of variance checked that the data are approximately even in spread between the different races (Howell, 2013). Levene's test was used to examine the equal variances assumption. Significance for both tests would suggest that the assumptions were not met.

The significance of the overall ANOVA was evaluated by the *F* test, which makes the overall comparison between races. Post-hoc analyses were conducted to evaluate the pairwise comparisons between races. Significance for all tests was evaluated at the conventional, $\alpha = .05$.

Cronbach's alpha values were calculated for the series of survey items comprising Wood's Shared Leadership Perception Survey. Applying guidelines suggested by George and Mallery (2016), the reliability for shared leadership perceptions was excellent (α = .90). The Cronbach's alpha statistics are reported in Table 2.

Table 2. Cronbach's alpha reliability statistics for shared leadership perceptions

Scale	No. of Items	A
Shared leadership perceptions	19	.90

RQ1: What are the levels of overall shared leadership among IT management?

To address research question one, descriptive statistics were used to explore the trends of shared leadership perceptions among the sample. Shared leadership scores ranged from 22.00 to 75.00, with M = 55.75 and SD = 9.25. To meet the criteria for normality, skewness should fall between -2.0 and 2.0 and kurtosis should fall between -7.0 and 7.0 (Kline, 2010). Both the skewness and kurtosis values fell within the thresholds. Table 3 presents the findings of the descriptive statistics.

Table 3. Descriptive statistics for shared leadership perceptions (overall sample)

Variable	Min.	Max.	*M*	*SD*	Skew	Kurtosis
Shared leadership perceptions	22.00	75.00	55.75	9.25	-0.68	0.84

RQ2: What are the levels of overall shared leadership among IT managers of different races?

To address research question two, descriptive statistics were used to explore the trends of shared leadership perceptions for each ethnicity. Shared leadership scores for white participants ranged from 22.00 to 75.00, with M = 55.65 and SD = 9.15. Shared leadership scores for black participants ranged from 28.00 to 72.00, with M = 54.82 and SD = 11.93. Shared leadership scores for Asian participants ranged from 41.00 to 73.00, with M = 57.17 and SD = 9.67. Shared leadership scores for Hispanic participants ranged from 39.00 to 68.00, with M = 57.15 and SD = 6.90. Shared leadership scores for other ethnicities ranged from 46.00 to 64.00, with M = 56.00 and SD = 7.78.

Table 4. Descriptive statistics for shared leadership perceptions by ethnicity

Ethnicity	*n*	Min.	Max.	*M*	*SD*	Skew	Kurtosis
White	131	22.00	75.00	55.65	9.15	-0.76	1.16
Black	22	28.00	72.00	54.82	11.93	-0.67	0.20
Asian	18	41.00	73.00	57.17	9.67	0.08	-0.93
Hispanic	20	39.00	68.00	57.15	6.90	-0.92	1.46
Other	8	46.00	64.00	56.00	7.78	-0.40	-2.11

There did not appear to be clear differences in shared leadership perceptions by ethnicity. However, Asian participants scored highest and Black participants scored lowest on the survey. Skewness and kurtosis values for each ethnicity fell within the acceptable ranges. Table 4 presents the findings of the descriptive statistics. Figure 2 presents a bar chart with the shared leadership scores for each ethnicity.

Figure 2. Shared leadership perceptions scores by ethnicity

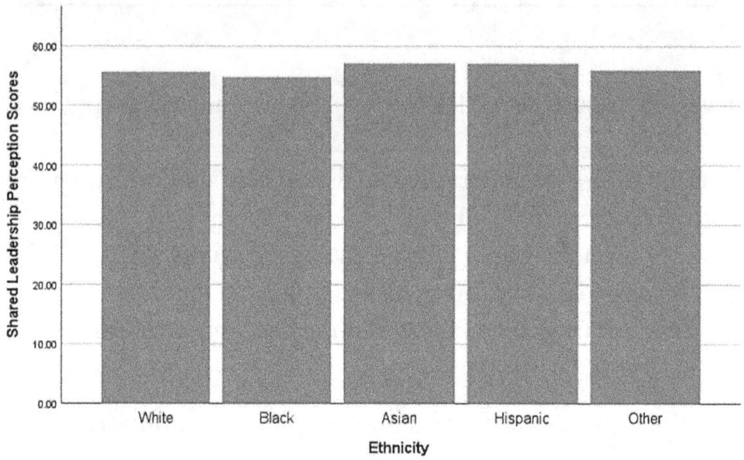

RQ3: What significant differences exist in levels of overall shared leadership amongst IT managers of different races (White, Black, Asian, Hispanic, Other)?

$H_0$3: Significant differences do not exist in levels of overall shared leadership amongst IT managers of different races.
H_A3: Significant differences do exist in levels of overall shared leadership amongst IT managers of different races.

To address research question three, an analysis of variance (ANOVA) was conducted to assess for differences in perception of shared leadership scores by ethnicity (White, Black, Asian, Hispanic, Other). Prior to running the ANOVA, the assumptions of normality and homogeneity of variance were tested by examination of the Kolmogorov-Smirnov (KS) test and Levene's test, respectively. The KS test determined that the normality assumption was not met ($p < .001$). However, the F test is a robust inferential analysis to normality violations, especially when the sample size is larger than 30 cases (Howell, 2013). Using Levene's test, the assumption for homogeneity of variance was met ($p = .277$). Due to the assumption of normality not being met, the non-parametric Kruskal-Wallis test was reported after conducting the ANOVA.

Results of the ANOVA were not statistically significant by ethnicity, ($F(4, 194) = 0.27$, $p = .896$, partial η^2=.006). The findings of the ANOVA indicated that there were not statistically significant differences in shared leadership scores by ethnicity. Due to non-significance, post-hoc tests were not further examined. The Kruskal-Wallis test further confirmed the findings of the ANOVA, ($H(4) = 0.53$, $p = .971$), suggesting that there were not significant differences in perception of shared leadership scores by ethnicity. The null hypothesis ($H_0 3$) could not be rejected. The findings of the univariate ANOVA is presented in Figure 1. The descriptive statistics of perception of shared leadership by ethnicity are presented in Table 5. The findings of the Kruskal-Wallis test are presented in Table 6.

Table 5. Descriptive statistics for shared leadership perception scores by ethnicity

Ethnicity	*n*	*M*	*SD*
White	131	55.65	9.15
Black	22	54.82	11.93
Asian	18	57.17	9.67
Hispanic	20	57.15	6.90
Other	8	56.00	7.78

Table 6. Kruskal-Wallis test for shared leadership perception scores by ethnicity

Term	*H*(4)	*p*
Ethnicity	0.53	.971

CONCLUSION AND RECOMMENDATIONS

Shared leadership presents a great opportunity for leaders and managers to improve organizational efficiency and is a leadership strategy that may be underutilized in IT organizations. In the ultracompetitive industry of information technology, the integration of shared leadership could provide organizations with a competitive edge. While this study did not assess overt racism or inequality, it assessed how managerial perceptions of shared leadership vary according to their racial backgrounds. Findings did not reveal any significant differences in levels of Pearce et al.'s (2007) theory of shared leadership based on race according to the 200 managers in IT who were surveyed. However, findings indicated that levels of shared leadership perceptions were moderate across all racial groups surveyed, as perception of shared leadership did not appear to differ across racial lines.

Racial differences in levels of overall shared leadership perceptions may serve as a signal to IT organizations to help all leaders better understand the value of shared leadership through leadership training or in-service seminars. As IT leaders embrace the power dynamics and potential of shared leadership, this study may provide a starting point for further research on possible inequities that underlie this unique leadership style.

Results indicate perceptions of shared leadership among a sample of U.S. IT managers was moderate. The implications are that room for improvement may exist in the degree to which IT managers leverage shared leadership. Consequently, IT managers who engage in shared leadership may maintain their competitive edge in this ultracompetitive field. This finding indicates an opportunity for organizational improvement in the field of IT, as research suggests that shared leadership is associated with increased organizational performance in IT (Hui-Ying & Jian-Peng, 2013). Shared leadership is integral to efficient operations (Stagnaro & Piotrowski, 2014). This results from the individual who leads a particular project to not be the overall department manager but is likely to be the worker who possesses the highest level of expertise and experience related to that project (Stagnaro & Piotrowski, 2014). Thus, shared leadership is an asset that leaders in the field of IT must recognize.

Leaders of IT organizations may take interest in the study results and may consider offering leadership training that facilitates shared leadership among managers. This training could include the objective of increasing behavioral changes appropriately conducive to increase communication styles that provide for genuine interactions with sincerity. As socially appropriate political skills in team members has been found to increase shared leadership in a diverse arena of workers (Xu et al., 2019), training in increasing political skills could be incorporated in business.

FUTURE RESEARCH DIRECTIONS

Findings from the current investigation indicate several opportunities for future research. As organizations with traditional hierarchical structures may have leaders who demonstrate less shared leadership perceptions than organizations that are adhocratic, an analysis of organizational culture may shed more light on differences that exist in perceptions of shared leadership. National culture may also play a significant role in shared leadership. Cultures that emphasize individualism, such as the United States, may be less likely to employ shared leadership than those that are collectivist. Future researchers may compare differences in shared leadership perceptions across different cultures by examining the concept within multinational organizations.

Not only can future research be conducted in cultural environmental influences on shared leadership, but a study may be investigated within different organizational environments, including other industries. Thus, future researchers may explore shared leadership in a variety of other industries to detect whether some industries seem to leverage shared leadership to a greater degree than others. While the focus of the current investigation was IT, little research exists on perceptions of shared leadership in other industries among managers or non-managers. Most research conducted has focused on the individuals within the organization as Wu and Cormican (2021) did with engineering design teams.

Because of the low response rate, participants only from LinkedIn, and to get another perspective then another direction for future research is to replicate the study with a larger scope of IT employees, including those in non-managerial positions. It is possible that managers and non-managers may have different perceptions of shared leadership in the field of IT. A study that utilizes team members as well as managers might reveal more about shared leadership in IT and highlight the discrepancies that may exist in perceptions of shared leadership, based on position. Another addition with obtaining perceptions of IT team members would be to assess the predictive power of race on the team's perceptions of shared leadership. Additionally, various teams could be coded for diversity and surveyed to see if the level of diversity affects the similarity of perception of shared leadership. Furthermore, future research could be conducted with an agreement measure to find out if the same level of shared leadership is perceived within a team by team members.

Through future research, there is the possibility of developing a model of a strategic framework for creating an appreciation of shared leadership in diverse teams. A strategic framework could also be developed that would provide effective strategies to increase ethnic minorities within the organization regardless of gender. Research could be conducted to examine the negative and positive impact occurring based upon perception of shared leadership.

Finally, there are several additional variables that may affect individuals' perceptions of levels of overall shared leadership, including age, gender, cultural background, personality type, marital status, years of experience, educational level, and the cultures and structures of their employing organizations. However, these variables were outside the scope of the current study, which was limited to assessing how race may affect levels of overall shared leadership perceptions among IT managers. Future researchers may consider examining the moderating effects of such demographic variables on shared leadership perceptions.

REFERENCES

Agnihotri, A., & Agnihotri, A. (2020). *Comparative study of team characteristics under shared leadership in large and small companies in IT industry in India* [Paper presentation]. 2020 8th International Conference on Reliability, Infocom Technologies and Optimization (Trends and Future Directions) (ICRITO), Noida, India. 10.1109/ICRITO48877.2020.9197938

Anwesha, M. (2020). Leadership for creating sustainability within the organization: An empirical study. *IUP Journal of Organizational Behavior, 19*(3), 7–17.

Avolio, B. (1994). The "natural": Some antecedents to transformational leadership. *International Journal of Public Administration, 17*(9), 1559–1581. doi:10.1080/01900699408524956

Avolio, B., Walumbwa D. A., & Weber, T. J. (2009). Leadership: Current theories, research, and future directions. *Annual Review of Psychology, 60*, 8.1-8.29.

Avolio, B. J., Jung, D., Murry, W., & Sivasubramaniam, N. (1996). Building highly developed teams: Focusing on shared leadership process, efficacy, trust, and performance. In D. A. Beyerlein, D. A. Johnson, & S. T. Beyerlein (Eds.), *Advances in interdiscinplinary studies of work teams* (pp. 173–209). JAI Press.

Bass, B. (1990a). From transactional to transformational leadership: Learning to share the vision. *Organizational Dynamics, 18*(3), 19–31. doi:10.1016/0090-2616(90)90061-S

Bass, B., & Avolio, B. (1991). *Multifactor Leadership Questionnaire (Form 5X)*. Center for Leadership Studies.

Bell, B. S., & Kozlowski, S. W. J. (2002). A typology of virtual teams: Implications for effective leadership. *Group & Organization Management, 27*(1), 14–49. doi:10.1177/1059601102027001003

Berman, G. (2008). *Harnessing diversity: Addressing racial and religious discrimination in employment*. Victorian Multicultural Commission and the Victorian Equal Opportunity and Human Rights Commission.

Beyer, J. M. (1999). Taming and promoting charisma to change organizations. *The Leadership Quarterly, 10*(2), 307–330. doi:10.1016/S1048-9843(99)00019-3

Bindl, U. K., & Parker, S. K. (2010). Proactive work behavior: Forward-thinking and change oriented action in organizations. In S. Zedeck (Ed.), *APA handbook of industrial and organizational psychology* (pp. 567–598). American Psychological Association.

Brace, N., Kemp, R., & Snelgar, R. (2012). *SPSS for psychologists* (5th ed.). Lawrence Erlbaum Associates.

Brown, M., Brown, R. S., & Nandedkar, A. (2019). Transformational leadership theory and exploring the perceptions of diversity management in higher education. *Journal of Higher Education Theory & Practice*, *19*(7), 11–21.

Brown, W. (2017). *Exploring the impact of shared leadership styles and nonprofit performance* [Doctoral Dissertation, Walden University]. ScholarWorks.

Burns, J. (1978). *Leadership*. Harper & Row.

Buttner, E. H., & Lowe, K. B. (2010). Diversity climate impact on employee of color outcomes: Does justice matter? *Career Development International*, *15*(3), 239–258. doi:10.1108/13620431011053721

Campion, M. A., Medsker, G. J., & Higgs, A. C. (1993). Relations between work group characteristics and effectiveness: Implications for designing effective work groups. *Personnel Psychology*, *46*(4), 823–850. doi:10.1111/j.1744-6570.1993.tb01571.x

Chen, C. C., Wu, J., Yang, S. C., & Tsou, H.-Y. (2008). Importance of diversified leadership roles in improving team effectiveness in a virtual collaboration learning environment. *Journal of Educational Technology & Society*, *11*(1), 304–321.

Chen, C. C., Wu, J., Yang, S. C., & Tsou, H.-Y. (2008). Importance of diversified leadership roles in improving team effectiveness in a virtual collaboration learning environment. *Journal of Educational Technology & Society*, *11*(1), 304–321.

Chickowski, E. (2009). Five trends changing the face of BI. *eWeek*, *26*(16), 18.

Cohen, J. (1988). *Statistical power analysis for the behavioral sciences* (2nd ed.). West Publishing Company.

Coleman, M. (2012). Leadership and diversity. *Educational Management Administration & Leadership*, *40*(5), 592–609. doi:10.1177/1741143212451174

Cox, J., Pearce, C., & Perry, M. (2003). Toward a model of shared leadership and distributed influence in the innovation process. In C. Pearce & J. Conger (Eds.), *Shared leadership: Reframing the hows and whys of leadership* (pp. 48–76). Sage. doi:10.4135/9781452229539.n3

Creswell, J. W. (2009). *Research design: Qualitative, quantitative, and mixed methods approaches* (3rd ed.). Sage.

Creswell, J. W. (2009). *Research design: Qualitative, quantitative, and mixed methods approaches* (3rd ed.). Sage.

D'Innocenzo, L., Mathieu, J. E., & Kukenberger, M. R. (2014). A meta-analysis of different forms of shared leadership – Team performance relations. *Journal of Management*, 1–28. doi:10.1177/0149206314525205

Dai, Y.-D., Dai, Y.-Y., Chen, K.-Y., & Wu, H.-C. (2013). Transformational vs transactional leadership: Which is better? *International Journal of Contemporary Hospitality Management*, *25*(5), 760–778. doi:10.1108/IJCHM-Dec-2011-0223

Day, D., Gronn, P., & Salas, E. (2004). Leadership capacity in teams. *The Leadership Quarterly*, *15*(6), 857–880. doi:10.1016/j.leaqua.2004.09.001

de Ron, A. J. (1998). Sustainable production: The ultimate result of a continuous improvement. *International Journal of Production Economics*, *56-57*, 99–110. doi:10.1016/S0925-5273(98)00005-X

Deetz, S. (2000). Discipline. In K. Grint (Ed.), *Work and society* (pp. 142–162). Polity.

Erkutlu, H. (2012). The impact of organizational culture on the relationship between shared leadership and team productivity. *Team Performance Management*, *18*(1-2), 102–119. doi:10.1108/13527591211207734

Faul, F., Erdfelder, E., Buchner, A., & Lang, A. G. (2014). *G*Power Version 3.1.9* [computer software]. Uiversität Kiel. Retrieved from https://www.gpower.hhu.de/en/html

Fausing, M. S., Joensson, T. K., Lewandowski, J., & Bligh, M. (2015). Antecedents of shared leadership: Empowering leadership and interdependence. *Leadership and Organization Development Journal*, *36*(3), 271–291. doi:10.1108/LODJ-06-2013-0075

Fitzgerald, T., & Gunter, H. (2006). Teacher leadership: A new form of managerialism. *New Zealand Journal of Educational Leadership*, *21*(2), 44–57.

Gan, Y., & Cheung, F. M. (2010). From proactive personality to organizational citizenship behavior: Mediating role of harmony. *Psychological Reports*, *106*(3), 755–765. doi:10.2466/pr0.106.3.755-765 PMID:20712164

George, D., & Mallery, P. (2016). *SPSS for Windows step by step: a simple guide and reference, 11.0 update* (14th ed.). Allyn and Bacon. doi:10.4324/9781315545899

Gockel, C., & Werth, L. (2010). Measuring and modeling shared leadership: Traditional approaches and new ideas. *Journal of Personnel Psychology*, *9*(4), 172–180. doi:10.1027/1866-5888/a000023

Groves, K. S., & LaRocca, M. (2010). *Leader ethical values as key antecedents to transformational and transactional leadership.* In Annual Meeting of Western Academy of Management, Kona, HI.

Hargreaves, A., & Fink, D. (2008). Distributed leadership: Democracy or delivery? In A. Harris (Ed.), *Distributed leadership: Different perspectives*. Springer.

Harris, A. (2013). Distributed leadership: Friend or foe? *Educational Management & Leadership*, *41*(5), 545–554. doi:10.1177/1741143213497635

Hartley, D. (2009). Educational policy, distributed leadership and socio-cultural theory. *Educational Review*, *61*(2), 139–150. doi:10.1080/00131910902844721

Hiller, N. J. (2002). *Understanding and measuring shared leadership in work teams.* Unpublished manuscript. University Park, PA: Pennsylvania State University.

Hinds, P., Liu, L., & Lyon, J. (2011). Putting the global in global work: An intercultural lens on the practice of cross-national collaboration. *The Academy of Management Annals*, *5*(1), 135–188. doi:10.5465/19416520.2011.586108

Hinkin, T. R., & Schriesheim, C. A. (2008). An examination of "nonleadership": From laissez-faire leadership to leader reward omission and punishment omission. *The Journal of Applied Psychology*, *93*(6), 1234–1248. doi:10.1037/a0012875 PMID:19025245

Hoch, J. E. (2014). Shared leadership, diversity, and information sharing in teams. *Journal of Managerial Psychology*, *29*(5), 541–564. doi:10.1108/JMP-02-2012-0053

Hoch, J. E., & Kozlowski, S. W. (2014). Leading virtual teams: Hierarchical leadership, structural supports, and shared team leadership. *The Journal of Applied Psychology*, *99*(3), 390–403. doi:10.1037/a0030264 PMID:23205494

Hoegl, M., & Gemuenden, H. G. (2001). Teamwork quality and the success of innovative projects: A theoretical concept and empirical evidence. *Organization Science*, *12*(4), 435–449. doi:10.1287/orsc.12.4.435.10635

Hofstede, G. (1980). Culture's consequences: International difference in work related values. *Sage (Atlanta, Ga.)*.

Howell, D. C. (2013). *Statistical methods for psychology* (8th ed.). Wadsworth Cengage Learning.

Hui-ying, M., & Jian-peng, W. (2013). The impact of shared leadership on innovation performance. *2013 International Conference on Management Science and Engineering 20th Annual Conference Proceedings*. 10.1109/ICMSE.2013.6586452

Jarvenpaa, S. L., & Ives, B. (1994). The global network organization of the future: Information management opportunities and challenges. *Journal of Management Information Systems*, *10*(4), 25–57. doi:10.1080/07421222.1994.11518019

Judge, T. A., & Piccolo, R. F. (2004). Transformational and transactional leadership: A meta-analytic test of their relative value. *The Journal of Applied Behavioral Science*, *89*(5), 755–768. doi:10.1037/0021-9010.89.5.755 PMID:15506858

Katz, D., & Kahn, R. L. (1978). *The social psychology of organizations* (2nd ed.). Wiley.

Kayworth, T. R., & Leidner, D. E. (2002). Leadership effectiveness in global virtual teams. *Journal of Management Information Systems*, *18*(3), 7–40. doi:10.1080/07421222.2002.11045697

Kendrick, J. (2011). Transformational leadership changing individuals and social systems. *Professional Safety*, *56*(11), 14. https://www.assp.org/publications/professional-safety

Kirkman, B. L., Gibson, C. B., & Kim, K. (2012). Across borders and technologies: Advancements in virtual teams research. In S. W. J. Kozlowski (Ed.), *Oxford Handbook of Organizational Psychology* (Vol. 2, pp. 789–858). Oxford University Press.

Kirkman, B. L., & Mathieu, J. E. (2005). The Dimensions and Antecedents of Team Virtuality. *Journal of Management*, *31*(5), 700–718. doi:10.1177/0149206305279113

Kline, R. B. (2010). *Principles and practice of structural equation modeling* (3rd ed.). The Guilford Press.

Kriger, N., Kaddour, A., Koenen, K., Kosheleva, A., Chen, J. T., Waterman, P. D., & Barbeau, E. M. (2011). Occupational, social, and relationship hazards and psychological distress among low-income workers: Implications of the 'inverse hazard law'. *Journal of Epidemiology and Community Health*, *65*(3), 260–272. doi:10.1136/jech.2009.087387 PMID:20713372

Leithwood, K., Mascall, B., & Strauss, T. (2009). *Distributed leadership according to the evidence*. Routledge. doi:10.4324/9780203868539

Lumby, J. (2013). Distributed leadership: The uses and abuses of power. *Educational Management Administration & Leadership*, *41*(5), 581–597. doi:10.1177/1741143213489288

Lumby, J., & Morrison, M. (2010). Leadership and diversity: Theory and research. *School Leadership & Management*, *30*(1), 3–17. doi:10.1080/13632430903509717

McClesky, J. A. (2014). Situational, transformational, and transactional leadership and leadership development. *Journal of Business Studies Quarterly*, *5*(4), 117–130. https://jbsq.org/wp-content/uploads/2014/06/June_2014_9.pdf

Mendez, M. J., & Busenbark, J. R. (2015). Shared leadership and gender: All members are equal … but some more than others. *Leadership and Organization Development Journal*, *36*(1), 17–34. doi:10.1108/LODJ-11-2012-0147

Meuthel, M., Gehrlein, S., & Hoegl, M. (2012). Socio-demographic factors and shared leadership behaviors in dispersed teams: Implications for human resource management. *Human Resource Management*, *51*(4), 525–548. doi:10.1002/hrm.21488

Muganda, N., & Pillay, K. (2013). Forms of power, politics and leadership in asynchronous virtual project environment. *International Journal of Managing Projects in Business*, *6*(3), 457–484. doi:10.1108/IJMPB-11-2011-0075

Nedzinskaite-Maciumiene, R., & Merkyte, S. (2019). Shared leadership of teachers through their interpersonal communication competence. *Acta-Paedagogica-Vilnensia, 42,* 85-98. doi:10.15388/ActPaed.42.6

Neubert, M. J., & Taggar, S. (2004). Pathways to informal leadership: The moderating role of gender on the relationship of individual differences and team member network centrality to informal leadership emergence. *The Leadership Quarterly*, *15*(2), 174–194. doi:10.1016/j.leaqua.2004.02.006

Niederman, F., & Tan, F. B. (2011). Managing global IT teams: Considering cultural dynamics. *Communications of the ACM*, *54*(4), 24–27. doi:10.1145/1924421.1924431

O'Leary, M. B., & Mortensen, M. (2010). Go con(figure): Subgroups, imbalance, and isolates in geographically dispersed teams. *Organization Science*, *21*(1), 115–131. doi:10.1287/orsc.1090.0434

Okcu, V. (2014). Relation between secondary school administrators' transformational and transactional leadership style and skills to diversity management in the school. *Educational Sciences: Theory and Practice*, *14*(6), 2162–2174. doi:10.12738/estp.2014.6.2128

Paradies, Y., Chandrakumar, L., Klocker, N., Frere, M., Webster, K., Burrell, M., & McLean, P. (2009). *Building on our strengths: A framework to reduce race-based discrimination and promote diversity in Victoria*. Victorian Health Promotion Foundation.

Pearce, C. L., Hoch, J. E., Jeppesen, H. J., & Wegge, J. (2010). New forms of management: Shared and distributed leadership in organizations. *Journal of Personnel Psychology*, *9*(4), 151–153. doi:10.1027/1866-5888/a000022

Pearce, C. L., Manz, C. C., & Sims, H. P. (2014). *Share, don't take the lead.* Information Age.

Pearce, C. L., & Sims, H. P. (2002). Vertical versus shared leadership as predictors of the effectiveness of chance management teams: An examination of aversive, directive, transactional, transformational, and empowering leader behaviors. *Group Dynamics, 6*(2), 172–197. doi:10.1037/1089-2699.6.2.172

Perry, M. L., Pearce, C. L., & Sims, H. P. Jr. (1999). Empowered selling teams: How shared leadership can contribute to selling team outcomes. *Journal of Personal Selling & Sales Management, 19*(3), 35–51. doi:10.1080/08853134.1999.10754180

Porter-O'Grady, T., & Wilson, C. K. (1995). *The leadership revolution in health care: Altering systems, changing behaviors.* Aspen Publishers, Inc.

Purvanova, R. K., & Bono, J. E. (2009). Transformational leadership in context: Face-to-face and virtual teams. *The Leadership Quarterly, 20*(3), 343–357. doi:10.1016/j.leaqua.2009.03.004

Ramthun, A. J., & Matkin, G. S. (2012). Multicultural shared leadership: A conceptual model of shared leadership in culturally diverse teams. *Journal of Leadership & Organizational Studies, 19*(3), 303–314. doi:10.1177/1548051812444129

Rose, D. M., & Gordon, R. (2015). Age-related cognitive changes and distributed leadership. *Journal of Management Development, 34*(3), 330–339. doi:10.1108/JMD-07-2013-0094

Routhieaux, R. L. (2015). Shared leadership and its implications for nonprofit leadership. *Journal of Nonprofit Education & Leadership, 5*(3), 139–152.

Sitthiwarongchai, C., Wichayanuparp, W., Chantakit, P., & Charoenboon, P. (2020). Impact of organization's leadership style on motivation of its employees. *Systematic Reviews in Pharmacy, 11*(3), 48–56.

Slater, L. (2008). Pathways to building leadership capacity. *Educational Management Administration & Leadership, 36*(1), 55–69. doi:10.1177/1741143207084060

Small, E. E., & Rentsch, J. R. (2010). Shared leadership in teams: A matter of distribution. *Journal of Personnel Psychology, 9*(4), 203–211. doi:10.1027/1866-5888/a000017

Soutphommasane, T. (2013). Anti-racism on the job: Tackling discrimination in employment and the workplace. *Proctor*, 42-44.

Spitzberg, B., & Changnon, G. (2009). Conceptualizing intercultural competence. In D. Deardorff (Ed.), *The Sage handbook of intercultural competence* (pp. 2–52). Sage.

Stagnaro, C., & Piotrowski, C. (2014). Shared leadership: A critical component in IT project management. *Journal of Technology Research.*

Tabachnick, B. G., & Fidell, L. S. (2013). *Using multivariate statistics* (6th ed.). Allyn and Bacon.

Tracey, J., & Hinkin, T. (1998). Transformational leadership or effective managerial practices? *Group & Organization Management, 23*(3), 220–236. doi:10.1177/1059601198233002

Trenery, B., & Paradies, Y. (2012). Organizational assessment: An overlooked approach to managing diversity and addressing racism in the workplace. *Journal of Diversity Management*, *7*(1), 11–26. doi:10.19030/jdm.v7i1.6932

Tucker, B., & Russell, R. (2004). The influence of the transformational leader. *Journal of Leadership & Organizational Studies*, *10*(4), 103–111. doi:10.1177/107179190401000408

Wang, D., Waldman, D., & Zhang, Z. (2014). A meta-analysis of shared leadership and team effectiveness. *The Journal of Applied Psychology*, *99*(2), 181–198. doi:10.1037/a0034531 PMID:24188392

Wiecek, W. M., & Hamilton, J. L. (2014). Beyond the Civil Rights Act of 1964: Confronting structural racism in the workplace. *Louisiana Law Review*, *74*, 1095–1160.

Wood, M. S. (2005). Determinants of shared leadership in management teams. *International Journal of Leadership Studies*, *1*(1), 64–85.

Xu, N., Chiu, C., & Treadway, D. C. (2019). Tensions between diversity and shared leadership: The role of team political skill. *Small Group Research*, *50*(4), 507–538. doi:10.1177/1046496419840432

Yukl, G. (2010). *Leadership in organizations* (7th ed.). Prentice Hall.

Yukl, G., & Mahsud, R. (2010). Why flexible and adaptive leadership is essential. *Consulting Psychology Journal*, *62*(2), 81–93. doi:10.1037/a0019835

Zhou, W., Vredenburg, D., & Rogoff, E. G. (2015). Informational diversity and entrepreneurial team performance: Moderating effect of shared leadership. *The International Entrepreneurship and Management Journal*, *11*(1), 39–55. doi:10.100711365-013-0274-3

ADDITIONAL READING

Hoch, J. E. (2013). Shared Leadership and Innovation: The Role of Vertical Leadership and Employee Integrity. *Journal of Business and Psychology*, *28*(2), 159–174. doi:10.100710869-012-9273-6

Kocolowski, M. D. (2010). Shared Leadership: Is it Time for a Change? *Emerging Leadership Journeys*, *3*(1), 22–32.

Wang, D., Waldman, D. A., & Zhang, Z. (2014). A meta-analysis of shared leadership and team effectiveness. *The Journal of Applied Psychology*, *99*(2), 181–198. doi:10.1037/a0034531 PMID:24188392

KEY TERMS AND DEFINITIONS

Distributed Leadership: Another term for shared leadership (Pearce et al., 2014).

Information Technology: The use of hardware and software applications to manage organizational data (Ullah & Lai, 2013).

Informational Diversity: Individual differences in perspectives and knowledge that workers bring to a team setting or project (Zhou, Vredenburg, & Rogoff, 2015).

Racism: Unfair treatment based on race, ethnicity, religion, or culture that results in unequal distribution of power, resources, or opportunities (Trenerry & Paradies, 2012).

Shared Leadership: A dynamic behavioral process depicted by team member influence, collaboration, and the exhibition of leadership by a group (Stagnaro & Piotrowski, 2014).

Transformational Leadership: Leadership that is inspirational, empowering, and inspires workers' commitment to an organization's overall goals (Bass, 1990a).

Chapter 8
Communicating Conscious Business Practice at an Ecologically-Conscious Architectural Studio:
A Case of Mr. Zero

Pinaki Nandan Pattnaik
NALSAR University of Law, India

Mahendra Kumar Shukla
NALSAR University of Law, India

ABSTRACT

This chapter presents an exploratory case study of how Mr. Zero, a pencil developed by the Ecologically Conscious Architectural Studio (ECAS) at Auroville, India integrates product micro-culture and the concept of conscious business in deriving sustainable practices with an aim of achieving a sustainable future. Through this chapter, the authors make an attempt at developing a deeper understanding of the concept of conscious business and its importance. Finally, the authors, through a qualitative analysis of a case study of Mr. Zero, map the practice of connecting conscious business movement through the adoption of product micro-culture at ECAS to evaluate its applicability in modern day business. At the end, the authors record findings on the interplay between product micro-culture and the conscious business movement for adoption by other businesses or even adaptation by others depending upon the context for viable sustainable solutions.

DOI: 10.4018/978-1-7998-3964-4.ch008

INTRODUCTION

"The world needs more love to awaken the lost human coefficient, and in the process environmental issues shall find its best solution." - Mr. ZERO

In his book, An Inquiry into the Nature and Causes of the Wealth of Nations, Volume 2, Smith (1778) states that it is self-interest, that empowers the invisible hand that eventually leads to economic as well as the overall prosperity of the society. Following self-interest, capitalism promulgates a state of affairs where workers work for wages and capital gets income (Jahan & Mahmud, 2015; Scott, 2009). Such practices enable a harmonious existence and provides for political freedom (Friedman, 2009) by taking out poverty from around the world (Palmer, 2011). With time, self-interest distorts into selfishness, leading it to becoming over-glorified. To that extent, people have increasingly become hypocritical even about other statements on morality (Smith, 1759).

Mackey (2011) identifies that businesses are neglecting the higher needs of human nature like altruism. Organizations, not only generate monetary wealth, but also produce emotional, spiritual, and intellectual wealth. Conscious organizations spread prosperity and joy among all their stakeholders and consistently innovate to create and deliver ever greater value for each one of them (Asphalt, 2020). These organizations succeed in the long run at a significantly higher level and with a considerably broader definition of success than traditional business (Sisodia, 2013).

As Hamel (2008) states, organizations cannot purchase peoples' creativity, passion and enthusiasm; they need to earn them, and most have not demonstrated deserving of them. Conscious organizations discharge this enormous source of renewable, generative human energy into the world. This, more than anything else, is the reason of their sustained success. Any individual or business can practice what they do either consciously or unconsciously. Such organizations that practice business consciously, settle on better choices since they have a complete comprehension of the considerable number of facts, undistorted by individual agendas. Additionally, the clarity that accompanies conscious business practices drives specifically to higher individual fulfilment from their work (Khalsa, 2010).

This chapter attempts to describe the concept and importance of conscious business movement. It also proposes its practice through product micro-culture. The authors, though a case study of Mr. Zero map the practices of conscious business movement at ECAS.

CONSCIOUS BUSINESS: A CONCEPTUAL UNDERSTANDING

"Being conscious means to be mindful and awake. Living consciously means to be open to perceiving the world around and within us, to understand our circumstances, and to decide how to respond to them in ways that honor our needs, values, and goals [. . .]. A conscious business fosters peace and happiness in the individual, respect and solidarity in the community, and mission accomplishment in the organization" (Kofman, 2008)

At times, conscious business and conscious capitalism are seen in usage as synonyms. However, conscious capitalism only refers to a wider sense of doing business (Hess, & Fuller, 2017; Srinivasan, 2011) whereas, conscious business is not just a business strategy or business model rather it is a comprehensive philosophy of doing business (Franceschelli, Santoro & Candelo, 2018). Available literature indicates the need for and values of corporates having a strong set of ideals as well a purpose to pursue. But, it is also to be noted that there are several others who affect as well as get affected by the decisions that are taken in corporates. Focusing on employees and customers is a vital aspect of the business, although this is not the only area of focus (Akbar, Jin, & Salam, (2018). Conscious capitalism suggests that businesses and business leaders should undertake activities that accrue benefits to all stakeholders viz. Society, Partners, Investors, Customers, Employees and Environment (Yangzom & Singh, 2019). A conscious business, on the other hand, endeavours to achieve a common set of benefits that satisfy all stakeholders. In the order of the priority of stakeholders, the society is placed at the top (Sisodia, 2013).

In consonance with the evolution of the societal consciousness, the philosophy as well as the definition of conscious capitalism continues to evolve (Frémeaux & Michelson, 2017; Mackey, 2011; Sisodia, 2013). At the core of conscious capitalism lies the idea "virtuousity" or seeking to "do well by doing good" (Okorochkova, 2017). It is built on the tenets of the purpose of being in business, managing stakeholder interests, leadership, and the general culture of the business. It is believed by conscious capitalism advocates, that organizations that embrace the tenets of conscious capitalism will in a long run out-perform other organizations in dimensions including financial performance, ultimately making a positive effect on the world (Conaway, Regester, Martin, Nixon, & Senior, 2018; Pilly & Sisodia, 2011).

Conscious Leadership

The primary motivation of conscious leaders is the purpose of the firm rather than money or power and they lead by motivating, mentoring, developing and inspiring individuals. An essential feature of being a conscious leader is the ability to perceive the contrast amongst legality and ethicality (Marques, 2017). Really conscious leaders can perceive this key distinction and act in a befitting manner (Thigpen, 2011). Mackey (2011) exhibits how vital conscious leadership is as he expresses, "the different stakeholders of a company, particularly the employees, look to administration to 'walk-the talk'. It is expressly essential that the CEO and other senior leadership symbolize the higher purpose for the corporation, as opposed to looking to boost their very own power or remuneration".

Conscious leaders, who have strong ideals, believe in the purpose and are able to craft composite benefits for all stakeholders, they are pivotal to establish a conscious culture in the organization (Voss, 2018). Conscious culture is identified by Mackey (2011) as having qualities like Trust, Authenticity, Caring, Transparency, Integrity, Learning and Empowerment. These, he referred to as TACTILE. Conscious businesses, thus, create a workplace that builds a community, and not individuals, which is in pursuit to flourish and self-actualize (Smith, 2017). Such an environment shall foster an enriching experience leading to employee satisfaction, which in turn, translate into customer satisfaction creating a possibility of all involved stakeholders having a rather fulfilling takeaway from the transaction with the business (Parung, 2019; Wallace, 2020).

Drivers of Conscious Business Movement

Human development can be understood as 'an unfolding, emergent, oscillating, spiraling process' marked by progressive upward movement through growingly complex stages. This upward development is an adaptive response to our changing life conditions. So as our lives become more complex (i.e. more connected), we are prompted to develop higher, more complex thinking and behaviors in order to cope. With regards to business, it is similarly expected that transactions be undertaken with a higher purpose in mind and not simply with a view to amplifying profits. A compelling and strong sense of purpose causes a phenomenal level of engagement for all stakeholders and catalyzes the creation and radiation of massive volumes of organizational energy (Sisodia, 2007). Just as humans have aspiring ideals; organizations must have ideals to pursue. Mackey (2011) identified these ideals as:

- The Good: Service to others by enhancing physical and mental well-being, education, communication and life quality.
- The True: Discovering and expanding human knowledge.
- The Beautiful: Creation of beauty, excellence and aesthetics.
- The Heroic: Courage to do what is right to change and pursuit to make the world a better place.

Strong (2011) argues that there are two noticeable global shifts in the world that are progressively rewarding the conscious business model: a) Massive advancement of the Maslow's hierarchy of needs, and b) Radical transparency with the rapid adoption of technology. Researchers around the world are re-focusing on the value of the Maslow's Hierarchy of Need in the context of modern day corporations. In his hierarchy of needs theory, Maslow examines human psychology and motivations that drive human motivation based on different levels of needs. Through his work, he introduced five incremental need levels that had basic physiological needs at the base of the pyramid and then moved from security to social belongingness, empathy and finally to an advanced state of self-actualization or consciousness. It has also been observed that wealthy countries are achieving advanced state of consciousness and climbing the hierarchical pyramid (Wilson, 2014). Enlightened leaders are delving on existentially critical questions at an organizational level seeking to achieve outcomes at a conscious as well as responsible level (Pruzan, 2001; Zsolnai 2017). Research also indicates that there has been a gradual shift in their attitude from being ego-centric 'ME' to becoming world-centric 'WE' (Coates, 2015; Pruzan, 2001). In parlance to the millennial, these might be the values that will assume control over the business field in decades to come (Soni & Simpson, 2013) as a large portion of future employees will search for meaningful work, career advancement, reasonable harmony and qualities that foster holistic contribution (Pruzan, 2001).

Businesses, today, have been impacted by technology and through the continuous development in technology as well. Technology has rendered conventional business plans and models, non-competitive or rather less competitive to those driven by technology alone (Bocken, Boons & Baldassarre 2019). More importantly, the World Wide Web is making deceptive conduct known internationally in just a blink of an eye, introducing a period of unprecedented transparency (Sisodia, 2013). Technology, thus, is also driving responsible behavior by businesses.

Similarly, educational programs at business schools are incorporating methods of reasoning so that graduates joining organizations would be responsible for their actions, mindful of all stakeholders, employ reason and add meaning to business (Lo, 2018; Simons, 2013). Incorporation of meaning into products adds value to brands leading to sustainable growth. In certain cases, such meaning is mandated through mandatory labeling, geo-tagging, health security seals etc. that reflect a conscious business approach. Such practices enable progressive growth in income and wealth for both businesses and consumers as well as. Organizations communicating such transition in practices are received positively by consumers and drive a change in the mindset. This results in a transition of consumers, from being random to being conscious. These conscious customers incorporate reason and meaning in their decision making leading to a larger development of the human kind (Pruzan, 2001; Strong, 2011; Yarimoglu, & Binboga, 2019). Development of moral, ethical and reasonable contracts for use in business has, of late, gotten known worldwide with academicians like Oliver Hart and Bengt Holmström being granted a Nobel Prize for their contribution to the social contract theory (Holmstrom, 2017).

RESEARCH METHODOLOGY

This work follows an exploratory research design to understand the concept of conscious business practices and map these practices in the case of Mr. Zero. To understand conscious business process, a single case study approach has been adopted for rich description and in-depth analysis (Yin, 2017). Case study research is suitable in this context as it make use of in-depth insights of the empirical phenomena. Miles and Huberman (1994) advocates a case study approach as it gives flexibility, richness and holism to the researcher, to understand the phenomenon of interest, especially in complex context.

For this study, secondary data are retrieved. In a research setting where ethical issues are involved, secondary data provides several advantages over primary sources. Secondary data reduces "both social desirability response bias and the reluctance to respond to explicit ethical questions" (Harris, 2001, p. 193). Also, researchers advocate collecting secondary data in studies where historical insights are required, as such type of data provides real and unchecked dimensions of the events being examined, and thus, overcomes difficulties of recollect. This study collects data from website, internal records, social media pages, and blogs of Mr. Zero and Ecologically Conscious Architectural Studio (ECAS) in December 2019. In the analysis, written documents retrieved from the secondary sources were examined using content analysis technique. The content analysis was found to be an appropriate technique to analyse the data as in this technique an "objective analysis of messages. . . is accomplished by means of explicit rules" (Berg, 2004, p. 224).

ECOLOGICALLY CONSCIOUS ARCHITECTURAL STUDIO: A CASE STUDY

In sync with the concept of the conscious business movement, the ECAS was established at Auroville, India. At the core of ECAS lies the philosophy that it is humanity that shapes our ecological environment and that such an environment, in turn, shapes our behavioral patterns. At ECAS, it is believed, that it is within the realm of possibility to bring about lasting positive impact for the society through an environmental conscious lifestyle. ECAS is pronounced as ek-aas, which has its origin in the Hindi language and is made from two syllables, which are 'ek' and 'aas'. 'Ek' means one, whereas 'aas' means longing or desire. Therefore, a literal translation of ECAS in Hindi means ONENESS, whereas the words depict togetherness, which explains a lot about the place and its people. ECAS is not merely a place or organization, but a feeling of oneness which binds all beings together with harmony and growth in the process of attaining peace. It is essentially a platform for passionate learners to come together with a conscious approach to contribute creatively and generate solutions towards a viable future.

ECO Design Cafe

ECO stands for Era of Conscious Architecture, which represents ecological and eco-sensitive approach as per the philosophy of ECAS. It handles the Research & Development department, which is responsible for research, invention, innovation and discoveries which are aligned with the philosophy and principles of conscious architecture. At the ECO Design Café, experts and artists of different professions meet, explore and attempt to design a better world.

Vision and Objectives

The studio has a vision to create a platform for conscious architecture embedded in self-consciousness, our evolution and our environment. The first objective of the studio is to develop a place for mutual exchange of expertise of varied background to incubate conscious business ideas. Secondly, it also endeavours to popularise the ECO Design Cafe, which aims at providing design-based services in all fields based on the philosophy of conscious architecture (designs that follow an eco-sensitive approach) to develop a platform for Innovation, Invention and Discoveries for the sensible survival of human being. Finally, ECAS also makes all efforts to generate skill-based employment opportunities for locals to revive traditional art and engage in such activities that aim to unite the world through its conscious approach.

Among various attempts made at ECAS that are having positive impacts on the environment, one stands out where the core philosophy of ECAS is showcased. Also, with rising interest in the product, it is evident that conscious business models are acceptable as viable solutions by the society.

Mapping Conscious Business Practices through MR ZERO Pencils

Mr. ZERO pencil is an ambitious yet inspiring initiative that has the capability of spreading the concept of conscious business to the present as well as the future generations. An ordinary pencil is a tool for great creations. However, the environmental impact of a pencil can be easy to overlook.

According to the life-cycle studies by World Watch Institute, forests having a mature ecosystem are frequently cut down completely to harvest lumber for pencil production. Furthermore, after re-plantation, saplings take on an average 14 years to grow into trees before being felled to become raw materials for producing pencils. There are multiple instances where production of pencil wood resulted in depleted forest reserves, contaminated waterways, and choked the air with pollutants. Also, it is often observed that herbicides are sprayed over the forest to kill plants that compete with saplings which lead to soil pollution. According to Kelly (2013), approximately 15-20 billion pencils are consumed annually and approximately 92,000 trees are cut each year to meet the annual global demand. That is exhaustion of a considerable amount of wood, graphite, rubber and aluminum that results in significant and often irreversible loss of habitats of many species.

The world population is estimated to increase at 83 million per year (Leridon, 2020) and so does our insatiable voracity for consumer goods. As most of the goods we consume seem relatively benign they tend to wreak havoc collectively. Accordingly, as the demand for pencils increase, ecological habitats will be destroyed and an enormous amount of carbon dioxide will be emitted due to the production. On an average 33.5 gram of carbon emission happens on production of one industrial pencil. In fact, a single industrial pencil entails an average of 0.52 Mega Joules of embodied energy due to heavy machinery, process and transportation, and the said energy is mostly extracted and transformed from fossil fuels and other non-renewable sources (Mr. ZERO, 2018).

According to a locally conducted survey by ECAS to understand the need and consumption behavior associated with pencils. Around 90% people never used the bottom part of pencil. According to the respondents in the survey, pencils were either lost or the grip became too uncomfortable for using a short pencil (Mr. ZERO, 2018). Moreover, industrial pencils available in the market use a chemical coat on the outer part of the pencil, making it difficult for the pencil to get properly decomposed into the soil. Further, after decomposition, it contaminates the land with toxic elements, causing soil erosion. It is true that pencils produced in industries can better meet the increasing demand and offer the maximum value in terms of pricing due to their operability at scale but that view is short sighted. A world bereft of trees and soil rich with harmful chemicals can have a devastating and cascading effect on our future generations at immeasurable levels as well.

In the light of these concerns, solutions were explored in the ECO Design Café at ECAS. Mr. ZERO pencil was designed to spread awareness of sustainable lifestyle solutions. It is a direct and creative solution for an environmental concern. Mr. ZERO aims to start a silent revolution for an ecologically friendly lifestyle. Being unique in a sense, Mr. Zero is an eco-friendly, carbon-negative, non-toxic and zero-waste pencil. It is a rustic wooden twig pencil with a seed, which can be recycled (replanted) after its usage. While one end of the pencil is used for writing, the other end of the pencil is customized to hold seeds. The art of zero wastage is clearly visible in the pencil's 'circle of life' design principle which emphasizes that nothing goes to waste. The pencil when recycled gives birth to a tree. Once the tree grows, it sheds wooden twigs which in turn are made into a pencil.

Designers at the ECO Design Studio faced their first hurdle in finding space within a standard pencil with 180 mm of solid graphite to insert seeds. It was addressed by reducing the length of the graphite to 100 mm from the bottom of the pencil. The remaining space was designed as a wood casing for the seeds. Once the graphite is fully utilized, the remainder of the pencil can be immersed in water for 24 hours before planting it in the soil. This helps the germination of seeds and the growth of the tree. The absence of industrial processing or the burning of the waste of the pencil prevents any release of carbon in the environment, thus not creating an imbalance in the carbon cycle. The pencil is handcrafted with consciousness and joy by using naturally available wooden twigs shed by local trees in the region of east Tamil Nadu, India.

Mr. ZERO is available in different wood types like Neem, Tulip, Guava, Soundal, Bamboo, Eucalyptus and Blackberry. They are capped with seeds of Australian Paper Tree, Bottle Brush and Sacred Fig. Its natural finish, wooden texture, forms and grip gives its users a unique artistic experience. The manufacturing process involves minimal energy. The main process is the collection of wood and artistically carving and assembling them. Unlike industrial pencils, which, involves heavy machinery operated by fossil fuels and other non-renewable sources, Mr. Zero pencils are energy minimalistic and reduce release of carbon dioxide into the environment.

The wooden twigs that provide the casing are transformed into carbon bank by transforming into a pencil. Zero tolerance for toxins is another shining quality of the pencil. Unlike Industrial pencils, glue used to affix the graphite and the wooden twig for this pencil is non-toxic in nature. It is derived from casein, a fully compostable compound. After graphite is used fully, the remaining twig and glue acts as natural fertilizer for the tree seed, which helps with the germination of the enclosed seed.

Even the packaging used for Mr. Zero pencils display the conscious business philosophy of ECAS. The packaging is unique and memorable as well as easy. A memorable Mr. Zero package is made by folding recycled paper using Origami art techniques without using any adhesive at all. Additionally, it also acts as a pencil holder for easy storage, thereby, helping people not lose their pencils. Mr. Zero spreads the message of joy in expression. The element of this awareness and joy is present at every stage of the pencil's life process: whether in collecting fallen twigs for pencil; in making a pencil that energy minimalistic & non-toxic; and in recycling the used pencil into a new tree that will support many other life forms.

CASE INSIGHTS

The case study presents an applicative model of the conscious business philosophy in action. ECAS has a vision to create a platform for conscious architecture embedded in self-consciousness, our evolution and our environment. The philosophy of Mr. Zero is to spread the message of joy through expression which has been the foundational tenet of civilization itself. Their purpose of being in business is not just profit but profits that accrue from being conscious of ourselves and the environment that we live in. They have adopted the most basic of nature's cycle and adapted their pencil to the environment and for the sustenance of the environment through design elements. This displays a higher purpose of being in business.

Situated at Auroville, they have drafted local needs of generating livelihood for many who engage in planting trees, collecting twigs, making pencils, packing them as well as selling them. At the same time, they also cater to the larger societal interests of a green planet. Customer delight in using the pencil and experiencing the growth of a plant from a seed to a tree is embedded in the concept of joy as well. Although their stakeholders do not see their money grow, their interests of intrinsic satisfaction do get accomplished.

The leadership at ECAS was conscious of the purpose that they wanted to be in business for. Their actions and initiatives were backed by the intent of being ecologically sensitive and at the same time being driven towards innovative solutions. The best example of a conscious mindset is observed in the ECO Design Café that promulgated the concept of conscious architecture embedded in self-consciousness, human evolution and the environment. Similarly, incubating ideas that are embedded in providing design-based services in all fields based on the philosophy of conscious architecture to develop a platform for Innovation, Invention and Discoveries for the sensible survival of human being is evidence of the leadership's steadfastness in the original purpose.

ECAS has established a culture of spreading Joy as they believe it is innate to our nature of being. It can be observed in the purpose of Mr. Zero. It is designed to spread joy of expression and can be experienced at all stages of making, using as well as disposing the pencil. The culture of giving back to nature finds prominence in the very essence of ECAS and the kind of social ventures that it supports. Also, at ECAS all efforts are made to generate skill-based employment opportunities for locals, to revive traditional art and to engage in such activities that aim to unite the world through its conscious approach.

Our findings from the synthesis of the conscious business model and the functioning of ECAS clearly indicate that they follow the four tenets of being a conscious business. The set of objectives envisaged by Mr. Zero towards creating a positive impact on the environment and the outcomes achieved thus far is presented at Figure 1.

CONCLUSION

The case study discussed in this chapter draws parallels to the concept of conscious business practice at play at the Era of Conscious Architecture (ECO) Design Café at ECAS at Auroville in India. The authors attempted to examine the global trend of the shift of human consciousness and its profound impact on businesses, society and the environment. A detailed analysis of the conscious business culture provided the basic tenets of such practices that entailed societal consciousness and not the narrow interests of profit accrual. Unlike the usual understanding of the conduct of business, conscious business practices are holistic and embed tenets like having a higher purpose of being in business, managing stakeholder interests in ways that are not only in sync with the purpose of being in business but also create a state of self-actualization, provide for a sustainable leadership and create a general culture of togetherness rather than individual gains in business. Apart from being viewed as a broad minded conscious organization, the economic gains from such practices include a positive and stronger consumer sentiment that translates to better revenues. Satisfied consumers result in helpful word of mouth publicity that encourages others to adopt the product. Similarly, it also provides an edge over the competition resulting in sustained differentiation and profits. Such practices, thus, satisfy the triple bottom line approach of organizations that include consciousness towards people, planet and profits.

Figure 1.

Initiatives	*Outcomes*
Fighting Climate change	By substituting existing industrial pencils with Mr. ZERO pencils, they successfully avoided further carbon emissions in the environment.
Reducing non-renewable energy consumption	Mr. ZERO pencils are handcrafted and therefore, don't require any heavy machinery, which minimize energy consumption during manufacturing.
Zero Wastage	The design principle of Mr. ZERO Pencils is circle of life, which ensures that nothing goes to waste. The Pencil gives birth to a tree, which sheds wooden twigs periodically, which in turn becomes pencils.
Prevent Soil erosion	Mr. ZERO pencil use non-toxic glue that has no chemical coating on the surface, unlike other industrial pencil. Further, remaining twig acts as fertilizer for the seed sown. The plants and trees prevent erosion of the soil as well.
Encouraging Afforestation	Post usage as a pencil, Mr. ZERO acts as a natural agent of afforestation by sowing the seed that gives life to a new tree.
Encouraging Local craftsmanship	Revival of traditional arts, skill development and employment generation to the local village people are outcomes that Mr. Zero has achieved.

The case of Mr. Zero pencils is a unique experiment at the ECO Design café wherein environmental concerns forms the higher purpose of being in business. The pencil is envisaged to spread joy of expression and is embedded in its manufacturing to disposal process. Made of fallen twigs, it provides for seeds that are to be replanted for our future generations to experience the green planet that we have. An examination of their vision shows that they satisfy the critical element of having a higher purpose that enables them to practice conscious business practices in their operations. Similarly, the leadership is committed to such practices and lead the way in actualizing their vision. Stakeholders like the business leaders, workers and the consumers find solace in contributing back to the society through being environmentally conscious.

Our research shows that it is possible to adopt conscious business practices and translate them into reality with intent and resilience to the purpose. However, it should be contextualized and communicated to the stakeholders. A culture should be established with top leadership leading the way forward. Success of such endeavours depends on strategic and effective communication to both internal as well as external stakeholders. Through actions including Corporate Social Responsibility activities, social marketing and cause related marketing attention can be garnered from interested consumers. Similarly a broad base awareness towards the possible positives from the usage of the product may initiate suitable consumption action from consumers. A well designed and integrated marketing communication should be developed and broadcasted so that the same can generate conversations around the topic. Channels like digital and electronic media can be optimally utilized to send the message across to the mass audience whereas blogs can be used to target specific sets of interested consumers.

REFERENCES

Akbar, K., Jin, Y., & Salam, S. (2018). Barriers to environmentally-conscious manufacturing innovation. *Human Systems Management*, *37*(4), 453–462. doi:10.3233/HSM-17251

Asphalt, E. (2020). Conscious, innovative solutions from Shisalanga. *IMIESA, 7.*

Berg, B. L. (2004). *Methods for the social sciences. In Qualitative Research Methods for the Social Sciences*. Pearson Education.

Bocken, N., Boons, F., & Baldassarre, B. (2019). Sustainable business model experimentation by understanding ecologies of business models. *Journal of Cleaner Production*, *208*, 1498–1512. doi:10.1016/j.jclepro.2018.10.159

Coates, D. (2015). *Capitalism: The Basics*. Routledge. doi:10.4324/9780203798799

Conaway, R. N., Regester, K., Martin, S., Nixon, C., & Senior, B. (2018). Amazon Whole Foods: When E-Commerce Met Brick-and-Mortar and Saved the Brand of Conscientious Capitalism. *Journal of Marketing Development and Competitiveness*, *12*(3).

Frémeaux, S., & Michelson, G. (2017). The common good of the firm and humanistic management: Conscious capitalism and economy of communion. *Journal of Business Ethics*, *145*(4), 701–709. doi:10.100710551-016-3118-6

Friedman, M. (2009). *Capitalism and Freedom*. University of Chicago press.

Hamel, G. (2008). The Future of Management. *Human Resource Management International Digest*, *16*(6). doi:10.1108/hrmid.2008.04416fae.001

Harris, H. (2001). Content analysis of secondary data: A study of courage in managerial decision making. *Journal of Business Ethics*, *34*(3-4), 191–208. doi:10.1023/A:1012534014727

Hart, O., & Holmstrom, B. (2017). The Sveriges Riksbank Prize in Economic Sciences in Memory of Alfred Nobel, 2016. *The Scandinavian Journal of Economics*, *119*(3), 487–488. doi:10.1111joe.12252

Hess, D., & Fuller, C. (2017). *The Evolving Language of Conscious Capitalism*. Academic Press.

Hubberman, A. M., & Miles, M. B. (1994). *Qualitative data analysis*. Academic Press.

Jahan, S., & Mahmud, A. S. (2015). What is capitalism. *Finance & Development*, (June), 44–45.

Kelly, J. (2013). *Satisfying Consumer Desires doesn't have to mean consumption*. Retrieved from Vancouver Sun: http://www.vancouversun.com/technology/satisfying+consumer+desires+doesn+have+mean+consumption/8623190/story.html

Khalsa, A. S. (2010). *Conscious Business: Based on the teachings on Yogi Bhajan*. Kundalini Research Institute.

Kofman, F. (2008). *Conscious business: How to build value through values* (Vol. 1). ReadHowYouWant.com.

Leridon, H. (2020). World population outlook: Explosion or implosion? *Population et Sociétés*, (1), 1–4. doi:10.3917/popsoc.573.0001

Lo, K. D. (2018). Fritz J. Roethlisberger Memorial Award Goes to "Business Not as Usual: Developing Socially Conscious Entrepreneurs and Intrapreneurs". *Journal of Management Education*, *42*(4), 564–566. doi:10.1177/1052562918778874

Mackey, J. (2011). What conscious capitalism really is: A response to James O'Toole and David Vogel's "Two and a Half Cheers for Conscious Capitalism". *California Management Review*, *53*(3), 83–90. doi:10.1525/cmr.2011.53.3.83

Marques, J. C. (2017). Industry business associations: Self-interested or socially conscious? *Journal of Business Ethics*, *143*(4), 733–751. doi:10.100710551-016-3077-y

Mr. Zero. (2018). *A Pencil is tool for great creations! ZERO Pencil is non-toxic rustic wooden twig Pencil, which could planted after using it as Pencil!* [Facebook status update]. Retrieved from https://www.facebook.com/pg/mr.zero.ecas/posts/?ref=page_internal

Okorochkova, A. A. (2017). Corporate social responsibility in the era of "conscious capitalism". *Russian Entrepreneurship*, *18*(7), 1253–1272.

Palmer, T. G. (Ed.). (2011). *The morality of capitalism: what your professors won't tell you*. Jameson Books.

Parung, C. A. (2019). How do the Indonesian ecologically conscious millennials value upcycled clothing? *IOP Conference Series. Materials Science and Engineering*, *703*(1), 012031. doi:10.1088/1757-899X/703/1/012031

Pillay, S. S., & Sisodia, R. S. (2011). *A case for conscious capitalism: Conscious leadership through the lens of brain science*. Ivey Business Journal.

Pruzan, P. (2001). Corporate reputation: Image and identity. *Corporate Reputation Review*, *4*(1), 50–64. doi:10.1057/palgrave.crr.1540132

Scott, B. R. (2009). *The concept of capitalism*. Springer Science & Business Media. doi:10.1007/978-3-642-03110-6

Simons, R., Dávila, A., & Kaplan, R. S. (2000). *Performance measurement & control systems for implementing strategy*. Prentice Hall.

Simpson, S., Fischer, B. D., & Rohde, M. (2013). The conscious capitalism philosophy payoff: A qualitative and financial analysis of conscious capitalism corporations. *Journal of Leadership, Accountability and Ethics*, *10*(4), 19–29.

Sisodia, R. S. (2013). Understanding the performance drivers of conscious firms. *California Management Review*, *55*(3), 87–96. doi:10.1525/cmr.2013.55.3.87

Smith, A. (1759). *The Theory of Moral Sentiments* (D. D. Raphael & A. L. Macfie, Eds.). doi:10.1093/oseo/instance.00042831

Smith, A. (1778). *An Inquiry Into the Nature and Causes of the Wealth of Nations: By Adam Smith....* Strahan.

Smith, G. T. (2017). *The Impact of Socially Conscious Initiative Announcements on Coffee Company Stock Values*. Academic Press.

Strong, M. (2011). What are the Limits to Conscious Capitalism? A Response to James O'Toole and David Vogel's "Two and a Half Cheers for Conscious Capitalism". *California Management Review*, *53*(3), 109–117. doi:10.1525/cmr.2011.53.3.109

Thigpen, P. (2011). Can We Find Another Half a Cheer? A Response to James O'Toole and David Vogel's "Two and a Half Cheers for Conscious Capitalism". *California Management Review*, *53*(3), 118–123. doi:10.1525/cmr.2011.53.3.118

Voss, C. (2018). Conscious Leaders Practicing Conscious Capitalism: Developing Conscious Leadership in Business. In Academy of Management Proceedings (Vol. 2018, No. 1, p. 12886). Briarcliff Manor, NY: Academy of Management.

Wallace, N. (2020). Conscious Leadership: Moving to an Intentional Focus for a Thriving Workplace Culture. *Leader to Leader*, *2020*(97), 53–57. doi:10.1002/ltl.20512

Wilson, S. (2014). *A design for life: An hour with Alain de Botton*. Delloite Insights. Retrieved from https://www2.deloitte.com/insights/us/en/deloitte-review/issue-14/dr14-design-for-life.html

Yangzom, C., & Singh, J. S. K. (2019). Ecologically Conscious Buying Behaviour of Organic Products: A Quantitative Study in Thimpu, Bhutan. *Malaysian Journal Of Consumer and Family Economics*, *22*(1), 92–113.

Yarimoglu, E., & Binboga, G. (2019). Understanding sustainable consumption in an emerging country: The antecedents and consequences of the ecologically conscious consumer behavior model. *Business Strategy and the Environment*, *28*(4), 642–651. doi:10.1002/bse.2270

Yin, R. K. (2017). *Case study research and applications: Design and methods*. Sage Publications.

Zsolnai, L. (2017). *Ecologically Conscious Leadership*. Academic Press.

Chapter 9
Communicating in Media Dark Areas

Dinesh Kumar
https://orcid.org/0000-0003-3698-8770
Jagran Lakecity University, India

Punam Gupta
Career College, India

ABSTRACT

Companies have to communicate with their consumers and deliver value. This is achievable in areas where consumers are educated and have access to media – and these conditions exist in markets in the developed world and also in urban areas in developing countries. But communicating to distant, scattered villages, or areas where the majority of the population is poor—areas called media-dark—poses a great challenge for business. Further, the target audience may also have no access to education or media. Communicating in these markets physically is simply not economical or feasible. This chapter describes the challenges of reaching consumers in media dark environments. It explores how companies are getting over these obstacles. Drawing on case studies describing innovative use of communication methods, it explains how initiatives can succeed in BOP areas using innovative approaches. A media communication mix is proposed for successfully reaching out to consumers in BOP markets.

INTRODUCTION

This paper stems from a deep concern for people who are ignored by policy makers, who are either too distant or too poor to be included in the development process. Policies of the government and marketing strategies formulated by companies usually focus on the rich, educated and accessible customers. A change in approach is required to reach the 50% or so of the world's population ignored by the development process – people living on less than $2.50 a day. This paper tries to solve the riddle of communicating with such customers in media dark environments and suggests ways of devising strategies to reach them and involve them in the mainstream.

DOI: 10.4018/978-1-7998-3964-4.ch009

The idea that companies should serve consumers in the neglected bottom-of-the-pyramid (BOP) markets was popularised by Prahalad (2004). Given that urban markets and those in the developed world were saturated, the idea was that companies could serve the often neglected consumers in BOP markets and thereby make a fortune out of it. But companies wishing to tap such markets faced enormous challenges. The problem of establishing supply chains to small, remote markets has been mentioned by many writers. But perhaps an equally big challenge is to find ways to communicate with people in such areas which usually media-dark.

The problems of communicating with customers in media-dark areas are illustrated by the experience of Dr Muhammad Yunus, who pioneered the concepts of 'microcredit' and 'microfinance' in Bangladesh. When he started out with his idea of giving micro loans to people who were living in extreme poverty, he found that he could not communicate with the intended beneficiaries – the women in BOP households. He describes in his book, *Banker to the Poor* (2007), how he could get people to participate in the banking system he wanted to create, a system based on mutual trust, strict supervision, accountability, participation, and creativity, instead of collaterals and guarantees which the poor could not provide.

BEYOND TRADITIONAL THINKING

But how could he explain the concept to women and organising them in groups in a highly traditional society? There was no media that was accessed by such women, who lived in strict traditional social norms and habits. One of the first problems that Dr Yunus faced was talking to women in a society where males were not allowed to interact with them. But talking was the only option, since written messages could not be sent or read, no advertisements were possible and no media existed. For a manager working in developed markets, such problems would well be un-imaginable.

Dr Yunus writes in his book that it was a long and patient process, "Because of the rules of *purdah*, we never dared enter women's houses in the villages we visited. So when I went to meet village women, I never knocked on their doors. Instead, I would stand in a clearing between several houses, so that everyone could see me and observe my behaviour. I usually brought one of my female students with me. This go-between would enter the house, introduce me, and speak on my behalf. She would then bring back any questions the women might have. I would answer the questions, and back the girl would go. Sometimes she would shuttle back and forth for over an hour. We wasted a lot of time. Often the young girl would not catch all my ideas or the women's questions would get jumbled. It was an inefficient system".

Though inefficient, it was the only way to get the message across. The experience described by him sums up the challenges of operating in BOP societies. It was clear that in such societies, traditional methods of communication just do not work: he operated in an area in which media was not available, the people were poor with literacy and exposure problems, bound by strict traditional norms. Quite rightly, Dr Yunus wondered, "How would we find women borrowers in a country where most poor women had never even seen a bank and where 85 per cent could not read our billboards or advertisements?"

COMMUNICATION CHALLENGES IN BOP MARKETS

The challenges faced by Dr Yunus shows the problem of business communication in many under-developed or media-dark markets. He found that the solution was simple person-to-person communication but that requires a lot of painstaking effort. Managers educated in urban business or communication schools and used to working with the media find themselves out of their element in BOP markets. Not surprisingly, many initiatives to reach such markets have ended in disaster.

Businesses must find out a way of communication if they have to reach customers in BOP markets. The first step is to understand media-dark environments. These are characterised by: (a) populations scattered over long distances, (b) without adequate media vehicles, (c) marked by poverty and illiteracy, (d) bound by traditions that limit exposure of a section of the population, or (e) are virtually cut-off from the development process. Either condition or a combination of these would qualify as BOP markets.

It is interesting to study attempts by companies to overcome these hurdles. Using a completely innovative approach and an out-of-the-box thinking, these companies have succeeded in communicating with customers who live in neglected, far-off markets in an effort to tap the fortune at the base of the pyramid. Globally, more than 4 billion people live in BOP markets, representing a huge potential. These people are not simply poor: the International Finance Corporation (IFC) defines the base of the pyramid as "not just lack of income, but lack of access to basic goods, services, and economic opportunities." This could include:

- Smallholder farmers
- Slum dwellers in urban areas
- People living in scattered villages
- Informal sector workers
- Populations with lack of access to basic goods and services such as water, electricity, sanitation, or credit

Though papers have been written that are sceptical of serving such isolated markets, many companies have succeeded in their efforts. The companies that have succeeded in this rough terrain have done so with a complete change in strategy, using completely innovative methods. While urban educated managers use the techniques that they are most familiar with – using advertising and clever campaigns – the ideas for reaching BOP markets come from the grassroots levels. Communication channels that solve long standing problems of the target market are more likely to succeed than replication methods from urban markets.

This paper identifies and describes the difficulties of reaching consumers in media dark areas, consisting of low literacy, media reach and exposure, limited penetration of print media, limited access to television and radio, communicating in diverse cultures and languages, scattered audiences, and lack of internet and communication infrastructure. This makes one-size-fits-all strategy irrelevant. Companies, used to urban oriented mass campaigns, find it difficult to tailor-make campaigns specific for every language and every region.

Any communications strategy in media dark areas will work only if the problems of BOP markets are addressed. Companies are getting over these obstacles in the most interesting ways. Drawing on case studies ranging from Grameen Bank (Bangladesh), Unilever (India), Kumbh Mela (India) and others; and describing media vehicles such as rural radio, newspaper and mobile phones, we explain how initiatives can succeed using innovative approaches. We show how communications with a two-way dialogue can succeed better in media dark environments. Thanks to technology, this is possible today, but calls for huge efforts and investments.

When companies think out-of-the-box, companies have come up with ways to communicate with customers living in scattered villages of India. The rural communication mix is described and some innovative ways are drawn from case studies that are used by businesses to communicate with such customers. It will help readers to understand the challenges of communicating in BOP markets and also to work out strategies for communicating with the proverbial "last man" described by Mahatma Gandhi – the person in a rural area or living in poverty in an area cut off from the development process.

Figure 1. People living in hill states in developing countries tend to be scattered and isolated, making business communication quite difficult.
Photograph by the author.

LITERATURE REVIEW

The issue of communicating in media dark areas has attracted the attention of researchers in the development field. There are a few papers written about marketing communication in media dark areas, and much of the research is focused on using information and communication technologies (ICTs) in BOP markets. However, while there is a general call for using such technologies, few papers suggest concrete proposals of getting over the problem of communicating in media-dark environments.

Tarafdar, Anekal and Singh (2012) examine the role of information and communication technologies in BOP markets. They write that communication technologies have a threefold role, consisting of "automate–informate–transform market mechanisms." They conclude that ICT facilitates development of market mechanisms in cut-off markets. Walsham and Sahay (2006) examine the current landscape and future aspects of information technology for development, and how information systems research can make a positive difference in developing countries. Kuriyan et al (2008) describe the use of low-cost but advanced technologies for the well-being of the poor through market-based solutions. They describe a project in South India that uses computer-service kiosks and strives for social development through access to computers and also seeks financial viability.

Rahman (2014) provides a descriptive analysis of CSR advertising and concludes that tapping the BOP markets has far-reaching developmental and economic implications for developing countries.

Pizzagalli et al (2018) examine marketing to low-income consumers and conclude that companies must be creative in their formulating their marketing strategies in order to engage with BOP consumers. They also conclude that companies should also cater to BOP consumers' needs in order to foster strong and enduring relationships.

Describing the challenges and opportunities of the last mile for BOP in Brazil, Barki and Parente (2020) report that companies should give priority and serve BOP markets while understanding its needs and peculiarities. They should develop an empathic and two-way communication in such markets. Simanis and Milstein (2012) write that companies must make BOP relevant to their core business. They write that managers must leave behind emotionally-tinged claims in favor of concrete, bounded opportunities that exist in such markets.

Jagtap and Kandachar (2009) stress on the need for innovation for BOP markets and show that satisfying needs of customers from BoP markets requires companies to be radically innovative. Such markets appear to be suitable for disruptive innovations.

A number of authors have stressed the role of communication in the development process and to improve the lives of the poor. Blowfield (2012) writes that business has various roles to play in the development of poorer countries and examines the circumstances under which business becomes a "development agent," that is, striving to deliver and be accountable for developmental outcomes. McAnany (2012) provides an outline of how communication technologies can impact social change and improve human lives. Quarry and Ramirez (2009) write that "good development contains good communication" and describe the movement away from the development world's fascination with large, obsessively planned results-based approaches.

There are few papers written from the point of view of marketing communications. While the role of ICTs is stressed by papers, there is little understanding about how these must be used. Apps created for BOP markets have thus not succeeded since many consumers do not have smart-phones. Nor do the apps provide any useful function for the poor consumer.

This chapter describes the practical attributes of communicating in BOP markets. It describes case studies where innovative, on the ground communication helped companies penetrate into villages and cut-off markets. This paper is written from the point of view of marketing communications but has relevance for development communicators also.

LIMITATIONS IN BOP MARKETS

To work out effective communication models for BOP markets, first the limitations have to be understood. The methods used in traditional marketing communications consist of spraying consumers with beautiful images through advertising. Beautiful models are shown in a state of *nirvana* by consuming one product or the other. The method has been compared to somewhat like using insect sprays, which kills insects for a while. In the same manner, advertising is sprayed and then companies wait for customers to turn up to buy their products. These sprays, however, do not work in media dark markets, simply because neither is media available nor is it economical for scattered markets. Companies have to follow different rules in BOP markets since these campaigns are useful only in areas where they can be reached through media vehicles. BOP markets are characterized by the following:

- ***Low literacy levels***: Many BOP consumers suffer from low literacy levels, hence written messaging is not feasible. There is a limited penetration of print media in BOP markets. Such markets are dominated by customs and traditions, which makes adoption of new products and practices difficult. Companies therefore face a challenge to develop an effective communication mix that can break the literacy barrier.
- ***Media reach and exposure:*** Though media reach is improving over the years, it is still poor in many areas. In villages, there is limited access to television, radio and print so people have limited exposure. In many areas, even mobile signals are difficult to get. Hence, suitable media vehicles just do not exist.
- ***Diverse audiences***: Populations in scattered areas show diverse cultures and languages. They also have varied customs, traditions and lifestyles. This makes one-size-fits-all strategy, used by managers in many corporations, irrelevant. Companies find it difficult to tailor-make campaigns for every region that matches the local languages, cultures and lifestyles.
- ***A dearth of information:*** There is a shortage of information and lack of service providers in BOP markets. Local content is also lacking.
- ***Scattered audiences:*** Many communities, especially in rural areas, are spread over a very large land-mass. People live in small clusters or villages which makes them inaccessible through mass media vehicles. Difficult terrains compound the problem of reaching these clusters.
- ***Lack of well developed ICT infrastructure:*** Internet penetration is limited because of lack of ICT infrastructure. This is slowly changing as there is increasing use of mobile phones in BOP markets but the condition varies from region to region.

Any BOP communications strategy will work only if the above problems are addressed. Fortunately, modern technology allows overcoming some of these limitations. Companies can now communicate with individual customers and hence mass communication channels can be bypassed. A BOP communication channel must therefore use modern technologies in the most innovative ways.

BOP MARKETS COMMUNICATION STRATEGY

Because of the limitations described in the previous section, a BOP communications strategy cannot consist of a mass media campaign but as an interactive, two-way dialogue. Thanks to technology this is possible today, but calls for change of methods and huge efforts by companies as it means creating new channels. It means combining traditional channels with modern technology.

Rather than using a channel like a radio station or newspaper, the two-way communication model that works in BOP markets is a "demand-driven" model, one in which users request to get important relevant information through the channel. The channel is then also used to send brand messages. For instance, farmers use a mobile app which they access to get information on weather and farming applications, and the channel can also be used to send business messages. Companies have learnt that providing services that are needed by BOP consumers is an effective way to make them use the channel, and the advertising messages piggyback on the channel thus created.

In addition, modern technology helps overcome illiteracy barriers by conveying ideas in an audio and visual form, that is, making messages understood through pictures and demonstration. Companies must therefore develop and execute an interface between modern and traditional communication methods. They must also illustrate new ideas and techniques, using internet, multimedia, personal visits and below-the-line (BTL) techniques. What works in BOP markets are audio-visual materials that are easily understood, communicated through mobile vans or through mobile phones. Some companies rely on trained village communicators who can connect with rural customers with localized content resonant with local cultural norms and ethos.

Kumar and Gupta (2017) illustrate this with examples of several companies that have used technology with huge success. They use a model in which consumers demand relevant information and use channels to get it. Communication strategies in most media-dark areas must adhere to some basic requirements, such as:

1. **Overcome literacy barriers:** A BOP communications strategy must overcome literacy barriers by conveying ideas in an audio and visual form that goes beyond the written word and is well understood by the audience. Communication must be in the local language. This calls for developing an interface between modern and traditional communication methods.
2. **Use multimedia techniques:** Companies must generate new ideas and techniques, using multimedia or personal visits and BTL techniques to overcome the paucity of mass media. They must create audio-visual materials that are easily understood, and delivered through mobile phones or physically through mobile vans.
3. **Use local communicators:** Companies have to learn to work through local communicators who convey ideas through stories in the local language and local idiom. Investments are required to develop and train a cadre of village communicators who can connect with rural customers. Managers are not familiar with these methods and will have to acquire new capabilities.
4. **Develop localized content:** Campaigns must use local content, language and images rather than simply repeat promotion messages made for urban markets. All messages must adhere to the local cultural norms.
5. **Use mobile technology:** With the spread of smart-phones, companies may have a way of reaching messages to distant customers. Mobile technology has been used most innovatively by some companies.

Ironically, this means that companies learn the traditional methods of one-person-one-message communication. Even while using modern technology, it means returning to the age-old method of person to person communication.

One-to-one communication using multimedia techniques overcomes many of the communication problems faced in BOP markets. Modern technology is very useful in creating these channels which become very useful for sending relevant information to users and also to engage them in a company's promotion. Such channels are becoming popular. In India, Unilever created an entertainment channel which could be accessed by mobile phones, and users give a missed call to the number. They immediately receive a call-back from the company that provides fifteen minutes of free entertainment. This channel also sends advertising messages. Companies can think of innovating in similar ways and then use them to send messages to consumers. Such a strategy is able to overcome illiteracy barriers by conveying ideas in an audio and visual form, illustrate new ideas and techniques, use innovative communication techniques, and use localized content resonant with local cultural norms and ethos. The modified marketing communication mix for BOP markets consists of using elements that cover all the above mentioned points.

THE MARKETING COMMUNICATIONS MIX

The marketing communications mix for BOP markets is much more complicated than working out a communication program for urban markets, which tend to have population in high density areas, which makes communication easy. But in BOP markets a large number of factors come into play from dealing with fragmented markets to adhering to cultural norms. Companies use a mix of methods and channels to reach their target audience. This specific blend of the marketing communications mix consists of a number of communication methods, each one modified for special situations. Based on what works in rural areas, we can define the BOP communications mix as a combination of ten components (fig 2):

- Community Radio/ local channels
- Village newspapers/local editions of large newspapers
- TV – Regional language channels
- Rural Sales Force
- Wall Paintings
- BTL techniques, Vans and demonstrations
- Local theatre and performing arts
- Melas and fairs
- Mobile
- Internet

Advertising

Advertising is defined as any paid form of non-personal presentation and promotion of ideas, goods, or services by an identified sponsor. Most advertising is done on mass media such as print, broadcast and outdoor, but since the reach of mass media in BOP markets is limited, advertising is more effective if done through wall paintings, posters, or simply by a mobile announcer with a loudspeaker. Sellers usually stick posters on walls to communicate with their customers in media-dark markets (fig 3)

Personal Selling

Personal selling consists of using a company's sales force to meet customers and build relationships with them. Personal selling is generally thought of as making sales presentations and offering incentive programs. In BOP markets personal selling becomes an effective tool of influencing customers but companies have to manage traveling costs of their salespeople against the volume of sales generated. Travelling salesmen and merchants are popular in these areas and fill the gap between customers and companies. Personal contact and encouraging trials through mobile vans are important to generate sales with BOP rural customers.

Figure 2. The rural communications mix

Sales Promotion

Sales promotion is defined as short-term incentives to encourage the purchase of a product. People in BOP markets are more likely to respond to such schemes because of cost considerations. For a company venturing into distant markets for the first time, or to increase trials and sales, a sales promotion offering a discount, coupon or a savings scheme is an effective way to engage customers. Companies have to invest in displays, premiums, discounts, coupons, and demonstrations. However, the problem remains reaching consumers living in wide, scattered areas.

Public Relations

In urban areas, public relations includes building good relations with the press, but in BOP markets, it means cultivating local communities and local opinion leaders who speak well of the company and its products. This is helpful in influencing people who are otherwise not exposed to advertising.

Direct Marketing

Direct marketing refers to communications with targeted individuals directly to obtain an immediate response. The use of mail, telephone, fax, e-mail, SMS and other tools help reach specific consumers. As smart-phones and internet spread among disadvantaged markets, these methods can now be used more frequently than in the past. A direct contact with customers through mobile phones is sometimes the only method of reaching BOP consumers.

Apps

Another tool of communication that has emerged in recent times is through apps. If BOP consumers can be persuaded to download and use apps on their smart-phones, the company can capture data of the user and make targeted offers on them. However, the app must solve a specific problem of the consumer in order to be useful.

Social Media

Smart-phones enable rural consumers to make profiles on social media sites and interact with others. This becomes an important tool for brands to communicate with them. BOP customers are becoming active on social media as internet availability improves. New channels such as apps and social media have encouraged more companies to move from mass media to targeted communication and engage in one-on-one dialogue, building close relationships with customers. Villages can be seen as narrowly defined micro-markets, and social media could well be the cheapest way to reach them.

Today, ICT helps companies not only to keep close track of customer needs and communicate with them, but have information about consumers at the individual and household levels. The new technologies provide new avenues for reaching smaller villages with specific and tailored messages.

Wall Paintings

Wall paintings (fig 4) are effective in far-off villages. These are cheap, have a long life and serve as fixtures on walls with high visibility. Local painters do the job and villagers welcome these messages as the paint helps to protect walls. A direct marketing push combined with wall paintings and attractive schemes can give a lot of mileage in rural markets. Many large companies are tapping rural markets through wall paintings and they have made significant inroads. Wall painting is the most widespread form of advertising and well accepted among rural consumers, and so is an effective promotional tool, because they constantly remind rural people about name and logos.

The methods and their applications are summarized in Table 1.

Form the above we can see that companies must use communication methods and technology with the most innovative methods. Companies have to learn to think local while trying to reach BOP markets. This is not easy for managers who have operated in urban markets or those managers who are deputed by multinational corporations to work in under-developed countries. Such managers find that business conditions are entirely different in BOP markets and are therefore not able to imagine the kind of channels and promotions that they must choose. For example, it would be unimaginable for a Western manager to learn that advertising consists of merely writing a message on a wall. Such are the innovative methods and the realities in BOP markets that are not taught in business schools. Case studies of successful and innovative methods are therefore very valuable to work out sustained communication strategies.

Figure 3. Rural advertising is done through wall posters.
Photograph by the author.

Figure 4. Wall paintings in local languages are a preferred way of rural advertising. Small advertisers simply write their message on a wall – see the message on the wall with a mobile number on the left hand side of the picture.
Photograph by the author.

Table 1. Methods to reach BOP markets and their use.

TV The 2011 Census figures for India reveals that one third of rural homes have a TV and only 3% of these homes have an Internet connection. About 5% of rural households own a computer or laptop. However, 90 per cent of districts in rural India have experienced positive growth in TV and mobile penetration.	**Mobile Vans** Using mobile vans is one of the most effective communication channels for BOP consumers, since it combines interpersonal communication with direct experience. Van campaigns in rural areas pull crowds. Vehicles carrying innovative advertisements always grab attention. Rural service camps and creation of local brand ambassadors also serve as means of effective communication. Some companies put stalls at prominent locations. Other crowd pullers in rural areas are rural games and tournaments.
Village Newspaper Mass circulated newspapers do not reach distant markets; and coverage of these markets in mainstream media is extremely low. Apart from news of a suicide or an accident, villages find very little coverage on nationally circulated newspapers. Some regional language newspapers or regional editions of larger newspapers are popular in towns but have very little reach.	**Community Radio** Community radio serves a limited area. It caters to the interests of local communities, broadcasting content that is popular to a local audience. Globally, community radios have proliferated and provide information to people living in remote or isolated areas, but in India, the government restricts its spread and is not popular.
Fairs Fairs see very large turnouts and represent opportunities for communication in BOP markets. The biggest such gathering in India is the Kumbh mela, described as the world's largest gathering and provides a chance for companies to reach their consumers. Many companies use these opportunities fruitfully. *Melas* (village fairs) are important in rural marketing because they offer access to a mass of rural people who are otherwise diverse and hard to reach. For BOP families, fairs are welcome annual or six monthly outings.	**Mobile Phones** Cheap smart-phones have given a boost to BOP mobile internet users. Cheap handsets and affordable connectivity charges have resulted in a deep penetration of mobile phones. However, in many places getting mobile signals is a problem.

SUCCESSFUL AND INNOVATIVE METHODS

Since companies cannot reach distant markets, below-the-line (BTL) campaigns can introduce the "touch and feel" element to products, and also allow two-way communication through which people can understand what the product is capable of doing and clarify their doubts. A product demonstration is very effective to convince rural customers. Using local and popular form of entertainment like folk dances and art-forms, a company can increase brand awareness building. Many companies have used some of the methods effectively.

BTL campaigns must be designed so that they touch emotions of local folk and create excitement around the brand. BOP markets drive a quantum jump in sales if they are simple, direct and social. Hyundai, for example, used the wedding season in India to create a themed offer built on social occasions. More important are the effective use of modern technologies to create channels for communication. Among the innovative channels are: a demand-based radio station that can be accessed through mobile, audio bus stands, and using mobile technology during fairs. These illustrate how technology can be used to reach BOP customers.

Audio Bus Stations

Buses are the most common method of transportation in BOP markets and audio ads at bus stations are innovative and useful for BOP market communications. A person waiting for a bus hears a recorded program of entertainment, advertising and bus announcements. It helps reach thousands of bus travellers who listen to the ads as they wait for announcements. The audio advertisements are played along with the bus arrival/departure announcements. Called AudioWala Station, it consists of speakers installed at bus shelters. Ads are interspersed between the announcements. Since the waiting travellers are usually interested in bus arrival or departure announcements, the advertisements get an assured audience. Advertisements are aired 16 hours every day, from 6 am to night 10 pm daily. The frequency of advertisement broadcast can be set from an interval of 5 minutes to 60 minutes. Apart from the audio messages, companies can also display and sell their products at bus stations. The Parle biscuit company, for instance, used the bus stations to promote a campaign offering free tea on purchase of Parle Marie biscuits, which customers could get by visiting the nearest canteen.

Unilever's Kan Khajura Tesan

One of the most innovative ways of communication has been created by Hindustan Unilever Limited, manufacturer of a wide range of consumer goods. The company developed its own communication channel through a completely out-of-the-box thinking for distant customers. It started a free entertainment channel on the mobile platform: a radio-on-demand service called *Kan Khajura Tesan* (KKT) to reach out to people in remote areas. *Kan Khajura* translates as 'ear centipede' and *tesan* is the local lingo for 'station.' It became immensely popular, and has gathered a large number of subscribers. KKT is an amazing innovation in rural communication. It is India's first free and on-demand entertainment mobile radio channel. It now operates in many states of the country. The tagline of the station, in local language is: "Give a missed call, get free entertainment." The user gives a missed call to the number 180030000123 and immediately gets a return call that plays an entertainment programme, along with the company's advertisements, for 15 minutes. In this way, the user gets an entertainment mix of songs, movie dialogues, radio jockey talk and jokes on their mobile phone, in areas where there is no FM station. The company says that there is a lot of demand for content or entertainment in media-dark areas and mobiles become their only medium for it. The advantage is that the company can keep track of the people who are dialing and listening in. It gathers data of the users and develops rich profiles of its listeners, which becomes extremely helpful in planning customised strategies for its brands. The company has stopped advertising on radio in these states as its own channel reaches more people than any radio station. The company has printed the phone number for the channel on some of its product packs and has put up banners outside stores to increase its reach (fig 5).

The company monitors usage of KKT on a 'live dashboard' that highlights the number of users and the areas from where calls are received. Mobile data helps it to identify the localities and the times of maximum traffic. The company is also able to access other useful information such as the frequency of the calls, the time of day the calls come in, the numbers from which repeat calls are made, and perhaps most importantly, the exact point when the caller decides to hang up. The dashboard also provides live information about the number of ad impressions for different brands.

Colgate at the Kumbh Mela

Another innovative method was employed by Colgate. The company wanted to increase the use of its toothpaste in rural India by educating consumers about oral hygiene and the benefits of using toothpaste regularly. It decided to use the popularity of a mega event, the Maha Kumbh Mela in India. Using mobile and location-based technologies, it was able to reach out to consumers at the biggest fair of India.

Figure 5. KKT prints its number for people to make a missed call from their mobiles.

Realizing that most of the pilgrims were from areas with low literary rates, it used voice-based communications via a mobile phone. The technology used was location-based targeting: whenever a mobile phone came within 3-5 km of the area of the Kukbh mela, it received a telephone call. A virtual circle was created around the pilgrimage site by tagging three cellular towers. Colgate entered into a partnership with the telecom service provider company, Airtel, which generated the phone call to the visitors. This way, people received a call the moment they entered the virtual circle around the Maha Kumbh Mela. The call consisted of a message by a celebrity Indian radio personality Amin Sayani, telling them to visit the Colgate booth for free samples, a chance to win prizes, and entertainment. It was the first campaign of its kind in India. The company was able to generate foot traffic to the Colgate booth attracting over 700,000 visitors. By this communication strategy, the company reported a sharp increase in the number of visitors as compared to the pre-promotion period.

DISCUSSION

BOP markets represent unique challenges. Companies find it difficult to communicate in areas where media is not available or where people are too scattered to reach. While modern internet and communication technologies promise to bridge over this gap, the problem remains how to use these technologies for marketing purposes. While many papers advocate innovative use of communication technologies, it is left to companies to figure out what these ways might be. This paper describes ways in which some companies have developed their own channels or deployed technologies in unique and innovative ways. The case studies serve as examples to show that companies can reach consumers in media dark areas through a combination of marketing genius and communication technology. Indeed, many other methods have been experimented and deployed to involve vast numbers of rural or disadvantaged populations in the development process. Today mobile phones are being used for financial and banking transactions by people who did not have access to banks earlier.

The methods to reach cut-off populations are limited only by the imagination of the companies and their managers. Technology itself is not the answer; companies must find ways to engage the consumers.

CONCLUSION

Reaching BOP consumers is no doubt a huge challenge for companies, but the seemingly insurmountable problems can be overcome with modern technology and innovative campaigns. The rewards are huge, as the channels can help realise the fortune at the bottom of the pyramid. Indeed, companies that have invested in such channels report a sizeable improvement in their revenues. However, it is evident that companies have to change their approach – from a mass media based approach to an individualised approach that provides both communication and local experiences. This is not easily done, since companies have to work on advertisements that are localised for each micro-region, using local languages and images that conform to local cultures. For large multinational companies, this is often difficult because their agencies produce like to create large campaigns with huge media spends. Simply translating these campaigns in local languages results in disconnect with BOP customers. Quite often, it creates communication disasters.

This is to say that companies must develop the ability to communicate with individual customers. As Gawande (2013) explains, "Though we yearn for technological solutions, people talking to people is still the way that habits change". He describes how oral rehydration therapy was popularised in the country to save children suffering from dysentery. The problem was attacked in a way that is routinely dismissed as impractical and inefficient: by going door-to-door, person by person, and just talking, as shown by Chowdhury and Cash (1996) in their book, *A Simple Solution.* Modern technology provides the means by which this can be done.

REFERENCES

Barki, E., & Parente, J. (2014). Challenges and opportunities of the last mile for the base of the pyramid: The case of Brazil. *Field Actions Science Reports, 12*(Special Issue). https://journals.openedition.org/factsreports/3671

Blowfield, M. (2012). Business and development: Making sense of business as a development agent. *Corporate Governance: International Journal of Business in Society, 12*(4), 414–426. doi:10.1108/14720701211267775

Chowdhury, A. M. R., & Cash, R. A. (1996). *A Simple Solution - Teaching Millions to Treat Diarrhoea at Home.* The University Press Limited (UPL).

Gangal, A. (2014). Kan Khajura Tesan: The Full Story. *afaqs!* https://www.afaqs.com/news/story/41226_Kan-Khajura-Tesan-The-Full-Story

Gawande, A. (2013). Slow Ideas: Some Innovations Spread Fast. How Do You Speed the Ones That Don't? *The New Yorker.* https://www.newyorker.com/reporting/2013/07/29/130729fa_fact_gawande

Hindustan Unilever runs Bihar's most popular radio on mobile phones. (2014, Mar. 4). *The Economic Times.*

HUL plans to let other firms use its mobile marketing channel Kan Khajura Tesan. (n.d.). https://www.hul.co.in/news/news-and-features/2014/kan-khajura-tesan-sets-world-record.html

Jagtap, S., & Kandachar, P. (2009). Towards Linking Disruptive Innovations and BOP Markets. In *DS 58-1: Proceedings of ICED 09, the 17th International Conference on Engineering Design The Design Society*. https://www.designsociety.org/publication/28611/towards_linking_disruptive_innovations_and_bop_markets

Kumar, D., & Gupta, P. (2017). *Rural Marketing: Challenges and Opportunities*. Sage Publishing.

Kuriyan, R., Ray, I., & Toyama, K. (2008). Information and Communication Technologies for Development: The Bottom of the Pyramid Model in Practice. *The Information Society*, *24*(2), 93–104. doi:10.1080/01972240701883948

Masuoka, T. (2011). *Reaching the Base of the Pyramid through Inclusive Business Models, International Finance Corporation*. IFC.

McAnany, E. G. (2012). *Saving the world: A brief history of communication for development and social change*. University of Illinois Press. doi:10.5406/illinois/9780252036774.001.0001

Pizzagalli, L., Sharma, A., & Lascu, D.-N. (2018). Marketing at the Bottom of the Pyramid: Serving, and in the Service of Low-Income Consumers. *Innovative Marketing*, *14*(2), 35–40. doi:10.21511/im.14(2).2018.04

Prahalad, C. K. (2004). *The fortune at the base of the pyramid*. Wharton School Publishing.

Quarry, W., & Ramirez, R. (2009). *Communication for Another Development: Listening before Telling*. Zed Books. doi:10.5040/9781350219274

Rahman, M. (2014). Advertising to bottom of the pyramid consumers: Descriptive analysis of CSR advertising. *Review of Enterprise and Management Studies*, *1*(2), 63–69.

Simanis, E., & Milstein, M. (2012). Back to Business Fundamentals: Making "Bottom of the Pyramid" Relevant to Core Business. *Field Actions Science Reports*, *2012*(4). https://journals.openedition.org/factsreports/1581

Tarafdar, M., Anekal, P., & Singh, R. (2012). Market development at the bottom of the pyramid: Examining the role of information and communication technologies. *Information Technology for Development*, *18*(4), 311–331. doi:10.1080/02681102.2012.690172

Walsham, G., & Sahay, S. (2006). Research on information systems in developing countries: Current landscape and future prospects. *Information Technology for Development*, *12*(1), 1, 7–24. doi:10.1002/itdj.20020

Yunus, M., & Jolis, A. (2007). *Banker to the Poor: Micro-lending and the Battle Against World Poverty*. Public Affairs.

Chapter 10
Benefits of a Liberal Arts Education on Effective Business Communication

Rachel Wilson
Wittenberg University, USA

Amanda Reboulet
Jacoulet, USA

ABSTRACT

With the growing popularity of science, technology, engineering, and mathematics (STEM) degrees, it is important to understand the value of a business degree coupled with a liberal arts education. Business degrees provide one with a multitude of beneficial skills including analytical thinking, problem solving, decision making, critical thinking, and project management. When coupled with a liberal arts education, business degrees become even more powerful providing young professionals with a competitive advantage by creating a more well-rounded individual with a broader education base. In addition to the benefits of a business degree, the liberal arts education provides increased leadership skills, creativity and innovation, adaptability, and both richer native communication and foreign language skills. This chapter focuses on how a liberal arts education provides one with more pronounced, stronger communication skills both written and orally, which directly provides value to businesses.

INTRODUCTION

Quintessentially American (Koblik & Graubard, 2000), liberal arts colleges provide graduates with a uniquely powerful education in terms of critical and creative thought. According to Jiang and Guo (2017) a liberal arts education "uses an interdisciplinary curriculum to cultivate critical thinking, creativity, moral reasoning, analytical skills, and a sense of social responsibility" (p. 268), and "values self-examination, participatory and informative citizenship" (p. 269). But once acquired, how does one typically make use of this investment in developing one's intellect? In what has become a famous, if not infamous, quote,

DOI: 10.4018/978-1-7998-3964-4.ch010

President Coolidge (1925) explained, "the chief business of the American people is business. They are profoundly concerned with producing, buying, selling, investing and prospering in the world." The pull towards enterprise is significant, regardless of undergraduate major. In fact, when looking at six popular degree areas of: a) language and philosophy, b) social science, c) business, d) communications, e) engineering and f) information technology, research suggests that employment in some form of business activity is typically listed as one of the top ten job outcomes for each of the six majors and of all college graduates in the United States with 54% working in major business functions (Fain, 2019).

While it may seem that there is a natural synergy between the education one would receive at a liberal arts college and the demand for people to contribute meaningfully to business success, tensions persist.

Suspicions of legitimacy both plague and haunt business schools in colleges and universities. Grey (2001) explained that "business schools, more than perhaps any other part of universities...have often experienced, the scorn of other, more traditional subjects" (p. S27). Such misgivings are perhaps even more pressing within liberal arts colleges. As Styhre (2009) described, "business school disciplines are often regarded as being less prestigious than traditional disciplines" (p. 30), because management is a "plebian science in terms of dealing with actual everyday life problems rather than liberal arts or abstract philosophies" (p. 31). Overcoming such tensions between departments engenders a space for mutual benefit to develop. As reported by Schneider (2015), "what we're faced with is not so much a dichotomy between liberal arts and technical skills but rather the task of bridging foundational knowledge with the practicality of the real world and what is happening in business" (p. 111). When coupled with a liberal arts education, business degrees become even more powerful providing young professionals with a competitive advantage by creating a more well-rounded individual with a broader education base, one with more pronounced, stronger communication skills both written and orally. In turn, the professional success of these graduates highlights the essential benefit derived from the critical and creative thinking which comprise the core of a liberal arts education.

Before such synergies can be developed, and tensions reduced, between business schools and the traditional liberal arts, it is important to understand the degree to which liberal arts colleges in the United States already incorporate business, and business-related, degrees. A descriptive research methodology was used as the basis for assessing this phenomenon. Prior to addressing the methodology and results, the survey of literature is presented next to build sufficient context for understanding and interpretation.

SURVEY OF LITERATURE

Without education the mind can easily become yoked to one's most base nature. Most scholars credit Greek philosophers such as Plato and Roman orators such as Cicero for developing the idea of a liberal educations (Arsene, 2012; Kimball, 1995) with the goal of liberating the mind. Indeed, the Greek desire to have cities ruled by citizens required a thoughtfully educated citizen with knowledge of the "fundamental 'liberating' arts of grammar, logic, and rhetoric" (Simmons, 2018, p. 100). Of course, while the idea of a liberal education survived the middle ages, the Renaissance and Reformation for the larger part of human history, such an ideal education was reserved for the elite and almost exclusively male.

Perhaps more than any other western country, the US embraced the liberal arts heritage of training a gentle man in the classics of philosophy and oration not in preparation for work but rather for a more meaningful life. Naturally, it must be noted that it wasn't until the last century that universal education gained support and not until 1918 that every state in the US required at least an elementary education for the common good (Graham, 1974). But it was the supply of private US colleges that first opened in the 17th century that proved to be a bastion for a liberal education and competitive advantage worldwide. Those US students fortunate enough to afford college were taught "how to think across academic disciplines, exploring connections and crossing subject boundaries in the humanities, the social sciences, the natural sciences and the fine arts" (Arsene, 2012, p. 107). However, when the supply of private liberal arts colleges failed to meet the demand for a more educated citizenry, Congress passed the Morrill Land-Grant Acts in 1862 sanctioning the sale of federal lands for the creation of land-grant colleges (Logan & Curry, 2015). State colleges departed from the pure liberal education and quickly began offering training which was considered to be more directly practical and the value of a liberal education came into question. Ironically, today other countries are now recognizing the importance of liberal education. Hong Kong has spent the last 15 years adding a one-year general education programs onto its three-year specialist programs at its eight public universities in an attempt to escape from its British modeled specialized university education (Logan & Curry). Similarly, the Netherlands and Germany are responding to the fast-paced changes of today and tomorrow as the begin to imitate US liberal arts models (Arsene).

While the ancients upheld the goal of liberating the mind from ignorant enslavement through philosophy and oration, overtime debate has developed about which disciplines are included in a liberal education. Today, it is most commonly referred to as the "liberal arts & sciences" in recognition of a widening disciplinary lenses. Many agree with John Dewy's notion that how a discipline is taught matters more than the substance (Dewy, 1944). Stoddard's seminal piece in 1974 described a liberal education where the subject matter is enduring and whole with teaching methods adjusted to the nonspecialized interests of the students and without reference to application (Bevins, 2012).

The debate over a liberal education is far from settled. Over the last few decades technological and social advances and as well as globalization have shifted workforce demands and individual consciousness. Employment in high-paying jobs is no longer found in manual and physical work but rather in the knowledge-based sectors. Lucrative employment in the most rapidly growing sectors of our economy increasingly demands not only technical skills but also analytical as well as emotional and social skills (Pew Research Center, 2016). These new trends suggest the importance of marrying the technical and the critical education.

Even with national trends towards pragmatic education, there have long been calls to marry the liberal arts education for professional training. In 1952, the Bell Telephone company, one of the largest companies at the time, partnered with the University of Pennsylvania to create the Institute of Humanistic Studies for Executives as it recognized the need for managers adept at leading instead of merely obeying orders from above (Davis, 2010). Later in that decade two articles in the Harvard Business Review prophesied that many of the quantitative parts of the executive's job would be replaced by a computer and called for increase of liberal arts education for the breadth and depth of judgement needed to lead the modern business (Nelson, 1958; Pamp, 1955). Indeed, the authors extolled that the essence of the humanities could best aid in the development of creativity and a search for values. Recent thought leaders also argue for business education to embrace the liberal arts as a way to build a more equitable and sustainable economy in an increasingly complex world that requires broader knowledge than any single person commands. (Durden, 2003; Goldenberg, 2001; Johnston et al, 1988; MacDonald & Ramagliann, 2004).

Students themselves seem to recognize the importance of both the liberal and the practical. For more than 50 years the University of California Los Angeles (UCLA) has been surveying first year students. A comparison of student responses to reasons for going to college in 1971 and 2015 provides insight into shifts in perspectives. Over the last 25 years there has been a significant increase in the percentage of students whose decision to go to college was greatly impacted by both monetary (from 44.5% in 1971 to 69.9% in 2015) and intellectual development (62.7% in 1971 to 71.5% in 2015). Clearly, these motivations are not mutually exclusive. And yet student demand as shown in national major trends reveal students are demanding classes according to "what the global economy appears to need, rather than on what the college believes they need in order to develop into adults" (Logan & Curry, 2015, p. 72). College leaders must find creative ways to both prepare students for work and a meaningful life.

How Liberal Arts and Sciences Majors Fare in Employment, a report written by The Association of American Colleges and Universities in 2014, used data from U.S. Census Bureau's American Community Survey covering the years 2010 to 2011 to investigate the career impact of a Liberal Arts and Science education (Humphreys & Kelly, 2014). The report reveals that the initial earnings gap between bachelor's degree holders in humanities or social sciences with pre-professional/professional not only closes but reverses by peak earning years (56-60 years of age). However, some of this reversal is attributed to the propensity for humanities and social science majors to pursue advanced graduate degrees.

Still, business is now the largest undergraduate major in the United States (Neem, 2019). Business education is dynamic and evolving. It is far removed from the historical business college of the early 20th century teaching narrowly specialized classes. Many curriculums are shifting from the assumption that financial gain should be the sole motivator of behavior and instead focusing on the social value of business in a broader context. The interconnectedness of today's social-media world is holding businesses to higher ethical standards than ever before so that the shareholder is no longer the only constituent but now all stakeholders from consumers to employees to the environment matter. In fact, this year's Business Roundtable of almost 200 chief executives, including the leaders of Apple, Pepsi and Walmart, met this summer to reimagine the role of business in society to one that focuses on more than just shareholder value (Gelles & Yaffe-Bellany, 2019).

In discussing Purdue University's Gallup-Purdue Index survey of college graduates, President Mitch Daniels said, "Our survey clearly indicated that it wasn't so much where you go to college as much as it is how you go to college — what you extract from the campus experience. Students and their families are making a significant investment in college, and it should be done with eyes wide open" (Gallup-Perdue, 2014). Unfortunately, when it comes to work interest and purpose well-being the same Gallup-Purdue Index reveals that business graduates fall behind graduates in other disciplines (Marken, 2020). By holding to each end of the rope, college educators can help to create graduates who are full of business knowledge but not lacking the art of business or the wholistic sense of economy in society.

A global pandemic and societal unrest highlight how important it is for a country to have citizens that can adapt and have flexible minds while considering the impact of actions in the communities they live and work. Our world has perhaps never experienced such an increasing number of wicked problems with multiple conflicting stakeholders. Diversity of thought in economy is more important than ever so we can identify the questions worth asking. Basic job-performance skills are necessary but not sufficient. Students, and by extension employees, benefit from being able to think critically and creatively. Perhaps the most effective business curriculum is intrinsically liberal in the approach to teaching rather than a subset of disciplines. Business programs and liberal education when viewed as complements for a holistic education produce a type of employee the market values. This perspective is substantiated by the results of this corpus linguistics analysis of a mini-corpus of job descriptions. The methodology used to create and analyze this corpus is presented in the following section.

METHODOLOGY

Corpus linguistic approaches allow one to establish patterns in language usage which can be investigated quantitatively and qualitatively (Krennmayr, 2015). Richards and Pilcher (2016) noted that it is generally accepted that, "the key way that corpora answer questions is through their affordability to generate frequency counts of words, multi-word phrases or stylistic occurrences" (p. A125). When constructing a corpus, one confronts a decision related to size. Larger corpora provide more data, and the results tend to be more robust and generalizable. However, smaller corpora are quicker to construct. Ultimately, the corpus size depends on the research questions being asked and the types of insights desired (Brezina, 2018). A mini-corpus (Banks, 2005) was considered appropriate here since the intent of this study is simply to ascertain what types of skills frequently occur in business management job postings. The use of a mini-corpus is acceptable if value can be obtained through its analysis (Anthony, 2013). The corpus for this study was constructed using the following protocol.

A researcher-developed corpus was built from compiled job descriptions from a search conducted at Google Careers (https://careers.google.com/jobs/results/) on 27 November 2020. The search parameters were on the term *business manager*, limited to the geographic region of the United States and those jobs which require a bachelor's degree. As such, these parameters provide a substantial delimitation for the study. More specifically, the corpus was constructed to narrowly focus on the types of job skills desired from college graduates in the United States upon entering the business world. Consequently, the results are of potential value to business schools as they develop, assess and refine their curricula. Once the corpus was created thematic analysis of bigrams was conducted along with an analysis of collocations. A little context if useful for each of these elements.

Words and phrases contain insight into the content of texts. N-grams allow one to specify the desired length of phrase one intends to analyze. Such units of analysis could be a unigram (e.g., *work*, *management*), a bigram (*hard work*, *management team*) or a larger phrase consisting of n-words (Selmeczy & Dobbins, 2013). Research from D'hondt, Verberne, Koster and Boves (2013) indicated that "classifiers trained on combinations of unigrams and n-grams composed of at most three words performed better than classifiers that only use unigrams; no improvement as obtained when using larger n-grams" (p. 757). This holds implications for methodological approach. As they subsequently noted, "because trigrams are sparser than bigrams, most of the subsequent research has focused on optimizing the combination of unigrams and bigrams" (D'hondt et al., p. 757). As such, bigrams and unigrams in the form of collocates to a selected key word form the basis of analysis for this study. Once these words and phrases were obtained, they were analyzed and aggregated based on emergent themes. The approach used for the thematic analysis is presented next.

Thematic analysis seeks to establish conceptual recurrences which emerge across multiple data sources (Nairn, 2020). Such an approach seeks to make sense of information by creating a semantic structure which enables one to see how individual pieces of information assemble together. Once assembled one is able to then assess similarities and differences in terms of thematic density, usage and interrelation. The approach to thematic analysis used for this study was similar to that used by Mumtaz and Saqulian (2020). Initial themes were identified and compared. When thematic differences were identified, each was discussed thoroughly and subsequently resolved through consensus. The themes were analyzed in terms of density (e.g., number of bigrams contained within each theme). With these elements provisionally established, it is useful to describe the specific aspects of corpus creation and analytic techniques.

#LancsBox 5.1.2 (http://corpora.lancs.ac.uk/lancsbox/) was used to create and analyze this mini-corpus focused on business job requirements in the United States (Brezina, Weill-Tessier & McEnery, 2020). The bigrams and collocations were calculated consistent with the internal protocol resident in the software (Brezina, McEnery & Wattam, 2015). Once the initial results were generated an external refinement protocol was adopted to narrow the analytic focus to the essential insights. A list of 127 common words (e.g., *you, it, what*) was used to bring attention to those terms which can be considered frequently occurring but generally uncommon. The assessment of bigrams was conducted in terms of relative frequency of these uncommon, but frequently occurring bigrams. To be included in the final results, a bigram had to occur at least 2 times per 10K words. The resulting bigrams were then aggregated into emergent themes. Only those bigrams considered to be directly related to liberal arts education were focused upon for comment and exploration in the results section. A similar approach was adopted for the analysis of collocations.

The collocations were those words which were appeared within a span of five words to the left or the right of the search term *business*. The threshold value for the collocates was those values with a t-statistic greater than 3. Using the z-score approximation (which is reasonably appropriate given the number of observations) a t-statistic greater than 3 is over a 99% confidence level. As such, this cutoff provides a reasonable threshold for avoiding spurious associations. Like the bigrams, the list of collocations was reduced by omitting common words. Similarly, the list of collocations was assessed for terms which are generally associated with a liberal arts education. Collectively, the bigrams and collocations provide evidence that is suggestive that a liberal arts education is of value for business management and execution within the United States. This insight is developed more fully in the results section of this chapter.

RESULTS

As established in the literature review, the synergetic intersection of a business major with a liberal arts education is important to examine. The methodology section outlined the approached utilized to identify key words and bigrams across two hundred Google job announcements. After an exhaustive textual analysis of these job postings using the key word search 'business manager' in the 'United States,' there were several key findings that can suggest a unique and positive role for liberal arts in conjunction with business majors.

While it is important to distinguish that a liberal arts business degree isn't necessarily better than one from a state school, degrees from a liberal arts school provide individuals with a niche skillset that many employers value. An important aspect of a liberal arts education is the integration across disciplines with a focus on critical and creative thinking. Traditionally, business programs from state schools focus on depth and skill development in specific areas such as accounting, finance, marketing, statistics or management. While both forms of education are important and provide a foundation for a successful career, business programs from liberal art colleges have an inherent advantage in developing the integrated, creative skills that employers seek.

For the purposes of this chapter, a textual analysis on the two hundred Google job announcements using the descriptions and responsibilities was accomplished with a more in-depth analysis specifically on the bigrams and collocates. The mini-corpus consisted of 70,746 tokens and 3,943 types, with a type-token ratio value of 0.056. A summary of the bigram analysis in provided in Table 1.

Table 1. A Summary of Key Bigram Themes

Key Themes	Number of Bigrams	% of Total
Business, Management & Teams	69	55%
Data/Tech/Engineering	30	24%
Customer Focus	15	12%
Liberal Arts	12	10%
Total	**126**	**100%**

Not surprisingly, the majority of bigrams (55%) fall under the broad theme of business, management and teams. Among the bigrams for this category were: *business growth*, *business objectives*, *execution cycle*, *identifying risks* and *supply chain*. Along with the customer focus theme (12%), these are areas in which public universities and liberal arts colleges could provide business-focused education comparably well. Bigrams for the customer focus theme included, among others, the phrases: *customer care*, *customer solutions*, *internal customers* and *user experience*. Often liberal arts colleges do not have robust engineering programs; therefore, the data/tech/engineering category was not considered in this analysis. So, for business applications which are engineering-based or infused, this is an area in which public universities could hold a competitive advantage. The last theme, liberal arts (10%), provides the bigrams which are collectively suggestive of the unique role that liberal arts colleges can fill when offering business majors. Among the bigrams included in the area were: *complex multi-disciplinary*, *innovative solutions*, *multi-disciplinary project* and *unique problem*.

At 10%, the special and unique contribution of liberal arts-based business majors is certainly niche; however, these skills and perspectives are potentially among the more complex, challenging and rewarding within applied business. These insights are amplified further through the results of the assessment of collocates. Using the key word "business" as an anchor, collocates, which were in this case words within plus or minus five words of the key search term, were identified. Within a liberal arts context, there were several words that appeared with the word 'business': connecting, create, critical, cross-functional, insights, and understand.

After sorting out common English words (e.g., at, for, before, etc.), there were 89 uncommon collocates identified. Of these terms, six (~7%) were considered as being meaningfully connected to the learning outcomes generally associated with a liberal arts education. These terms will be explored in greater detail. One of the collocates that appeared frequently was the word *connecting*. As liberal art colleges tend to emphasize a broader education with exposure across more disciplines, connecting with both people and specialty areas are embedded in the educational composition. Employers such as Google, rely on this unique skillset to help them bridge the gap between many of their focus areas and business entities. Liberal arts colleges should focus on enhancing this unique skillset of connecting and encourage students to expand and build upon it specifically when looking for a job.

Another collocate that is essential to discuss in the context of liberal art college advantage is the word *create*. Being able to create or develop a product or idea was highlighted as an important skill that companies specifically Google search for when hiring. Liberal arts colleges pride themselves in teaching students to create and develop ideas through their educational approach. Often in more traditional, state schools, creativity is reserved for courses focusing on innovation, product development, or strategy and not necessarily embedded as a key aspect of general education courses.

Critique can likely be considered the *sine qua non* of a liberal arts education. As such, the word *critical* could be considered the quintessential collocate to highlight from this analysis. One of the key benefits of higher education is the ability to think critically and this is especially true for business managers. This concept of critically thinking is more apparent with a liberal arts education as many of the courses are designed to incorporate a critical thinking approach. Additionally, the exposure to a wide variety of subjects gives students a broader context in which to critically think as well as provides them with more approaches to tackle problems and find solutions. Typically, more traditional, public universities encourage students to think rationally and logically within a single, business context. By having a more extensive context from various types of courses, liberal arts business students can more critically think and contribute to problems perhaps differently.

Another collocate word that benefits from a liberal arts college approach is *cross-functional.* As the world benefits more from globalization, being able to successfully work and contribute to a cross-functional team is imperative. More traditional business schools define cross-functional as different disciplines within a business context. As an example, a finance person, an HR specialist, a manager, and a marketing manager are considered on a cross-functional team. It could be argued that this is a narrow cross-functional team with similar methods and approaches. Within a liberal arts college context, business students learn to work cross-functionally across many different specialties and majors, which is better suited for the expansive demands faced by a business manager. This approach contributes to a broader sense of working on a cross-functional team and perhaps enables students to be better equipped to deal with and consolidate disparate views.

Insights is another collocate worthy of discussion. From the job announcements, Google is searching for employees who can form insights. Much like the ability to critically think, insights tend to be broader and more comprehensive for liberal art college business students as they draw on many different disciplines and specialties. For example, business schools at public universities teach identifying insights, but it is from a business context. Liberal art college business students have the ability to draw insights from among other disciplines, the arts, languages and sciences. This key difference in insights should be expanded upon and highlighted within liberal art colleges since it's critical for a business manager.

Lastly, the collocate *understand* is pivotal to explore form a liberal arts college perspective. Liberal art college business students are expected and encouraged to take courses across a broader spectrum of disciplines. As students learn about language, cultures, arts and sciences they are learning the important act of understanding defined holistically. Often, they are better prepared to understand new ideas and concepts that may not be within a traditional business manager role. The term business manager tends to have a broad, generic description; therefore, it is imperative for them to have an understanding of many disciplines to build a strong team.

Going forward, it is important for liberal arts colleges to embrace the niche skills identified through this analysis of job search bigrams and collocates and develop them further into their curriculum. Equally important, liberal arts colleges should communicate the significance of these distinctive skills to students for job searches and interviews. As more people obtain college degrees and compete in the job market, differentiating oneself will become increasingly crucial to obtaining desired jobs.

While a liberal arts business degree isn't necessarily better than one from a public university, degrees from a liberal arts school provide business students with a broader, more comprehensive skillset that employers, specifically Google, search for when hiring. The focus between liberal arts and traditional business schools are slightly different and that difference creates unique opportunities for both liberal arts and public university students to create a comparative advantage in the job market. The inherent advantages and niche skills provided through a liberal arts education should be further developed by both the liberal arts college and students. Through this textual analysis, several key benefits of a liberal arts school business education were highlighted providing areas for these schools to focus on and further develop with students.

CONCLUSION

After a thorough corpus linguistic analysis of Google job postings for a *business manager* in the United States, several key benefits of a liberal arts education were identified. One of the key benefits is that attributes for which Google is searching are an inherent part of a liberal arts curriculum. These attributes include, but aren't limited to terms such as, *connecting*, *create*, *critical*, *cross-functional*, *insights*, and *understand*. Many of the skills Google searches for in professionals are those intangible attributes that are inherent within a liberal arts education. The intrinsic synergy created from a liberal arts education with a business degree provides an individual with a competitive advantage, which is rooted in critical, creative thinking and strong communication skills.

There were several limitations to this study. This study did not look at benefits or advantages of public universities. While there are certainly advantages to this type of education, it was not considered as part of this study and only the benefits of liberal arts colleges were considered. Additionally, only Google as an employer was considered for the purposes of this analysis. There may be small nuances in the skills and knowledge employers search for in future employees. Broadening the search to job postings across the spectrum of potential employers of business graduates would likely provide additional insight. Lastly, only one day of job postings was analyzed. While such a snapshot is not inherently problematic it is possible that such a limited collection of job postings could skew the understanding of the types of characteristics for which employers search.

Future studies in this area could include a more comprehensive analysis of advantages produced by both liberal arts and public colleges. This analysis is only from the perspective of a liberal arts college and did not look at those collocates that could benefit from a public education. Additionally, this analysis could be expanded to a wider spectrum of the job market and include more companies, locations, as well as more job postings across time. There could be nuances between what companies search for that might have importance to graduates searching for specific attributes in a future employer. While liberal arts colleges may require more general education courses than public colleges; this does not mean that liberal arts graduates will integrate these different disciplines in their jobs.

As liberal art colleges further develop curriculum, it is important that they embrace the niche skills identified through this analysis. This analysis illustrated how Google searches for future employees with these niche skills. Almost of the same importance as embracing this competitive advantage from a curriculum perspective, it is important for liberal arts colleges to communicate the significance of these differentiable skills to students and help them prepare for the post-graduation job market. The ability to differentiate oneself from competition is an important consideration for graduates to obtain jobs. It is important to state that while liberal arts business degrees aren't necessarily better in quality than those degrees obtained from other schools, the type of education liberal art schools potentially allow business students to have a broader, more comprehensive foundation that top employers search for in their hiring decisions. Going forward in an uncertain environment, liberal arts colleges should embrace inherent advantage such as these niche skills discussed in this analysis and future develop them with students.

REFERENCES

Anthony, L. (2013). A critical look at software tools in corpus linguistics*. *Linguistic Review*, *30*(2), 141–161.

Arsene, M. (2012). The Living Tradition: Liberal Arts Education. The U.S. Campus Heritage. *East-West Cultural Passage*, *12*(2), 106–114.

Banks, D. (2005). The case of Perrin and Thomson: An example of the use of a mini-corpus. *English for Specific Purposes*, *24*(2), 201–211. doi:10.1016/j.esp.2004.01.001

Bevins, S. (2012). STeM: Moving the Liberal arts education into the 21st century. *Technology and Engineering Teacher*, *71*(4), 10–13.

Brezina, V. (2018). *Statistics in Corpus Linguistics: A Practical Guide*. Cambridge University Press. doi:10.1017/9781316410899

Brezina, V., McEnery, T., & Wattam, S. (2015). Collocations in context: A new perspective on collocation networks. *International Journal of Corpus Linguistics*, *20*(2), 139–173. doi:10.1075/ijcl.20.2.01bre

Brezina, V., Weill-Tessier, P., & McEnery, A. (2020). *#LancsBox v.5.x* [software]. Available at: http://corpora.lancs.ac.uk/lancsbox

Coolidge, C. (1925). *Address to the American Society of Newspaper Editors*. https://www.presidency.ucsb.edu/documents/address-the-american-society-newspaper-editors-washington-dc

D'hondt, E., Verberne, S., Koster, C., & Boves, L. (2013). Text representations for patent classification. *Computational Linguistics*, *39*(3), 755–775. doi:10.1162/COLI_a_00149

Davis, W. (2010, June 16). The 'Learning Knights' of Bell Telephone. *The New York Times*.

Dewey, J. (1944). The Latter Works. *The American Scholar*, *14*(3), 276-80.

Durden, W. G. (2003). The Liberal Arts as a Bulwark of Business Education. *The Chronicle of Higher Education*, *49*(45).

Eagan, K., Stolzenberg, E. B., Ramirez, J. J., Aragon, M. C., Suchard, M. R., & Rios-Aguilar, C. R. (2016). The American Freshman: Fifty-Year Trends 1966-2015. Higher Education Research Institute Graduate School of Education & Information Studies University of California, Los Angeles.

Fain, P. (2019, August 2). Philosophy degrees and sales jobs. *Inside Higher Ed*. Retrieved from: https://www.insidehighered.com/news/2019/08/02/new-data-track-graduates-six-popular-majors-through-their-first-three-jobs

Fischer, K. (2012, February 5). Bucking cultural norms, Asia tries liberal arts. *Chronicle of Higher Education*. Retrieved from http://chronicle.com/article/Bucking-Cultural-Norms-Asia/130667/

Gallup-Perdue. (2014). *Measuring the Most Important Outcomes of Higher Education*. Retrieved July 01, 2020, from https://www.purdue.edu/newsroom/gallup/

Gelles, D., & Yaffe-bellany, D. (2019, August 19). *Shareholder Value Is No Longer Everything, Top C.E.O.s Say*. Retrieved from https://www.nytimes.com/2019/08/19/business/business-roundtable-ceos-corporations.html?action=click&module=TopStories&pgtype=Homepage

Goldenberg, E. N. (2001). Teaching Key Competencies in Liberal Arts Education. *New Directions for Teaching and Learning*, *2001*(85), 85. doi:10.1002/tl.2

Graham, P. A. (1974). *Community and Class in American Education, 1865–1918*. Wiley.

Grey, C. (2001). Re-imagining relevance: A response to Starkey and Madan. *British Journal of Management*, *12*(Special Issue), S27–S32. doi:10.1111/1467-8551.12.s1.3

Humphreys, D., & Kelly, P. (2014). *How Liberal Arts and Sciences Majors Fare in Employment: a report on earnings and long-term career paths*. Association of American Colleges and Universities.

Jiang, Y. G., & Guo, H. (2017). Transcending the nature of refinement: The policy development on liberal arts education in China. *Chinese Education & Society*, *50*(3), 268–283. doi:10.1080/10611932.2017.1331009

Johnston, J. S., Shaman, S., & Zemsky, R. (1988). *Unfinished Design: The Humanities and Social Sciences in Undergraduate Engineering Education*. Association of American Colleges.

Kimball, B. A. (1995). *Orators and philosophers: A history of the idea of liberal education*. College Entrance Board Examination.

Koblik, S., & Graubard, S. (2000). *The distinctively American: Residential liberal arts colleges*. Transaction Publishers.

Krennmayr, T. (2015). What corpus linguistics can tell us about metaphor in use in newspaper texts. *Journalism Studies*, *16*(4), 530–546. doi:10.1080/1461670X.2014.937155

Logan, J., & Curry, J. (2015). A Liberal Arts Education: Global Trends and Challenges. *Christian Higher Education*, *14*(1-2), 66–79. doi:10.1080/15363759.2015.973344

MacDonald, D. B., & Ramagliann, J. A. (2004). Teaching International Business Law: A Liberal Arts Perspective. *Journal of Legal Studies Education*, *22*(1), 39–64. doi:10.1111/j.1744-1722.2004.00010.x

Marken, A. (2020, January 5). *In U.S., Business Grads Lag Other Majors in Work Interest*. Retrieved July 01, 2020, from https://news.gallup.com/poll/177638/business-grads-lag-majors-work-interest.aspx

Mumtaz, N., & Saqulain, G. (2020). Hospital and health administrator level barriers and priorities for national neonatal hearing screening in Pakistan: A thematic analysis. *Pakistan Journal of Medical Sciences*, *36*(5), 1036–1041. doi:10.12669/pjms.36.5.1965 PMID:32704285

Nairn, A. (2020). What is with all the hate? A thematic analysis of New Zealanders' attitudes to the human rights commission's "Give nothing to racism" social marketing campaign. *New Zealand Sociology*, *35*(1), 97–122.

Neem, J. (2019, August 13). *Abolish the Business Major!* Retrieved from https://www.chronicle.com/interactives/2019-08-13-abolish-the-business-major

Nelson, C. A. (1958). Liberal Arts in Management. *Harvard Business Review*, *36*, 91–99.

Pamp, F. (1955). Liberal Arts as Training for Business. *Harvard Business Review*, *33*(3), 42–50.

Pew Research Center. (2016). *The State of American Jobs: How the shifting economic landscape is reshaping work and society and affecting the way people think about the skills and training they need to get ahead*. Author.

Richards, K., & Pilcher, N. (2016). An individual subjectivist critique of the use of corpus linguistics to inform pedagogical materials. *Dialogic Pedagogy*, *4*, A122–A141. doi:10.5195/dpj.2016.163

Schneider, A. B. (2015). The liberal arts in business education: Perspectives of a multi-time CEO. *Jesuit Higher Education*, *4*(2), 108–116.

Selmeczy, D., & Dobbins, I. G. (2014). Relating the content and confidence of recognition judgments. *Journal of Experimental Psychology. Learning, Memory, and Cognition*, *40*(1), 66–85. doi:10.1037/a0034059 PMID:23957366

Simmons, E. L. (2018). Vocation for planetary citizenship: Lutheran liberal arts education in the Anthropocene. *Dialog*, *57*(2), 99–106. doi:10.1111/dial.12389

Stoddard, G. (1974). *The outlook for American education*. Southern Illinois University Press.

Styhre, A. (2009). The phantom menace: Conducting practitioner-informed research without losing academic liberties. In J. W. Cox, T. G. LeTrent-Jones, M. Voronov, & D. Weir (Eds.), *Critical management studies at work: Negotiating tensions between theory and practice* (pp. 29–39). Edward Elgar Publishing. doi:10.4337/9781848449497.00009

Chapter 11
Prelude of Investment:
Freshman's Dilemma in the Insurance Sector Investments

Shilpi Gupta
https://orcid.org/0000-0003-4382-3616
Amity University, Chhattisgarh, India

Monica Shrivastava
Shri Shankaracharya Technical Campus (SSGI), Chhattisgarh, India

ABSTRACT

The government of India has taken multiple economic reforms such as Jan Dhan Yojna, UPI, demonetization, and digitalization moving India towards a cashless economy. The financial landscape of India has undergone a radical change with the insurance sector bearing the torch on the road of exponential growth. The insurance penetration recorded was only 3.69% in 2017. The shockingly low participation of individuals indicated the existence of challenges that need to be addressed. The first section of the chapter explores the various factors creating a dilemma for investment in the insurance sector. The other sections of the chapter focus on the current scenario of Insurance investment and the paradigm shift in the perception of customers towards insurance products. The basic purpose is to implement systems thinking of looking at the whole and holistic picture with the highest inclusion towards nation-building and improving the penetration percentage and density of insurance in India.

INTRODUCTION

In "Rigiveda" we find the term "Yogakshema Bahamayam" which is more or less akin to the well-being and security of people. This makes it clear that the traces of sharing the future losses were available even in ancient India (S. M. Jha, 2003). Though there is a long history in the legacy of India, the Insurance sector lacks behind from other economies in terms of penetration and density. The basic reason can be attributed to the perception of Insurance as a tax saving instrument since times immemorial in India specially. There is always a dilemmic situation in one's mind about whether to invest in Insurance

DOI: 10.4018/978-1-7998-3964-4.ch011

securities or save the money for future? What should be the motivation to pay high premiums when easy and better options of increasing money at a guaranteed pace is available in the banks in the form of saving's account, Recurring deposit and fixed deposits? If one doesn't encounter the future contingency like accidents, the high premiums paid on insurance is lost.

Let's view this situation from a different perspective. The primary aim of forecasting the contingencies is identification of full range of possibilities, not just based on illusory certainties. Whether a specific prediction of accident, incurable ailment, retirement benefits actually turns out to be accurate or not is only a part of the unreleased picture. The most difficult thing in this world is an attempt to forecast the future and more difficult is controlling the uncertainties hidden in it (Paul Saffo, Six Rules for Effective Forecasting, HBR, July-August 2007). Insurance is a way to handle the hidden uncertainties.

As per a survey of Business Standard the investment of India in health care is only 5% compared to the developed countries. The low figure indicates the immense potential present in India. (Saraswathy, "Business Standard, March, 20, 2013).

Insurance is a necessity in the countries where there is a system of single earning member and no provision for social security. But Insurance sector has its own series of challenges and hurdles. This factor makes India the most favourable market for Insurance Investments (Sadhak, 2009). Insurance reduces the social liability of a developing country like India by increasing the aura of risk coverage and financial security. There is no amount of fixed requirement of money that can be kept aside for future use by the family members. Growth of money and return on investment is an important criterion in the society. After LPG in 1991, a milestone was achieved when the nation decided to privatise the industry along with requisite regulations. The Insurance sector in India has completed a full circle from being an open competitive market to nationalisation and back to a liberalised market again (Chaudhury & Das.2014).

The opportunity cost and the trade-offs between money and insecurity is too high. This is a problem every individual specially the novice investors face. While investing in the Insurance securities of the stock market only the theoretical part and perspective is considered but the problem lies in interpretation or perception of the theory inhaled subject to the varying mind set of the people involved.

The psychology of the individuals is never constant in every similar situation. A human mind always does the multitasking of thinking and evaluating multiple factors at a time based on their current situation and future expectations.

But things are changing. The 21st century known as the knowledge era brought with it a boom in the minds of investors in the Insurance sector. Overall insurance penetration reached 3.69% in 2017 from 2.71% in 2001 but this is still very low compared to the global market as indicated in figure1. A lot changed though very slowly and a lot is still to be changed in the next 5 years. The thought process of the matured investors of the stock market in the Insurance sector needs to be challenged and redirected to assure the novice players of a clean, clear and bias free market where the process is more important than the outcomes. Many of the novice participants exhibit a poor intuitive judgement of how co-variation of risk and return affects portfolio, acting as if diversifying always is the safest option even when facing contradictory evidence in the data (Hedesström, 2006). With small and dedicated effort we need to increase the participation of youngsters in the Insurance sector investments. Whether one is financially literate or not, every citizen has the objective of profit and wealth maximization in his own parlance for a better and secured future. This is a high time to think in a positive way, follow the interconnected grid of development and travel the road of Insurance Investment ahead with trust and confidence challenging the internal biases as well as external blocks existing in the system.

Figure 1. Comparison of insurance penetration in India with respect to the world
Source: IRDAI, Annual Report (2016-17).

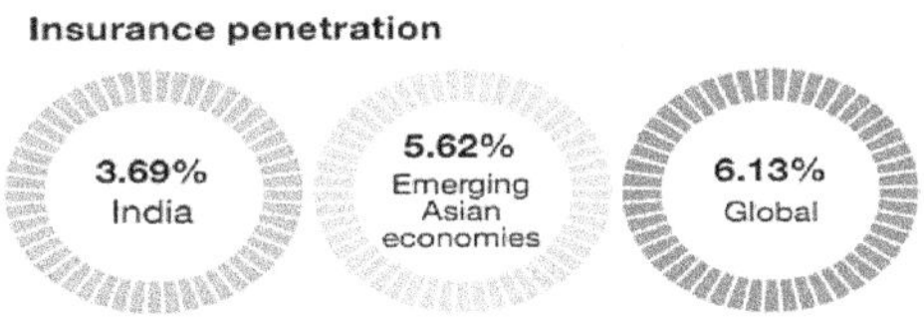

The abysmal level of insurance culture in developing economies has attracted relative interests among researchers and practitioners alike (Udry, 1994). The S&P 500 market share of around 80% is running by intangibles, and still Insurance is limited to physical assets only. A well-developed insurance sector can provide long-term funds for infrastructure development (Charumathi, 2012)

THEORETICAL PERSPECTIVES: INDUSTRIAL REVOLUTION THE FATHER OF INSURANCE

History is proof to the fact that protection from risk and uncertainty is the basic tendency of human beings. Since time immemorial the industries provided financial security in the form of death protection, accidental protection and retirement benefits. So it can be said that Industrial revolution was the father of Insurance. Insurance is not based on just outgrowing number of investors at any time but built on preservation of trust and lifelong mutual benefits (PWC Report,2019,Competing in a new age of insurance).

The insurance industry in India is expected to reach US$ 280 billion by 2020. Life insurance industry in the country is expected grow by 12-15 per cent annually for the next three to five years. In life insurance segment, private players had a market share of 25.29 per cent in new business in FY19 (IBEF, October 2019).

Life insurance in India has a huge growth potential. By 2020, it is expected to account for 35 per cent of India's total savings. (IBEF, December 2019). Amazon India is also expected to enter the insurance market as an agent.

Harnessing the Growth Potential in India- The Untapped Market

The year 2020 will mark huge increase in the young workforce of the population. There is no set social and financial security available to the individuals. The life Insurance sector can extend its arms to them and provide financial security. This factor acts as a catalyst for the Insurance companies to increase its market growth and market share with a touch of social cause which is beneficial to all. The demographic dividends as a result of young population awareness for investment in Insurance can act as a boom for the infrastructural growth and capital market mobility. The Indian insurance market is poised for strong growth, with the insurable population expected to touch 750 million in 2020, and life expectancy reaching 74 years(India Insurance—Going from Teens to Twenties, BCG-FICCI, October 2019).

The present population of India as on 2020 is approximated to be 138 Crores (Worldometer, Jan 1, 2020).The percentage of population in rural India and Urban India is 65.5% and 34.5% (Worldometer Report, 2019).The insurance penetration of India as on 2017 was 3.69%. The target was to increase the insurance penetration by 2020 as there is existence of huge untapped potential in the Indian insurance market and the low consumption level depicts an alarming situation in India. The low consumption level has been attributed to many psychological, social, Economic, political and other factors. Yaari (1965) and Hakansson (1969) confirm that if the insurance penetration and insurance density margins are low, it is an indication that the overall consumption of insurance is low. Many countries in Asia are experiencing a rapid growth in the population of middle class which gives a favourable market dynamics to the Insurance Investment Industry.

Insurance: The Game Changer for the Indian Economy

The Insurance is considered to be the game changer as it is a social tool for counteracting the unforeseen losses and contingencies existing in the society by diverting the gross premiums collected towards capital investments and development of the Indian economy. The forecasted value of the Insurance premium collected till FY 2019 is depicted in Figure 2.

Figure 2. Forecasted value of the insurance premium collected till FY 2019
Source: IBEF December 2019

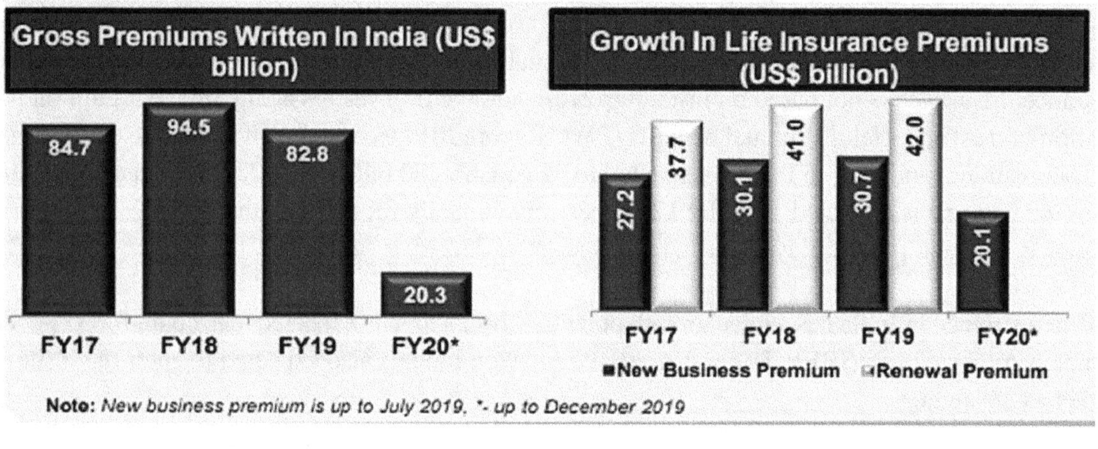

The figure 2 explains the growing New Insurance Business Premium in FY 2019 as 30.7 (US $ billion) compared to Renewal premium of 42 (US $ billion) depicting a steady rise in Insurance Investments in the near future due to increased awareness amongst the people of India. The FY 20 till December 2019 showed collection of New business premium of 20.1(US $ billion). The huge collection of money in the form of premiums can act as a lubricating agent for the capital formation in the economy.

The growth of Insurance industry is critical to the exponential advancement of a developing economy like India because the underlying assets covered in insurance is long term capital investments which can be channelized to Infrastructural growth of a country.

Secondly it is the only investment which covers the pool of risk of individuals, corporates and smoothening the growth of the country. Hence multiple benefits are reaped from a single drug.

Demographic shifts around the world have exposed the Insurance investments to both risk and opportunities. In India the expected life span has reached 74 years due to medical advancements. The increasing life style diseases due to food culture and sedentary work culture amongst the middle class have opened the door to the Insurance Industry. The birth rates and ever growing middle class population has in turn supported the necessity of Insurance Investment.

The governments have withdrawn pension and retirement benefits. In this way addressing the high expected life span and the gaps to meet the requirements related to it, the Insurance Industry can actually add to the growth of new products and secure the future of the individuals. This will largely contribute to the development of the Indian economy both in terms of Infrastructure and liquidity.

The Insurance is a game changer as it acts as a value addition to the financial service sector by employing a more dynamic workforce, technologically skilled agents, loyalty and trust based industry. It promotes demand and supply flexibility, customized and tailor made investment opportunities and above all working for the best transformative customer experiences increasing the innovativeness and changing the face of the Indian economy.

Swimming Through the Ocean: The Fundamental Challenges

The term insurance itself boggles the mind of a common man. The basic reason for this is that the novice investor has to invest money for the future benefit which is a bit scary because people believe in following the outcome more than the process. Moreover people follow the outcome more than the process. After globalization and privatization the whole world became one market and millions of investment opportunities were lying in line. The whole world could be accessed by the click of a mouse. Secondly the huge asymmetry in the information channels and perception misquoting also poses a major threat to the Insurance Industry. Every industry is working for customer satisfaction. The tangible immediate benefits are visible in a short span of time but the advantages of Insurance intangible is difficult to be forecasted rationally.

The 21st century is often quoted as the IT age. The information technology is capable of bringing the masses under one roof with a common purpose. As a result the transmission of information is at a lightning speed thus generating awareness and knowledge. The knowledge can be both helpful and harmful for the Industry and the product as the absorption of the information and its decoding is quite personal to the individual and the information can be perceived in multiple ways. Every investor is keen on a quality and service centric product.

The Behavioural finance field has captured the market in the last 2 decades as cognitive behaviour and emotions of an individual effect to a large extent the investment pattern of individuals and Insurance sector is an integral part of it. Behavioural finance combines behavioural and cognitive psychological theory with conventional economics and finance to understand decisions investors make (Ackert and Deaves, 2009)

The investment behaviour has its bed rock foundations on the inherent attitudes of the people based on many psychological, social, economic, political and miscellaneous factors which directly or indirectly affect their decision making ability. The widespread view is that attitudes are complex systems made up of three components. These are; cognitive component referring to the person's thoughts, affective component referring to person's feelings, and the conative component referring to the person's behavioural tendencies (Ajzen and Fishbein, 1980).According to Shiller (2000), the Efficient Market Hypothesis is based on total rational behaviour of people, processing of all available information and maximization of expected utility perfectly. All these factors pose challenges to the Insurance Industry. If the winds of these biases can be adjusted to the right direction, it can provide immense opportunities for the betterment of the novice and matured investors and also for the economy. The common short term view of the novel investors to make short term luring profits needs to be changed from a very early stage of investment.

Factors Responsible for the Promotion of Investment Dilemma in the Insurance Sector Investment

Psychological Biases That Contributes Towards Insurance Sector Investment Dilemmas

As per Expected Utility theory investors are rational and use 100% of the information available in the market. But the market crashes in the stock market falsifies this belief. Every novel investors as well as matured investors search for instant gratification and quick results. Now a days 20-20 cricket matches are preferred over five day test match due to the fast results within 3 hours. This is an integral part of psychological bias. As per the Research done by Ritter (2003), behavioural finance is based on the foundation of psychology which enumerates that human decision making capability and processes are subject to several cognitive illusions. These illusions are divided into two groups: illusions caused by heuristic decision process and illusions rooted from the adoption of mental frames grouped in the prospect theory (Waweru et al. 2008)

The behavioural factors were divided into 2 categories by Kahneman and Tversky .They were the pioneers for studying the factors belonging to heuristics theory and introducing three factors namely representativeness, availability bias, and anchoring (Kahneman and Tversky, 1974). Waweru et al. also list two factors under heuristic theory named Gambler's fallacy and Overconfidence into heuristic theory (Waweru et al. 2008).

Prospect theory focuses on subjective decision-making influenced by the investors' value system, whereas Expected Utility Theory concentrates on investors' rational expectations (Filbeck, et al. 2005). Prospect theory describes some states of mind affecting an individual's decision-making processes including Regret aversion, Loss aversion and mental accounting (Waweru et al. 2008).

Heuristic Factors

Heuristic Biases are based on a simple psychology of referring to last 10 years question paper for preparation of 12thboard exams. Why? Because it will reduce the burden of going through each and every topic mentioned in the book. Can it be called a mental shortcut? Yes. It is the framing of the mind which reduces the judgement making procedure in complex situations. This is exactly what happens in Insurance Investment decisions. The new investors are always in a dilemma of investing in the most profit earning scheme of Insurance, or the security whose information is available easily, or an Insurance security that promises for the highest returns, or the Insurance that has topped the charts of NSE and BSE in the last few years or the belief that the investor himself is the best judge for creating portfolio suited to his needs based on one's limited knowledge. The biases related to the above mentioned issues are discussed in the following points.

1. **Representativeness**: Investors are aware of the benefits of investing in diversified portfolios as suggested by Harry Markowitz. Every novel investors have framed a particular goal in mind like high return, more coverage, growth, safety, amount of premium, lock in period, tenure of premium,

relaxation in terms and conditions, etc. The novice investors before investing in insurance attach their decisions to the brand image, star companies, representation of the securities or the past performance of the company. But is this always true? No, all these factors can be misrepresented by enhanced promotional and advertisement activities. The frequency of availability of information about an Insurance company enhances the Representativeness bias in the minds of the investors. This in turn can lead to a mismatch between the objectives and outcomes of investment by a novice investors in the long run.

2. **Availability Bias**: The front page advertisements in any newspaper and magazine demands a high premium compared to the other pages as human beings tend to rely on the most readily information available. For example, if the advertisement of Life Insurance investments is shown in social media covering rare and broad spectrum of diseases then the novice investors tend to believe that this is the best investment ever for future without a deep insight or knowledge of the other insurance investments matching their twin requirement of risk and return. The new and in some cases the matured investors do not bother to go through the fundamental analysis of the company related to the share. This misguides the investor and hence increases the misjudgement of the market. IRDA makes it compulsory to publish the annual reports of insurance companies with details regarding financial claims met, Gross premiums during the year, contribution to GDP etc through IFRS standards to have more transparency and reliability of the market.
3. **Anchoring:** Humans always have the tendency to attach a thought to some reference point. Especially the novel investors try to refer to a previous experience or the experience of somebody else and base their decisions on that. The fresh investors always look for a benchmark of figures and attach their expectation to it without considering the fundamental and technical details of the sectorial investments. An Insurance security which is priced at 90 and a novel investor thinks it to be overpriced. The moment the price sweeps down to 65, the investors immediately jump to buy the share without further analysis and patience for the price to come down. Was it because they believed that the price will not fall down further? No it was because they anchored to the 90 value as an anchor price and the moment it fell down they bought it without further inspection of the industry performance or the analysis of the company's statistics. This tendency of rooting to a benchmarked figure can cause harm to the market and the investor both in the long run.
4. **Overconfidence:** Investment platforms are a cakewalk for very few people. Many a times there is a huge unexpected gain in the very first investment. That boosts the confidence of the new investors of his perfect and accurate knowledge of the market. But as it is said that the first win can be a just due to sheer luck. Some investors build the notion of knowing the market very well after the first achievement. But the fact remains that the market is always volatile and very difficult to be forecasted. As Warren Buffet said the market can never be forecasted. Overconfidence leads to more trading, over ranking of his performance and a false vibration in the market. This is a common mistake in many Insurance investments as they are usually long term and the fruits of it are borne after a long period, so proper analysis of the company and the industry is a must for target achievement in terms of risk and reward.
5. **Gambler's Fallacy:** This biasness is based on the fact that if an insurance security has topped the chart for 2 years, the highest probability of its excelling in the coming years is also attached to it. This can lead to serious consequences in some cases. For example if ICICI prudential has topped the chart from 2016-2018, does it assure that it will continue the legacy in the coming years too. No? The past performance or the event can in no way guarantee or govern the probability of oc-

currence of any game in the future. The market cannot be predicted for even 24 hours, left aside the coming year. The new investors lose the sight of probability in occurrence of an event and take the recent experience as the trend.

6. **Confirmation Bias:** Every person has got an inherent tendency of forming an opinion in their mind about a financial product and filtering information provided from various sources as per their convenience. For example investment in stock market is like walking in a Jurassic park. The new investors in the beginning are sceptical of their investment and so they resort to the views of others. In gathering the views and information from others an image is formed in their minds with its imaginary characteristics which may or may not be true. Further analysis only leads to confirmation of the beliefs an investor has formed side lining the fundamental analysis and some real negative facts about the investment. The new investors become selective listeners and retainers to the facts depicted. For example if an investor is willing to invest in HDFC Life Insurance, he will accept all the supporting documents and information related to its positivity and filter the negatives and shortcomings related to it in his portfolio construction. This can affect the return of the investor and effect market perceptions. The learning comes the hard way at the cost of market fluctuations and personal investment instability.

Prospect Factors

Since time immemorial humans have attached more weight to expected gains than expected losses. This is a bias which has affected the Insurance industry hugely. Every new investor tries to judge any investment based on short term gains or in terms of expected utility from a reference point rather than absolute measurable gains. This thought process gives rise to the following biases.

1. **Regret Aversion:** Every human act in the best of interests but still sometimes their decision and judgements go wrong. This is because decisions originate from an emotional space deep inside. The insurance forecasting is based on individuals framing and reframing of buying too little if a large loss is to be incurred or too much insurance that is never used. Thus, anticipation of regret should prevent an individual from making extreme decisions (Braun, M., & Muermann, A. (2004). The novice investors try to reduce the feeling of regret by making decisions based on emotions.
2. **Loss Aversion:** Warren Buffet said "if you cannot stand 50% paper loss on your stock, stay away from the markets." Prospect theory predicts that novel as well as many experienced investors suffer from bounded rationality to such an extent that they view term life insurance as non-rewarding and risky investment. The investor believes that if any bad incident doesn't happen within the specified time, they will lose on the Insurance premium amount. The investors usually have a myopic vision. These investors prefer to invest in a safer option like fixed deposits or savings account or government securities where the return is fixed compared to the uncertainty of events in future. This act usually is the result of the hidden sentiment that the pain of a loss is double as powerful as the pleasure of the profit.
3. **Mental Accounting:** t is "the set of cognitive operations used by individuals and households to organize, evaluate, and keep track of financial activities" (Thaler, 1999). Mental accounting is the categorization of funds in the minds of individuals based on commonalities. Every new investor categorizes funds based on their origin. Investors divide their income into regular income or sudden gains. The first psychology of human is to meet the daily necessities by their regular income.

Insurance is a far option for the new investors prioritizing the tangible assets like house, car and others. The expected life of an individual in India has increased to 74 years, so it is believed that there is ample time for investing in Insurance funds and pension funds. But what is not forecasted are the uncertainties, the lifestyle ailments, the problem of dependents and many more in the list which is not dependant on the demographics like age and present condition of an investor? Mental accounting creates potential mismatch in the timing of when categorization of income and expenses are done and when consumption opportunities arise that can lead to suboptimal financial decision making.

Environmental Factors Conducive for the Growth of Insurance Investments Dilemma

The world is suffering from life style diseases like Diabetes, blood pressure, stress and obesity. These ailments are increasing in India also at an alarming rate. In the last 10 years cancer has been the talk of the town. Its rate has increased approximately by 33% in the world in the last 10 years. In spite of health awareness and well-being campaigns conducted frequently in India, the ecosystem of life insurance and health insurance is sparsely penetrated. The young workforce concentrates more on the tangible investments than the intangible necessary commitments. The following environmental factors add to the dilemma of the new investors in the Insurance investments.

1. **Epidemics/Pandemics**: Several uncontrollable natural disasters, epidemics and Pandemics have a huge impact on Insurance investments for inducing a dilemma in the minds of investors. COVID-19 had a huge impact in India. No Insurance Policy had a straight cover on epidemics and infectious diseases. The common man thinks it as a negative aspect of Insurance investment without considering the fact that human mentality is conservative. If the investors needs to be convinced for the investments in the regular uncertainties of life like accidents and ailments then how is it possible to convince them to invest in once in a decade probable and rare occurrence of infectious and deadly pandemics. Humans have a very conservative attitude towards loss prediction and optimistic attitude towards gain probability.
2. **Shifting Demographics**: The changing demographics are a challenge for the Insurance Sector. The demographic factors have a huge impact on Investments. In India the growing middle class and the new young workforce is in need of multiplication of money as well as security. But this class has a pre-set allocation of funds in their minds in the various compartments of life. This mind-set acts as a challenge as well as a catalyst for the growth of Insurance investment in a developing country like India. The dilemma of investing in Insurance for future benefit is always less appealing than consuming money for immediate satisfaction and entertainment. This creates a sense of following of the crowd in the middle class population for comparison of standard of living and the tangible factor always excels. Another demographic factor is ageing which impacts the insurance investment. The aged population increases the dependency ratio in the Indian society creating a need for Insurance coverage.
3. **Basic amenities**: The physical environment of investors has a huge impact on their Investment outlook. Any person surviving on the basic minimum of daily wages, struggling for basic education and livelihood cannot invest in Insurance. The basic needs always cover the major concern. This acts as an important factor in demotivating the fresh investors in investing in this sector and firstly

building the empire of a decent lifestyle. The rising cost of living in the metro and smart cities of India adds on to their dilemma for investing in an unforeseen contingency.

Ethical Aspects for Promoting Dilemma in Insurance Investment

1. **Ambition beyond profit**: The Insurance industry has complicated terms and terminologies as they cover a wide spectrum of ailments and deal with different individuals with different expectations. The Insurance agents sometimes play with the investment sentiments of new investors to meet their personal targets, take advantage of unawareness of the investors for achieving their short term benefits and achieve a prestigious position. This unethical attitude of insurance agents breaks the trust of common man in Insurance companies. The integrity of the insurance agents paves way for promotion of Investment in the Insurance sector.
2. **Lack of Confidence in the existing system**: The huge and lengthy paperwork involved in claiming insurance is another factor which effects the Investment in this industry and creates a fear in the minds of investors of the complications involved in the whole process. The system of encashment in times of hardship and need and duration of follow up is scary to the investors.

Economic Factors Facilitating Insurance Sector Investments Dilemmas

Economic conditions can impact the decision making power of novel investors drastically and in turn affect the demand for Insurance products. Insurance companies make money by investing premium payments and hence they help in the maintenance of the liquidity and infrastructural development of the country. But some factors creates dilemma in the minds of the investors.

1. **Cost Efficiency (Cost optimization):** The recession faced by the economy increases the cost of Insurance investments and reduces the R & D capital allocated to Insurance Innovation. The less innovativeness and high premium claimed increases the dilemma and bias in the minds of individual investors for further claims and hence reduces their trust and investment in this Industry. Lack of innovation in the Insurance product front makes the transformative customers less attracted to this sector.
2. **Low Interest Rates**: The constantly low interest rates prevailing in the present scenario has a negative impact on the Insurance Investment in the minds of fresher's as it results in less annuity and return. Insurance is expected to yield more proportionate returns based on the length of investment and amount of premium paid. The lowering credit quality motivates the novel investors to look for alternative investment avenues for using their excess liquidity to invest in illiquid assets that yields more returns than the existing interest rates. Very low interest rates diverts the wealth from Insurance Industry to other basic avenues as it leads to higher cost of annuities and creates a withdrawing attitude in investors.

Political Factors Stimulating Dilemma in Insurance Investment

The change in government regulation has a huge and long lasting impact on fresher's action plan of investment. Insurance is basically considered as a push product. Many young people invest in Insurance for claiming tax deduction in Income tax Return. Hence it serves the dual purpose of safety with savings. The biggest example is the "Black Monday" in May 2004, when the markets dropped down by 700 points as the BJP went out of power and Congress took over. There was nothing wrong with the performance of the companies whose stock prices crashed. But it was just the reflexivity of investors at work without rationalization.

1. **Partnership role in pension Reforms:** As governments pull back from providing pensions and the retirement savings gap grows, the investors develop a distrust in the ideology of investment even when insurance companies assure about providing packages of pension and other retirement benefits. This dilemma is a product of the uncertainty and longevity of the private players related to the safety of novel and matured investors. This dilemma discourages the innovation on the product front.

Technological Factors Enhancing the Dilemma for Insurance Sector Investments

1. **Fin-tech:** The Customized Development of product models with the help of Digitalization has changed the perception of the world towards industries and the banking and financial services are equally affected by it. The financial technology popularly known as the fin-tech is facilitating or hindering the minds of the Investors is still unexplainable and unexplored. The digital platform of investment adds to the insecurity of new investors due to operational and confidentiality issues. The variety of products available by the click of a mouse may confuse the investor about the short term and long term returns.
2. **Unified Platform**: Lack of Localized experiences adds on to the dilemma of investing in the Insurance sector. India is an agricultural country and more than 70% of the population is concentrated in the rural areas. The lack of awareness and understandability by the uneducated creates a hinge in the minds of the rural people regarding private sector players and their preferences. The unified common platform misguides the less educated or financially less literate people. The Ketan Parekh K10 stocks are a learning example for this. Mr. Parekh was considered the pied piper of technology stocks. He had a huge investor following but when the technology boom ended it became evident that the funds were diverted from different banks. This led to information cascades in the novel investors' minds and more irrationality in the rural people.
3. **Telematics**: Telematics is the convergence of telecommunication and informatics. Many Insurance companies are using this technology in the vehicle industry in the form of apps. India is an agricultural country and the financial inclusion is in its growth stage. The rural areas where electricity is a problem, can internet and the big jargons be expected to be operated influentially? No. These technologies create a detrimental attitude to investment making it an urban class luxury.

Miscellaneous Factors

1. **Customer Expectations:** The insurance agents appointed by the Insurance companies are unable to inculcate a sense of trust and loyalty in the minds of investors. An element of doubt remains hidden in the targeted customers. The dilemma of conglomeration and doubt lowers the customer expectations in many parameters. The right talent of agents appointed can altogether satisfy the customer expectations in the long run and this real deal can reduce the dilemma in the new investors.

2. **Financial Literacy**: Financial literacy can be explained as the wisdom to know how money matters work and the most judicious utilisation of money. India accommodates 17.5% of the world's population and as per recent survey nearly 76% of its adult population does not understand even the basic financial concepts (http://www.assocham.org).

The Insurance is one of the basic area in which every individual in urban and rural population needs to invest for the future road untraveled. Multiplication of money is important but retaining and utilization of the money earned is far more important. The novice investors are affected by the views and perceptions of the people who are not very financially literate, who takes decisions based on impulse and are overconfident of their market knowledge. Besides the new investors are unable to plot a graph and trend of risk return trade-off

SOCIETAL OUTREACH OF INSURANCE: THE CURRENT SCENARIO

The key sector stocks of Insurance in the last few years are GIC, HDFC Standard Life, ICICI Lombard, ICICI Prudential, SBI Life Insurance and The New India Assurance. The whole world has witnessed a customer's dominance in terms of shift of power from product centric Industries to customer centric industries. Figure 3 depicts the change in customer perception from just informed decisions to tailored products and possession of the products immediately. The importance of information, speed, agility and 200% satisfaction from the product is the demand of the day.

Figure 3. The changing perception of the customer towards Insurance

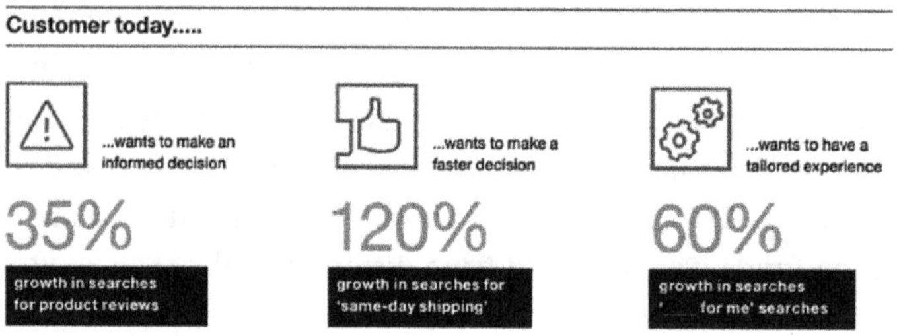

The insurance industry is presently facing huge economic turbulence due to low interest rates, fluctuating equity market and strict regulations imposed by the government. To a certain extent the psychology and perspectives of the individual investors also pose huge challenge to the Insurance Industry. With the help of digitalization every consumer wants to access the financial platform through mobiles and computers. Presently there are various websites providing online database for comparison between different policies and companies like bankbazaar.com, policybazaar.com. They compare the prices of various products along with the offerings, technological developments and future prospects changing the purview of investments. The insurance demands vary between matured and emerging markets and hence different strategies are needed to target the customers of the two different markets. The consumer preferences needs to be more customized and tailor made to align local demands with national demands for encouraging Insurance investment.

The Foreign direct Investment limit for the Insurance sector has been increased from 26% to 49% in 2014which has increased the capital investment in this sector with a motive of rise in overall performance and profitability. The urge to compete globally makes the insurance services more technology friendly increases the employment ratio in India and results in innovative products for demand in the world market

In Union budget 2020, Finance Minister, Nirmala Sitharaman, proposed that Life Insurance Companies existing for more than 10 years can go public through issue of IPO.LIC proposed to issue shares through IPO to meet its highest disinvestment target of $2.1 trillion. Fitch argues that once LIC gets listed, it will be subject to stringent disclosure requirements stipulated by the SEBI. "This will create a strong culture of compliance and accountability within the insurer. We think the insurer's investment allocation decisions will be rationalised too, as major investment decisions could be subjected to additional scrutiny and approvals," Fitch said.(ETBFSI, February 26,2020)

The information bombardment presently through various social media platforms like Facebook, blogs, company websites and their annual reports, Linkedin, twitter and many more makes the investors proactive and confused. The information is searched and sometimes interpreted in a distorted and asymmetrical manner. But the present generation is updated about the latest global trends.

The Indian Insurance market is on its success journey travelling the road from monopolistic and regulated environment to customer driven market behaviour. This has paved the way to innovative and competitive products in this dynamic market. The initiative of the government in permitting FDI from 26% to 49% changed the landscape of investment in insurance. The exposure to global market brought about a revolution in the Indian Insurance industry and to maintain a competitive edge at parlance with international standards the megatrends were set.

The present consumers of Insurance products demand for customized policies addressing their needs and candid policies which can be easily understood by the common man. The convenience of claiming the returns with less complexities and the time lag in expecting the return is at the top of their priority list.

Figure 4 depicts the expected market growth of Insurance forecasted by IRDA in 2019. Till FY 2025 the CAGR is expected to grow by 14%-15%. The Compounded annual growth rate is the rate at which initial investment grows till the maturity period when the principal is compounded annually. The above prediction is a very positive indication for the Insurance industry as it will lead to infrastructural growth, capital formation and fulfil the cause of security and growth targeting the masses.

SETTING THE CONTEXT–THE PARADIGM SHIFT: THE ROAD AHEAD

The internet penetration in India is rising day by day. The number of users in India was 429 million in 2017 which is expected to increase by 829 million in 2021 (Assocham-PwC study Report 2019). The rate of increase is expected to be 17.9%, which will consist mainly of the young population, which is going to influence all the industries of India and Insurance will also not remain untouched by it. So their needs to be a paradigm shift in the offerings and financial landscape of India with the customer base. This will facilitate

1. **New Transformative model for Insurance:** The traditional age old offerings of insurance products altered, as the financial landscape has changed in India. Consolidation of Insurance companies with changes in Investment strategies to handle risk is the need of the hour. The present generation believes in conquering the world with just a mobile and click of a mouse. So Digitally enabled risk

prevention policies and schemes through mobile can increase the investment and consumption of the Insurance Sector. In India. Fin-tech is already providing financial budgeting to the individuals by controlling and tracking their income and expenditure in their pre-set categories as per their personal risk return desirability.

2. **Developing a Value chain:** A value chain can be developed by outsourcing of the services of insurance when and wherever necessary to reduce the cost and increase the accessibility of rural and remote areas so that no one is left untouched under the financial inclusion objective of the government. A strict control needs to be kept on the value chain for effective and transparent rendering of the services for the benefit of all. The agents forming an integral part of the value chain should be ethically and socially responsible for their loyalty and accountability.
3. **Differentiation:** Customised insurance policies are difficult to be framed by regulatory agencies but differentiation of Insurance products with respect to demographics, need covering of basic ailments and income groups can take the Insurance products to a different platform. The work has already started and taken to a different level by many companies. In March 2017, HDFC Life in collaboration with Haptik, has announced the launch of the country's first life insurance chat-box which will help the customer as a financial guide to aid them to choose the most suitable plans befitting their needs. The rate of grievance handling of investors can be speeded up in the digital platform.

Figure 4. The expected CAGR growth in the Insurance market of India
Source: IRDAI, Company Public Disclosures, BCG analysis, 2019

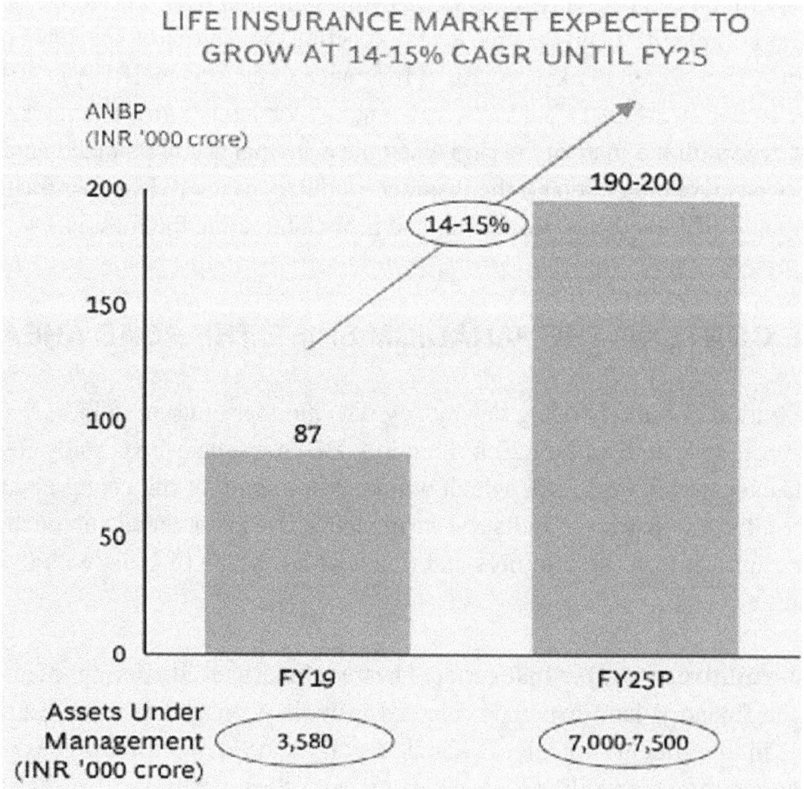

4. **Group Insurance and Micro Insurance:** Financial Inclusion is the motto of the government for the development of the whole economy. The government is working towards all round development of each and every individual in India and Group Insurance and Micro insurance are the important steps taken towards it. Micro insurance is a privilege to the poor where they can pay just for the insurance they actually need. The affordability and penetration of insurance increases in the economy even in the rural areas. The group insurance covers the mass of employees of an organization or group of members at a reduced cost. This increase the retention and loyalty of the professionals, employees and the insured towards their organization .Number of lives covered under private life insurance companies reached 36.20 million up to June 2018, showing year-on-year growth rate of 27.48(IBEF, July 2019).
5. **Life Insurance companies going public:** As per Budget 2020, the finance minister announced that LIC will go public and get listed. This will facilitate transparency and accountability of the firm and attract more foreign investment resulting further in foreign capital inflows which will act as a boom to the Indian Insurance Industry and the Indian economy. The listing of Insurance securities will upgrade the standards of disclosure and make them more answerable to the investors and society increasing the faith of the new investors in all parlances.
6. **Digitalization:** Though a difficult task but creating personalized customer experiences for the rural and urban people on different parameters is necessary as the accessibility and preferences are different in the two distinct worlds. Digitalization is a key catalyser of disintermediation and allows insurers to meaningfully engage and influence customer experience directly. It serves all the facilities at the tip of hand. Figure 5 depicts the difference between the digitally matured and digitally un-matured investors. The digitally matured investors go for online survey and online buying but the digitally less matured investors still avail the offline route of buying Insurance as per the survey of BCG-FICCI 2019.
1. **Parametric Insurance:** The parametric insurance provides coverage for a predefined uncontrollable event that can cause a loss in future drastically. This step increases the belief of the investors in the insurance investments. The present case of COVID-19 is the best example to explain this concept. Since December 2019 the virus had spread its wings in China. It was highly expected to be spread to all parts of the world due to continuous migration of people. The Informal surveillance systems of the country which aggregates the official surveillance reports and informs about the future pandemics, epidemics and unpredictable infections could have avoided the spread by restricting the movability of people and goods from one place to another. This step creates the bed rock of growth decreasing the loss to the economy.

ROLE OF REGULATORY BODIES IN BRIDGING THE GAP

To bridge the gap between expectations and reality the help of Regulatory bodies is mandatory. The segmentation of insurance investors by regulatory bodies helps in proper formulation of Insurance products customised to the needs and requirements at the local level. The financial intermediaries needs to focus primarily on the customers interests and their changing life cycle modulating the Insurance product services and coverage to the extent possible

Figure 5. Research and Purchase behaviour of Insurance in 2019
Source: BCG-FICCI Insurance survey (2019)

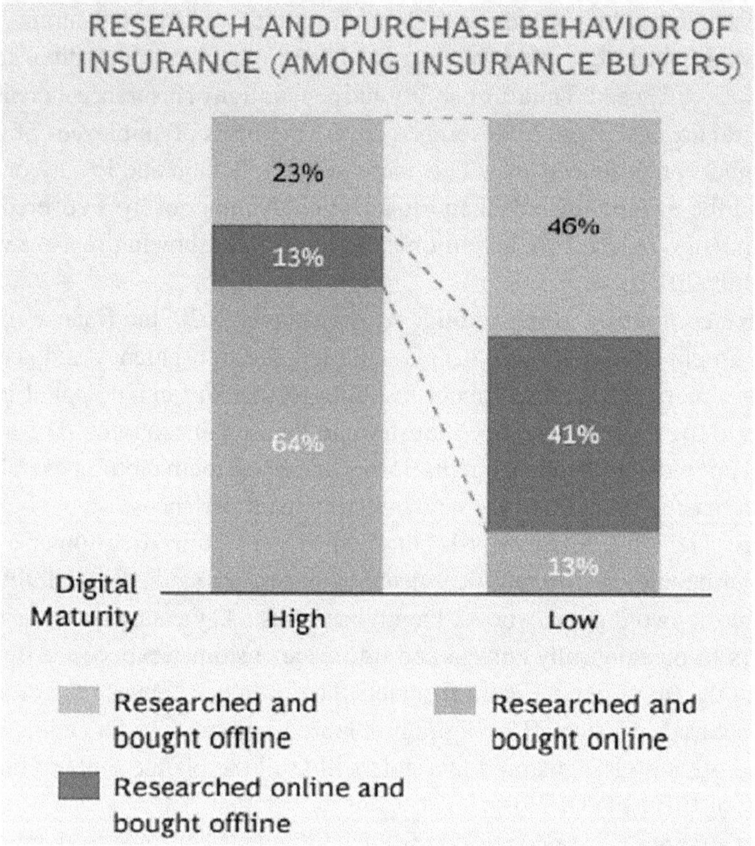

Stimulation experiments for risk profiling of the target customers for Insurance Investment based on demographics, dependants, needs and expectations are to be figured out. The experiments are costly to perform but have a long lasting result in the minds of investors and contribute on the societal platform by building trust amongst the naïve investors of this sector.

The higher Education department should make the basic techniques of investments and their application in the stock market a compulsory subject in higher schools and colleges as the students of today are the prospective investors or financial consultants of the future. The inherent biases cannot be removed from an individual but keeping aside the biases and using the non-compliance and uncontrollable factors as points of judgement towards the optimum decision making in the Insurance sector can be promoted for a balanced economy.

The withdrawal of pension and other retirement benefits by the government has opened new avenues to create differentiation of instruments amongst the private players of the Insurance Industry. The focus of every investor is optimal earning and a comfortable life after retirement and this psychology can easily be used to motivate investment in this direction with a transparent and customised policy.

Collaborative workshops and customer awareness programmes of the government with the private institutions, banks, universities, NGO's, media and influential personalities reflecting the vision and mission can be a step towards capturing the attention of the investors and getting different viewpoints for customization, modernization and diversification of the existing plans and policies.

Blogs, forums and other social media should be used as a medium of customer education and imbibe a sense of right choice of Insurance investment promoting early purchase and reasonable premium payments suited to the needs and pockets of the investors.

The government of India had already taken multiple economic reforms such as Jan Dhan Yojna, UPI, demonetization, digitalization and Linkage of Aadhar with the bank accounts and moving India towards a cashless economy. These reforms will initiate a megatrend for gearing up the new age technology.

The establishment of strong and supporting baseline levels of education, sanitation, health and nutrition by the government will be a step towards a better India. The control levels during implementation needs to be strict and regulated for proper utilization of resources and increasing the per capita income of people.

Extension of hands from all perspectives will give India an edge in the Insurance sector investment as depicted in Figure 6 and forecasted by IBEF report in December 2019.

Figure 6. Forecasted growth in GDP per capita at current prices
Source: IBEF December 2019

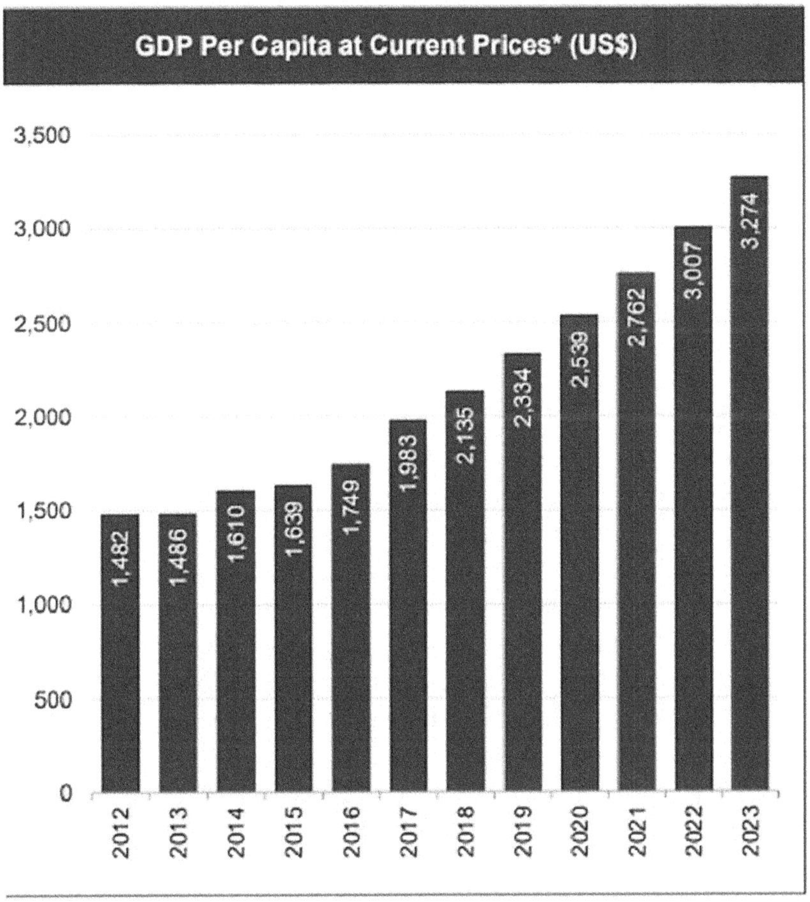

Source: IBEF December 2019

Figure 6 indicates that bridging the gap with the help of the regulatory bodies can improve the per capita GDP of India. As per the forecasting of IBEF, the Per capita GDP of India is expected to reach US$3274 in 2023 from US$2135 in 2018. This is only possible if the white spaces of the economy are addressed by seeking opportunities and combating the challenges.

THE UNTOLD STORY

The latest innovations in tune with globalization have totally changed the financial landscape and scenario of Indian consumers. But till date no firm conclusion have been drawn regarding the improved financial behaviour and judgement capability enhancement in the common man due to the changed and improved situations. Many anti-technology oriented consumers specially the senior citizens for whose well -being approximately 30% of the Insurance offers are devoted, it's still a toss whether for them technology is an aid or a curse.

Industrial revolution is the father of Insurance as it came into light predominantly after that. The technological advancements of the information age in an agricultural dominant country like India where two-thirds workforce is involved in agricultural and allied business, may prove sometimes to be disruptive if not taken in the right stride.

CONCLUSION

The Indian Insurance sector is on the road of exponential growth. The growth will not be materialized if the insurers are not aware of the various dilemmas in their minds, the developments in the world, the need for the basic insurance and of the emerging innovative and customised trends taking place in the Insurance Industry of India. An organized and well developed stock market is essential for promoting economic growth by channelizing the savings and lubricating the flow of funds. The investors are more exposed to foreign investments and the risk is diversified converting savings to investments. If the products can be customised and designed for the most rational person and the most perfect market, then we design for nobody in the world. But if we instead use behavioural science to decode the thinking capability and direction of investors the results can be really amazing. Besides the psychological factors the other factors like technology, environment, legal, economic and political factors needs to hold hands in shaping the perspective of the individual investors towards insurance investments. The insights of the advanced technology will make the uninsurable risks also insurable in the future. Though the concept of digitalization is given so much importance today but the implementation and execution of the business strategies will be very difficult. The epicentre of the Insurance Industry is the people no matter how developed the technology becomes. The core purpose of Insurance is serving the needs of the people. The government acts as a bridge in filling the gap for future strategic planning. The government through its regulatory lens must promote only those companies which provide a clear purpose to the young generation by articulating the importance of insurance needs to the society. The reinforcement and building of trust amongst the general public is the foundation of this sector. Just technology and automation is not enough to remove the inefficiencies prevalent in the society or removing of dilemmas from the minds of individuals. Customers just need simple Insurance products with stress on human centric design compared to product design in the insurance Industry. No matter what facts and figures are presented for the shortfall of the Insurance Investment, we as individuals are solely responsible for removing these in conjunction with the government, realizing that Insurance is not just a tax saving, money channelizing or avenue for growing funds but Insurance has the sole purpose of serving the mankind. Insurance companies were highly involved in the rat race of short term profit making and growth and this led to collection of high commissions but resulted in misrepresentation of the basic product.

The knowledge and expertise of the financial consultants and advisors is to be propelled for reviewing an investor's portfolio and planning for a better one. Some really very serious and regulated efforts are to be initiated by the insurers to remove the loopholes and providing the required services to the clients building a sense of loyalty and trust. The big challenge presently is to search the right talent as financial intermediaries as they are the key element for quality service and satisfaction to the customer. The organizations of today need to be more dynamic than the volatile market conditions. The competitive edge of the business is to be enhanced by differentiation of the product at the local level also known as globalization. After the Listing of Insurance products in the stock market through IPO's the diversity of shareholders will increase in the industry with the young workforce bearing the torch of expectations and satisfaction.

There are many industries which serves the dual purpose of profitability with a social cause. The pulse of the investors is the basic foundation for the growth and development of this industry and also for our nation. Technology should never rule the pulse of a country else the sight of social responsibility will be lost. Technology has acted as a bedrock foundation for spreading the information, increasing the operational efficiencies and touching lives with care and trust.

To manage in this world of volatility customer centricity is the core value. It is basically an imperative tool for each and every individual for meeting the future uncertainties of our lives and providing a shield to our loved ones. We all need to join hands and work for the transformation and growth in a holistic way. Insurance is the lighthouse of the 21st century.

REVIEW QUESTIONS

1. What are the challenges imposed by traditional financial theories in getting a proper insight of the Investment psychology of an individual?
2. Technology is a blessing or a curse in facilitating the behaviour of investments of individuals?
3. "Low Financial literacy rate is a major cause of the various biases in individuals." Explain the statement.
4. What are the techniques to promote suitable investment culture in India?
5. What are the various innovations needed in the Insurance Industries to attract the investors?
6. Can customised Insurance portfolios be constructed for rural and urban people separately depending on their demands?
7. What are the various social outreach programmes run by the government of India for welfare of the masses and promoting investment in the Insurance sector?

REFERENCES

Ackert, L., & Deaves, R. (2009). *Behavioral finance: Psychology, decision-making, and markets*. South-Western Pub.

Ajzen, I., & Fishbein, M. A. (1980). Attitudes and the Attitude–Behavior Reasoned Automatic Processes. Published. In W. Stroebe & M. Hewstone (Eds.), *European Review of Social Psychology*. John Wiley & Sons.

Black, K., & Skipper, H. D. (2000). *Life and Health Insurance*. Prentice-Hall.

Braun, M., & Muermann, A. (2004). The impact of regret on the demand for insurance. *The Journal of Risk and Insurance*, *71*(4), 737–767. doi:10.1111/j.0022-4367.2004.00110.x

Charumathi, B. (2012). On the determinants of profitability of Indian life insurers: An empirical study. *Proceedings of the World Congress on Engineering, WCE 2012.*

Chaudhury, S. K., & Das, S. K. (2014). Trends in marketing of new insurance schemes and distribution: An empirical study on Indian life insurance sector. *Journal of Business and Technology (Dhaka)*, *9*(2), 61–81. doi:10.3329/jbt.v9i2.26196

Filbeck, G., Hatfield, P., & Horvath, P. (2005). Risk aversion and personality type. *Journal of Behavioral Finance*, *6*(4), 170–180. doi:10.120715427579jpfm0604_1

Hakansson, N. H. (1969). Optimal Investment and Consumption Strategies under Risk, and Under Uncertain Lifetime and Insurance. *International Economic Review*, *10*(3), 443–466. doi:10.2307/2525655

Harvard Business Review. (2007). *Six rules for effective forecasting*. Available at www.Hbr.org/2007/07.htmlAccessed on 11/04/2020

Hedesström, T. M. (2006). *The psychology of diversification: Novice investors' ability to spread risks*. Academic Press.

IBEF. (2018). *Indian Insurance Industry Analysis*. Retrieved from https://www.ibef.org/archives/industry/insurancereports/indian-insurance-industry-analysis-september-2018

IRDAI. (2017). *Annual report 2016-17*. Author.

Jha, S. M. (2003). Services Marketing. Himalaya Publishing House.

PWC. (2019). Competing *in a new age of insurance: How India is adopting emerging technologies. CII.* Available at https://www.pwc.in/assets/pdfs/consulting/financial-services/competing-in-a-new-age-of-insurance.pdf

PwC and CII. (2018). *Leveraging customer persona for insurance in a digital era*. Available at https://www.pwc.in/assets/pdfs/publications/2018/leveraging-customer-persona-for-insurance-in-a-digital-era.pdf

Ritter, R. J. (2003). Behavioral Finance. *Pacific Basin Finance Journal, 2*(14), 429-437.

Sadhak, H. (2009). *Life Insurance in India: Opportunities, Challenges and Strategic Perspective*. SAGE Publications India.

Sha, A., Mehrotra, P., & Marathe, A. (2019). *India Insurance going from teens to twenties.* Boston Consulting Group. Available at http://ficci.in/spdocument/23133/BCG-FICCI-Report-October-2019.PDF

Shiller, R. J. (2000). *Irrational Exuberance*. Princeton University Press.

Swiss Re Institute. (2018). *Sigma 03/2018: World insurance in 2017: solid, but mature life markets weigh on growth.* Available on https://www.swissre.com/institute/research/sigma-research/sigma-2018-03.html

Thaler, R. H. (1999). Mental accounting matters. *Journal of Behavioral Decision Making*, *12*(3), 183–206. doi:10.1002/(SICI)1099-0771(199909)12:3<183::AID-BDM318>3.0.CO;2-F

Think with Google report. (2018). https://www.thinkwithgoogle.com/consumer-insights/

Tversky, A., & Kahneman, D. (1974). Judgment under uncertainty: Heuristics and biases. *Science*, *185*(4157), 1124–1131. doi:10.1126cience.185.4157.1124 PMID:17835457

Udry, C. (1994). Risk and Insurance in a Rural Credit Market: An Empirical Investigation in Northern Nigeria. *The Review of Economic Studies*, *61*(3), 495–526. doi:10.2307/2297901

Waweru, N. M., Munyoki, E., & Uliana, E. (2008). The effects of behavioral factors in Nairobi Stock Exchange. *International Journal of Business and Emerging Markets*, *1*(1), 24–41. doi:10.1504/IJBEM.2008.019243

Yaari, M. E. (1965). Uncertain Lifetime, Life Insurance, and the Theory of the Consumer. *The Review of Economic Studies*, *32*(2), 137–150. doi:10.2307/2296058

Chapter 12
Driving Insights via Processes of Socioemotional Being and Becoming

Catherine Hayes
University of Sunderland, UK

Ian Corrie
University of Cumbria, UK

Toby Lloyd Rowland
Defence Medical Academy, UK

ABSTRACT

Being able to transcend disciplinarity in the development of effective strategies for the communication of insights in business is pivotal to progressive development and dynamic processes of change management. The unique cultural and situational specificity of military life has a long recognised and multifactorial impact on lives lived in active service, and veteran retirement is the focus of this chapter. This is highlighted via a consideration of how understanding the nature of 'self' is epistemologically determined by human capacity to make meaning of experience, to reflect on the pre-existing of historical memories, and perhaps, most significantly of all, to formulate a reflexive and proactive response to the future. The situated nature of military service provides the chapter with a means of examining the fundamental nature of knowledge and ways of knowing, interpretation, and processes of meaning making transcend several fields of individual knowledge, such as philosophy, social science, medical science, psychology, and faith.

INTRODUCTION

Being able to transcend disciplinarity in the development of effective strategies for the communication of insights in business is pivotal to progressive development and dynamic processes of change management. The unique cultural and situational specificity of military life has a long recognised and multifactorial

DOI: 10.4018/978-1-7998-3964-4.ch012

impact on lives lived in active service and veteran retirement (Cooper et al, 2018). There are reciprocal lessons from both business and the military which have a shared epistemological basis and as such a high degree of relevance to the communication of insights in business. Understanding the nature of 'self' is epistemologically determined by human capacity to make meaning of experience, to reflect on the pre-existing of historical memories, and perhaps, most significantly of all, to formulate a reflexive and proactive response to the future (Button, Jinkerson and Bryan, 2017). The situated nature of military service, is such that the fundamental nature of knowledge and ways of knowing, interpretation and processes of meaning making transcend several fields of individual knowledge, such as philosophy, social science, medical science, psychology and faith (Merriman et al, 2017). This chapter will embrace these potentially transferrable facets of praxis to drive discussion of how processes of socioemotional being and becoming can serve to potentially also improve insights in business settings.

The acquisition of knowledge pertaining to the self, forms the basis of epistemological debate which has endured across mankind for thousands of years (Muis, Chevrier and Singh, 2018). Providing a contextual and situational approach to understanding the complexity of military personnel and veteran perceptions of self will be the focus of this chapter rather than engaging in any deep philosophical debate of how, rather than why, knowledge is stored and accessed on a daily basis, and alongside this, how it has the potential to inform processes of immediate and long term decision making as a consequence of making meaning of experience (Campbell, 2018).

Military services have never been more in need of coping mechanisms that accommodate systemic inequity and the need to function effectively on both an individual and collective level (Olson, 2018; Rodd and Sanders, 2018). At the heart of the capacity to establish these coping mechanisms, is the need to address the emotional self in the military workplace (Conley, Durlak and Kirsch, 2015). Awareness of the concept of emotional intelligence has increased radically over the last decade (Kilgore, 2017; Garcia Zea et al, 2019). Intergenerational solidarity and understanding have never been at the fore of positive function across society in an array of differing contexts and correspondingly new approaches to supporting people in reflecting on their experiences have been developed and implemented (Williams-Klotz and Gansemer-Topf, 2017). Belying any holistic wellbeing, whether organisationally or individually, is mental health. As a consequence of this advocating, promoting and facilitating the positive health and wellbeing of staff has been identified as a key priority for address and sustained integration into educational and vocational training practice (Ghiya, 2019; Schonert-Reichl and Roeser, 2016).

The chapter serves to provide an insight into how understanding the concepts of cognition, metacognition and epistemic cognition can be used to frame and define how meaning making of military service, will be integrated, both at the point of experience and after active service is complete. Both are used to form the basis of what, in the longer term, have the potential to become the long-held assumptions and presuppositions usually surrounding internal and external life worlds. Being able to make sense of both is pivotal in supporting and addressing the issues with which military service personnel and veterans present across the societies they have served in active service.

The central aims of this chapter are threefold. Firstly, the authors have aimed to provide a theoretical rather than an applied approach to the context of business, which provides a backdrop of conceptual aspects worthy of consideration around the acquisition of knowledge and ways of knowing. Secondly, the authors aim to provide an insight into the integration of philosophical approaches into the facilitation of critical introspection and reflective practice. The third and final aim of the chapter is to increase an awareness of predisposing factors of a decline in the mental health and wellbeing of military service personnel and military veterans and to highlight the direct relevance of this to business contexts.

Shared Connections, Shared Perspectives and Shared Learning

Military and business identity have shared perspectives in relation to the universal complexity of organisational infrastructure, which forms the contextual basis for the development and operationalisation of culture, professional practice and governance. Considering different perspectives for those working in business is important if a degree of perspective on interprofessional and interpersonal relationships is to be understood from the perspective of risk, credibility and trust. Nowhere are these better typified than in a military setting where education and training form the basis of how relationships and interactions develop and shape the organisation as well as the relationships of those within it.

The Legitimacy of Military Epistemology

In relation to the social construction of reality, seminal historical research still informs how social constructionism has shaped and continues to shape understanding of how and why meaning making occurs at all (Burger and Luckmann, 1966). The context specificity of the military has the capacity in temporal terms, not only to influence the attitude and behaviour of personnel through the acquisition of habitual and learned behaviour but also to alter the psychological capacity of them to re-adjust back to civilian life as they become military veterans (Abraham et al, 2017). The long-held pre-suppositions and assumptions that accumulate via experiences in everyday life constitute the potential basis of interrelationships and effective communication with others that is either unhindered by epistemological bias or completely overshadowed by it (Gerken, 2017). Context specific language and discourse add further complexity to this, as meaning making is articulated, shared and disseminated (James, 2017). The notion of institutionalisation is apparent when personnel become so acclimatised to using similar (context specific) language and acceptable behaviours and attitudes become a social norm and expectation across working life in the military (Gibson et al, 2017). To educate personnel about this is the first mechanism to enacting positive change in relation to it but perhaps most importantly in the potential transferability understanding the significance of their insights to business practice.

Whilst current research has shifted the research landscape to the point where it is acceptable for analysis of social worlds to become commonplace, there has been limited study of the potential role of education and training in providing a protective mechanism for the future health and wellbeing of both active and military veterans. This chapter addresses this point and offers insight into mechanisms and approaches to supporting both and the contribution they could make during active duty and, subsequently, for the veteran population (Rukavishnikov and Pugh, 2018), many of which can be transferred to business contexts. Indeed, it is the legitimacy of military education and training schools which provides an ideal platform for the sharing of best practice in preparing, supporting and protecting the mental health and wellbeing of service men and women during the course of their military duties and the experiences they have within it (Sookermany, Meyer and Land, 2017). Traditional culture has also ensured that social structures have replaced accepted norms to such an extent that they are normalised in military contexts so that human constructions of reality are framed by new philosophical lenses. The most significant components of reality construction will be captured as a means of understanding how best knowledge might be progressively deconstructed as an integral part of critical introspection and reflexivity.

Since epistemology is an area of philosophy concerned with the nature and justification of knowledge in humans and features areas of liminal transdisciplinary between education, philosophy and psychology. King (2009) annotated the progressive development of students from Feldman and Newcomb's (1969) operational defining of the delineation between growth and change through a lens which provided clarity into how ability, capacity and capability of understanding could be temporally developed. The implicit link between this and the work of Mezirow (1990; 2000 and 2009) is that habits of mind are far more durable than points of view and that they are context specific in relation to the assumptions that guide their core decision making processes.

Contextual Backdrop

Facilitating the capacity of military personnel how to think rather than what to think as an integral part of their educational training has emerged as a consequence of a relatively recent recognition and value of challenging assumption and pre-supposition. This value emanates from the need to delineate perceived reality from actual reality and consequently the ascertainment of truth beyond that which can be regarded as only rationally valid instead of reflexively ascertained.

This paradigm shift in military education has largely been influenced by approaches in design thinking – an active process of integrating and discerning processes of reflexivity into complexity theory, again permitting a cognitively more flexible mechanism of delineating between truth and verisimilitude.

The context specificity of military education and training within the broad concept of institutionalism has dictated how the reflexive turn in military epistemology is becoming progressively operationalised across military praxis. Traditionally conscientious decision making, was by its very nature posited as something only to be judged through the lens of empiricism or objectivity. However, at a functional level the capacity to think intuitively often overrides capacity for rationalism and in this sense military epistemology sees a shift to the immediate integration of implicit, tacit or epistemic knowledge. Consolidating what is epistemic, with cognate knowledge of certainty rather than pre-supposition has become the keystone of assemblage theoretical perspectives on what constitutes both efficiency and efficacy in the context of military service and the critical thinking underpinning them.

HISTORICAL AND PHILOSOPHICAL PERSPECTIVES ON TRUTH

Establishing the truth in historical perspectives is illustrated widely across philosophy and academic literature, where the establishment of truth and being able to discern between actual rather than perceived reality has been posited as the central crux of rationalistic decision making for centuries. Within this, there was also the much later acknowledgement of how the emotional can override the rational, due to human conscience and capacity for reflexivity in action. However, the complexity of military service means these philosophical standpoints can be contested and debated as to whether the aim of military education and training is to reach a position of truth, or, rather, the best or least bad outcome in circumstances where lives are at stake. This demands much of military personnel making the decisions and their ability to act, under pressure, often with incomplete information and with lives very much at stake. Trying to identify a truth in military decision making is further complicated when an active and skilled enemy is involved, seeking to win victory by all the means at their disposal, including deception. In such circumstances it is absolutely imperative that a decision maker may actively choose to wait and delay a critical decision until more information or clarity is available or discernible. To remain inactive in such circumstances is the military equivalent of a mortal sin, as it invites the enemy to seize the initiative and gain a potentially decisive advantage. Military education and training seek to avoid this by linking the need to be decisive in uncertain circumstances, with the necessity for individual moral courage:

We must have the moral courage to make tough decisions in the face of uncertainty – and accept full responsibility for those decisions – when the natural inclination would be to postpone the decision pending more complete information. To delay action in an emergency because of incomplete information shows a lack of moral courage. We do not want to make rash decisions, but we must not squander opportunities while trying to gain more information. (General A M Gray and Major J Schmitt, Warfighting, United States Marine Corps, 1989)

In relation to the core issues of transferability and ecological validity that surround research with a specific contextual setting or situated nature, these can be important factors to consider, both in relation to active military service and in how military candidates are educated and trained with a sense of civic as well as institutional responsibility. For those in the context of decision making where temporality is a key driver of decision making (i.e. thinking in the moment) the question of being able to ascertain truth stems from the question of whether that truth is purely a matter of objective binary decision making, or whether it is an epistemic means of consolidating both pre-existing and sometimes co-existing beliefs and assumptions. The aim of establishing truth is therefore twofold. The value of truth is firstly rooted in the value of having a true belief and secondly the devaluing of having beliefs that are false.

As a general rule, human belief is not based on any innate sense of intentionality. Usually there is a source of tangible evidence to support assumptions or pre-suppositions of perceived truth and actuality, the basis of which are used to proactively formulate decision making by mankind. From this assertion, it is also possible to posit that humans have an aim of epistemic rationality, which underpins their beliefs and their systemic bases of truth and perceived reality. Extending this idea further, it might also be posited that people have an aim of believing by being epistemically rational but that this poses a fundamental challenge because of human emotion at an epistemic level. This is particularly dangerous when assumptions and pre-suppositions remain unchallenged or unacknowledged. It is what leads to the concept of methods driven instead of question led research, where in the attempt to find truth, it becomes possible to believe only in the pursuit of it. Framing human capacity in this respect, is determined by the fundamental and blatantly apparent relationship between knowledge, truth and belief. The purpose of establishing truth in the context of decision making, ought to be to guide intrinsic belief to the actual evidence available on any given issue or stance of relevance to the potential outcome. What may rightly or wrongly regarded as evidence then, clearly resonates as an issue for further consideration. This has particular resonance in the context of immediate and instantaneous decision where the ramifications of a wrong decision can potentially mean the difference between life and death in military service. If self-belief is the source of guidance in the establishment of truth, then epistemically it can be posited that ways of framing belief are nullified in terms of their generalisable or transferable value since they are couched in the aim of truth being belief alone. The individuality of mind is central to the concept of epistemology. This has also become a fundamental basis for deciding who ought to be taught *how* as well as *what* to think in relation to military organisational hierarchies.

Propositions stem from the constructions of people, for whom research into a specific area or discipline is a motivating factor and this is common to all situations and contexts, not just military settings. The ability to critically appraise and evaluate claims of truth are the very hallmarks of 21st Century research synthesis and these are echoed by Descartes' discussion of the clarity of truth in original debates of the legitimacy of metaphysics (Descartes, 1641). This was extended into current practice by Leibniz (1989), whose 'Theory of Truth' formed the basis of modern systematic inquiry.

HEURISTICS AND BIASES

In relation to the potential transferability of knowledge between the context of military and business epistemology, there are key operational definitions, which although similar in semantics have entirely different meanings in epistemological praxis. In military settings the organisational knowledge hierarchy is structured into strategic then operational then tactical, whereas in business the terminology is reflective of strategic thinking at an executive level, being operationalised by work at the front line of business. This subtle but resonant difference is reflective of the equally resonant difference to the consequence of a poor decision being made. Ultimately the stakes are high in both contexts but the clear line of delineation in the military is the potential for immediate loss of life or devastating injury, which is incomparable to an error in the context of everyday business performance. In the contexts of decision making which is fundamental to both environments, the seminal work of Tversky and Kahneman (1974) from the discipline of economic psychology is most overlooked. 'Judgement under Uncertainty: Heuristics and Biases', remains as relevant to the context of human decision making today as it was at the time it was published, when it challenged the theory of human rationality. It is the situated context of workplace ambiguity that lends itself so well to the concept that uncertainty impacts upon the human capacity to make informed decisions. Nowhere is this of greatest relevance than to the field of military epistemology and the potential transferability of military epistemology to those situational contexts and settings where higher order critical thinking 'in situ', has greatest resonance. What Tversky and Kahneman revealed, was the predictability in those errors of judgement, made in the context of ambiguous evidence and in the face of multi-combinatorically framed complexity, where several intraneous and extraneous variables might potentially be at work. They framed the term 'heuristics' and 'biases' as explanatory mechanisms of the subconscious mental shortcuts that underpin the sometimes necessarily spontaneous decision making in applied contexts and settings.

The methodological approaches that examined the interpretive and analytical approaches surrounding Tversky's and Kahneman's approach to heuristics modelled, exactly, how high-level quality interpretation is fundamental to correspondingly high-level criticality in applied professional practice. Those subconscious processes underpinning this high-quality interpretation, are pivotal to the function of the human mind and have provided a platform of psychological theory and conceptual thinking that has not only shaped modern-day economics in the case of the authors. Beyond this, the approach has transcended disciplinarity to become of relevance to every professional identity where subconscious thought can sway and influence the optimal chance of making sense of ambiguity in practice.

With a career trajectory and respected background in military psychology, Kahneman had been responsible for the assessment of soldier capability and the fact he had been raised in a war-torn country provided the motivation for him to intellectually prefer applied, rather than purely theoretical knowledge. This has the potential to influence capacity for valid decision making in practice. Recognising the subconscious influences impacting on human judgement in action was a fundamental landmark in the study of human psychology.

The Influence of Cognitive Biases in Practice

The erroneous decision making that stems from making automatic judgements in the process of complex decision making were identified by Tversky and Kahneman as being attributable to two concepts. These were termed 'heuristics' and 'bias' – the two are subtly but significantly different in terms of their impact on practice. Cognitive bias constitutes systematic errors in thinking which can often be attributed to the nature and presentation of problems. This fundamentally challenged the model of rational choice theory that was a keystone of social sciences research at the time. Tversky and Kahneman highlighted the limitations of human cognition and highlighted that the reality of human decision making is rooted in the capacity of humans to know the outcome of options available to them. Fundamentally and of exceptional significance to practice based learning and research, Tversky and Kahneman provided a means of educating members of society by introducing mechanisms of being able to understand that the limitation of human reasoning is shaped by the subconscious biases that frame human thinking. Important considerations of human emotion in the context of departing from rational thinking were considered in 'Judgement under Certainty' (1974). These are the resultant systematic errors in thinking when people are emotionally impacted upon by issues are something which are automatic and that humans have no subconscious control of. As such the complexity of human nature is one which has to be considered in any aspect of research claiming to be purist in its objectivity, since it is debateable whether this is achievable at all.

Sociological Perspectives in Heuristics and Biases

Social scientists have traditionally posited decision making as being either descriptive or normative – the delineating features, of which, are that description posits experience in the past, whereas a normative approach advocates the core concept of reflexivity. Placing cognitive limitation at the heart of what it is to be a human decision maker, opens avenues of understanding that had never been recognised before and which are of huge relevance in decision making today. This stems from the challenge that identifying workplace issues for address, understanding and wider dissemination necessitate. Ambiguity adds another dimension to reasoning capability and what Tversky and Kahneman highlight before all else is that the unlimited cognitive capacity to predict certain outcomes simply does not exist in the human brain, since cognitive capacity for it is limited.

Defining the study of heuristics is relatively straightforward when applied to human decision making. Most straightforwardly, heuristics can be regarded as the cognitive illusions that the human mind uses to bypass complex decision making with the consequence they are often unintentionally, yet irrefutably, wrong. In the same manner in which heuristics are context specific and bound by the situated nature of key events and practices, so too is validity, which has important ramifications for the concepts of perceived reality, actual reality, verisimilitude and trustworthiness in practice. It is the predictability of heuristics and the consequent errors that manifest from them which are tangible and, in this respect, predictable. Within 'Judgement under Uncertainty', the three heuristics identified for specific concern are the concepts of representativeness, availability and adjustment (otherwise termed anchoring). Stereotypical assumptions fall under the bracket of representativeness, where human judgement can be very evidently skewed by the pre-cognition that people enter the construction of meaning making with. Humans therefore construct perceptions of reality based on their previous experience and the epistemically cognitive pre-suppositions and assumptions they hold about them in practice. As a consequence of this, representativeness can potentially be fundamentally wrong and as a direct consequence of this, can ultimately lead to misdirected or simply wrong conclusions about the information available to the human mind.

Informing Judgement

The availability heuristic is dependent on how common an experience something has been, the meaning attributed to it and the capacity of people to make meaning and judgement in the light of it. It could potentially account for the subtle nuances of organisational culture that go unnoticed because of their relative degree of frequency. Memory was thus posited by Tversky and Kahneman to distort as well as inform judgement, leading to an increasing likelihood of human error. Their work at this point made significance of the connection between cognitive bias and heuristics. Whereas heuristics were benchmarks of context and time, cognitive biases were acknowledged for the first time as being far more straightforward systematic errors of thinking.

Kahneman was later keen to clarify that this connection does not necessarily denigrate heuristics as something bad, but rather something to be acknowledged and aware of. What the impact of this was though, was to frame intuition as something fundamentally flawed but nevertheless valued in the absence of wider knowledge access at given points in time (Kahneman, et al, 1982). The wider implication of this now historical research is that, for the first time, it identified a dualistic model of thinking, in which some of the time humans have the capacity to think quickly, intuitively and rashly, which is prone to error and the other part of the time humans are considered, reflective and less influenced by the mental shortcuts that characterise quick thinking. It is these recognitions, which have consequently been used to explicate human capacity for reasoning and the projection of behaviour in practice-based settings.

Linking both intuition and research is a third element, 'military experience'. The value of practical application of military skills during warfare or training is recognised as key, as much for the ability to function under pressure and to give orders and make plans that by their nature are well-suited to the complex and confusing environment that is battle:

Battle experience overcomes friction, from troopers up to the divisional commander. (Von Clausewitz, On War, tr Michael Howard and Peter Paret, 1976)

Yet while direct experience of battle will help prepare an individual for further action in future, supplementing it with wider knowledge can help prepare for the wider challenges which occur during warfare and when societal norms no longer apply:

Direct experience is inherently too limited to form an adequate foundation either for theory or for application. At best it produces an atmosphere that is of value in drying and hardening the structure of thought. The great value of indirect experience lies in its greater variety and extent. (Captain Sir Basil Liddell Hart, Strategy: The Indirect Approach, 1954)

Kahneman (2013) first recognised dual processing theory via discussion of the dichotomy between two modes of thought, termed (the fictional) system 1 "instinctive and emotional" and (the fictional) system 2 "deliberative and more logical". This was used as a metaphorical understanding of how behaviour is a direct consequence of proactive response, where system 1 processes are intuitive, fast, autonomous, and high capacity in contrast to system 2 processes, which are reflective, slow, and resource intensive. System 1 processes are hypothesised to provide default outputs that may be acted upon as explicit representations manipulated in working memory via System 2 processing, (Evans & Stanovich, 2013a & Thompson, 2013). The important and relevant points from Kahneman's work are;

System 2 can potentially be less objective and more ambiguous and multifaceted in contrast to System 1. When System 2 is engaged belief stems from knowledge provided by System 1 and contrary to scientific belief the tendency is for humans to rely on data, which consolidates and supports their own perspectives (confirmation bias). System 2 necessitates deliberate effort, focused attention and slow thinking constructs mechanisms of deliberate self-control. In situations of cognitive overload in the System 2, the System 1 overrides thinking processes and as a consequence questions to System 2 are raised by System 1. Whereas System 2 searches the memory to find a measured response, System 1 continues to constantly monitoring the external world.

Substitution occurs when a cognitive shutdown of System 1 occurs, which a consequence of no answer is being found to a hard question and the brain searching for an alternative easier question. System 2 is capable of constructive critique but is somewhat reliant upon presupposition and assumption rather than evidence-based decision making. Since System 1 has developed to prioritise potentially negative information and threats to mankind, there is a tendency to give priority to threat as opposed to opportunity, which is of huge consequence to perception of risk and perception of opportunity. Kahneman termed this 'broad negativity dominance', or negative bias, which provides a basis for why it is never difficult to recall a critical incident yet instances of excellent performativity may be overlooked.

Schwartz developed and extended this work on human emotion in practice and attributed it to the fuelling of heuristics in the formulation of subjective opinion (Schwartz, 2000). The notion of conscious brain activity is central to the context of critical thinking, critical introspection and reflexivity. Claxton (2015) highlighted how so many aspects of human experience lie in stark contrast to the concept of common sense that mankind would often like to think characterise personhood, as somehow making it credible as a species. Whilst intellectuals may disagree on the subtle nuances of what constitutes the conscious awareness of the human mind, it is startling how their consensus all collides in the context of humanity being inveterate storytellers, who automatically make meaning of the world around them, then assimilate it into a story to be told. It is a distinctive characteristic of the species that delineates and disarticulates it from the rest of the animal species occupying the world. It has sustained mankind for generations in its capacity to provide explanation and rationale for being and for perceiving.

Experience belies all perceptual reality and the mind, in all its complexity, is responsible for the glory of what is now badged under the label and taxonomy of human experience. This capacity to formulate and regale stories, whether to ourselves or others, is pivotal to the process of being able to reflect and consolidate knowledge of what has been, what is and what has the potential to be in the world:

What is the good of experience if you do not reflect? (Frederick the Great, quoted in JFC Fuller, Decisive Battles of the USA, 1953)

THE POWER OF COLLECTIVE NARRATIVE

Collective narrative provides a context for the establishment of socio-cultural context, history and works far beyond the context of description and elaboration in being able to frame future action and dependency on pre-existing meaning. Story telling is intergenerational, cross generational and characterises us as being distinct in being able to traverse and incorporate representations in a process of sense-making that characterises existence itself. Claxton's observation that the perceptual world exists on the outside and memories, thoughts and feelings are on the inside does much to unpack the significance of the unconscious mind in action.

The temporal nature of consciousness is also something of huge significance to experience, particularly experience of a particular point or time in history. Key words amidst our capacity to make sense of things are rationality, sense-making and explication. How fantastic is it then, which the most celebrated of man's achievements are characterised by the capacity to take risk, think laterally and thrive on ambiguity and the complexity of human life on earth. This does not deliberately or flippantly question our capacity as a fundamentally unique species, but rather addresses the beautiful irony that frames our existence and the meaning we ascribe to it.

HEURISTICS AND BIASES IN ACTION

As outlined earlier, heuristics and biases serve as cognitive shortcuts to aid and support the processing information given to the brain, upon which decisions can not only be made, but which can also can lead to significant errors of judgement (Tversky & Kahneman, 1974). Recent authors have contributed to the heuristics and biases knowledge extending it beyond the parameters of this original work. Key authors in the field (Shepperd et al, 2008; Funkhouser, 2007; Mather et al, 2000 and Pettigrew, 1979) have added several recognitions, that also contribute greatly to the discussion around self-deception and the understanding of self:

The first of these is the concept of 'self-enhancement biases' – describing oneself more positively than a normative criterion would predict, Krueger (1998). In contrast to the theory of self-verification theory, which proposes that humans fundamentally gave a desire to be perceived by others as they perceive themselves, this can drive motivation for this affirmation in practice. Moving from this theory is the concept of group biases, which facilitates a sense of active belonging to collective groups and communities of praxes. In contrast, self-serving attribution biases refer to the interpretation of events in a way which can be regarded as self-serving in the claiming of responsibility for positive outcomes and externalising responsibility for those which have the potential to be negative. Status quo biases arise in instances when sometimes it can be perceived as being somewhat better to do nothing when faced with adversity, it can also be perceived as stemming from the need not to change that which is already working in practice. Optimism bias is the capacity to predict the near future based on an overestimation of a potentially positive outcome, which differs from the illusion of control bias where the human mind can perceive being able to influence outcomes despite there being no causal connection to them (Langer, 1975). Memory biases can be divided into the selective recall of information, which incorporates Festinger's (1957) work on cognitive dissonance, and self-serving to achieve a positive self-assessment of our past choices, (Mather et al, 2000). Confirmation bias is the concept of searching for new evidence to support our perspective and interpretation of evidence in a skewed manner whereas belief preservation bias is wishing beliefs could to remain the same when we are unwilling to admit when we are wrong, or to admit uncertainties or fallibilities.

PERFORMATIVITY

The concept of performativity as elucidated by Lyotard also has a striking impact on individual capacity to express and articulate meaning of experiential learning and positioning. What is of greatest significance to the deconstruction of long held pre-suppositions and assumptions from individual realities and lived experiences is his acknowledgement of the fact that structuralist approaches denigrate and largely ignore the intraneous and extraneous figural components, which serve to function beyond the constraints of representational frameworks and structures. Positionally, Lyotard states the mutual reciprocity of the two and the relative implications of this to fundamental fields of academic disciplinarity such as linguistics and phenomenology. Perhaps most significant to research praxis was Lyotard's acknowledgement of the relevance of temporal and spatial specificity, which links directly to the situated nature of research-based practice. Experience and experiential articulation of sensorial self in an external world, therefore become an imperative to the credibility of language structure and discursive accounts of it. This essentially destabilises traditional thinking, ensuring that the world of interpretivist research remains free to celebrate the value of ambiguity and chaos that is a life lived and to abandon all hope of binary thinking in consideration of a 'real world' It is this stance that permits us to frame professional identity, regardless of discipline or profession, in the context of truth, positionality and knowledge, as epistemic reflexivity, in contrast to purely descriptive autobiographical narrative. This is in keeping too, with the dynamic shifts in professional identity that a career trajectory based in the midst of politics, governmental change and upheaval and consequently professional practice can ensure.

INTUITION AND KNOWLEDGE

Since the whole emphasis of workplace research is placed on the sensorial awareness of experience from professional practice, then the notion of intuition and the role intuition plays in the motivation and formulation of new knowledge cannot be ignored. Whether belief based on intuition is knowledge is a long-contested debate and perceptual reality occupies the same philosophical reasoning space. Since perceptual realities also lead to belief via sensorial experience then to frame intellectual understanding in this seems reasonable, which in turn makes it constitute knowledge, regardless of whether or not it is true. In turn, the notion of making sense of intellectual awareness can be regarded as socially constructed knowledge formulation, regardless of how abstract the intellectual awareness actually is. For either to be possible it is necessary to firstly delineate intuitive from perceptual knowledge. Perception is inherently more advanced than simply having a sensorial experience or an acknowledgement of externality. The two are inextricably intertwined in the sense that perceptual reality is largely dependent upon priori knowledge of sensorial experiences.

In the context of the social world there is no singular truth but a continuum of truth which acts as a lens of interpretation for the execution of pragmatic research. This stance is termed relativism. Relativism is often closely associated with the concept of triangulation, in particular the triangulation of research findings from the context of research-based practice or practice-based research, or most often work based research. Triangulation might be used to assess congruency or consistency rather than repeatability, the concept of the testifiability of knowledge is largely redundant because of the temporality of knowledge i.e. it is only true for that particular snapshot of time within which it is captured. Multiple realities within the context of positionality are also worth considering, since human perception is subject to maturation, change and adaptation in the light of additional human experience and perception. This in itself raises important debates in relation also to what perceptual knowledge is.

Delineating between what is perceptual and what is sensorial is a key mechanism of distinguishing between different states of mind and the meaning the mind makes of information supplied to it. The fact is that being sensorily aware of something is inherently different from perceiving it. The two are very much interrelated in that it is possible to perceive without first having had sensorial experience of something. There is a non-stasis of positionality that aligns with this, that accounts for this capacity for change. For each perception in the world, there is a representation of a propositional truth about the world. In this sense, knowledge that derives from human perception is therefore experientially valid but not necessarily true. This forms the basis of the delineation between perceived and actual reality.

THE STRUCTURE AND AGENCY OF EXPERIENTIAL BEING

Structure and agency have determined that the situated nature of experience is specific to our life trajectories, individual experiences and personal perceptions of them. For every context specific interpretation, there will be as many realities of it as there are experiencers of it. It is here that the fundamental question of how we can prioritise and give salience to emergent themes becomes an issue. Locating the specifics of our own situated nature as interpretive researchers, making experience of these realities, is imperative to this process of acknowledgement. Failing in this respect lends itself to the processes of overgeneralising, rather than making specific informed decision making as to whether emergent theory may have potential transferability to similar contexts and settings rather than generalising and making universal claims about the value of data interpretation. Constraints of the process lie in the capacity of researchers to be sufficiently reflective and reflexive in accounts of themselves. The process is inherently reliant on self-evaluation and the acknowledgement and meaning of self that not all interpretivist researchers necessarily achieve. Perhaps it is the difficulty of recognising and critiquing concepts of personality, as opposed to just positionality, which makes this discourse so potentially challenging in practice. The concept of the personal, as opposed to purely the positional, integrates the concept of emotional intelligence into the dilemma of how best to present self. Personality itself can be seen as a paradigm influencing interpretive stance.

Simplistically posited, the unique universality of human experience from the perspective of all individuals means that interpretivist approaches to research, arguably like any other human research are influenced by the combinatorial variables that shape and inform the human mind. Personality can be defined though, as the paradigmatic characteristics of perception, thought, feeling and behaviour expression that can delineate one individual from another and which is recognisable between temporal and situational contexts. Emotional intelligence hinges on all of these and for the majority of people, personality remains fundamentally stable throughout life. It is this which can influence chosen ontological and epistemological stance as opposed to the specific ontological or epistemological stance of the questions and research areas we propose for study, however as unique individuals, these are all inherently unique. The implication with this is that our personalities can be argued to be the sum of our positionalities however this can be contested with debates of whether personality is socially constructed. It is not our aim through this text to debate this sociological frame of perspective but it ought to be recognised that for the large part the concept of human universality actually transcends situation, context and time and that this is what actually frames human research endeavour.

Introspection and Critical Judgement

Introspection is directly linked to the notion of human consciousness, a process of intraneous self-examination and explication of internal thoughts, feelings and memories with the resultant outcome of critical self-reflection (Cherry 2016). There is nothing new in curiosity surrounding levels of consciousness or the liminality of conscious mental states and historically this was also a focus for research (Wundt, 1879). Initial studies examined how conscious mental states (elements of consciousness) could be scientifically studied using introspection as an integral part of formal experimental processes and as a consequence leading the field as a founder of cognitive psychology. Wundt's attribution to the establishment and progressive development of structuralism, forms the fundamental basis of understanding thoughts, sensation and perception. Consequently, it was contested that self-analysis was not feasible since individuals did not possess an appreciation of the processes or mechanisms of their own mental processes, Blumenthal (2002) & Danziger (1980).

CONCLUSION

Since the armed forces are an extension of national/government policy and there to undertake its bidding, not serve as a judiciary seeking to determine 'truth', it ought to be clearly acknowledged that this lies in contrast to business settings. The military has to interpret and seek to apply government policy and intent within a highly dynamic and contested environment, that in recent years has had the added complexity of dealing with the potential for all decision making to be circulated and publicised online, in real-time. As a direct consequence of this, even minor tactical issues can have a strategic impact, which is essentially what General Charles Krulak referred to as the 'Strategic Corporal'. It is clear that there are the added implications of this for the mental health and wellbeing of those who make and implement military decisions. Further research is required to understand the impact of whether this is too 'managed through' a heuristic approach, with the consequences only recognised by the individual well after the event.

This raises further questions of direct relevance to both military and business contexts of how reflection on learning and experience be incorporated in practical terms into military education and training. This brings in the potential for the integration of the teaching of 'positionality' or 'positional stance' across everyday academic and military curricula. Within the military context this is traditionally it is done by rank held, sometimes by the types of appointment to which someone will be assigned, but both are only after someone has been selected for that rank or appointment. This raises the far more contentious debate of whether the capacity for critical reflection and reflexivity ought to be taught and the ability to do so, confirmed as a pre-requisite for promotion or appointment throughout a career trajectory in the military or business?

Military education and training need to strike an appropriate balance between indirect experience (study), direct experience, reflection/reflexive behaviour and heuristics. It is arguable that business is no different. The nature of interdisciplinary research is such that linking these areas for knowledge construction together through collaborative effort, could be of significant reciprocal value to both.

REFERENCES

Abraham, T., Cheney, A. M., & Curran, G. M. (2017). A Bourdieusian analysis of US military culture ground in the mental help-seeking literature. *American Journal of Men's Health, 11*(5), 1358–1365. doi:10.1177/1557988315596037 PMID:26229053

Button, C. J., Jinkerson, J., & Bryan, C. J. (2017). Making Meaning After Combat Trauma and Moral Injury. In *Reconstructing Meaning After Trauma* (pp. 167–184). Academic Press. doi:10.1016/B978-0-12-803015-8.00011-5

Campbell, L. (2018). An epistemology for practical knowledge. *Canadian Journal of Philosophy, 48*(2), 159–177. doi:10.1080/00455091.2017.1341073

Claxton, G. (2015). *Intelligence in the flesh: Why your mind needs your body much more than it thinks*. Yale University Press.

Conley, C. S., Durlak, J. A., & Kirsch, A. C. (2015). A meta-analysis of universal mental health prevention programs for higher education students. *Prevention Science, 16*(4), 487–507. doi:10.100711121-015-0543-1 PMID:25744536

Cooper, L., Caddick, N., Godier, L., Cooper, A., & Fossey, M. (2018). Transition from the military into civilian life: An exploration of cultural competence. *Armed Forces and Society, 44*(1), 156–177. doi:10.1177/0095327X16675965

Descartes, R. (1641). *Discourse on method and the meditations* (F. E. Sutcliffe, Trans.). Penguin Books.

Eisner, E. W. (1998). *The enlightened eye: Qualitative inquiry and the enlightenment of educational practice*. Prentice Hall.

Feldman, K. A., & Newcomb, T. M. (1969). *The impact of college on students*. Transaction Publishers.

Freire, P. (2000). Pedagogy of the oppressed (30th ann. ed.). New York, NY: Continuum.

Garcia Zea, D., Sankar, S., & Isna, N. (2019). The impact of emotional intelligence in the military workplace. *Human Resource Development International*, 1–17.

Gerken, M. (2017). *On folk epistemology: How we think and talk about knowledge*. Oxford University Press. doi:10.1093/oso/9780198803454.001.0001

Ghiya, G. D. (2019). Promoting Spiritual Health and Holistic Wellness. *Journal of Health Management, 21*(2), 230–233. doi:10.1177/0972063419835104

Gibson, S., Baskerville, D., Berry, A., Black, A., Norris, K., & Symeonidou, S. (2017). Including students as co-enquirers: Matters of identity, agency, language and labelling in an international participatory research study. *International Journal of Educational Research, 81*, 108–118. doi:10.1016/j.ijer.2016.11.008

Gleiser, M. (2014). *The Island of knowledge: The limits of science and the search for meaning*. Basic Books.

James, P. G. (2017). Discourse analysis. In *The Routledge Handbook of Language and Dialogue* (pp. 62–77). Routledge. doi:10.4324/9781315750583-5

Kahneman, D., Slovic, S. P., Slovic, P., & Tversky, A. (Eds.). (1982). *Judgment under uncertainty: Heuristics and biases*. Cambridge university press. doi:10.1017/CBO9780511809477

Killgore, W. D. (2017). *Refinement and Validation of a Military Emotional Intelligence Training Program*. University of Arizona Tucson United States.

Leibniz, G. W. (1989). Meditations on knowledge, truth, and ideas. In *Philosophical Papers and Letters* (pp. 291–295). Springer. doi:10.1007/978-94-010-1426-7_34

Merriman, P., Peters, K., Adey, P., Cresswell, T., Forsyth, I., & Woodward, R. (2017). Interventions on military mobilities. *Political Geography, 56*, 44–52. doi:10.1016/j.polgeo.2016.11.003

Mezirow, J. (1990). How critical reflection triggers transformative learning. *Fostering Critical Reflection in Adulthood, 1*(20), 1-6.

Mezirow, J. (2000). Learning as Transformation: Critical Perspectives on a Theory in Progress. The Jossey-Bass Higher and Adult Education Series. Jossey-Bass Publishers.

Mezirow, J., & Taylor, E. W. (Eds.). (2009). *Transformative learning in practice: Insights from community, workplace, and higher education*. John Wiley & Sons.

Muis, K. R., Chevrier, M., & Singh, C. A. (2018). The role of epistemic emotions in personal epistemology and self-regulated learning. *Educational Psychologist, 53*(3), 165–184. doi:10.1080/00461520.2017.1421465

Olson, M. D. (2018). Exploring military social work from a social justice perspective. *International Social Work, 61*(1), 119–129. doi:10.1177/0020872815606792

Rodd, P., & Sanders, K. (2018). The imperative of critical pedagogy in times of cultural austerity: A case study of the capacity to reimagine education as a tool for emancipation. *New Zealand Sociology, 33*(3), 33.

Rukavishnikov, V. O., & Pugh, M. (2018). Civil-military relations. In *Handbook of the Sociology of the Military* (pp. 123–143). Springer. doi:10.1007/978-3-319-71602-2_7

Savin-Baden, M., & Major, C. H. (2013). *Qualitative Research: The Essential Guide to Theory and Practice. In Qualitative Research: The Essential Guide to Theory and Practice*. Routledge.

Schonert-Reichl, K. A., & Roeser, R. W. (Eds.). (2016). *Handbook of mindfulness in education: Integrating theory and research into practice*. Springer. doi:10.1007/978-1-4939-3506-2

Schwartz, N. (2000). Emotion, Cognition and Decision Making'. *Cognition and Emotion, 14*(4), 433–430. doi:10.1080/026999300402745

Sookermany, A., Meyer, E. L., & Last, D. M. (2017). Military Sciences–The Backbone of Military Educational Institutions? *Book of abstracts ISMS 2017.*

Tallant, J. (2017). *Truth and the World: An Explanationist Theory*. Routledge. doi:10.4324/9781315143491

Williams-Klotz, D. N., & Gansemer-Topf, A. M. (2017). Identifying the camouflage: Uncovering and supporting the transition experiences of military and veteran students. *Journal of the First-Year Experience & Students in Transition, 29*(1), 83–98.

ADDITIONAL READING

Badour, C. L., Blonigen, D. M., Boden, M. T., Feldner, M. T., & Bonn-Miller, M. O. (2012). A longitudinal test of the bi-directional relations between avoidance coping and PTSD severity during and after PTSD treatment. *Behaviour Research and Therapy*, *50*(10), 610–616. doi:10.1016/j.brat.2012.06.006 PMID:22835842

Christensen, T., & Lægreid, P. (2020). The coronavirus crisis—Crisis communication, meaning-making, and reputation management. *International Public Management Journal*, *23*(5), 713–729. doi:10.1080/10967494.2020.1812455

Christensen, T., & Lægreid, P. (2020). The coronavirus crisis—Crisis communication, meaning-making, and reputation management. *International Public Management Journal*, *23*(5), 713–729. doi:10.1080/10967494.2020.1812455

Copley, L., & Carney, J. (2020). Using Gestalt Techniques to Promote Meaning Making in Trauma Survivors. *The Journal of Humanistic Counseling*, *59*(3), 201–218. doi:10.1002/johc.12145

Grusky, O. (2017). The effects of succession: A comparative study of military and business organization. In *Organizational Careers* (pp. 369–374). Routledge. doi:10.4324/9781315125909-58

Sorin-George, T., & Catalin, G. (2016). From Military Strategy To Business Strategy. *Management Strategies Journal*, *31*(1), 227–233.

Tran, J. (2020). *The Business of War: Theological and Ethical Reflections on the Military-Industrial Complex*. Wipf and Stock Publishers.

Viney, R. A. E., Clarke, J., & Cornelissen, J. (2017). Making Meaning from Multimodality: Embodied Communication in a Business Pitch Setting. *Sage (Atlanta, Ga.)*.

KEY TERMS AND DEFINITIONS

Assumption: Something that is accepted as true or as certain to happen, without factual or evidence-based proof.

Coping: Is the process of making a conscious effort to deal with problems or issues causing psychological stress or inner conflict which impact on psychological functionality.

Epistemology: The theoretical perspectives of knowledge, especially with regard to its methodology, methods, validity, and scope, and the distinction or delineation between justified belief and opinion

Interpretation: The process of explaining the meaning of something or an explanation or way of explaining.

Knowledge: The facts, information, and skills acquired through experience, action, research, or education; the theoretical or practical understanding of a specific subject or discipline.

Meaning Making: A process of making sense of what is meant by experience, words, text, concepts, philosophies, or action.

Philosophy: The study of the theoretical basis of a particular branch of knowledge or experience.

Post-Traumatic Stress Disorder (PTSD): A mental health condition, which can be directly attributed to the experience of trauma.

Reflection: A process of serious contemplative thinking or active or consideration of past events.

Reflexivity: Is the consequent processual meaning making on experience beliefs, judgments and practices which influences future direction, as opposed to reflection, a process of contemplating past events.

Chapter 13
Becoming Who You Are Through Authentic Organizational Communication

Ross Jackson
https://orcid.org/0000-0002-5358-966X
Wittenberg University, USA

ABSTRACT

Business communication is comprised of standards designed for efficiency. Like commodities, official correspondences are often indistinguishable. Adherence to templates provides uniformity in arrangement if not also content. When this approach works well, it is both efficient and effective. However, the universal applicability of this paradigm is suspect. Such standardization stifles creativity. When one is responsible for communicating insights in business, a radical break with convention might be beneficial in terms of gaining attention and provoking thought. Deviating from established norms is risky. Further, while one learns key tenants of business communication at work and in college, one is seldom informed as to when to stop following the rules and forge a new communicative path forward. In this chapter, existential insights are combined with communication theory to illustrate how authentic organizational communication can assist in one becoming who one is while also communicating insights in a business in a way that the form and content are strategically aligned.

INTRODUCTION

Business communication is comprised of standards (Mechenbier, 2011). Internally, these stylistic choices are designed for operational improvements since homogenization is often associated with efficiency (Church & Naugler, 2019; Davis, 2016). Externally, communication design choices are influenced by considerations of organizational branding (Abecassis-Moedas & Benghozi, 2012). Like commodities on a production line, official correspondences are often indistinguishable from one another. This is by design. Once generated, standardized templates allow workers to *fill in the blanks*, and be assured that the document is consistent with general expectations. Adherence to templates provides uniformity in

DOI: 10.4018/978-1-7998-3964-4.ch013

arrangement if not also content. Benefits of this approach exist for supervisors and subordinates alike. Workers have the confidence of clear expectations. Managers have the ability to scan documents quickly and locate the desired information. Given these positive attributes, why would anybody think of deviating from the operational norm? As the adage asserts, there is no sense in reinventing the wheel.

When this approach works well, it is both efficient and effective. However, the universal applicability of this paradigm is suspect. There are occasions for which organizational templates become barriers to effective communication. Through standardization it is possible that internal consumers of information are only passively reading the document, as errors frequently increase with routine procedures (Byrne & Davis, 2006). This could adversely affect organizational decision making. Additionally, standardization, by design, stifles creativity. This limits authenticity and could eventually erode one's confidence as one perpetually subordinates self to organization. When one is simply communicating transactional information within an organization these limitations are perhaps of only minor significance. When the information being conveyed is sufficiently novel, these limitations could be consequential if not also detrimental. This suggests there is a need for those in organizations to distinguish when, where and how insights in business are to be effectively communicated.

When one is responsible for communicating insights in business, a radical break with convention might be beneficial in terms of gaining attention and provoking thought; however, deviating from established norms is perceived as risky even though there isn't an apparent relationship between career advancement and compliance (Carmeli, Shalom & Weisberg, 2007). Further, while one learns key tenants of business communication at work and in college, one is seldom informed as to when to stop following the rules and forge a new communicative path forward. Stated somewhat differently, people are enculturated for compliance and obedience but not for deviation and disobedience. Each approach offers something to organizations and individuals. Value can be derived through an exploration of the tension which exists organizationally and individually between these diametrically opposed forms of being and communicating.

In this chapter, existential insights are combined with communication theory to illustrate how authentic organizational communication can assist in one becoming who one is while also more effectively communicating business insights in a way that form and content are strategically aligned. To do this, an interpretative qualitative research approach was used. The methodological approach is presented in the following section entitled, *making sense of what others have talked about*. After the methodology is presented, four areas are developed. The first conceptual area (i.e., *coloring inside the lines*) focuses on the notions of obedience and compliance. The second theme (i.e., *deviating from the path*) explores the notion of disobedience and noncompliance. The third thematic area (i.e., *authenticity and performance*) examines the existential aspects associated with owning one's decisions to either comply or deviate from organizational expectations as one communicates insights in business. The last section (i.e., *communicating insights*) is presented to explore how one might decide to navigate the terrain between compliance and noncompliance in respect to organizational templates.

MAKING SENSE OF WHAT OTHERS HAVE TALKED ABOUT

Interpretative qualitative research forms the core of this study. The empirical material of analysis was derived from a semi-structured literature review with an interpretative frame informed by Critical Management Studies (CMS) perspectives. Since this research was based on a synthesis of previous research, one might say that the focus of this study is on *making sense of what others have talked about*. Making sense requires acts of interpretation which means this approach is partially subjective. While such methodological approaches are none too common in business research, there have been previous applications (Agarwal & Tanniru, 1990; De Waal, 2013; Riach & Wilson, 2007). Monin (2004) explained why such a research methodology is appropriate in business by noting that, "management inquiry is rhetorical because all texts are rhetorical" (p. 3). In this particular case, the interpretation of management is critical. As a consequence, establishing some basic context of CMS research is appropriate.

So, what is CMS research? Alvesson and Deetz (2000) explained that the aim of critical research was to, "disrupt ongoing social reality for the sake of providing impulses to the liberation from or resistance to what dominates and leads to constraints in human decision making," with emphasis placed on "the specific practices that reproduce asymmetry in will formation, decision making, and...the construction of social reality" (p. 1). The focus for this study is ultimately on how employees navigate the difficult terrain associated with complying with or deviating from official communication templates within organizations. For an employee, deviating from a standard template represents a risk. Employees in such a situation might simply decide that compliance is a more pragmatic response and therefore avoid the risk altogether. Even when one approaches the question academically, there could be a tendency for playing it safe. As Clarke (2009) explained, for those engaged in conducting business research, "we are usually discouraged from asking dangerous questions and pursuing and expressing such clarity, sincerity, normative orientations and experience-based understanding" (p. 77). From a CMS perspective, this work aims to examine how an employee might think beneficially about acts of compliance and deviation in official organizational communications with the ultimate aim being both improved communication and authenticity. To achieve this objective, a survey of existing literature was conducted.

While a survey of literature is frequently a section within an applied research study, the insights established through a survey of literature provide suitable ground on which theory might be developed (Webster & Watson, 2002). Such a synthesis of previous research lacks the narrow specificity of applied research but holds latent potential for powerful insights to emerge through aggregation. Based on this, it is possible for an extended survey of literature to be considered a sufficient research effort in its own right. As Snyder (2019) explained, "by integrating findings and perspectives from many empirical findings, a literature review can address research questions with a power that no single study has" (p. 333). Key to obtaining the benefit of this approach is the selection process used to identify research of merit for inclusion in one's review.

Selection is essential in survey research. Snyder (2019) indicated that when conducting research based on a survey of literature the "inclusion and exclusion criteria is one of the most important steps," and that it is important "to provide reasoning and transparency concerning all choices made; there must be logical and valid motives" (p. 337). The selection protocol reflects determinations as to *what* is the point of focus for a given study. Once the selection criteria are established, it is important to give thought to how conceptualization will take place within the study. As Webster and Watson (2002) explained, "a literature review is concept-centric. Thus, concepts determine the organizing framework of the review" (p. xvi). The conceptualization scheme reflects a *way of thinking* about a given element of inquiry. With this in mind, it is possible to turn attention to the specific selection protocol and conceptualization scheme used for this this qualitative study.

Peer-reviewed, scholarly articles were selected using the academic search engine, EBSCOHost (https://www.ebsco.com). Search terms for *obedience*, *compliance, deviation, existentialism* and *authenticity* were each paired with the term *business* to identify the population of articles of interest. A near/far selection process was applied to each article cohort. First, articles with the most recent publication dates were selected and reviewed. These sources were used to provide insight into the state of current research and thinking in the respective research area. Additionally, these articles were used as the basis for the identification of the articles which can be considered seminal in each of the respective areas. Second, once established the articles with the most distant publication dates were selected and reviewed. Those articles were used to provide foundational knowledge on the topic. Given the constraints of space and the intent of this chapter these near/far selections were synthesized to provide the minimum conceptualization necessary to delimit each of the respective research themes. Such an approach is open to critique. While admittedly cursory and quasi-subjective, the insights derived can be aimed towards the liberation of workers constrained by policy.

As indicated, there are grounds on which the methodological approach of this study can be legitimately critiqued. But such reproaches, while serious, are not necessarily invalidating. Alvesson and Deetz (2000) explained, "more important than data collection techniques are the questions asked and the intent of analysis, how social reality is understood, and the cognitive interest pursued" (p. 67). Since the aim of this research is to inform and empower workers to gain confidence in themselves and autonomy in their communicative acts, the technical limitations in the methodology approach are considered secondary. With the methodology of this interpretive, qualitative study briefly sketched, it is now possible to examine obedience and compliance within an organizational context.

COLORING INSIDE THE LINES

Organizations execute work according to procedures (Bolles & Hubbard, 2006; Ferrari, Witschel, Spagnolo & Stefania, 2018; Wiesner, 2000). Such procedures collectively form what comes to be the operational routine within a business. When one is newly hired learning *how* the organization operates and conforming to those norms and expectations is part of one's onboarding, indoctrination or professional socialization process (Ferri-Reed, 2013; Klein, Polin & Leigh Sutton, 2015). Metaphorically, this phase of existence and execution can be described as the time during which an employee *colors inside the lines*. Expectations for appearance, language, schedule and performance are set by management, along with senior members of the staff, and employees tend to operate according to those explicit and implicit guidelines. Operating within such a sphere requires a degree of conformity and obedience. But gaining acceptance as a legitimate member of the organization comes at a price as one sacrifices a degree of authenticity for approval. The loss of *self* which is associated with conformity is a popular theme in dystopian literature.

Dystopian works like *We* (Zamyatin, 2016), *1984* (Orwell, 2001) and *Player Piano* (Vonnegut, 2006) highlight corrosive effects of obedience and conformity. Such illustrations while not new, have recently been found to hold application potential for those operating within organizations. Burrell and Dale (2002) explained, "organization is a vortex in which very little is secure. And we find when these notions are untamed and vortices come together that we come close to some concepts of *dystopia*" (p. 124, emphasis retained). Similarly, for Seeger and Davison-Vecchione (2019) "dystopian fiction provides constructive grounds for real-world social and political interventions" (p. 61). Of particular importance within an organizational context is the power dynamic between managers and subordinates. Sava (2016) explained "modern utopias, which almost invariably turn into dystopias, share common elements regarding the use of power in new kinds of societies, societies that invariably turn into totalitarian systems" (p. 14). The literary themes of power, work and loss of self which figure prominently in dystopian literature are mere shadows of a darker organizational reality. From the safe distance provided by literature, one is able to think about the inherent tradeoffs between belonging and autonomy. Through review one is able to see the protagonists of these dystopian works often feel a tension between the sense of security which comes from being *in* the dominant group and the loss of *self* required for admission. Such tension is not simply a literary theme, but one that living individuals confront within their professional existence.

While literature is an informative way to assess elements of conformity and obedience from a point of detachment, these aspects are perhaps more constructively understood in reality. Doing so requires an examination of both conformity and obedience. Given the power dynamics are more overt in regard to obedience, it is beneficial to start one's exploration there. Milgram's (1963, 1965) experiments provide evidence which suggest a human tendency towards obedience. According to Milgram, "obedience is as basic element in the structure of social life as one can point to" (1963, p. 371). In assessing individual proclivities towards obedience, Milgram (1965) explained, "obedient dispositions are deeply ingrained, and are engaged irrespective of their consequences for others," and that "the subject becomes implicated in a situation from which he cannot disengage himself" (p. 72). Admittedly, there are certainly ethical concerns associated with the Milgram experiment (Clark, 2019) as well as subsequent findings that are inconsistent with the popular interpretation of this study's results (Perry, Brannigan, Wanner & Stam, 2020). One potential modification to the dominant view of Milgram's results is to view his work as focusing on *engaged followership* rather than obedience (Griggs, 2017). While these nuances hold operational significance in a narrow sense, for the purpose of this study, the question of obedience (loosely defined) holds important implications for those working in organizations insofar as one's place of employment is enacted within a context from which it is difficult to disengage oneself and in which doing what one is told to do is expected. Consequently, while conceptually linked, within the context of organizational dynamics, employees' actions may be more narrowly defined in terms of conformity and compliance rather than obedience.

Conformity can be understood as "the internal decision one makes" after measuring the "personal moral costs and benefits of behaving in accordance with other's directives" (Watson & Berkley, 2009, p. 464). Conformity is an area which has a relatively rich and established pedigree. In terms of conformity, Asch (1956) found that an individual, when confronted by a majority perspective, exhibits a pronounced tendency to adopt the view held by others rather than assert one's own perspective. While there is debate around the findings of the Asch conformity study (Larsen, 1974; Mori & Arai, 2010), the results are fairly robust in terms of replication (Kyrlitsias & Michael-Grigoriou, 2018; Lamb & Alsikafi, 1980). Such conformity has potentially impactful consequences for individuals and organizations. As Gandossy and Sonnenfeld (2005) noted, "while groups can pathologically suppress problem-solving skills through diffusions of responsibility, groupthink and other dysfunctional responses, they can additionally react pathologically once the resulting crisis breaks open through misguided attempts to contain the damage or 'circle the wagons'" (p. 239). Further, Watson and Berkley show that there is a link between punishment and compliance. These findings are consistent with those which are observable in organizations.

Becoming a manager might not only represent assuming a new position; it could also entail determining and adopting the organizationally sanctioned way of being. In other words, becoming a manager might be associated with an existential transformation. As Gagnon (2008) explained, "much identity work done by program participants consisted in trying to conform, to fit the model that was expected of them as managers and future leaders, in order to advance their careers and become 'better' or closer to what management wanted" (p. 384). From the perspective of management, one may conform to expectations in order to obtain or maintain a promotion, and the adoption of the appropriate persona could be viewed by the newly appointed manager as part of the deal. While there is potentially a degree of agency associated with managerial conformity, the same is not necessarily true for subordinates. Sosik, Chun and Zhu (2014) described that "followers may lack the wherewithal, power, and sense of moral autonomy/authority to challenge" (p. 77). Therefore, subordinate conformity is potentially different from that of management. A key determination is whether or not subordinates are able to ascertain and leverage a sense of individual agency. When they do, research suggests that they are able to question authority.

As early as 1971 Blackie noted that within organizations "obedience is no longer an automatic response to a command" (p. 47). In fact, Larsen's (1974) research found that Asch's results on conformity could have been influenced by the McCarthyism which was occurring in the United States in the 1950s. For this reason, Larsen suggested "different time periods create different pressures toward conformity, which in turn may be reflected in different levels of conformity behavior" (p. 304). Watson and Berkley (2009) indicated that "identifying the factors that make it possible to resist complying with unethical directives as well as those factors encouraging compliance is important to the progress of organizational ethics" (p. 475). Informed by these perspectives one has a better understanding of obedience and conformity. With this in mind, one can now examine its converse, deviation and disobedience.

DEVIATING FROM THE PATH

Obedience to authority and compliance with rules and regulations is pragmatic. This is perhaps most organizationally relevant at the beginning of one's career when one is figuring out the company's way of doing business and one's place in it. However safe and comforting conformity may be, there is value in learning how to deviate from the path. More specifically, within organizations one needs to determine under what circumstances one is willing to be disobedient or noncompliant, and for what reasons one is willing to enact those deviations from established norms and protocols. One important reason which is potentially beneficial to the organization as well as the individual is *progress*. Fromm (2010) explained "man has continued to evolve by acts of disobedience" and that intellectual development is "dependent on the capacity for being disobedient" (p. 3). Understood from this perspective, moving beyond the *status quo* often requires noncompliance with the protocols which entrench the current operational reality. More broadly, disobedience can be viewed as a check against authority slipping into autocracy and for stimulating social change (Passini & Morselli, 2013). Narrowing the focus to disobedience in an organizational context is useful for understanding how this general phenomenon relates to those engaged in work.

In dealing with organizational disobedience, two questions emerge which are worthy of consideration. First, under what circumstances (if any) is it permissible for one within an organization to disobey established procedures? Second, when it is determined to be permissible for one to disobey, it is possible to enact? The answers to these two questions have consequences for individuals and organizations. From a legal perspective, Ostas (2010) explained that it was "often acceptable" to disobey "inane busines regulations" (p. 310). So, there is some legal justification which suggests that if the something is nonsensical enough or if the consequence of conforming to the rule is significantly great, deviation may be permissible. Clearly, the presence of noncompliance suggests that one can, in fact, disobey within organizational contexts (Pollman, 2019; Rennstam & Kärreman, 2020). A deeper question is if such a capability is internalized at the worker level. Fromm (2010) explained, "the organization man has lost the capacity to disobey, he is not even aware of the fact that he obeys" (p. 12). Fromm highlighted the important role of awareness for action. If one is aware of the structure of obedience which permeates organizations, one can then transcend it through disobedience. In such a way, *awareness* is an important precondition for the freedom one is ultimately able to achieve.

Linkages between freedom and disobedience are complex and multifaceted. While challenging to define precisely, one can generally claim that freedom figures prominently in disobedience. The interrelationship between the two is both cause and consequence and potentially compounding. Seeing the connection between these two forces is perhaps most directly observable within colleges and universities as these are traditionally sites in which there are both specific freedoms and social engagements. For Green (2003), "academic freedom is the environment that ideas like best – including ideas about civil disobedience" (p. 405). Admittedly, these same freedoms and engagements typically do not exist in businesses. Differences in responsibilities, commitments, and social function make direct comparisons between colleges and businesses problematic. However, a similar questioning attitude and informed engagement are possible. To a degree, the very freedom needed to disobey in business might emerge from the act of noncompliance. As Fromm (2010) explained, "A person can become free through acts of disobedience by learning to say no to power. But not only is the capacity for disobedience the condition for freedom; freedom is also the condition for disobedience. If I am afraid of freedom, I cannot dare to say "no," I cannot have the courage to be disobedient" (p. 9). Saying no within an organization requires courage. Doing so places one in potential conflict with management.

Organizationally, a paradox potentially emerges if management advocates for disobedience. According to Kacerauskas (2016) "usually, any management reduces creativity since it requires following the rules of an organization, i.e. to obey the work routine that is inconsistent with creativity. In the case of creativity stimulation, the managers risk to provoke the disobedience for their instructions including an instruction to develop creativity" (p. 39). In a classic *Catch-22*, if management directs disobedience and the workforce complies, subordinates are simply continuing to comply with authority. This complicates the situation. Part of the benefit, organizationally and individually, is not that disobedience is officially sanctioned, but that individuals learn when and how to strategically disobey management based on an authentic appraisal of self and the needs of the situation. Organizationally, acts of disobedience can potentially be observed in official communications.

When it comes to communicating organizational insights, adherence to templates, like compliance in general, could be pragmatically useful. However, such an approach is not without risk. Within the context of teaching business communications, Mechenbier (2011) explained that there are "dangers of 'copying a template'" (p. 194). These dangers focused primarily on plagiarism and abuses of business ethics. In highlighting both benefits and drawbacks associated with a template-based communication approach in business, Schultz (2006) described that standard approaches to business communication (i.e., templates) "are efficient and that variations would cause readers to lose time searching for pertinent information;" but breaking from the standard could be "received more favorably" and that "the reader will likely feel that the author…will be more apt to bring fresh, creative ideas" (p. 408). As one engages in routine tasks, it is possible for one to disengage with the task or information at hand as one's mind wanders (Cheyne, Solman, Carriere & Smilek, 2009). If one is communicating something new, and one wants the idea to be perceived as such, deviating from the official template might be a more conducive means of conveying that content. Making the determination as to when to comply with and when to deviate from organizational convention is neither straightforward nor unproblematic. Assessing context is essential.

Pragmatically, one might decide that obedience and compliance to organizational norms and directives is expedient in terms of career advancement and acceptance. Yet, disobedience has been shown to be beneficial for progress. Within businesses there is some room identified for the legal deviation from directives in extreme cases. In the more banal aspects of work execution, a worker deviates from expectations at one's own risk. Taking that risk can lead to greater freedom and creativity. Between the two extremes of compliance and disobedience, a middle path is needed. As Fromm (2010) described the situation, "if a man can only obey and not disobey, he is a slave; if he can only disobey and not obey, he is a rebel…he acts out of anger, disappointment, resentment, yet not in the name of a conviction or a principle" (p. 5). The principle advocated for here is *authenticity*. Engaging in strategic disobedience in official correspondences within the organization holds the potential for both greater authenticity and organizational performance.

AUTENTICITY AND PERFORMANCE

Intensely philosophical and personal, determinations of identity and purpose permeate throughout one's life and relationships. Who are you? What are you doing? Why are you doing those activities as opposed to others? If the answers to these questions are to be anything more than superficial platitudes, one must dig deeply inwards and spend some time reflecting on one's values, motivations and aspirations. Through the process one might be able to achieve self-awareness, self-confidence and authenticity. This is beneficial organizationally as authenticity has been linked to improved performance (Gardner, Cogliser, Davis & Dickens, 2011; Ilies, Manzi et al., 2021; Mehmood, Hamstra, Nawab & Vriend, 2016; Morgeson & Nahrgang, 2005; Wei, Li, Zhang & Liu, 2018). Before exploring the connection between authenticity and performance, it is useful to first examine authenticity itself more closely. Conceptions of existential and communicative authenticity are addressed here. Given its foundational quality, the concept of existential authenticity is presented first.

Existential authenticity deals with the work associated with *being* who one truly is. It might seem odd to frame one's project of self as *work*. After all, *being* could be alternatively conceptualized as something which is automatic. However, conceptualizing the creation and maintenance of one's *self* as work, resides at the core of existentialist philosophy. Understanding and communicating this conception is part of the human condition as variously envisioned by existentialists. In his major philosophical text, *Being and Nothingness*, Jean-Paul Sartre (1994) explained "I emerge alone and in aguish confronting the unique and original project which constitutes my being; all the barriers, all the guard rails collapse, nihilated by the consciousness of my freedom…I have to realize the meaning of the world and of my essence; I make my decision concerning them – without justification and without excuse" (p. 39). This conceptualization transforms *self as a given* to *self as a project*. Within this undertaking, each individual is responsible for defining and becoming oneself. Such an activity necessitates a degree of rebelliousness. Camus (1991) stated this succinctly when he said, "in order to exist, man must rebel" (p. 22). Through this rebellion, one creates and asserts one's authentic self into the world. While existentialism had its peak of influence in post-war France, the concerns about existential authenticity continue today.

Modern applications of existential authenticity can be found in both the fields of psychology and sociology. This suggests that existential authenticity is important in both individual and collective contexts. In a recent exploration of existential psychology, Bradford (2019) explained, "on the foundation of honest self-reckoning, we become more willing and able to be open to experience as it is, enabling a more radical authenticity" (p. 122). While clearly important for the individual, the implications of existential authenticity are not confined solely to self. Pierce (2015) noted how there is overlap between individual and collective authenticity by noting that "one's individual identity is constructed in large part by reference to the groups which he or she belongs, and a group's identity is constructed by and through the contributions of its individual members" (p. 442). This insight is particularly relevant here as the primary focus is on how an individual balances the tensions between self and others within business organizations. Informed by these notions of existential authenticity, it is possible to extend the notion of authenticity further to that of communicative authenticity.

Communicative authenticity describes the degree to which the essence of an insight is accurately conveyed. In examining communicative authenticity, one should also consider the degree to which the medium selected to communicate the insight enhances its conveyance. In this regard, authenticity can be seen as an aid to effective communication. The concern for communicative authenticity rests at the core of analysis and understanding. For Hardt (1993), communication is central "in analyses of authenticity and alienation" (p. 50). While this concern exists within a multitude of potential contexts, communicative authenticity is particularly important for the purpose of this work as it is made manifest within organizations. From a business perspective, linkages between authenticity and communication are perhaps most observable within marketing. At least as a metaphor, branding can be considered an existential concern for organizations since branding is how organizational *identity* is asserted into the public sphere. Marketing communications have been found to play a role in consumer assessments of brand authenticity (Abhishek & McDonald, 2018). While branding is an outward facing concern, concerns with leadership rhetoric are largely inward facing. Linkages between communication and authenticity are observable in senior leadership (Robertson, 2005). Organizationally, communicative authenticity is a concern internally as well as externally. The concern for authenticity is amplified further due to its connection with organizational performance.

Authenticity and improvements in performance are observable across a variety of contexts. In terms of education, authenticity was found to improve learning outcomes (Cavenett, 2017). A similar dynamic is observable in regard to business performance. Authentic leadership has been found to improve organizational outcomes (Gardner, Cogliser, Davis & Dickens, 2011; Ilies, Mehmood, Hamstra, Nawab & Vriend, 2016; Morgeson & Nahrgang, 2005). Wei, Li, Zhang and Liu (2018) contend that "leaders' authenticity may play an important role in improving followers' job performance, and these performance improvements are in the form of both task performance and organizational citizenship behavior" (p. 771). Further still, linkages between individual authenticity and work performance have also been established (Manzi et al., 2021). Collectively, research suggests that authenticity improves performance in education and business and at both the manager and subordinate levels.

The concept of authenticity was explored along two paths: a) existential authenticity and b) communicative authenticity. These two threads bring focus on being who one is (i.e., existential authenticity) and having the self-confidence required to deviate from established norms in terms of the mindless adoption of organizational templates (i.e., communicative authenticity). From these two threads interrelationships between authenticity and performance were presented. These connections reveal the latent potential associated with an empowered workforce to bring their authentic selves to work and through the process improve organizational outcomes. A framework for how an employee might navigate the difficult terrain of authentically communicating insights in organizations is presented next.

COMMUNICATING INSIGHTS

Based on this interpretative qualitative research, aspects of obedience, compliance, disobedience, authenticity and performance were explored to develop a context for thinking about how to more effectively communicate insights in organizations through using or eschewing organizational templates. While templates create a standardized approach that is beneficial for execution within organizations, deviating from these templates can be valuable.

Examining the deviation from organizational templates benefits from both a managerial and practitioner perspective. Deviating from the templates provides leadership with a visible indication that change is occurring and that thinking differently could benefit the organization. In this first application, the search for creativity and autonomy could be executed in a semi-sanctioned fashion. Often when templates and standard approaches are used, they create a stagnant way to execute recurring business. While efficient and effective, this stifles creativity and it's often necessary to innovate and find better ways of doing business. One way to avoid this stagnation is to have organizations revaluate standard templates periodically to understand if there is a better way of executing workload. Through such an assessment, organizations achieve the benefits that templates offer while allowing for creativity from the workforce at agreed upon intervals.

Second, deviating from standard templates provides a method for communicating that an idea *itself* is worthy of presenting in a different, more creative way. This allows the audience to digest the messaging and recommendation in a different way, which can be used to highlight the importance or creativity behind it. Additionally, by communicating an idea by deviating from the standard template, one can illustrate its relative importance by taking it out of the daily execution routine. From a workforce perspective, this becomes a method to encourage and guide management to approach or think about a problem or solution set differently. Also, it allows an individual or team to communicate that they are different and innovative in an approach, which could potentially draw more attention to the recommendation or decision. Such an approach holds value for teams as well as individuals.

When one has a team that they want to approach something with a fresh perspective or creatively, removing the templates which forces compliance and assimilation of ideas can be beneficial. The very act of removing the barriers presented by a template can be the catalyst a team needs to obtain a new idea and allows those working it to have maximum latitude to create and innovate. The elimination of barriers in thought and expression could be an effective tool to communicate the necessity for creativity to the workforce. As an example, projects that don't need to follow a template are those which require maximum creativity. In such cases, the organization is acknowledging that there are tradeoffs between standardization and creativity and allows for context to influence where along the execution spectrum a team is operating. One contextual element worth considering is the degree to which the work being communicated is transactional in nature.

Transactional workload likely requires the use of templates to be efficient; however, if an organization's workload isn't highly transactional, it may be worthwhile to eliminate templates altogether. This could also be true if an organization has a high number of individuals who thrive on creativity and developing their own materials. While templates and standard approaches benefit managers through the ability to be quickly apprised, it can lead to a bored, disengaged workforce. Allowing for creativity and different ways to tackle a project provides those with a creative mind an outlet to excel. By utilizing templates, managers may be missing out on some truly valuable techniques to communicate ideas. As indicated, when considering these opportunities and concerns, managers might decide to allow subordinate to deviate from organizational templates. But what should an individual do if management is not on board with this approach?

The previous scenarios described situations in which the deviation from organizational templates is either sanctioned or semi-sanctioned by management. Deviation in these cases poses little risk to the individual. To clarify, in these cases one is deviating from the organizational template but not the organizational policy. There are potentially cases when an individual might want to communicate insights in business by not only deviating from the use of the organizational template but to do so in an unauthorized fashion. Similar contextual elements to those previously discussed (e.g., conceptual novelty, the need for creativity, non-transactional workload) exist in this case and therefore do not require development again here. The only difference in this context is that management has not created cases for which deviation from the organizational template is permitted. Such a situation places the weight of decision on the individual.

In the absence of an organizational policy for deviation from templates, the individual needs to determine *if* and *when* a certain situation would be more effectively communicated through an alternative means. Such an action entails risk. The guiding principles of *authenticity* and *autonomy* could be useful in informing one's determination. Using a critical reflective process, one might be able to ascertain why one is considering eschewing the organizational template. If such a determination is based on ego, rebelliousness, or contrarian impulses, it is likely better to adhere to the template. If however, the insight is sufficiently novel and the need to provoke thought compelling, deviation might be more effective. When taking such a risk the subordinate might want to convey prudence, sincerity and respect towards management as one demonstrate one's courage and creativity. Taking this risk requires balance.

Hopefully, it is clear that there are no easy answers. Using an organizational template is sometimes the best approach; sometimes it is not. Likewise, sometimes deviating from templates is more effective; sometimes not. Individuals benefit from assessing the situation (i.e., reading the room), examining the attributes of what is being communicated, reflecting on their motivations to adhere to or reject the template and using their agency to authentically communicate insights within an organization. Summarizing the key insights developed in this chapter should reinforce their salience.

CONCLUSION

Autonomy is asserted, not granted. Organizationally, individuals frequently navigate the difficult terrain between compliance and disobedience in regard to policies and procedures. Both approaches offer something to an employee and one's organization. But benefits are seldom derived without cost. Determining which strategy is to be pursued requires context in terms of situation, intent and motivation. An examination of the use of organizational templates for communicating insights in business provides an illustrative case study for understanding the dynamics of this phenomenon.

A semi-structured literature review, with an interpretative frame informed by CMS perspectives, formed the methodological basis for this interpretative qualitative research. To illustrate the individual and organizational potential of authentic communication, existential insights were combined with communication theory. Early in one's career there is pragmatic utility in terms of learning norms and gaining acceptance through compliance with organizational templates. This can be thought of metaphorically as *coloring inside the lines*. After gaining legitimacy within an organization, it is potentially useful to explore strategies of noncompliance with organizational norms (i.e., *deviating from the path*). During this phase, an employee tests the parameters of the institution to find out how much latitude one has in tradeoffs between compliance and effectiveness. Informed by the lessons learned from both compliance and disobedience, one is able to develop a unique path forward marked by both authenticity and improved performance. In this phase, the ability to effectively communicate insights becomes the primary focus and adherence to, or deviation from, organizational templates becomes a secondary concern.

There are several strategies developed here as to how one might communicate insights more effectively in one's organization. First, if there is a need to be creative and innovative, a template won't capture this effectively. Additionally, for certain projects, it's beneficial to allow maximum flexibility and an alternative means to communicate insights. Finally, allowing the workforce to decide can empower them to make the best decision on approach and methodology dependent on the requirements of the project. While this information was grounded in the conceptual and empirical findings presented in this chapter, there are certainly limitations to consider.

First, this study was based on a semi-structured literature review. While such an approach is useful, it has limitations in regard to completeness. As such, one should be careful to not overgeneralize the findings. This study would benefit through its extension by applying a structured, meta-study methodological approach. Second, this study was a qualitative study. Extending the research in this area to quantify the time spent in various forms of compliance with or deviation from organizational templates and the associated effect on organizational outcomes would add empirical weight to the perspectives developed here. Lastly, this study focused narrowly on compliance and deviation in the use of organizational templates. The concerns associated with autonomy and subjugation of employees extends to other areas of organizational existence. Measuring the degree of authenticity permitted within organizations and the associated organizational outcomes are important both individually and collectively. Even with these limitations in mind, the importance associated with effectively communicating insights in organizations remains.

Concerns for authenticity bring focus to the value of internal coherence and external validity. Ideally, organizations are sites in which emplyoees are able to *be* and *communicate* authentically. There can exist both authentic and inauthentic compliance as well as authentic and inauthentic noncompliance. Employees benefit from examining this situation strategically when deciding what to do. When the situation or content being expressed is significantly novel using an organizational template may fail to adequately deliver the message. In such situations one might need to exercise strategic noncompliance and select a communication style which provokes thought and brings attention to the fact that what is being discussed is not *business as usual*. Novel insights might require novel communication approaches. Such deviations hold potential organizational benefit if the deviation allows for quicker understanding and action. Organizations can facilitate this through empowerment, but only individuals can enact it through the assertion of their autonomy.

REFERENCES

Abecassis, M. C., & Benghozi, P. (2012). Efficiency and innovativeness as determinants of design architecture choices. *Journal of Product Innovation Management*, *29*(3), 405–418. doi:10.1111/j.1540-5885.2012.00914.x

Abhishek, D., & McDonald, R. (2018). Building brand authenticity in fast-moving consumer goods via consumer perceptions of brand marketing communications. *European Journal of Marketing*, *52*(7), 1387–1411. doi:10.1108/EJM-11-2016-0665

Agarwal, R., & Tanniru, M. R. (1990). Knowledge acquisition using structured interviewing: An empirical investigation. *Journal of Management Information Systems*, *7*(1), 123–140. doi:10.1080/07421222.1990.11517884

Alvesson, M., & Deetz, S. (2000). *Doing Critical Management Research*. Sage Publications. doi:10.4135/9781849208918

Asch, S. E. (1956). Studies of independence and conformity: I. A minority of one against a unanimous majority. *Psychological Monographs*, *70*(9), 1–70. doi:10.1037/h0093718

Blackie, W. (1971). Authority. *S.A.M. Advanced Management Journal*, *36*(4), 47.

Bolles, D. L., & Hubbard, D. G. (2006). 11. Creating policies, plans, and procedures: 11.1 Determining the need. In *Power of Enterprise-Wide Project Management* (pp. 117–119). American Management Association International.

Bradford, K. (2019). Radical authenticity. *Existential Analysis: Journal of the Society for Existential Analysis*, *30*(1), 115–127.

Burrell, G., & Dale, K. (2002). Utopiary: Utopias, gardens and organization. *Sociological Review. Monograph*, *50*(2), 106–127. doi:10.1111/j.1467-954X.2002.tb03581.x

Byrne, M. D., & Davis, E. M. (2006). Task structure and postcompletion error in the execution of a routine procedure. *Human Factors*, *48*(4), 627–638. doi:10.1518/001872006779166398 PMID:17240711

Camus, A. (1991). *The Rebel*. Vintage.

Carmeli, A., Shalom, R., & Weisberg, J. (2007). Considerations in organizational career advancement: What really matters. *Personnel Review*, *36*(1/2), 190–205. doi:10.1108/00483480710726109

Cavenett, S. (2017). Authentically enhancing the learning and development environment. *Australasian Journal of Engineering Education*, *22*(1), 39–53. doi:10.1080/22054952.2017.1372031

Cheyne, J. A., Solman, G. J. F., Carriere, J. S. A., & Smilek, D. (2009). Anatomy of an error: A bidirectional state model of task engagement/disengagement and attention-related errors. *Cognition*, *111*(1), 98–113. doi:10.1016/j.cognition.2008.12.009 PMID:19215913

Church, D. L., & Naugler, C. (2019). Benefits and risks of standardization, harmonization and conformity to opinion in clinical laboratories. *Critical Reviews in Clinical Laboratory Sciences*, *56*(5), 287–306. doi:10.1080/10408363.2019.1615408 PMID:31060412

Clark, K. R. (2019). Ethics in research. *Radiologic Technology*, *90*(4), 394–397. PMID:30886035

Clarke, N. (2009). Footless and fancy free? On some means to move beyond the self-induced and institutional constraints of CMS. In J. W. Cox, T. G. LeTrent-Jones, M. Voronov, & D. Weir (Eds.), *Critical management studies at work: Negotiating tensions between theory and practice* (pp. 64–81). Edward Elgar. doi:10.4337/9781848449497.00011

Davis, P. T. (2016). Process standardization is key. *COBIT Focus*, 1-3.

De Wall, B. M. E. (2013). User participation practice: To overcome the objective-subjective dichotomy. *IADIS International Journal of Computer Science & Information Systems*, *8*(1), 142–158.

Ferrari, A., Witschel, H. F., Spagnolo, G. O., & Gnesi, S. (2018). Improving the quality of business process descriptions of public administrations. *Business Process Management Journal*, *24*(1), 49–66. doi:10.1108/BPMJ-05-2016-0096

Ferri-Reed, J. (2013). Onboarding strategies to supercharge millennial employees. *Journal for Quality and Participation*, *36*(2), 32–33.

Fromm, E. (2010). *On Disobedience: Why Freedom Means Saying "No" to Power*. HarperCollins Publishers.

Gagnon, S. (2008). Compelling identity: Selves and insecurity in global, corporate management development. *Management Learning*, *39*(4), 375–391. doi:10.1177/1350507608093710

Gandossy, R., & Sonnenfeld, J. (2005). "I see nothing, I hear nothing": Culture, corruption and apathy. *International Journal of Disclosure and Governance*, *2*(3), 228–243. doi:10.1057/palgrave.jdg.2040055

Gardner, W. L., Cogliser, C. C., Davis, K. M., & Dickens, M. P. (2011). Authentic leadership: A review of the literature and research agenda. *The Leadership Quarterly*, *22*(6), 1120–1145. doi:10.1016/j.leaqua.2011.09.007

Green, L. (2003). Civil disobedience and academic freedom. *Osgoode Hall Law Journal*, *41*(2/3), 381–405.

Griggs, R. A. (2017). Milgram's obedience study. *Teaching of Psychology*, *44*(1), 32–37. doi:10.1177/0098628316677644

Hardt, H. (1993). Authenticity, communication, and critical theory. *Critical Studies in Mass Communication*, *10*(1), 49–69. doi:10.1080/15295039309366848

Ilies, R., Morgeson, F. P., & Nahrgang, J. D. (2005). Authentic leadership and eudaemonic well-being: Understanding leader-follower outcomes. *The Leadership Quarterly*, *16*(3), 373–394. doi:10.1016/j.leaqua.2005.03.002

Kacerauskas, T. (2016). The paradoxes of creativity management. *Ekonomie a Management*, *19*(4), 33–43. doi:10.15240/tul/001/2016-4-003

Klein, H. J., Polin, B., & Leigh Sutton, K. (2015). Specific onboarding practices for the socialization of new employees. *International Journal of Selection and Assessment*, *23*(3), 263–283. doi:10.1111/ijsa.12113

Kyrlitsias, C., & Michael, G. D. (2018). Asch conformity experiment using immersive virtual reality. *Computer Animation & Virtual Worlds, 29*(5). doi:10.1002/cav.1804

Lamb, T. A., & Alsikafi, M. (1980). Conformity in the Asch experiment: Inner-other directedness and the "defiant subject.". *Social Behavior and Personality*, *8*(1), 13–16. doi:10.2224bp.1980.8.1.13

Larsen, K. S. (1974). Conformity in the Asch Experiment. *The Journal of Social Psychology, 94*(2), 303–304. doi:10.1080/00224545.1974.9923224

Manzi, C., Sorgente, A., Reverberi, E., Tagliabue, S., & Gorli, M. (2021). Double jeopardy-analyzing the combined effect of age and gender stereotype threat on older workers. *Frontiers in Psychology, 11*, 606690. doi:10.3389/fpsyg.2020.606690 PMID:33510682

Mechenbier, M. X. (2011). Cheating the business template: Filling in the blanks. *Business Communication Quarterly, 74*(2), 192–195. doi:10.1177/1080569911404055

Mehmood, Q., Hamstra, M. R. W., Nawab, S., & Vriend, T. (2016). Authentic leadership and followers' in-role and extra-role performance: The mediating role of followers' learning goal orientation. *Journal of Occupational and Organizational Psychology, 89*(4), 877–883. doi:10.1111/joop.12153

Milgram, S. (1963). Behavioral study of obedience. *Journal of Abnormal and Social Psychology, 67*(4), 371–378. doi:10.1037/h0040525 PMID:14049516

Milgram, S. (1965). Some conditions of obedience and disobedience to authority. *Human Relations, 18*(1), 57–76. doi:10.1177/001872676501800105

Monin, N. (2004). *Management Theory: A Critical and Reflective Reading*. Routledge. doi:10.4324/9780203356814

Mori, K., & Arai, M. (2010). No need to fake it: Reproduction of the Asch experiment without confederates. *International Journal of Psychology, 45*(5), 390–397. doi:10.1080/00207591003774485 PMID:22044061

Orwell, G. (2001). *Nineteen Eighty-Four*. The Folio Society.

Ostas, D. T. (2010). Civil disobedience in a business context: Examining the social obligation to obey inane laws. *American Business Law Journal, 47*(2), 291–312. doi:10.1111/j.1744-1714.2010.01095.x

Passini, S., & Morselli, D. (2013). The triadic legitimacy model: Understanding support to disobedient groups. *New Ideas in Psychology, 31*(2), 98–107. doi:10.1016/j.newideapsych.2012.06.002

Perry, G., Brannigan, A., Wanner, R. A., & Stam, H. (2020). Credibility and incredulity in Milgram's obedience experiments: A reanalysis of an unpublished test. *Social Psychology Quarterly, 83*(1), 88–106. doi:10.1177/0190272519861952

Pierce, A. J. (2015). Authentic identities. *Social Theory and Practice, 41*(3), 435–457. doi:10.5840oct heorpract201541323

Pollman, E. (2019). Corporate oversight and disobedience. *Vanderbilt Law Review, 72*(6), 2013–2046.

Rennstam, J., & Kärreman, D. (2020). Understanding control in communities of practice: Constructive disobedience in a high-tech firm. *Human Relations, 73*(6), 864–890. doi:10.1177/0018726719843588

Riach, K., & Wilson, F. (2007). Don't screw the crew: Exploring the rules of engagement in organizational romance. *British Journal of Management, 18*(1), 79–92. doi:10.1111/j.1467-8551.2006.00503.x

Robertson, L. (2005). The cost of missed opportunities. *Strategic Communication Management, 9*(3), 5.

Sartre, J.-P. (1994). *Being and Nothingness*. Gramercy Books.

Sava, T. (2016). From Plato to Swift and Orwell, from utopia to dystopia. *Journal of Humanistic and Social Studies*, *7*(1), 9–16.

Schultz, B. (2006). Business documents don't have to be boring. *Business Communication Quarterly*, *69*(4), 407–410. doi:10.1177/10805699060690041l

Seeger, S., & Davison-Vecchione, D. (2019). Dystopian literature and the sociological imagination. *Thesis Eleven, 155*(1), 45-63. doi:10.1177/0725513619888664

Snyder, H. (2019). Literature review as a research methodology: An overview and guidelines. *Journal of Business Research*, *104*, 333–339. doi:10.1016/j.jbusres.2019.07.039

Sosik, J., Chun, J., & Zhu, W. (2014). Hang on to your ego: The moderating role of leader narcissism on relationships between leader charisma and follower psychological empowerment and moral identity. *Journal of Business Ethics*, *120*(1), 65–80. doi:10.100710551-013-1651-0

Vonnegut, K. (2006). *Player Piano*. The Dial Press.

Watson, G., & Berkley, R. (2009). Testing the value-pragmatics hypothesis in unethical compliance. *Journal of Business Ethics*, *87*(4), 463–476. doi:10.100710551-008-9953-3

Webster, J., & Watson, R. T. (2002). Analyzing the past to prepare for the future: Writing a literature review. *Management Information Systems Quarterly*, *26*(2), xiii–xxiii.

Wei, F., Li, Y., Zhang, Y., & Liu, S. (2018). The interactive effect of authentic leadership and leader competency on followers' job performance: The mediating role of work engagement. *Journal of Business Ethics*, *153*(3), 763–773. doi:10.100710551-016-3379-0

Wiesner, P. (2000). The office walls. *ColoradoBiz*, *27*(8), 9.

Zamyatin, Y. (2016). *We*. McAllister Editions.

Compilation of References

Abarca, A. (1979). La toma de decisiones: un proceso de aprendizaje. *Revista educación, 3*(1). Recovered from https://revistas.ucr.ac.cr/index.php/educacion/article/view/18667

Abbasi, M. H., Siddiqi, A., & Azim, R. U. A. (2011). Role of effective communications for enhancing leadership and entrepreneurial skills in university students. *International Journal of Business and Social Science*, *2*(10).

Abecassis, M. C., & Benghozi, P. (2012). Efficiency and innovativeness as determinants of design architecture choices. *Journal of Product Innovation Management*, *29*(3), 405–418. doi:10.1111/j.1540-5885.2012.00914.x

Abhishek, D., & McDonald, R. (2018). Building brand authenticity in fast-moving consumer goods via consumer perceptions of brand marketing communications. *European Journal of Marketing*, *52*(7), 1387–1411. doi:10.1108/EJM-11-2016-0665

Abraham, T., Cheney, A. M., & Curran, G. M. (2017). A Bourdieusian analysis of US military culture ground in the mental help-seeking literature. *American Journal of Men's Health*, *11*(5), 1358–1365. doi:10.1177/1557988315596037 PMID:26229053

Achdut, N., & Refaeli, T. (2020). Unemployment and psychological distress among young people during the COVID-19 pandemic: Psychological resources and risk factors. *International Journal of Environmental Research and Public Health*, *17*(19), 7163. doi:10.3390/ijerph17197163 PMID:33007892

Ackert, L., & Deaves, R. (2009). *Behavioral finance: Psychology, decision-making, and markets*. South-Western Pub.

Agarwal, R., & Tanniru, M. R. (1990). Knowledge acquisition using structured interviewing: An empirical investigation. *Journal of Management Information Systems*, *7*(1), 123–140. doi:10.1080/07421222.1990.11517884

Agnihotri, A., & Agnihotri, A. (2020). *Comparative study of team characteristics under shared leadership in large and small companies in IT industry in India* [Paper presentation]. 2020 8th International Conference on Reliability, Infocom Technologies and Optimization (Trends and Future Directions) (ICRITO), Noida, India. 10.1109/ICRITO48877.2020.9197938

Aguirre, M. (2005). El impacto de la emoción en la toma de decisiones. *La Gaceta de Económicas*.

Ajzen, I., & Fishbein, M. A. (1980). Attitudes and the Attitude–Behavior Reasoned Automatic Processes. Published. In W. Stroebe & M. Hewstone (Eds.), *European Review of Social Psychology*. John Wiley & Sons.

Akbar, K., Jin, Y., & Salam, S. (2018). Barriers to environmentally-conscious manufacturing innovation. *Human Systems Management*, *37*(4), 453–462. doi:10.3233/HSM-17251

Al Sharoufi, H. (2014). The role of pragmatics in understanding human communication in an institutional setting. *Journal of Defense Resources Management*, *4*(2), 95–108.

Albuquerque, E., Seabra, L., Rolim, P., & Gomes, L. (2012). Riscos físicos em uma unidade de alimentação e nutrição: Implicações na saúde do trabalhador. *Revista da Associação Brasileira de Nutrição, 4*(1), 40–47.

Allen, M. (1997). *Visionary business: an entrepreneur's guide to success.* New World Library.

Almeida, F., Kennedy, A. J., Lin, B., & Nowak, I. (2019). Measuring innovation through a crowd source initiative. *International Journal of Innovation Science, 11*(3), 471–488. doi:10.1108/IJIS-04-2019-0046

Almeida, F., & Rocha, R. (2011). Introduction of a WIKI in an enterprise: Motives and challenges. *Journal of Systems Integration, 2*(4), 46–53. doi:10.20470/jsi.v2i4.101

Althaf, S., & Babbitt, C. W. (2020). Disruption risks to material supply chains in the electronics sector. *Resources, Conservation and Recycling*, 105248.

Alvesson, M., & Deetz, S. (2000). *Doing critical management research.* SAGE publications. doi:10.4135/9781849208918

Alves, T. P. (2010). *Melhoria contínua: Importância e aplicação no processo produtivo de uma indústria metalúrgica.* Manole.

Anthony, L. (2013). A critical look at software tools in corpus linguistics*. *Linguistic Review, 30*(2), 141–161.

Anwesha, M. (2020). Leadership for creating sustainability within the organization: An empirical study. *IUP Journal of Organizational Behavior, 19*(3), 7–17.

Appelo, J. (2011). *Management 3.0: Leading Agile Developers, Developing Agile Leaders.* Addison-Wesley Professional.

Appelo, J. (2014). *Management 3.0 Workout.* Happy Melly Express.

Appleby, Y., & Pikington, R. (2014). *Developing Critical Professional Practice in Education.* NIACE.

Araújo, L. E. (2009). *Nivelamento de capacidade de produção utilizando quadros Heijunka em sistemas híbridos de coordenação de ordens de produção* (Dissertação de Mestrado). Pós-Graduação em Engenharia de Produção, São Paulo, Brazil.

Araújo, C., & Pedron, C. D. (2016). The Importance of Soft Skills and it Project Managers' Personality Type. *International Journal of Professional Business Review, 1*(1), 40–59. doi:10.26668/businessreview/2016.v1i1.8

Ariely, D. (2009). *Predictably Irrational: The Hidden Forces That Shape Our Decisions.* Harper Collins Books.

Arora, M., & Sharma, R. L. (2017). Decoding diverse dimensions of entrepreneurial leadership with special emphasis on persuasive communication. *Management Dynamics, 17*(1).

Arora, M. (2020). Post-Truth and Marketing Communication in Technological Age. In *Handbook of Research on Innovations in Technology and Marketing for the Connected Consumer* (pp. 94–108). IGI Global. doi:10.4018/978-1-7998-0131-3.ch005

Arsene, M. (2012). The Living Tradition: Liberal Arts Education. The U.S. Campus Heritage. *East-West Cultural Passage, 12*(2), 106–114.

Artisan Alliance Enterprise. (2016). *Impact Report.* Alliance for Artisan Enterprise.

Asch, S. E. (1956). Studies of independence and conformity: I. A minority of one against a unanimous majority. *Psychological Monographs, 70*(9), 1–70. doi:10.1037/h0093718

Asphalt, E. (2020). Conscious, innovative solutions from Shisalanga. *IMIESA, 7.*

Audretsch, D. B. (2007). Entrepreneurship capital and economic growth. *Oxford Review of Economic Policy*, *23*(1), 63–78. doi:10.1093/oxrep/grm001

Autio, E., Kenney, M., Mustar, P., Siegel, D., & Wright, M. (2014). Entrepreneurial innovation: The importance of context. *Research Policy*, *43*(7), 1097–1108. doi:10.1016/j.respol.2014.01.015

Avolio, B., Walumbwa D. A., & Weber, T. J. (2009). Leadership: Current theories, research, and future directions. *Annual Review of Psychology, 60*, 8.1-8.29.

Avolio, B. (1994). The "natural": Some antecedents to transformational leadership. *International Journal of Public Administration*, *17*(9), 1559–1581. doi:10.1080/01900699408524956

Avolio, B. J., Jung, D., Murry, W., & Sivasubramaniam, N. (1996). Building highly developed teams: Focusing on shared leadership process, efficacy, trust, and performance. In D. A. Beyerlein, D. A. Johnson, & S. T. Beyerlein (Eds.), *Advances in interdiscinplinary studies of work teams* (pp. 173–209). JAI Press.

Azmi, A. M., Hairi, O. N., Lee, K. Y., & Fauziah, I. (2012). Entreprenuers success in business: Some critical factors. *International Business Management*, *6*(3), 369–373. doi:10.3923/ibm.2012.369.373

Bailey, C. (2017). *A Guide to Qualitative Field Research*. SAGE Publications.

Bang, H., & Midelfart, T. N. (2017). What characterizes effective management teams? A research-based approach. *Consulting Psychology Journal*, *69*(4), 334–359. doi:10.1037/cpb0000098

Banks, D. (2005). The case of Perrin and Thomson: An example of the use of a mini-corpus. *English for Specific Purposes*, *24*(2), 201–211. doi:10.1016/j.esp.2004.01.001

Bârgău, M. A. (2015). Types of leader in Organisation. *EIRP Proceedings, 10*(1), 559-565.

Barki, E., & Parente, J. (2014). Challenges and opportunities of the last mile for the base of the pyramid: The case of Brazil. *Field Actions Science Reports*, *12*(Special Issue). https://journals.openedition.org/factsreports/3671

Barua, S. (2020). *Understanding Coronanomics: The economic implications of the coronavirus (COVID-19) pandemic*. Academic Press.

Barzilay, R., Moore, T. M., Greenberg, D. M., DiDomenico, G. E., Brown, L. A., White, L. K., Gur, R. C., & Gur, R. E. (2020). Resilience, COVID-19-related stress, anxiety and depression during the pandemic in a large population enriched for healthcare providers. *Translational Psychiatry*, *10*(1), 1–8. doi:10.103841398-020-00982-4 PMID:32820171

Bass, B. (1990a). From transactional to transformational leadership: Learning to share the vision. *Organizational Dynamics*, *18*(3), 19–31. doi:10.1016/0090-2616(90)90061-S

Bass, B., & Avolio, B. (1991). *Multifactor Leadership Questionnaire (Form 5X)*. Center for Leadership Studies.

Bayrak, T. (2015). A review of business analytics: A business enabler or another passing fad. *Procedia: Social and Behavioral Sciences*, *195*, 230–239. doi:10.1016/j.sbspro.2015.06.354

BBVA Innovation Center. (2011). *Neuroeconomía: Mecanismos cerebrales implicados en la toma de decisiones financieras*. KnowSquare: red de conocimiento.

Bean, R., & Davenport, T. H. (2019). *Companies Are Failing in Their Efforts to Become Data-Driven*. https://hbr.org/2019/02/companies-are-failing-in-their-efforts-to-become-data-driven

Belk, R. W. (2020). Post-pandemic consumption: Portal to a new world? *Cadernos EBAPE.BR*, *18*(3), 639–647. doi:10.1590/1679-395120200175x

Bell, B. S., & Kozlowski, S. W. J. (2002). A typology of virtual teams: Implications for effective leadership. *Group & Organization Management, 27*(1), 14–49. doi:10.1177/1059601102027001003

Berg, B. L. (2004). *Methods for the social sciences. In Qualitative Research Methods for the Social Sciences.* Pearson Education.

Berkun, S. (2008). *Making Things Happen: Mastering Project Management.* O'Reilly Media.

Berman, G. (2008). *Harnessing diversity: Addressing racial and religious discrimination in employment.* Victorian Multicultural Commission and the Victorian Equal Opportunity and Human Rights Commission.

Berns, M. J. (1987). *Communication variables and female entrepreneurs: exploratory case studies of six former corporate executive women.* Academic Press.

Bertrand, J. W. M., & Fransoo, J. C. (2002). Operations management research methodologies using quantitative modeling. *International Journal of Operations & Production Management, 22*(2), 241–264. doi:10.1108/01443570210414338

Bevins, S. (2012). STeM: Moving the Liberal arts education into the 21st century. *Technology and Engineering Teacher, 71*(4), 10–13.

Beyer, J. M. (1999). Taming and promoting charisma to change organizations. *The Leadership Quarterly, 10*(2), 307–330. doi:10.1016/S1048-9843(99)00019-3

Bidzan-Bluma, I., Bidzan, M., Jurek, P., Bidzan, L., Knietzsch, J., Stueck, M., & Bidzan, M. (2020). A Polish and German Population Study of Quality of Life, Well-Being, and Life Satisfaction in Older Adults During the COVID-19 Pandemic. *Frontiers in Psychiatry*, 11. PMID:33281646

Bindl, U. K., & Parker, S. K. (2010). Proactive work behavior: Forward-thinking and change oriented action in organizations. In S. Zedeck (Ed.), *APA handbook of industrial and organizational psychology* (pp. 567–598). American Psychological Association.

Blackie, W. (1971). Authority. *S.A.M. Advanced Management Journal, 36*(4), 47.

Black, K., & Skipper, H. D. (2000). *Life and Health Insurance*. Prentice-Hall.

Blowfield, M. (2012). Business and development: Making sense of business as a development agent. *Corporate Governance: International Journal of Business in Society, 12*(4), 414–426. doi:10.1108/14720701211267775

Bocken, N., Boons, F., & Baldassarre, B. (2019). Sustainable business model experimentation by understanding ecologies of business models. *Journal of Cleaner Production, 208*, 1498–1512. doi:10.1016/j.jclepro.2018.10.159

Bois, J. S. (1975). *The art of awareness* (2nd ed.). William C. Brown Publisher.

Bolles, D. L., & Hubbard, D. G. (2006). 11. Creating policies, plans, and procedures: 11.1 Determining the need. In *Power of Enterprise-Wide Project Management* (pp. 117–119). American Management Association International.

Bolotova, A. K. (2012). Time parameters of nonverbal communication and personal communicative competence. *Psychology in Russia. State of the Art*, 289-300.

Bonadio, B., Huo, Z., Levchenko, A. A., & Pandalai-Nayar, N. (2020). Global supply chains in the pandemic (No. w27224). National Bureau of Economic Research.

Bose, R. (2009). Advanced analytics: Opportunities and challenges. *Industrial Management & Data Systems, 109*(2), 155–172. doi:10.1108/02635570910930073

Boyatzis, R. E. (2011). Managerial and Leadership Competencies A Behavioral Approach to Emotional, Social and Cognitive Intelligence. *Vision – The Journal of Business Perspective, 15*(2), 91-100.

Brace, L. (2016). *The Seven Principles of Managing for Creativity*. Retrieved from https://management30.com/blog/the-seven-principles-of-managing-for-creativity/

Brace, N., Kemp, R., & Snelgar, R. (2012). *SPSS for psychologists* (5th ed.). Lawrence Erlbaum Associates.

Bradford, K. (2019). Radical authenticity. *Existential Analysis: Journal of the Society for Existential Analysis*, *30*(1), 115–127.

Braun, M., & Muermann, A. (2004). The impact of regret on the demand for insurance. *The Journal of Risk and Insurance*, *71*(4), 737–767. doi:10.1111/j.0022-4367.2004.00110.x

Brezina, V., Weill-Tessier, P., & McEnery, A. (2020). *#LancsBox v.5.x* [software]. Available at: http://corpora.lancs.ac.uk/lancsbox

Brezina, V. (2018). *Statistics in Corpus Linguistics: A Practical Guide*. Cambridge University Press. doi:10.1017/9781316410899

Brezina, V., McEnery, T., & Wattam, S. (2015). Collocations in context: A new perspective on collocation networks. *International Journal of Corpus Linguistics*, *20*(2), 139–173. doi:10.1075/ijcl.20.2.01bre

Brockhaus, R. H. Sr. (1980). Risk taking propensity of entrepreneurs. *Academy of Management Journal*, *23*(3), 509–520.

Brooks, K. (1978). Evaluating the communicative act of oral interpretation. *Communication*, *7*(1), 167–180.

Brown, W. (2017). *Exploring the impact of shared leadership styles and nonprofit performance* [Doctoral Dissertation, Walden University]. ScholarWorks.

Brown, M., Brown, R. S., & Nandedkar, A. (2019). Transformational leadership theory and exploring the perceptions of diversity management in higher education. *Journal of Higher Education Theory & Practice*, *19*(7), 11–21.

Buchanan & O'Connell. (2006). A brief history of decision making. *Harvard Business Review*, *84*(1), 32–41.

Burns, J. (1978). *Leadership*. Harper & Row.

Burrell, G., & Dale, K. (2002). Utopiary: Utopias, gardens and organization. *Sociological Review. Mongraph*, *50*(2), 106–127. doi:10.1111/j.1467-954X.2002.tb03581.x

Burrow, J., & Kleindl, B. (2013). *Business Management* (13th ed.). South-Western, Cengage Learning.

Bushe, G. R., & Marshak, R. J. (2015). *Dialogic Organization Development: The Theory and Practice of Transformational Change*. Berrett-Koehler Publishers.

Buttner, E. H., & Lowe, K. B. (2010). Diversity climate impact on employee of color outcomes: Does justice matter? *Career Development International*, *15*(3), 239–258. doi:10.1108/13620431011053721

Button, C. J., Jinkerson, J., & Bryan, C. J. (2017). Making Meaning After Combat Trauma and Moral Injury. In *Reconstructing Meaning After Trauma* (pp. 167–184). Academic Press. doi:10.1016/B978-0-12-803015-8.00011-5

Byrne, M. D., & Davis, E. M. (2006). Task structure and postcompletion error in the execution of a routine procedure. *Human Factors*, *48*(4), 627–638. doi:10.1518/001872006779166398 PMID:17240711

Camerer, C. F., Loewenstein, G., & Prelec, D. (2005). Neuroeconomics: How neuroscience can inform economics. *Journal of Economic Literature, 43*(1), 9–64. doi:10.1257/0022051053737843

Cameron, E. E., Joyce, K. M., Delaquis, C. P., Reynolds, K., Protudjer, J. L., & Roos, L. E. (2020). Maternal psychological distress & mental health service use during the COVID-19 pandemic. *Journal of Affective Disorders*, *276*, 765–774. doi:10.1016/j.jad.2020.07.081 PMID:32736186

Campbell, L. (2018). An epistemology for practical knowledge. *Canadian Journal of Philosophy*, *48*(2), 159–177. doi:10.1080/00455091.2017.1341073

Campion, M. A., Medsker, G. J., & Higgs, A. C. (1993). Relations between work group characteristics and effectiveness: Implications for designing effective work groups. *Personnel Psychology*, *46*(4), 823–850. doi:10.1111/j.1744-6570.1993.tb01571.x

Camus, A. (1991). *The Rebel*. Vintage.

Carmeli, A., Shalom, R., & Weisberg, J. (2007). Considerations in organizational career advancement: What really matters. *Personnel Review*, *36*(1/2), 190–205. doi:10.1108/00483480710726109

Cavenett, S. (2017). Authentically enhancing the learning and development environment. *Australasian Journal of Engineering Education*, *22*(1), 39–53. doi:10.1080/22054952.2017.1372031

Cepani, L., & Lamani, D. (2013). Development of the accounting research methods in Albania. *Studies in Business & Economics*, *8*(3), 32–40.

Charumathi, B. (2012). On the determinants of profitability of Indian life insurers: An empirical study. *Proceedings of the World Congress on Engineering, WCE 2012*.

Chaudhury, S. K., & Das, S. K. (2014). Trends in marketing of new insurance schemes and distribution: An empirical study on Indian life insurance sector. *Journal of Business and Technology (Dhaka)*, *9*(2), 61–81. doi:10.3329/jbt.v9i2.26196

Chen, C. C., Wu, J., Yang, S. C., & Tsou, H.-Y. (2008). Importance of diversified leadership roles in improving team effectiveness in a virtual collaboration learning environment. *Journal of Educational Technology & Society*, *11*(1), 304–321.

Cheney, G., Christensen, L. T., Zorn, T. E., & Ganesh, S. (2011). *Organizational Communication in an Age of Globalization: Issues, Reflections, Practices*. Waveland Pr Inc.

Chen, S.-P., & Wu, W.-Y. (2010). A systematic procedure to evaluate an automobile manufacturer-distributor partnership. *European Journal of Operational Research*, *205*(3), 687–698. doi:10.1016/j.ejor.2010.01.036

Chen, Y., Yang, J., & Ribarsky, W. (2009). Toward effective insight management in visual analytics systems. *IEEE Pacific Visualization Symposium*, 49-56.

Cheyne, J. A., Solman, G. J. F., Carriere, J. S. A., & Smilek, D. (2009). Anatomy of an error: A bidirectional state model of task engagement/disengagement and attention-related errors. *Cognition*, *111*(1), 98–113. doi:10.1016/j.cognition.2008.12.009 PMID:19215913

Chickowski, E. (2009). Five trends changing the face of BI. *eWeek, 26*(16), 18.

Chowdhury, A. M. R., & Cash, R. A. (1996). *A Simple Solution - Teaching Millions to Treat Diarrhoea at Home*. The University Press Limited (UPL).

Cho, Y., & Choi, I. (2018). Writing from sources: Does audience matter? *Assessing Writing*, *37*, 25–38. doi:10.1016/j.asw.2018.03.004

Church, D. L., & Naugler, C. (2019). Benefits and risks of standardization, harmonization and conformity to opinion in clinical laboratories. *Critical Reviews in Clinical Laboratory Sciences*, *56*(5), 287–306. doi:10.1080/10408363.2019.1615408 PMID:31060412

Clarke, N. (2009). Footless and fancy free? On some means to move beyond the self-induced and institutional constraints of CMS. In J. W. Cox, T. G. LeTrent-Jones, M. Voronov, & D. Weir (Eds.), *Critical management studies at work: Negotiating tensions between theory and practice* (pp. 64–81). Edward Elgar. doi:10.4337/9781848449497.00011

Clark, K. R. (2019). Ethics in research. *Radiologic Technology*, *90*(4), 394–397. PMID:30886035

Claxton, G. (2015). *Intelligence in the flesh: Why your mind needs your body much more than it thinks.* Yale University Press.

Coates, D. (2015). *Capitalism: The Basics.* Routledge. doi:10.4324/9780203798799

Cohen, J. (1988). *Statistical power analysis for the behavioral sciences* (2nd ed.). West Publishing Company.

Colbran, R., Ramsden, R., Stagnitti, K., & Toumbourou, J. W. (2019). Advancing towards contemporary practice: A systematic review of organisational performance measures for non-acute health charities. *BMC Health Services Research*, *19*(132), 1–12. doi:10.118612913-019-3952-1 PMID:30795742

Coleman, M. (2012). Leadership and diversity. *Educational Management Administration & Leadership*, *40*(5), 592–609. doi:10.1177/1741143212451174

Conaway, R. N., Regester, K., Martin, S., Nixon, C., & Senior, B. (2018). Amazon Whole Foods: When E-Commerce Met Brick-and-Mortar and Saved the Brand of Conscientious Capitalism. *Journal of Marketing Development and Competitiveness*, *12*(3).

Conley, C. S., Durlak, J. A., & Kirsch, A. C. (2015). A meta-analysis of universal mental health prevention programs for higher education students. *Prevention Science*, *16*(4), 487–507. doi:10.100711121-015-0543-1 PMID:25744536

Coolidge, C. (1925). *Address to the American Society of Newspaper Editors.* https://www.presidency.ucsb.edu/documents/address-the-american-society-newspaper-editors-washington-dc

Cooper, L., Caddick, N., Godier, L., Cooper, A., & Fossey, M. (2018). Transition from the military into civilian life: An exploration of cultural competence. *Armed Forces and Society*, *44*(1), 156–177. doi:10.1177/0095327X16675965

Coronado, G., Cañan, F., & Herrera, B. (2007). *La Gestión del Conocimiento para la toma de decisiones. Serie Técnica No 5: Apoyando los esfuerzos en el manejo y protección de la biodiversidad tropical.* The Nature Conservancy.

Costa, A. S., Santana, L. C., & Trigo, A. C. (2015). Qualidade do atendimento ao cliente: Um grande diferencial competitivo para as organizações. *Revista de Iniciação Científica*, *2*(2), 155–172.

Cox, J., Pearce, C., & Perry, M. (2003). Toward a model of shared leadership and distributed influence in the innovation process. In C. Pearce & J. Conger (Eds.), *Shared leadership: Reframing the hows and whys of leadership* (pp. 48–76). Sage. doi:10.4135/9781452229539.n3

Creswell, J. W. (2009). *Research design: Qualitative, quantitative, and mixed methods approaches* (3rd ed.). Sage.

Cunningham, J. B., & Lischeron, J. (1991). Defining entrepreneurship. *Journal of Small Business Management*, *29*(1), 45–61.

D'hondt, E., Verberne, S., Koster, C., & Boves, L. (2013). Text representations for patent classification. *Computational Linguistics*, *39*(3), 755–775. doi:10.1162/COLI_a_00149

D'Innocenzo, L., Mathieu, J. E., & Kukenberger, M. R. (2014). A meta-analysis of different forms of shared leadership – Team performance relations. *Journal of Management*, 1–28. doi:10.1177/0149206314525205

Dai, Y.-D., Dai, Y.-Y., Chen, K.-Y., & Wu, H.-C. (2013). Transformational vs transactional leadership: Which is better? *International Journal of Contemporary Hospitality Management*, *25*(5), 760–778. doi:10.1108/IJCHM-Dec-2011-0223

Dali, M., Shah, N. R., Abdullah, M., Azman, A. R., Nordin, S. N., Muhammad, I., ... Nilai, B. B. (n.d.). *The Entrepreneurship Model Development Based on Truthfulness, Trustworthiness, Wisdom, and Communication Characteristics*. Academic Press.

Damasio, A. R. (1994). *Descartes' Error*. G.P. Putnam's Sons.

Darling, J. R., & Beebe, S. A. (2007). Effective entrepreneurial communication in organization development: Achieving excellence based on leadership strategies and values. *Organization Development Journal*, *25*(1), 76.

Dashti, Y., Schwartz, D., & Pines, A. M. (2011). High technology entrepreneurs, their social networks and success in global markets: The case of Israelis in the US market. *Current Topics in Management: Global Perspectives on Strategy, Behavior, and Performance*, *1*, 131.

Davenport, T. H., & Kim, J. (2013). *Keeping Up with the Quants: Your Guide to Understanding and Using Analytics*. Harvard Business School Publishing Corporation.

Davis, P. T. (2016). Process standardization is key. *COBIT Focus*, 1-3.

Davis, W. (2010, June 16). The 'Learning Knights' of Bell Telephone. *The New York Times*.

Davis, S. M. (1968). Entrepreneurial succession. *Administrative Science Quarterly*, *13*(3), 402–416. doi:10.2307/2391050

Day, D., Gronn, P., & Salas, E. (2004). Leadership capacity in teams. *The Leadership Quarterly*, *15*(6), 857–880. doi:10.1016/j.leaqua.2004.09.001

de Ron, A. J. (1998). Sustainable production: The ultimate result of a continuous improvement. *International Journal of Production Economics*, *56-57*, 99–110. doi:10.1016/S0925-5273(98)00005-X

De Wall, B. M. E. (2013). User participation practice: To overcome the objective-subjective dichotomy. *IADIS International Journal of Computer Science & Information Systems*, *8*(1), 142–158.

Deetz, S. (2000). Discipline. In K. Grint (Ed.), *Work and society* (pp. 142–162). Polity.

Descartes, R. (1641). *Discourse on method and the meditations* (F. E. Sutcliffe, Trans.). Penguin Books.

Deutscher, G. (2016). *Through the Language Glass: Why the World Looks Different in Other Languages*. Cornerstone Digital.

Dewey, J. (1944). The Latter Works. *The American Scholar*, *14*(3), 276-80.

Dolphin, R. (2005). Internal Communications: Today's Strategic Imperative. *Journal of Marketing Communications*, *11*(3), 171–190. doi:10.1080/1352726042000315414

Durden, W. G. (2003). The Liberal Arts as a Bulwark of Business Education. *The Chronicle of Higher Education*, *49*(45).

Dwomoh, G., Luguterah, A. W., & Duah, S. B. (2020). Hoteliers' human resource strategies for business sustainability during COVID-19 pandemic in Ghana. *The Journal of Business and Retail Management Research*, *14*(3). Advance online publication. doi:10.24052/JBRMR/V14IS03/ART-04

Eagan, K., Stolzenberg, E. B., Ramirez, J. J., Aragon, M. C., Suchard, M. R., & Rios-Aguilar, C. R. (2016). The American Freshman: Fifty-Year Trends 1966-2015. Higher Education Research Institute Graduate School of Education & Information Studies University of California, Los Angeles.

Eek, F., Larsson, C., Wisén, A., & Ekvall Hansson, E. (2021). Self-Perceived Changes in Physical Activity and the Relation to Life Satisfaction and Rated Physical Capacity in Swedish Adults during the COVID-19 Pandemic—A Cross Sectional Study. *International Journal of Environmental Research and Public Health*, *18*(2), 671. doi:10.3390/ijerph18020671 PMID:33466860

Eisner, E. W. (1998). *The enlightened eye: Qualitative inquiry and the enlightenment of educational practice*. Prentice Hall.

Elg, U., Ghauri, P. N., & Tarnovskaya, V. (2008). The role of networks and matching in market entry to emerging retail markets. *International Marketing Review*, *25*(6), 674–699. doi:10.1108/02651330810915583

Eraut, M. (2003). *Developing Professional Knowledge And Competence*. Routledge.

Erkutlu, H. (2012). The impact of organizational culture on the relationship between shared leadership and team productivity. *Team Performance Management*, *18*(1-2), 102–119. doi:10.1108/13527591211207734

Evans, M. (2006). El proceso de toma de decisiones como un espacio para el aprendizaje en las organizaciones. Revista Ciencias Estratégicas, 14(16), 153-169.

Fabeil, N. F., Pazim, K. H., & Langgat, J. (2020). The impact of COVID-19 pandemic crisis on micro-enterprises: Entrepreneurs' perspective on business continuity and recovery strategy. *Journal of Economics and Business*, *3*(2). Advance online publication. doi:10.31014/aior.1992.03.02.241

Fain, P. (2019, August 2). Philosophy degrees and sales jobs. *Inside Higher Ed*. Retrieved from: https://www.insidehighered.com/news/2019/08/02/new-data-track-graduates-six-popular-majors-through-their-first-three-jobs

Fairhurst, G. T., & Connaughton, S. L. (2014). Leadership: A communicative perspective. *Leadership*, *10*(1), 7–35. doi:10.1177/1742715013509396

Faul, F., Erdfelder, E., Buchner, A., & Lang, A. G. (2014). *G*Power Version 3.1.9* [computer software]. Uiversität Kiel. Retrieved from https://www.gpower.hhu.de/en/html

Fausing, M. S., Joensson, T. K., Lewandowski, J., & Bligh, M. (2015). Antecedents of shared leadership: Empowering leadership and interdependence. *Leadership and Organization Development Journal*, *36*(3), 271–291. doi:10.1108/LODJ-06-2013-0075

Feldman, K. A., & Newcomb, T. M. (1969). *The impact of college on students*. Transaction Publishers.

Fernald, L. W., Solomon, G. T., & Tarabishy, A. (2005). A new paradigm: Entrepreneurial leadership. *Southern Business Review*, *30*(2), 1–10.

Fernández, L. (2014). *El comportamiento online del consumidor: factores que aumentan la actividad de búsqueda de ewom en el sector turístico* (Master's thesis). Universidad de Oviedo, Oviedo, España.

Ferrari, A., Witschel, H. F., Spagnolo, G. O., & Gnesi, S. (2018). Improving the quality of business process descriptions of public administrations. *Business Process Management Journal*, *24*(1), 49–66. doi:10.1108/BPMJ-05-2016-0096

Ferri-Reed, J. (2013). Onboarding strategies to supercharge millennial employees. *Journal for Quality and Participation*, *36*(2), 32–33.

Fetterman, D. (2019). *Ethnography: Step-by-Step*. SAGE Publications.

Filbeck, G., Hatfield, P., & Horvath, P. (2005). Risk aversion and personality type. *Journal of Behavioral Finance*, *6*(4), 170–180. doi:10.120715427579jpfm0604_1

Filion, L. J. (1988). *The strategy of successful entrepreneurs in small business: vision, relationships and anticipatory learning* (Doctoral dissertation). University of Lancaster.

Fischer, K. (2012, February 5). Bucking cultural norms, Asia tries liberal arts. *Chronicle of Higher Education*. Retrieved from http://chronicle.com/article/Bucking-Cultural-Norms-Asia/130667/

Fitzgerald, T., & Gunter, H. (2006). Teacher leadership: A new form of managerialism. *New Zealand Journal of Educational Leadership*, *21*(2), 44–57.

Florea, N. V., & Duica, A. (2017). Improving Communication and Relationship with Customers using Models to Measure their Value. *Valahian Journal of Economic Studies*, *8*(1), 47–56. doi:10.1515/vjes-2017-0006

Folsom, M. B. (1924). The organization of a statistical department. *Harvard Business Review*, *2*(2), 178–193.

Foucault, M. (1980). *Power/Knowledge: Selected interviews & other writings 1972-1977*. Pantheon Books.

Frank, M. C., Everett, D. L., Fedorenko, E., & Gibson, E. (2008). Number as a cognitive technology: Evidence from Pirahã language and cognition. *Cognition*, *108*(3), 819–824. doi:10.1016/j.cognition.2008.04.007 PMID:18547557

Freire, P. (2000). Pedagogy of the oppressed (30th ann. ed.). New York, NY: Continuum.

Frémeaux, S., & Michelson, G. (2017). The common good of the firm and humanistic management: Conscious capitalism and economy of communion. *Journal of Business Ethics*, *145*(4), 701–709. doi:10.100710551-016-3118-6

Friedman, M. (2009). *Capitalism and Freedom*. University of Chicago press.

Fritz, M., & Canavari, M. (2008). Management of perceived e-business risks in food-supply networks: E-trust as pre-requisite for supply-chain system innovation. *Agribusiness*, *24*(3), 355–368. doi:10.1002/agr.20163

Fromm, E. (2010). *On Disobedience: Why Freedom Means Saying "No" to Power*. HarperCollins Publishers.

Gagnon, S. (2008). Compelling identity: Selves and insecurity in global, corporate management development. *Management Learning*, *39*(4), 375–391. doi:10.1177/1350507608093710

Gallup-Perdue. (2014). *Measuring the Most Important Outcomes of Higher Education*. Retrieved July 01, 2020, from https://www.purdue.edu/newsroom/gallup/

Gandossy, R., & Sonnenfeld, J. (2005). "I see nothing, I hear nothing": Culture, corruption and apathy. *International Journal of Disclosure and Governance*, *2*(3), 228–243. doi:10.1057/palgrave.jdg.2040055

Gangal, A. (2014). Kan Khajura Tesan: The Full Story. *afaqs!* https://www.afaqs.com/news/story/41226_Kan-Khajura-Tesan-The-Full-Story

Gan, Y., & Cheung, F. M. (2010). From proactive personality to organizational citizenship behavior: Mediating role of harmony. *Psychological Reports*, *106*(3), 755–765. doi:10.2466/pr0.106.3.755-765 PMID:20712164

Garcia Zea, D., Sankar, S., & Isna, N. (2019). The impact of emotional intelligence in the military workplace. *Human Resource Development International*, 1–17.

García, M., & Lena, F. (2018). Aplicación del método Delphi en el diseño de una investigación cuantitativa sobre el fenómeno FABLAB. *EMPIRIA. Revista de Metodología de Ciencias Sociales*, 129-166.

Gardner, W. L., Cogliser, C. C., Davis, K. M., & Dickens, M. P. (2011). Authentic leadership: A review of the literature and research agenda. *The Leadership Quarterly*, *22*(6), 1120–1145. doi:10.1016/j.leaqua.2011.09.007

Gartner, W. (1985). A Conceptual Framework for Describing the Phenomenon of New Venture Creation. *Academy of Management Review, 10*(4), 696–706. doi:10.5465/amr.1985.4279094

Gawande, A. (2013). Slow Ideas: Some Innovations Spread Fast. How Do You Speed the Ones That Don't? *The New Yorker*. https://www.newyorker.com/reporting/2013/07/29/130729fa_fact_gawande

Gelles, D., & Yaffe-bellany, D. (2019, August 19). *Shareholder Value Is No Longer Everything, Top C.E.O.s Say.* Retrieved from https://www.nytimes.com/2019/08/19/business/business-roundtable-ceos-corporations.html?action=click &module=TopStories&pgtype=Homepage

George, D., & Mallery, P. (2016). *SPSS for Windows step by step: a simple guide and reference, 11.0 update* (14th ed.). Allyn and Bacon. doi:10.4324/9781315545899

Gerken, M. (2017). *On folk epistemology: How we think and talk about knowledge.* Oxford University Press. doi:10.1093/oso/9780198803454.001.0001

Ghiya, G. D. (2019). Promoting Spiritual Health and Holistic Wellness. *Journal of Health Management, 21*(2), 230–233. doi:10.1177/0972063419835104

Gibson, S., Baskerville, D., Berry, A., Black, A., Norris, K., & Symeonidou, S. (2017). Including students as co-enquirers: Matters of identity, agency, language and labelling in an international participatory research study. *International Journal of Educational Research, 81*, 108–118. doi:10.1016/j.ijer.2016.11.008

Gleiser, M. (2014). *The Island of knowledge: The limits of science and the search for meaning.* Basic Books.

Glimcher, P., Camerer, C., Fehr, R., & Polorack, R. (2009). Neuroeconomics: Decision making and the brain. Academic Press Publications.

Glimcher, P. W., & Rustichini, A. (2004). Neuroeconomics: The Consilience of Brain and Decision. *Science, 306*(5695), 447–452. doi:10.1126cience.1102566 PMID:15486291

Gochhayat, J., Giri, V. N., & Suar, D. (2017). Influence of Organizational Culture on Organizational Effectiveness: The Mediating Role of Organizational Communication. *Global Business Review, 18*(3), 691–702. doi:10.1177/0972150917692185

Gockel, C., & Werth, L. (2010). Measuring and modeling shared leadership: Traditional approaches and new ideas. *Journal of Personnel Psychology, 9*(4), 172–180. doi:10.1027/1866-5888/a000023

Godinic, D., Obrenovic, B., & Khudaykulov, A. (2020). Effects of economic uncertainty on mental health in the COVID-19 pandemic context: Social identity disturbance, job uncertainty and psychological well-being model. *Int. J. Innov. Econ. Dev, 6*(1), 61–74. doi:10.18775/ijied.1849-7551-7020.2015.61.2005

Goldenberg, E. N. (2001). Teaching Key Competencies in Liberal Arts Education. *New Directions for Teaching and Learning, 2001*(85), 85. doi:10.1002/tl.2

González, C. (2011). *Pymes mexicanas, incubadoras del desarrollo y crecimiento económico del México actual* (Unpublished bachelor's thesis). Universidad Autónoma de San Luis Potosí, San Luis Potosí, RP.

González, M. (2016). 31% del PIB nacional es aportado por mujeres empresarias. *Informa BTL.* Recovered from https://www.informabtl.com/31-del-pib-nacional-es-aportado-por-mujeres-empresarias/

Graham, P. A. (1974). *Community and Class in American Education, 1865–1918.* Wiley.

Green, L. (2003). Civil disobedience and academic freedom. *Osgoode Hall Law Journal, 41*(2/3), 381–405.

Grey, C. (2001). Re-imagining relevance: A response to Starkey and Madan. *British Journal of Management, 12*(Special Issue), S27–S32. doi:10.1111/1467-8551.12.s1.3

Gries, T., & Naudé, W. (2010). Entrepreneurship and structural economic transformation. *Small Business Economics, 34*(1), 13–29. doi:10.100711187-009-9192-8

Griffin, R. W., Phillips, J. M., & Gully, S. M. (2016). *Organizational Behavior: Managing People and Organizations*. Cengage Learning.

Griggs, R. A. (2017). Milgram's obedience study. *Teaching of Psychology, 44*(1), 32–37. doi:10.1177/0098628316677644

Groves, K. S., & LaRocca, M. (2010). *Leader ethical values as key antecedents to transformational and transactional leadership*. In Annual Meeting of Western Academy of Management, Kona, HI.

Guenther, K. (2003). Assessing Web Site Usability. *Online (Bergheim), 27*(2), 65–69.

Haas, D. F., & Deseran, F. A. (1981). Trust and symbolic exchange. *Social Psychology Quarterly, 44*(1), 3–13. doi:10.2307/3033857

Hakansson, N. H. (1969). Optimal Investment and Consumption Strategies under Risk, and Under Uncertain Lifetime and Insurance. *International Economic Review, 10*(3), 443–466. doi:10.2307/2525655

Hamel, G. (2008). The Future of Management. *Human Resource Management International Digest, 16*(6). doi:10.1108/hrmid.2008.04416fae.001

Hansen, C. J. (1995). Writing the project team: Authority and intertextuality in a corporate setting. *Journal of Business Communication, 32*(2), 103–122. doi:10.1177/002194369503200201

Hardt, H. (1993). Authenticity, communication, and critical theory. *Critical Studies in Mass Communication, 10*(1), 49–69. doi:10.1080/15295039309366848

Hargreaves, A., & Fink, D. (2008). Distributed leadership: Democracy or delivery? In A. Harris (Ed.), *Distributed leadership: Different perspectives*. Springer.

Harris, A. (2013). Distributed leadership: Friend or foe? *Educational Management & Leadership, 41*(5), 545–554. doi:10.1177/1741143213497635

Harris, H. (2001). Content analysis of secondary data: A study of courage in managerial decision making. *Journal of Business Ethics, 34*(3-4), 191–208. doi:10.1023/A:1012534014727

Hartley, D. (2009). Educational policy, distributed leadership and socio-cultural theory. *Educational Review, 61*(2), 139–150. doi:10.1080/00131910902844721

Hart, O., & Holmstrom, B. (2017). The Sveriges Riksbank Prize in Economic Sciences in Memory of Alfred Nobel, 2016. *The Scandinavian Journal of Economics, 119*(3), 487–488. doi:10.1111joe.12252

Harvard Business Review. (2007). *Six rules for effective forecasting*. Available at www.Hbr.org/2007/07.htmlAccessed on 11/04/2020

Hatch, M. J. (2018). *Organization Theory: Modern, Symbolic, and Postmodern Perspectives*. Oxford University Press.

Hedesström, T. M. (2006). *The psychology of diversification: Novice investors' ability to spread risks*. Academic Press.

Heide, M., von Platen, S., Simonsson, C., & Falkheimer, J. (2018). Expanding the Scope of Strategic Communication: Towards a Holistic Understanding of Organizational Complexity. *International Journal of Strategic Communication, 12*(4), 452–468. doi:10.1080/1553118X.2018.1456434

Heney, P. (2008). Managing employees takes a sense of style. *Hotel & Motel Management, 223*(13), 6.

Henri, J. F. (2010). The Periodic Review of Performance Indicators: An Empirical Investigation of the Dynamism of Performance Measurement Systems. *European Accounting Review, 19*(1), 73–96. doi:10.1080/09638180902863795

Hernández, M., Feijo, M., & Zarza, A. (2010). *Razón e intuición: prácticas en la toma de decisiones de las empresas de economías emergentes*. Tecnológico de Monterrey. Recovered from http://acacia.org.mx/busqueda/pdf/04_PF304_Toma_de_Decisiones.pdf

Hernández, R. (2020). *Layoffs during the COVID-19 Pandemic: Four Findings from WARN Act Data*. Academic Press.

Hernández-Murillo, R., &Krolikowski, P. (2020). Assessing Layoffs in Four Midwestern States during the Pandemic Recession. *Economic Commentary*.

Herrera, C. (2010). Commentary: Ethics and the rhetorical context of human research. *International Journal of Epidemiology, 39*(1), 12–16. doi:10.1093/ije/dyp400 PMID:20100822

Hess, D., & Fuller, C. (2017). *The Evolving Language of Conscious Capitalism*. Academic Press.

Hiller, N. J. (2002). *Understanding and measuring shared leadership in work teams*. Unpublished manuscript. University Park, PA: Pennsylvania State University.

Hinds, P., Liu, L., & Lyon, J. (2011). Putting the global in global work: An intercultural lens on the practice of cross-national collaboration. *The Academy of Management Annals, 5*(1), 135–188. doi:10.5465/19416520.2011.586108

Hindustan Unilever runs Bihar's most popular radio on mobile phones. (2014, Mar. 4). *The Economic Times*.

Hinkin, T. R., & Schriesheim, C. A. (2008). An examination of "nonleadership": From laissez-faire leadership to leader reward omission and punishment omission. *The Journal ofApplied Psychology, 93*(6), 1234–1248. doi:10.1037/a0012875 PMID:19025245

Hlupic, V. (2014). *The Management Shift: How to Harness the Power of People and Transform Your Organization For Sustainable Success*. Palgrave Macmillan. doi:10.1057/9781137352958

Hoch, J. E. (2014). Shared leadership, diversity, and information sharing in teams. *Journal of Managerial Psychology, 29*(5), 541–564. doi:10.1108/JMP-02-2012-0053

Hoch, J. E., & Kozlowski, S. W. (2014). Leading virtual teams: Hierarchical leadership, structural supports, and shared team leadership. *The Journal of Applied Psychology, 99*(3), 390–403. doi:10.1037/a0030264 PMID:23205494

Hodgkinson, G., & Starbuck, W. (2008). *The Oxford Handbook of Organizational Decision Making*. Oxford University Press. doi:10.1093/oxfordhb/9780199290468.001.0001

Hoegl, M., & Gemuenden, H. G. (2001). Teamwork quality and the success of innovative projects: A theoretical concept and empirical evidence. *Organization Science, 12*(4), 435–449. doi:10.1287/orsc.12.4.435.10635

Hofstede, G. (1980). Culture's consequences: International difference in work related values. *Sage (Atlanta, Ga.)*.

Hougaard, R. (2018). *The Real Crisis In Leadership*. Retrieved from https://www.forbes.com/sites/rasmushougaard/2018/09/09/the-real-crisis-in-leadership/#62e6fd173ee4

Howell, D. C. (2013). *Statistical methods for psychology* (8th ed.). Wadsworth Cengage Learning.

Hubberman, A. M., & Miles, M. B. (1994). *Qualitative data analysis*. Academic Press.

Hui-ying, M., & Jian-peng, W. (2013). The impact of shared leadership on innovation performance. *2013 International Conference on Management Science and Engineering 20th Annual Conference Proceedings*. 10.1109/ICMSE.2013.6586452

HUL plans to let other firms use its mobile marketing channel Kan Khajura Tesan. (n.d.). https://www.hul.co.in/news/news-and-features/2014/kan-khajura-tesan-sets-world-record.html

Humphreys, D., & Kelly, P. (2014). *How Liberal Arts and Sciences Majors Fare in Employment: a report on earnings and long-term career paths.* Association of American Colleges and Universities.

IBEF. (2018). *Indian Insurance Industry Analysis.* Retrieved from https://www.ibef.org/archives/industry/insurancereports/indian-insurance-industry-analysis-september-2018

Ilies, R., Morgeson, F. P., & Nahrgang, J. D. (2005). Authentic leadership and eudaemonic well-being: Understanding leader-follower outcomes. *The Leadership Quarterly*, *16*(3), 373–394. doi:10.1016/j.leaqua.2005.03.002

INEGI. (2009). *Censo Económico. Micro, pequeña, mediana y gran empresa.* Recovered from https://www.inegi.org.mx/est/contenidos/espanol/proyectos/censos/ce2009/default.asp?s=est&c=14220

Insmail, S., Malone, M., & Van, Y. (2014). *Organizaciones Exponenciales: Por qué existen nuevas organizaciones diez veces más escalables y rentables que la tuya (y qué puedes hacer al respecto).* Singularity University Book.

IRDAI. (2017). *Annual report 2016-17.* Author.

Isson, J. P., & Harriott, J. (2013). Effective analytics communication strategies. In Win with Advanced Business Analytics: Creating Business Value from Your Data (pp. 301-319). John Wiley & Sons.

Ivancevich, J., Konopaske, R., Donelly, J., & Gibson, J. (2006). *Organizações: Comportamento, estrutura e processos.* McGraw Hill.

Jackson, R. A., & Reboulet, A. M. (2019). Parlant de business: An application of combined probability theory to inherent and translation-induced semantic ambiguity. *International Journal of Trade, Economics and Finance*, *10*(6), 162–170.

Jagtap, S., & Kandachar, P. (2009). Towards Linking Disruptive Innovations and BOP Markets. In *DS 58-1: Proceedings of ICED 09, the 17th International Conference on Engineering Design The Design Society*. https://www.designsociety.org/publication/28611/towards_linking_disruptive_innovations_and_bop_markets

Jahan, S., & Mahmud, A. S. (2015). What is capitalism. *Finance & Development*, (June), 44–45.

James, L. (2018). *Big data and business analytics spend to reach US$260 billion in 2022.* https://www.technologyrecord.com/Article/big-data-and-business-analytics-spend-to-reach-us260-billion-in-2022-72124

James, P. G. (2017). Discourse analysis. In *The Routledge Handbook of Language and Dialogue* (pp. 62–77). Routledge. doi:10.4324/9781315750583-5

Jamshed, S. (2014). Qualitative research method-interviewing and observation. *Journal of Basic and Clinical Pharmacy*, *5*(4), 87–88. doi:10.4103/0976-0105.141942 PMID:25316987

Jarvenpaa, S. L., & Ives, B. (1994). The global network organization of the future: Information management opportunities and challenges. *Journal of Management Information Systems*, *10*(4), 25–57. doi:10.1080/07421222.1994.11518019

Jha, S. M. (2003). Services Marketing. Himalaya Publishing House.

Jiang, Y. G., & Guo, H. (2017). Transcending the nature of refinement: The policy development on liberal arts education in China. *Chinese Education & Society*, *50*(3), 268–283. doi:10.1080/10611932.2017.1331009

Johannisson, B., & Nilsson, A. (1989). Community entrepreneurs: Networking for local development. *Entrepreneurship and Regional Development*, *1*(1), 3–19. doi:10.1080/08985628900000002

Johansson, C. (2015). *Empowering employees through communicative leadership*. Academic Press.

Johansson, C., Miller, V. D., & Hamrin, S. (2014). Conceptualizing communicative leadership. *Corporate Communications*. Advance online publication. doi:10.1108/CCIJ-02-2013-0007

Johnston, J. S., Shaman, S., & Zemsky, R. (1988). *Unfinished Design: The Humanities and Social Sciences in Undergraduate Engineering Education*. Association of American Colleges.

Judge, T. A., & Piccolo, R. F. (2004). Transformational and transactional leadership: A meta-analytic test of their relative value. *The Journal of Applied Behavioral Science*, *89*(5), 755–768. doi:10.1037/0021-9010.89.5.755 PMID:15506858

Kacerauskas, T. (2016). The paradoxes of creativity management. *Ekonomie a Management*, *19*(4), 33–43. doi:10.15240/tul/001/2016-4-003

Kahneman, D., Slovic, S. P., Slovic, P., & Tversky, A. (Eds.). (1982). *Judgment under uncertainty: Heuristics and biases*. Cambridge university press. doi:10.1017/CBO9780511809477

Kalogiannidis, S. (2020). COVID Impact on Small Business. *International Journal of Social Science and Economics Invention*, *6*(12), 387. doi:10.23958/ijssei/vol06-i12/257

Kasyoka, M. (2017). *The Non-Linear Nature Of Software Development*. Retrieved from https://www.otbafrica.com/index.php/otb/item/192-the-non-linear-nature-of-software-development

Katz, D., & Kahn, R. L. (1978). *The social psychology of organizations* (2nd ed.). Wiley.

Kayworth, T. R., & Leidner, D. E. (2002). Leadership effectiveness in global virtual teams. *Journal of Management Information Systems*, *18*(3), 7–40. doi:10.1080/07421222.2002.11045697

Keller, L. R. (1989). Decision research with descriptive, normative, and prescriptive purposes – some comments. *Annals of Operations Research*, *19*(1-4), 485–487. doi:10.1007/BF02283536

Kelley, D. J., Peters, L., & O'Connor, G. C. (2009). Intra-organizational networking for innovation-based corporate entrepreneurship. *Journal of Business Venturing*, *24*(3), 221–235. doi:10.1016/j.jbusvent.2008.05.010

Kelly, J. (2013). *Satisfying Consumer Desires doesn't have to mean consumption*. Retrieved from Vancouver Sun: http://www.vancouversun.com/technology/satisfying+consumer+desires+doesn+have+mean+consumption/8623190/story.html

Kendrick, J. (2011). Transformational leadership changing individuals and social systems. *Professional Safety*, *56*(11), 14. https://www.assp.org/publications/professional-safety

Khademi, B. (2020). Ecosystem value creation and capture: A systematic review of literature and potential research opportunities. *Technology Innovation Management Review*, *10*(1), 16–34. doi:10.22215/timreview/1311

Khalsa, A. S. (2010). *Conscious Business: Based on the teachings on Yogi Bhajan*. Kundalini Research Institute.

Kheirbek, R. E., Beygi, S., Zargoush, M., Alemi, F., Smith, A. W., Fletcher, R. D., Seton, P. N., & Hawkins, B. A. (2015). Causal analysis of emergency department delays. *Quality Management in Health Care*, *24*(3), 162–166. doi:10.1097/QMH.0000000000000067 PMID:26115064

Killgore, W. D. (2017). *Refinement and Validation of a Military Emotional Intelligence Training Program*. University of Arizona Tucson United States.

Kimball, B. A. (1995). *Orators and philosophers: A history of the idea of liberal education.* College Entrance Board Examination.

Kimbrough, S., Chou, C., Chen, Y.-T., & Lin, H. (2014). On developing indicators with text analytics: Exploring concept vectors applied to English and Chinese texts. *Information Systems and e-Business Management, 12*(3), 385–415. doi:10.100710257-013-0228-x

Kimura, F., Thangavelu, S. M., Narjoko, D., & Findlay, C. (2020). Pandemic (COVID-19) policy, regional cooperation and the emerging global production network. *Asian Economic Journal, 34*(1), 3–27. doi:10.1111/asej.12198

Kirkman, B. L., Gibson, C. B., & Kim, K. (2012). Across borders and technologies: Advancements in virtual teams research. In S. W. J. Kozlowski (Ed.), *Oxford Handbook of Organizational Psychology* (Vol. 2, pp. 789–858). Oxford University Press.

Kirkman, B. L., & Mathieu, J. E. (2005). The Dimensions and Antecedents of Team Virtuality. *Journal of Management, 31*(5), 700–718. doi:10.1177/0149206305279113

Klein, H. J., Polin, B., & Leigh Sutton, K. (2015). Specific onboarding practices for the socialization of new employees. *International Journal of Selection and Assessment, 23*(3), 263–283. doi:10.1111/ijsa.12113

Kline, R. B. (2010). *Principles and practice of structural equation modeling* (3rd ed.). The Guilford Press.

Kloosterhuis, H. (2000). Analogy argumentation in law: A dialectical perspective. *Artificial Intelligence and Law, 8*(2/3), 173–187. doi:10.1023/A:1008385531494

Koblik, S., & Graubard, S. (2000). *The distinctively American: Residential liberal arts colleges.* Transaction Publishers.

Kofman, F. (2008). *Conscious business: How to build value through values* (Vol. 1). ReadHowYouWant.com.

Kohavi, R., Rothleder, N. J., & Simoudis, E. (2002). Emerging trends in business analytics. *Communications of the ACM, 45*(8), 45–48. doi:10.1145/545151.545177

Krennmayr, T. (2015). What corpus linguistics can tell us about metaphor in use in newspaper texts. *Journalism Studies, 16*(4), 530–546. doi:10.1080/1461670X.2014.937155

Kriger, N., Kaddour, A., Koenen, K., Kosheleva, A., Chen, J. T., Waterman, P. D., & Barbeau, E. M. (2011). Occupational, social, and relationship hazards and psychological distress among low-income workers: Implications of the 'inverse hazard law'. *Journal of Epidemiology and Community Health, 65*(3), 260–272. doi:10.1136/jech.2009.087387 PMID:20713372

Kuhn, T. S. (1996). *The structure of scientific revolutions* (3rd ed.). The University of Chicago Press. doi:10.7208/chicago/9780226458106.001.0001

Kumar, A., & Sharma, R. (2000). *Principles of Business Management.* Atlantic Publishers and Distributors.

Kumar, D., & Gupta, P. (2017). *Rural Marketing: Challenges and Opportunities.* Sage Publishing.

Kung, C. H., & Solvberg, A. (1986). Activity Modeling and Behavior Modeling. In *Proceedings of the IFIP WG 8.1 Working Conference on Comparative Review of Information Systems Design Methodologies: Improving the Practice,* (145-171). North-Holland.

Kuriyan, R., Ray, I., & Toyama, K. (2008). Information and Communication Technologies for Development: The Bottom of the Pyramid Model in Practice. *The Information Society, 24*(2), 93–104. doi:10.1080/01972240701883948

Kurpjuweit, S., Reinerth, D., Schmidt, C., & Wagner, S. (2019). Implementing visual management for continuous improvement: Barriers, success factors and best practices. *International Journal of Production Research, 57*(17), 5574–5588. doi:10.1080/00207543.2018.1553315

Kutschera, I., & Ryan, M. (2009). Implications of intuition for strategic thinking: Practical recommendations for gut thinkers. *S.A.M. Advanced Management Journal, 74*(3), 12–20.

Kyrlitsias, C., & Michael, G. D. (2018). Asch conformity experiment using immersive virtual reality. *Computer Animation & Virtual Worlds, 29*(5). doi:10.1002/cav.1804

Lahav, Y. (2020). Psychological distress related to COVID-19–the contribution of continuous traumatic stress. *Journal of Affective Disorders, 277*, 129–137. doi:10.1016/j.jad.2020.07.141 PMID:32818776

Lakuma, P. C., Sunday, N., Sserunjogi, B., Kahunde, R., &Munyambonera, E. F. (2020). *How has the COVID-19 Pandemic impacted Ugandan businesses? Results from a business climate survey*. Academic Press.

Lamb, T. A., & Alsikafi, M. (1980). Conformity in the Asch experiment: Inner-other directedness and the "defiant subject.". *Social Behavior and Personality, 8*(1), 13–16. doi:10.2224bp.1980.8.1.13

Lamm, R. L., & Everett, J. (2009). *Dynamic argument* (2nd ed.). Cengage Learning.

Larsen, K. S. (1974). Conformity in the Asch Experiment. *The Journal of Social Psychology, 94*(2), 303–304. doi:10.1080/00224545.1974.9923224

Lechner, C., Dowling, M., & Welpe, I. (2006). Firm networks and firm development: The role of the relational mix. *Journal of Business Venturing, 21*(4), 514–540. doi:10.1016/j.jbusvent.2005.02.004

Lee, P. C., Xu, S. T., & Yang, W. (2021). Is career adaptability a double-edged sword? The impact of work social support and career adaptability on turnover intentions during the COVID-19 pandemic. *International Journal of Hospitality Management, 94*, 102875. doi:10.1016/j.ijhm.2021.102875

Leibniz, G. W. (1989). Meditations on knowledge, truth, and ideas. In *Philosophical Papers and Letters* (pp. 291–295). Springer. doi:10.1007/978-94-010-1426-7_34

Leithwood, K., Mascall, B., & Strauss, T. (2009). *Distributed leadership according to the evidence*. Routledge. doi:10.4324/9780203868539

Leridon, H. (2020). World population outlook: Explosion or implosion? *Population et Sociétés*, (1), 1–4. doi:10.3917/popsoc.573.0001

Leroy, H., Segers, J., Van Dierendonck, D., & Den Hartog, D. (2018). Managing people in organizations: Integrating the study of HRM and leadership. *Human Resource Management Review, 28*(3), 249–257. doi:10.1016/j.hrmr.2018.02.002

Lewin, K. (2010). Defining the field at a given time. *Psychological Review, 50*(3), 292–310. doi:10.1037/h0062738

Liao, S.-K., & Chang, K.-L. (2009). Select televised sportscasters for Olympic Games by analytic network process. *Management Decision, 47*(1), 14–23. doi:10.1108/00251740910929678

Liao, S.-K., Chang, K.-L., & Tseng, T.-W. (2010). Optimal selection of program suppliers for TV companies using an analytic network process (ANP) approach. *Asia-Pacific Journal of Operational Research, 27*(6), 753–767. doi:10.1142/S0217595910002983

Linke, A., & Zerfass, A. (2011). Internal communication and innovation culture: Developing a change framework. *Journal of Communication Management (London), 15*(4), 332–348. doi:10.1108/13632541111183361

Lins, N. V., & Holanda, M. S. (2011). *Proposta de gestão visual da produção naval em estaleiros*. XXII COPINAVAL - Congresso Panamericano de Engenharia Naval, Transporte Marítmo e Portuária, Buenos Aires, Argentina.

Locker, K., & Kaczmarek, S. (2013). *Business Communication: Building Critical Skills*. McGraw-Hill Education.

Logan, J., & Curry, J. (2015). A Liberal Arts Education: Global Trends and Challenges. *Christian Higher Education, 14*(1-2), 66–79. doi:10.1080/15363759.2015.973344

Lo, K. D. (2018). Fritz J. Roethlisberger Memorial Award Goes to "Business Not as Usual: Developing Socially Conscious Entrepreneurs and Intrapreneurs". *Journal of Management Education, 42*(4), 564–566. doi:10.1177/1052562918778874

Lonardi, E. (2017). *Como afecta las emociones en la toma de decisiones en las empresas Pymes, estudio de caso: Heladerías Persicco* (Master's thesis). Universidad de Buenos Aires. Recovered from ybibliotecadigital.econ.uba.ar/download/tpos/1502-0226_LonardiE.pdf

Londoño, C., Herrera, E., & Peláez, L. (2011). Diferencias de género en la toma de decisiones. *Cultura, Educación y Sociedad*. Recovered from https://revistascientificas.cuc.edu.co/culturaeducacionysociedad/article/view/930

Looy, A., & Shafagatova, A. (2016). Business process performance measurement: a structured literature review of indicators, measures and metrics. *SpringerPlus, 5*(1797), 1-24.

Loué, C., & Baronet, J. (2012). Toward a new entrepreneurial skills and competencies framework: A qualitative and quantitative study. *International Journal of Entrepreneurship and Small Business, 17*(4), 455–477. doi:10.1504/IJESB.2012.050164

Loxton, M., Truskett, R., Scarf, B., Sindone, L., Baldry, G., & Zhao, Y. (2020). Consumer behaviour during crises: Preliminary research on how coronavirus has manifested consumer panic buying, herd mentality, changing discretionary spending and the role of the media in influencing behaviour. *Journal of Risk and Financial Management, 13*(8), 166. doi:10.3390/jrfm13080166

Lumby, J. (2013). Distributed leadership: The uses and abuses of power. *Educational Management Administration & Leadership, 41*(5), 581–597. doi:10.1177/1741143213489288

Lumby, J., & Morrison, M. (2010). Leadership and diversity: Theory and research. *School Leadership & Management, 30*(1), 3–17. doi:10.1080/13632430903509717

Lunenburg, F. C. (2010). Communication: The process, barriers, and improving effectiveness. *Schooling, 1*(1), 1–10.

MacDonald, D. B., & Ramagliann, J. A. (2004). Teaching International Business Law: A Liberal Arts Perspective. *Journal of Legal Studies Education, 22*(1), 39–64. doi:10.1111/j.1744-1722.2004.00010.x

Mackey, J. (2011). What conscious capitalism really is: A response to James O'Toole and David Vogel's "Two and a Half Cheers for Conscious Capitalism". *California Management Review, 53*(3), 83–90. doi:10.1525/cmr.2011.53.3.83

Maister, D. H. (2013). The psychology of waiting lines. Managing employee/customer interaction in service businesses. In J. A. Czepiel, M. R. Solomon, & C. F. Surprenant (Eds.), (pp. 113–123). Lexington Books.

Maniviesa, P. (2019). Diferencias entre la dirección empresarial femenina y masculina. *Pymerang*. Recovered from https://www.pymerang.com/direccion-de-negocios/funciones-del-director-general/liderazgo/505-diferencias-entre-la-direccion-empresarial-femenina-y-masculina

Manzi, C., Sorgente, A., Reverberi, E., Tagliabue, S., & Gorli, M. (2021). Double jeopardy-analyzing the combined effect of age and gender stereotype threat on older workers. *Frontiers in Psychology, 11*, 606690. doi:10.3389/fpsyg.2020.606690 PMID:33510682

Marken, A. (2020, January 5). *In U.S., Business Grads Lag Other Majors in Work Interest.* Retrieved July 01, 2020, from https://news.gallup.com/poll/177638/business-grads-lag-majors-work-interest.aspx

Markovic, M. R., & Salamzadeh, A. (2018). The importance of communication in business management. In *The 7th International Scientific Conference on Employment, Education and Entrepreneurship* (pp. 11-28). Belgrade, Serbia: Academic Press.

Markovic, M. R., & Salamzadeh, A. (2018). The Importance of Communication in Business Management. *Proceedings of the 7th International Scientific Conference on Employment, Education and Entrepreneurship*, 11-28.

Marques, J. (2013). Understanding the Strength of Gentleness: Soft-Skilled Leadership on the Rise. *Journal of Business Ethics, 116*(1), 163–171. doi:10.100710551-012-1471-7

Marques, J. C. (2017). Industry business associations: Self-interested or socially conscious? *Journal of Business Ethics, 143*(4), 733–751. doi:10.100710551-016-3077-y

Marshall, I. Jr. (2008). *Gestão da qualidade* (6th ed.). Editora FGV.

Martinez-Millana, A., Lizondo, A., Gatta, R., Vera, S., Salcedo, V. T., & Fernandez-Llatas, C. (2019). Process mining dashboard in operating rooms: Analysis of staff expectations with analytic hierarchy process. *International Journal of Environmental Research and Public Health, 16*(2), 1–14. doi:10.3390/ijerph16020199 PMID:30642000

Mastrangelo, L. M., Benitez, D. G., & Cruz-Ros, S. (2017). How social entrepreneurs can influence their employees' commitment. *Journal of Promotion Management, 23*(3), 437–448. doi:10.1080/10496491.2017.1294878

Masuoka, T. (2011). *Reaching the Base of the Pyramid through Inclusive Business Models, International Finance Corporation.* IFC.

Mayer, J. (2006). *Waiting on the world to change. On Continuum.* Columbia Records.

Mazzei, A. (2010). Promoting active communication behaviours through internal communication. *Corporate Communications, 15*(3), 221–234. doi:10.1108/13563281011068096

McAdam, R., Leonard, D., Henderson, J., & Hazlett, S.-A. (2008). A grounded theory research approach to building and testing TQM theory in operations management. *Omega, 36*(5), 825–837. doi:10.1016/j.omega.2006.04.005

McAnany, E. G. (2012). *Saving the world: A brief history of communication for development and social change.* University of Illinois Press. doi:10.5406/illinois/9780252036774.001.0001

McClesky, J. A. (2014). Situational, transformational, and transactional leadership and leadership development. *Journal of Business Studies Quarterly, 5*(4), 117–130. https://jbsq.org/wp-content/uploads/2014/06/June_2014_9.pdf

McCracken, L. M., Badinlou, F., Buhrman, M., & Brocki, K. C. (2020). Psychological impact of COVID-19 in the Swedish population: Depression, anxiety, and insomnia and their associations to risk and vulnerability factors. *European Psychiatry, 63*(1), e81. doi:10.1192/j.eurpsy.2020.81 PMID:32843115

McGuire, R. R. (1977). Speech acts, communicative competence and the paradox of authority. *Philosophy & Rhetoric, 10*(1), 30–45.

Mechenbier, M. X. (2011). Cheating the business template: Filling in the blanks. *Business Communication Quarterly, 74*(2), 192–195. doi:10.1177/1080569911404055

Mehmood, Q., Hamstra, M. R. W., Nawab, S., & Vriend, T. (2016). Authentic leadership and followers' in-role and extra-role performance: The mediating role of followers' learning goal orientation. *Journal of Occupational and Organizational Psychology, 89*(4), 877–883. doi:10.1111/joop.12153

Mello, C. H. (1998). *Auditoria contínua: Estudo de implementação de uma ferramenta de monitoramento para sistema de garantia da qualidade com base nas normas NBR ISO9000* (Dissertação de Mestrado). EFEI, Minas Gerais, Brazil.

Mendez, M. J., & Busenbark, J. R. (2015). Shared leadership and gender: All members are equal ... but some more than others. *Leadership and Organization Development Journal*, *36*(1), 17–34. doi:10.1108/LODJ-11-2012-0147

Merriman, P., Peters, K., Adey, P., Cresswell, T., Forsyth, I., & Woodward, R. (2017). Interventions on military mobilities. *Political Geography*, *56*, 44–52. doi:10.1016/j.polgeo.2016.11.003

Meuthel, M., Gehrlein, S., & Hoegl, M. (2012). Socio-demographic factors and shared leadership behaviors in dispersed teams: Implications for human resource management. *Human Resource Management*, *51*(4), 525–548. doi:10.1002/hrm.21488

Mezirow, J. (1990). How critical reflection triggers transformative learning. *Fostering Critical Reflection in Adulthood*, *1*(20), 1-6.

Mezirow, J. (2000). Learning as Transformation: Critical Perspectives on a Theory in Progress. The Jossey-Bass Higher and Adult Education Series. Jossey-Bass Publishers.

Mezirow, J., & Taylor, E. W. (Eds.). (2009). *Transformative learning in practice: Insights from community, workplace, and higher education*. John Wiley & Sons.

Mihai, R. L. (2017). Corporate Communication Management: A Management Approach. *Valahian Journal of Economic Studies*, *8*(2), 103–110. doi:10.1515/vjes-2017-0023

Milgram, S. (1963). Behavioral study of obedience. *Journal of Abnormal and Social Psychology*, *67*(4), 371–378. doi:10.1037/h0040525 PMID:14049516

Milgram, S. (1965). Some conditions of obedience and disobedience to authority. *Human Relations*, *18*(1), 57–76. doi:10.1177/001872676501800105

Mofijur, M., Fattah, I. R., Alam, M. A., Islam, A. S., Ong, H. C., Rahman, S. A., ... Mahlia, T. M. I. (2020). Impact of COVID-19 on the social, economic, environmental and energy domains: Lessons learnt from a global pandemic. *Sustainable Production and Consumption*.

Moher, D., Liberati, A., Tetzlaff, J., & Altman, D. G. (2009). Preferred reporting items for systematic reviews and meta-analyses: The PRISMA statement. *PLoS Medicine*, *6*(7), 1–6. doi:10.1371/journal.pmed.1000097 PMID:19621072

Mohr, P., Biele, G., & Heekeren, H. (2010). Neural Processing of Risk. *Journal of Neuroscience. Vol*, *30*(19), 6613–6619. doi:10.1523/JNEUROSCI.0003-10.2010 PMID:20463224

Monahan, T., & Fisher, J. A. (2010). Benefits of "Observer Effects": Lessons from the Field. *Qualitative Research*, *10*(3), 357–376. doi:10.1177/1468794110362874 PMID:21297880

Monica, B., & Balaş, R. (2014). Social media marketing to increase brand awareness. *Journal of Economic and Business Research*, *20*(2), 155–164.

Monin, N. (2004). *Management Theory: A Critical and Reflective Reading*. Routledge. doi:10.4324/9780203356814

Mori, K., & Arai, M. (2010). No need to fake it: Reproduction of the Asch experiment without confederates. *International Journal of Psychology*, *45*(5), 390–397. doi:10.1080/00207591003774485 PMID:22044061

Morreale, S. P., Osborn, M. M., & Pearson, J. C. (2000). Why communication is important: A rationale for the centrality of the study of communication. *JACA-ANNANDALE*, *1*, 1–25.

Motyka, B. (2018). Employee engagement and performance: A systematic literature review. *International Journal of Management and Economics*, *54*(3), 227–244. doi:10.2478/ijme-2018-0018

Mr. Zero. (2018). *A Pencil is tool for great creations! ZERO Pencil is non-toxic rustic wooden twig Pencil, which could planted after using it as Pencil!* [Facebook status update]. Retrieved from https://www.facebook.com/pg/mr.zero.ecas/posts/?ref=page_internal

Muganda, N., & Pillay, K. (2013). Forms of power, politics and leadership in asynchronous virtual project environment. *International Journal of Managing Projects in Business*, *6*(3), 457–484. doi:10.1108/IJMPB-11-2011-0075

Muis, K. R., Chevrier, M., & Singh, C. A. (2018). The role of epistemic emotions in personal epistemology and self-regulated learning. *Educational Psychologist*, *53*(3), 165–184. doi:10.1080/00461520.2017.1421465

Mumtaz, N., & Saqulain, G. (2020). Hospital and health administrator level barriers and priorities for national neonatal hearing screening in Pakistan: A thematic analysis. *Pakistan Journal of Medical Sciences*, *36*(5), 1036–1041. doi:10.12669/pjms.36.5.1965 PMID:32704285

Murata, K. (2019). On the role of Visual Management in the era of digital innovation. *Procedia Manufacturing*, *39*, 117–122. doi:10.1016/j.promfg.2020.01.246

Murmann, J. P., & Sardana, D. (2013). Successful entrepreneurs minimize risk. *Australian Journal of Management*, *38*(1), 191–215. doi:10.1177/0312896212444114

Nada, D. (2013). *Project approval decisions: exploring success factors* (PhD thesis). University of Calgary, Canada.

Nairn, A. (2020). What is with all the hate? A thematic analysis of New Zealanders' attitudes to the human rights commission's "Give nothing to racism" social marketing campaign. *New Zealand Sociology*, *35*(1), 97–122.

Nakara, W. A., Benmoussa, F. Z., & Jaouen, A. (2012). Entrepreneurship and social media marketing: Evidence from French small business. *International Journal of Entrepreneurship and Small Business*, *16*(4), 386–405. doi:10.1504/IJESB.2012.047608

Naquin, S., & Holton, E. III. (2006). Leadership and Managerial Competency Models: A Simplified Process and Resulting Model. *Advances in Developing Human Resources*, *8*(2), 144–165. doi:10.1177/1523422305286152

NarayananS.SahaS. (2020). Urban food markets and the lockdown in India. SSRN 3599102.

Năstase, P., & Stoica, D. (2011). A new business dimension – Business analytics. *Accounting & Management Information Systems*, *9*(4), 603–618.

Nedzinskaite-Maciumiene, R., & Merkyte, S. (2019). Shared leadership of teachers through their interpersonal communication competence. *Acta-Paedagogica-Vilnensia, 42,* 85-98. doi:10.15388/ActPaed.42.6

Neem, J. (2019, August 13). *Abolish the Business Major!* Retrieved from https://www.chronicle.com/interactives/2019-08-13-abolish-the-business-major

Neese, M., & Kong, S. M. (2007). Driving lean through the visual factory: Visual instructions offer the simplicity employees need. *Circuits Assembly*.

Nelson, C. A. (1958). Liberal Arts in Management. *Harvard Business Review*, *36*, 91–99.

Neubert, M. J., & Taggar, S. (2004). Pathways to informal leadership: The moderating role of gender on the relationship of individual differences and team member network centrality to informal leadership emergence. *The Leadership Quarterly*, *15*(2), 174–194. doi:10.1016/j.leaqua.2004.02.006

Nguyen, T., Zhou, L., Spiegler, V., Ieromonachou, P., & Lin, Y. (2018). Big data analytics in supply chain management: A state-of-the-art literature review. *Computers & Operations Research*, *98*, 254–264. doi:10.1016/j.cor.2017.07.004

Niederman, F., & Tan, F. B. (2011). Managing global IT teams: Considering cultural dynamics. *Communications of the ACM*, *54*(4), 24–27. doi:10.1145/1924421.1924431

Nisha, K. M., & Khan, M. A. (2016). Leveraging economy through MSMEs: Recent trends and challenges of women's entrepreneurship in south India. *Journal of Entrepreneurship. Management & Innovation*, *12*(4), 127–149.

Normore, A. H. (Ed.). (2016). *Handbook of research on effective communication, leadership, and conflict resolution*. IGI Global. doi:10.4018/978-1-4666-9970-0

O'Leary, M. B., & Mortensen, M. (2010). Go con(figure): Subgroups, imbalance, and isolates in geographically dispersed teams. *Organization Science*, *21*(1), 115–131. doi:10.1287/orsc.1090.0434

O'Malley, M., & Baker, W. F. (2019). *Organizations for People: Caring Cultures, Basic Needs, and Better Lives*. Stanford Business Books. doi:10.1515/9781503611054

Ogar, E. C. V., Okuta, A. J., Okon, E. E., & Odama, A. J. (2021). Assessment of the Socioeconomic Impact of COVID-19 Pandemic on Small and Medium Scale Business Enterprises: Nigerian Youths in Perspective. *Journal of World Economic Research*, *10*(1), 18–27.

Okcu, V. (2014). Relation between secondary school administrators' transformational and transactional leadership style and skills to diversity management in the school. *Educational Sciences: Theory and Practice*, *14*(6), 2162–2174. doi:10.12738/estp.2014.6.2128

Okorochkova, A. A. (2017). Corporate social responsibility in the era of "conscious capitalism". *Russian Entrepreneurship*, *18*(7), 1253–1272.

Olson, M. D. (2018). Exploring military social work from a social justice perspective. *International Social Work*, *61*(1), 119–129. doi:10.1177/0020872815606792

Ornatowski, C. M. (1998). 2+2=5 if 2 is large enough. *Journal of Business and Technical Communication*, *12*(3), 316–342. doi:10.1177/1050651998012003003

Orwell, G. (2001). *Nineteen Eighty-Four*. The Folio Society.

Ostas, D. T. (2010). Civil disobedience in a business context: Examining the social obligation to obey inane laws. *American Business Law Journal*, *47*(2), 291–312. doi:10.1111/j.1744-1714.2010.01095.x

Packer, C. L., & Suski, C. (2013). *Gestão à vista na produção como ferramenta de trabalho*. Inova.

Palmer, T. G. (Ed.). (2011). *The morality of capitalism: what your professors won't tell you*. Jameson Books.

Pamp, F. (1955). Liberal Arts as Training for Business. *Harvard Business Review*, *33*(3), 42–50.

Paradies, Y., Chandrakumar, L., Klocker, N., Frere, M., Webster, K., Burrell, M., & McLean, P. (2009). *Building on our strengths: A framework to reduce race-based discrimination and promote diversity in Victoria*. Victorian Health Promotion Foundation.

Parks, R., & Thambusamy, R. (2017). Understanding Business Analytics Success and Impact: A Qualitative Study. *Information Systems Education Journal*, *15*(6), 43–55.

Parung, C. A. (2019). How do the Indonesian ecologically conscious millennials value upcycled clothing? *IOP Conference Series. Materials Science and Engineering*, *703*(1), 012031. doi:10.1088/1757-899X/703/1/012031

Passini, S., & Morselli, D. (2013). The triadic legitimacy model: Understanding support to disobedient groups. *New Ideas in Psychology*, *31*(2), 98–107. doi:10.1016/j.newideapsych.2012.06.002

Pearce, C. L., Hoch, J. E., Jeppesen, H. J., & Wegge, J. (2010). New forms of management: Shared and distributed leadership in organizations. *Journal of Personnel Psychology*, *9*(4), 151–153. doi:10.1027/1866-5888/a000022

Pearce, C. L., Manz, C. C., & Sims, H. P. (2014). *Share, don't take the lead.* Information Age.

Pearce, C. L., & Sims, H. P. (2002). Vertical versus shared leadership as predictors of the effectiveness of chance management teams: An examination of aversive, directive, transactional, transformational, and empowering leader behaviors. *Group Dynamics*, *6*(2), 172–197. doi:10.1037/1089-2699.6.2.172

Pérez, Y., & Coutín, A. (2005). La gestión del conocimiento: un nuevo enfoque en la gestión empresarial. *ACIMED*, *13*(6). Recovered from http://scielo.sld.cu/scielo.php?script=sci_arttext&pid=S1024-94352005000600004&lng=es&tlng=es

Perry, G., Brannigan, A., Wanner, R. A., & Stam, H. (2020). Credibility and incredulity in Milgram's obedience experiments: A reanalysis of an unpublished test. *Social Psychology Quarterly*, *83*(1), 88–106. doi:10.1177/0190272519861952

Perry, M. L., Pearce, C. L., & Sims, H. P. Jr. (1999). Empowered selling teams: How shared leadership can contribute to selling team outcomes. *Journal of Personal Selling & Sales Management*, *19*(3), 35–51. doi:10.1080/08853134.1999.10754180

Pew Research Center. (2016). *The State of American Jobs: How the shifting economic landscape is reshaping work and society and affecting the way people think about the skills and training they need to get ahead.* Author.

Pierce, A. J. (2015). Authentic identities. *Social Theory and Practice*, *41*(3), 435–457. doi:10.5840octheorpract201541323

Pillay, S. S., & Sisodia, R. S. (2011). *A case for conscious capitalism: Conscious leadership through the lens of brain science*. Ivey Business Journal.

Pink, D. H. (2011). *Drive: The Surprising Truth About What Motivates Us*. Riverhead Books.

Pizzagalli, L., Sharma, A., & Lascu, D.-N. (2018). Marketing at the Bottom of the Pyramid: Serving, and in the Service of Low-Income Consumers. *Innovative Marketing*, *14*(2), 35–40. doi:10.21511/im.14(2).2018.04

Plowman, K. D., & Willson, C. (2018). Strategy and Tactics in Strategic Communication: Examining their Intersection with Social Media Use. *International Journal of Strategic Communication*, *12*(2), 125–144. doi:10.1080/1553118X.2018.1428979

Polacinski, E. (2012). *Implantação dos 5Ss e proposição de um SGQ para uma indústria de erva-mate. Gestão Estratégica: Empreendedorismo e Sustentabilidade*. Congresso Internacional de Administração.

Pollack, J. (2007). The changing paradigms of project management. *International Journal of Project Management*, *25*(3), 266–274. doi:10.1016/j.ijproman.2006.08.002

Pollman, E. (2019). Corporate oversight and disobedience. *Vanderbilt Law Review*, *72*(6), 2013–2046.

Poppendieck, M. (2007). *Implementing Lean Software Development*. Addison-Wesley.

Porter-O'Grady, T., & Wilson, C. K. (1995). *The leadership revolution in health care: Altering systems, changing behaviors*. Aspen Publishers, Inc.

Prahalad, C. K. (2004). *The fortune at the base of the pyramid.* Wharton School Publishing.

Pruzan, P. (2001). Corporate reputation: Image and identity. *Corporate Reputation Review*, *4*(1), 50–64. doi:10.1057/palgrave.crr.1540132

Purvanova, R. K., & Bono, J. E. (2009). Transformational leadership in context: Face-to-face and virtual teams. *The Leadership Quarterly*, *20*(3), 343–357. doi:10.1016/j.leaqua.2009.03.004

PwC and CII. (2018). *Leveraging customer persona for insurance in a digital era*. Available at https://www.pwc.in/assets/pdfs/publications/2018/leveraging-customer-persona-for-insurance-in-a-digital-era.pdf

PWC. (2019). Competing *in a new age of insurance: How India is adopting emerging technologies. CII.* Available at https://www.pwc.in/assets/pdfs/consulting/financial-services/competing-in-a-new-age-of-insurance.pdf

Qiu, W., Rutherford, S., Mao, A., & Chu, C. (2017). The pandemic and its impacts. *Health, Culture and Society (Pittsburgh, Pa.)*, *9*, 1–11. doi:10.5195/HCS.2017.221

Quarry, W., & Ramirez, R. (2009). *Communication for Another Development: Listening before Telling*. Zed Books. doi:10.5040/9781350219274

Queirós, A., Faria, D., & Almeida, F. (2017). Strengths and Limitations of Qualitative and Quantitative Research Methods. *European Journal of Education Studies*, *3*(9), 369–387.

Queiroz, M. M., Ivanov, D., Dolgui, A., & Wamba, S. F. (2020). Impacts of epidemic outbreaks on supply chains: Mapping a research agenda amid the COVID-19 pandemic through a structured literature review. *Annals of Operations Research*, 1–38. PMID:32836615

Rabin, M. (1998). Psychology and Economics. *Revista de Economic Literature*, *36*(1), 11–46.

Rahim, A., & Bonoma, T. V. (1979). Managing organizational conflict: A model for diagnosis and intervention. *Psychological Reports*, *44*(3, suppl), 1323–1344. doi:10.2466/pr0.1979.44.3c.1323

Rahman, M. (2014). Advertising to bottom of the pyramid consumers: Descriptive analysis of CSR advertising. *Review of Enterprise and Management Studies*, *1*(2), 63–69.

Ramthun, A. J., & Matkin, G. S. (2012). Multicultural shared leadership: A conceptual model of shared leadership in culturally diverse teams. *Journal of Leadership & Organizational Studies*, *19*(3), 303–314. doi:10.1177/1548051812444129

Randazzo, C. (2012). Positioning resumes and cover letters as reflective-reflexive process. *Business Communication Quarterly*, *75*(4), 377–391. doi:10.1177/1080569912459267

Rangel, A. S., Silva, M. M., & Costa, B. K. (2010). Competitividade da indústria têxtil Brasileira. *Revista de Administração e Inovação*, *7*(1), 151–174.

Rashid, M., Caine, V., & Goez, H. (2015). The Encounters and Challenges of Ethnography as a Methodology in Health Research. *International Journal of Qualitative Methods*, *14*(5), 1–16. doi:10.1177/1609406915621421

Raupp, J., & Hoffjann, O. (2012). Understanding strategy in communication management. *Journal of Communication Management (London)*, *16*(2), 146–161. doi:10.1108/13632541211217579

Ray, D. M. (1993). Understanding the entrepreneur: Entrepreneurial attributes, experience and skills. *Entrepreneurship and Regional Development*, *5*(4), 345–358. doi:10.1080/08985629300000022

Rennstam, J., & Kärreman, D. (2020). Understanding control in communities of practice: Constructive disobedience in a high-tech firm. *Human Relations*, *73*(6), 864–890. doi:10.1177/0018726719843588

Riach, K., & Wilson, F. (2007). Don't screw the crew: Exploring the rules of engagement in organizational romance. *British Journal of Management*, *18*(1), 79–92. doi:10.1111/j.1467-8551.2006.00503.x

Richards, K., & Pilcher, N. (2016). An individual subjectivist critique of the use of corpus linguistics to inform pedagogical materials. *Dialogic Pedagogy*, *4*, A122–A141. doi:10.5195/dpj.2016.163

Ritter, R. J. (2003). Behavioral Finance. *Pacific Basin Finance Journal, 2*(14), 429-437.

Robertson, L. (2005). The cost of missed opportunities. *Strategic Communication Management*, *9*(3), 5.

Rodd, P., & Sanders, K. (2018). The imperative of critical pedagogy in times of cultural austerity: A case study of the capacity to reimagine education as a tool for emancipation. *New Zealand Sociology*, *33*(3), 33.

Rogowska, A. M., Kuśnierz, C., & Bokszczanin, A. (2020). Examining anxiety, life satisfaction, general health, stress and coping styles during COVID-19 pandemic in Polish sample of university students. *Psychology Research and Behavior Management*, *13*, 797–811. doi:10.2147/PRBM.S266511 PMID:33061695

Rose, D. M., & Gordon, R. (2015). Age-related cognitive changes and distributed leadership. *Journal of Management Development*, *34*(3), 330–339. doi:10.1108/JMD-07-2013-0094

Rothman, L., De Vijlder, F., Schalk, R., & Van Regenmortel, M. (2019). A systematic review on organizational empowerment. *The International Journal of Organizational Analysis*, *27*(5), 1336–1361. doi:10.1108/IJOA-02-2019-1657

Routhieaux, R. L. (2015). Shared leadership and its implications for nonprofit leadership. *Journal of Nonprofit Education & Leadership*, *5*(3), 139–152.

Rowley, J. (2002). Using case studies in research. *Management Research News*, *25*(1), 16–27. doi:10.1108/01409170210782990

Rukavishnikov, V. O., & Pugh, M. (2018). Civil-military relations. In *Handbook of the Sociology of the Military* (pp. 123–143). Springer. doi:10.1007/978-3-319-71602-2_7

Sadhak, H. (2009). *Life Insurance in India: Opportunities, Challenges and Strategic Perspective*. SAGE Publications India.

Sadler, E., & Shefy, E. (2004). The intuitive executive: Understanding and applying 'gut feel' in decision-making. *The Academy of Management Executive*, *18*(4), 76–91. doi:10.5465/ame.2004.15268692

Sahlin, J., & Angelis, J. (2019). Performance management systems: Reviewing the rise of dynamics and digitalization. *Cogent Business & Management*, *6*(1), 1–21. doi:10.1080/23311975.2019.1642293

Salah, S., Carretero, J. A., & Rahim, A. (2009). Six Sigma and Total Quality Management (TQM): Similarities, differences and relationship. *International Journal of Six Sigma and Competitive Advantage*, *5*(3), 237–250. doi:10.1504/IJSSCA.2009.028095

Salamzadeh, Y., Bidaki, V. Z., & Vahidi, T. (2018). Strategic thinking and organizational success: Perceptions from management graduates and students. *Global Business and Management Research*, *10*(4), 1–19.

Salinas, O. (2001). *La experiencia como conocimiento de la empresa*. Gestiopolis. Recovered from https://www.gestiopolis.com/experiencia-como-conocimiento-empresa/

Salloch, S., Wäscher, S., Vollmann, J., & Schildmann, J. (2015). The normative background of empirical-ethical research: First steps towards a transparent and reasoned approach in the selection of an ethical theory. *BMC Medical Ethics*, *16*(20), 1–9. doi:10.118612910-015-0016-x PMID:25889221

Sánchez, R. (2017). *Utilización de las TICs en la toma de decisiones de modo colaborativo* (Tesis de ingenería). Universidad de Valladolid. Recovered from https://uvadoc.uva.es/bitstream/handle/10324/23051/TFG-G2347.pdf;jsessionid=CCDC5F2838507A48AC7F932505CCCC4F?sequence=1

Sanfey, A. G., Loewenstein, G., McClure, S. M., & Cohen, J. D. (2006). Neuroeconomics: Cross-Currents in Research on Decision-Making. *Trends in Cognitive Sciences, 10*(3), 108–116. doi:10.1016/j.tics.2006.01.009 PMID:16469524

Sarka, H. (2014). Tools of Internal Communication from Knowledge Transfer Perspective. *Journal of Competitiveness, 6*(4), 50–62. doi:10.7441/joc.2014.04.04

Sartre, J.-P. (1994). *Being and Nothingness*. Gramercy Books.

Sava, T. (2016). From Plato to Swift and Orwell, from utopia to dystopia. *Journal of Humanistic and Social Studies, 7*(1), 9–16.

Savin-Baden, M., & Major, C. H. (2013). *Qualitative Research: The Essential Guide to Theory and Practice. In Qualitative Research: The Essential Guide to Theory and Practice*. Routledge.

Saxena, G. (2005). Relationships, networks and the learning regions: Case evidence from the Peak District National Park. *Tourism Management, 26*(2), 277–289. doi:10.1016/j.tourman.2003.11.013

Schivardi, F., & Guido, R. (2020). *A simple method to estimate firms' liquidity needs during the COVID-19 crisis with an application to Italy*. Academic Press.

Schneider, A. B. (2015). The liberal arts in business education: Perspectives of a multi-time CEO. *Jesuit Higher Education, 4*(2), 108–116.

Schonert-Reichl, K. A., & Roeser, R. W. (Eds.). (2016). *Handbook of mindfulness in education: Integrating theory and research into practice*. Springer. doi:10.1007/978-1-4939-3506-2

Schultz, B. (2006). Business documents don't have to be boring. *Business Communication Quarterly, 69*(4), 407–410. doi:10.1177/108056990606900411

Schumpeter, J. A. (2000). Entrepreneurship as innovation. *Entrepreneurship: The Social Science View*, 51-75.

Schwartz, N. (2000). Emotion, Cognition and Decision Making'. *Cognition and Emotion, 14*(4), 433–430. doi:10.1080/026999300402745

Scott, B. R. (2009). *The concept of capitalism*. Springer Science & Business Media. doi:10.1007/978-3-642-03110-6

Sebastião, S. P., Zulato, G., & Trindade, A. D. (2017). Internal communication and organisational culture: The management interplay in the view of the Portuguese communication consultant. *Public Relations Review, 43*(4), 863–871. doi:10.1016/j.pubrev.2017.05.006

Seeger, S., & Davison-Vecchione, D. (2019). Dystopian literature and the sociological imagination. *Thesis Eleven, 155*(1), 45-63. doi:10.1177/0725513619888664

Selmeczy, D., & Dobbins, I. G. (2014). Relating the content and confidence of recognition judgments. *Journal of Experimental Psychology. Learning, Memory, and Cognition, 40*(1), 66–85. doi:10.1037/a0034059 PMID:23957366

Sha, A., Mehrotra, P., & Marathe, A. (2019). *India Insurance going from teens to twenties*. Boston Consulting Group. Available at http://ficci.in/spdocument/23133/BCG-FICCI-Report-October-2019.PDF

Shannon, C. E. (1948). A Mathematical Theory of Communication. *The Bell System Technical Journal, 27*(3), 379–423. doi:10.1002/j.1538-7305.1948.tb01338.x

Sharma, R. L., & Arora, M. (2015). Communication as the mainstay of entrepreneurial leadership: A conceptual framework. *Management Dynamics, 15*(2).

Sharma, M., Luthra, S., Joshi, S., & Kumar, A. (2021). Accelerating retail supply chain performance against pandemic disruption: Adopting resilient strategies to mitigate the long-term effects. *Journal of Enterprise Information Management*. Advance online publication. doi:10.1108/JEIM-07-2020-0286

Sharp, H., Dittrich, Y., & de Souza, C. (2016). The Role of Ethnographic Studies in Empirical Software Engineering. *IEEE Transactions on Software Engineering*, *42*(8), 786–804. doi:10.1109/TSE.2016.2519887

Sheang Lee, K., Hua Lim, G., Jiuan Tan, S., & Hou Wee, C. (2001). Generic marketing strategies for small and medium-sized enterprises- conceptual framework. *Journal of Strategies Marketing*, *9*.

Sheridan, S., & Williams, P. (2011). Developing Individual Goals, Shared Goals, and the Goals of Others: Dimensions of Constructive Competition in Learning Contexts. *Scandinavian Journal of Educational Research*, *55*(2), 145–164. do i:10.1080/00313831.2011.554694

Shiller, R. J. (2000). *Irrational Exuberance*. Princeton University Press.

Silva, A., Roratto, L., Servat, M. E., Dorneles, L., & Polacinski, E. (2013). *Gestão da qualidade: Aplicação da ferramenta 5W2H como plano de ação para projeto de abertura de uma empresa*. Horizontina.

Silva, J. N., & Loos, M. J. (2017). Proposta de implementação da gestão à vista no auxílio à produtividade. *Revista Espacios*, *38*(27), 34–46.

Simanis, E., & Milstein, M. (2012). Back to Business Fundamentals: Making "Bottom of the Pyramid" Relevant to Core Business. *Field Actions Science Reports*, *2012*(4). https://journals.openedition.org/factsreports/1581

Simmons, E. L. (2018). Vocation for planetary citizenship: Lutheran liberal arts education in the Anthropocene. *Dialog*, *57*(2), 99–106. doi:10.1111/dial.12389

Simon, H. (1990). Invariants of human behavior. *Annual Review of Psychology*, *41*(1), 1-20.

Simon, H. (1957). *Administrative behavior*. Cambridge Univ Press.

Simons, R., Dávila, A., & Kaplan, R. S. (2000). *Performance measurement & control systems for implementing strategy*. Prentice Hall.

Simpson, S., Fischer, B. D., & Rohde, M. (2013). The conscious capitalism philosophy payoff: A qualitative and financial analysis of conscious capitalism corporations. *Journal of Leadership, Accountability and Ethics*, *10*(4), 19–29.

Sisodia, R. S. (2013). Understanding the performance drivers of conscious firms. *California Management Review*, *55*(3), 87–96. doi:10.1525/cmr.2013.55.3.87

Sitthiwarongchai, C., Wichayanuparp, W., Chantakit, P., & Charoenboon, P. (2020). Impact of organization's leadership style on motivation of its employees. *Systematic Reviews in Pharmacy*, *11*(3), 48–56.

Slater, L. (2008). Pathways to building leadership capacity. *Educational Management Administration & Leadership*, *36*(1), 55–69. doi:10.1177/1741143207084060

Small, E. E., & Rentsch, J. R. (2010). Shared leadership in teams: A matter of distribution. *Journal of Personnel Psychology*, *9*(4), 203–211. doi:10.1027/1866-5888/a000017

Smith, G. T. (2017). *The Impact of Socially Conscious Initiative Announcements on Coffee Company Stock Values*. Academic Press.

Smith, A. (1759). *The Theory of Moral Sentiments* (D. D. Raphael & A. L. Macfie, Eds.). doi:10.1093/oseo/instance.00042831

Smith, A. (1778). *An Inquiry Into the Nature and Causes of the Wealth of Nations: By Adam Smith...*. Strahan.

Smith, M. (1950). The communicative act. *The Journal of Social Psychology, 31*(2), 271–281. doi:10.1080/00224545.1950.9919012

Snyder, H. (2019). Literature review as a research methodology: An overview and guidelines. *Journal of Business Research, 104*, 333–339. doi:10.1016/j.jbusres.2019.07.039

Sokolic, D., Mrak, M. K., & Vretenar, N. (2017). Business management tools and firm performance. In *4th International Multidisciplinary Scientific Conference on Social Sciences and Arts – SGEM* (pp. 139-146). Sofia, Bulgaria: Academic Press.

Sookermany, A., Meyer, E. L., & Last, D. M. (2017). Military Sciences–The Backbone of Military Educational Institutions? *Book of abstracts ISMS 2017.*

Sosik, J., Chun, J., & Zhu, W. (2014). Hang on to your ego: The moderating role of leader narcissism on relationships between leader charisma and follower psychological empowerment and moral identity. *Journal of Business Ethics, 120*(1), 65–80. doi:10.100710551-013-1651-0

Soutphommasane, T. (2013). Anti-racism on the job: Tackling discrimination in employment and the workplace. *Proctor*, 42-44.

Souza, R. P., Hékis, H. R., Ribeiro, R. M., & Valentim, R. A. (2014). Avaliação e monitoramento de processos de produção utilizando recurso da gestão à vista em uma grande indústria do setor têxtil no estado do Rio Grande do Norte. *Revista de Administração e Inovação, 11*(1), 162–180. doi:10.5773/rai.v1i1.1142

Speroff, B. J. (1953). Empathy and role-reversal as factors in industrial harmony. *The Journal of Social Psychology, 37*(1), 117–120. doi:10.1080/00224545.1953.9921876

Speroff, B. J. (1955). Empathy and role-reversal as factors in communication. *The Journal of Social Psychology, 41*(1), 163–165. doi:10.1080/00224545.1955.9714259

Spitzberg, B., & Changnon, G. (2009). Conceptualizing intercultural competence. In D. Deardorff (Ed.), *The Sage handbook of intercultural competence* (pp. 2–52). Sage.

Stagnaro, C., & Piotrowski, C. (2014). Shared leadership: A critical component in IT project management. *Journal of Technology Research.*

Stare, A. (2013). Agile project management – a future approach to the management of projects? *Dynamic Relationship Management Journal, 1*(2), 43–53. doi:10.17708/DRMJ.2013.v02n01a04

Stoddard, G. (1974). *The outlook for American education.* Southern Illinois University Press.

Strong, M. (2011). What are the Limits to Conscious Capitalism? A Response to James O'Toole and David Vogel's "Two and a Half Cheers for Conscious Capitalism". *California Management Review, 53*(3), 109–117. doi:10.1525/cmr.2011.53.3.109

Styhre, A. (2009). The phantom menace: Conducting practitioner-informed research without losing academic liberties. In J. W. Cox, T. G. LeTrent-Jones, M. Voronov, & D. Weir (Eds.), *Critical management studies at work: Negotiating tensions between theory and practice* (pp. 29–39). Edward Elgar Publishing. doi:10.4337/9781848449497.00009

Suleman, F. (2007). *O valor das competências: um estudo aplicado ao sector bancário.* Horizonte.

Sunarsi, D., Suryani, N. L., & Jati, W. (2020). COVID-19 Pandemic Analysis Toward Productivity Giving Layoffs Effect in The Company of Industrial Sector around South Tangerang. *ProsidingICoISSE, 1*(1), 472–481.

Swiss Re Institute. (2018). *Sigma 03/2018: World insurance in 2017: solid, but mature life markets weigh on growth.* Available on https://www.swissre.com/institute/research/sigma-research/sigma-2018-03.html

Tabachnick, B. G., & Fidell, L. S. (2013). *Using multivariate statistics* (6th ed.). Allyn and Bacon.

Tallant, J. (2017). *Truth and the World: An Explanationist Theory*. Routledge. doi:10.4324/9781315143491

Taneja, S., & Toombs, L. (2014). Putting a face on small businesses: Visibility, viability, and sustainability the impact of social media on small business marketing. *Academy of Marketing Studies Journal*, *18*(1), 249.

Tarafdar, M., Anekal, P., & Singh, R. (2012). Market development at the bottom of the pyramid: Examining the role of information and communication technologies. *Information Technology for Development*, *18*(4), 311–331. doi:10.1080/02681102.2012.690172

Thaler, R. H. (1999). Mental accounting matters. *Journal of Behavioral Decision Making*, *12*(3), 183–206. doi:10.1002/(SICI)1099-0771(199909)12:3<183::AID-BDM318>3.0.CO;2-F

Thigpen, P. (2011). Can We Find Another Half a Cheer? A Response to James O'Toole and David Vogel's "Two and a Half Cheers for Conscious Capitalism". *California Management Review*, *53*(3), 118–123. doi:10.1525/cmr.2011.53.3.118

Think with Google report. (2018). https://www.thinkwithgoogle.com/consumer-insights/

Thorelli, H. B. (1986). Networks: Between markets and hierarchies. *Strategic Management Journal*, *7*(1), 37–51. doi:10.1002mj.4250070105

Tonkin, L. (1998). *Effective visual management: Bring excellence into sharper focus*. LTC.

Torghabehi, Y., Maki, A., Kurczewski, K., & Abdekhodaee, A. (2016). Visual management, performance management and continuous improvement: A lean manufacturing approach. *International Journal of Lean Six Sigma*, *7*(2), 187–210. doi:10.1108/IJLSS-09-2014-0028

Tracey, J., & Hinkin, T. (1998). Transformational leadership or effective managerial practices? *Group & Organization Management*, *23*(3), 220–236. doi:10.1177/1059601198233002

Trenery, B., & Paradies, Y. (2012). Organizational assessment: An overlooked approach to managing diversity and addressing racism in the workplace. *Journal of Diversity Management*, *7*(1), 11–26. doi:10.19030/jdm.v7i1.6932

Trochim, W. M. K. (2001). *The research methods knowledge base*. Atomic Dog Publishing.

Troy, L. C., Hirunyawipada, T., & Paswan, A. K. (2008). Cross-Functional Integration and New Product Success: An Empirical Investigation of the Findings. *Journal of Marketing*, *72*(6), 132–146. doi:10.1509/jmkg.72.6.132

Tucker, B., & Russell, R. (2004). The influence of the transformational leader. *Journal of Leadership & Organizational Studies*, *10*(4), 103–111. doi:10.1177/107179190401000408

Tufte, E. R. (1983). *The Visual Display of Quantitative Information*. Graphics.

Turismo Algarve. (2018). *Balanço turístico do ano 2018*. https://www.turismodoalgarve.pt/pt/noticias/7512/algarve-consolida-resultados-turisticos-em-2018.aspx#prettyPhoto

Tuzovic, S., & Kabadayi, S. (2020). The influence of social distancing on employee well-being: A conceptual framework and research agenda. *Journal of Service Management*. Advance online publication. doi:10.1108/JOSM-05-2020-0140

Tversky, A., & Kahneman, D. (1974). Judgment under uncertainty: Heuristics and biases. *Science*, *185*(4157), 1124–1131. doi:10.1126cience.185.4157.1124 PMID:17835457

Udry, C. (1994). Risk and Insurance in a Rural Credit Market: An Empirical Investigation in Northern Nigeria. *The Review of Economic Studies*, *61*(3), 495–526. doi:10.2307/2297901

UNESCO. (2001). *Artesanías creadoras*. París: UNESCO, Sección de Artesanías y Diseño.

Van Dooremalen, T. (2017). The pros and cons of researching events ethnographically. *Ethnography*, *18*(3), 415–424. doi:10.1177/1466138117709293 PMID:29081715

Van Gaans, M. (2018). *What is Management 3.0?* Retrieved from https://wuwei-inst.org/management-3-0-what-is-it-all-about/

Van Roosmalen, R. (2017). Doing It! AL Nuland, The Netherlands: Agile Strides.

Vercic, A. T., & Vokic, N. P. (2017). Engaging employees through internal communication. *Public Relations Review*, *43*(5), 885–893. doi:10.1016/j.pubrev.2017.04.005

Vogel, P., & Fischler-Strasak, U. (2014). Fostering sustainable innovation within organizations. In *Sustainable entrepreneurship* (pp. 191–205). Springer. doi:10.1007/978-3-642-38753-1_13

Vonnegut, K. (2006). *Player Piano*. The Dial Press.

Voss, C. (2018). Conscious Leaders Practicing Conscious Capitalism: Developing Conscious Leadership in Business. In Academy of Management Proceedings (Vol. 2018, No. 1, p. 12886). Briarcliff Manor, NY: Academy of Management.

Wachowicz, T. (2010). Decision support in software supported negotiations. *Journal of Business Economics & Management*, *11*(4), 576–597.

Wallace, N. (2020). Conscious Leadership: Moving to an Intentional Focus for a Thriving Workplace Culture. *Leader to Leader*, *2020*(97), 53–57. doi:10.1002/ltl.20512

Walsham, G., & Sahay, S. (2006). Research on information systems in developing countries: Current landscape and future prospects. *Information Technology for Development*, *12*(1), 1, 7–24. doi:10.1002/itdj.20020

Wang, D., Waldman, D., & Zhang, Z. (2014). A meta-analysis of shared leadership and team effectiveness. *The Journal of Applied Psychology*, *99*(2), 181–198. doi:10.1037/a0034531 PMID:24188392

Ward, T., & Dagger, T. (2017). The complexity of relationship marketing for service customers. *Journal of Services Marketing*, *21*(4), 281–290. doi:10.1108/08876040710758586

Waring, T. (2009). Emancipatory practice and information systems implementation: An action research project in an NHS acute trust. In J. W. Cox, T. G. LeTrent-Jones, M. Voronov, & D. Weir (Eds.), *Critical management studies at work: Negotiating tensions between theory and practice* (pp. 40–63). Edward Elgar Publishing. doi:10.4337/9781848449497.00010

Watson, G., & Berkley, R. (2009). Testing the value-pragmatics hypothesis in unethical compliance. *Journal of Business Ethics*, *87*(4), 463–476. doi:10.100710551-008-9953-3

Waweru, N. M., Munyoki, E., & Uliana, E. (2008). The effects of behavioral factors in Nairobi Stock Exchange. *International Journal of Business and Emerging Markets*, *1*(1), 24–41. doi:10.1504/IJBEM.2008.019243

Webster, J., & Watson, R. T. (2002). Analyzing the past to prepare for the future: Writing a literature review. *Management Information Systems Quarterly*, *26*(2), xiii–xxiii.

Weick, K. E. (1979). *The social psychology of organizing* (2nd ed.). Addison-Wesley Publishers.

Weick, K. E. (1995). *Sensemaking in organizations*. Sage Publications, Inc.

Wei, F., Li, Y., Zhang, Y., & Liu, S. (2018). The interactive effect of authentic leadership and leader competency on followers' job performance: The mediating role of work engagement. *Journal of Business Ethics*, *153*(3), 763–773. doi:10.100710551-016-3379-0

White, S. K. (2000). *Sustaining affirmations: The strengths of weak ontology in political theory*. Princeton University Press.

Whorf, B. L. (1956). Science and Linguistics. In J. B. Carrol (Ed.), *Language Thought, and Reality: Selected Writings of Benjamin Lee Whorf*. MIT Press.

Wiecek, W. M., & Hamilton, J. L. (2014). Beyond the Civil Rights Act of 1964: Confronting structural racism in the workplace. *Louisiana Law Review*, *74*, 1095–1160.

Wiesner, P. (2000). The office walls. *ColoradoBiz*, *27*(8), 9.

Williams-Klotz, D. N., & Gansemer-Topf, A. M. (2017). Identifying the camouflage: Uncovering and supporting the transition experiences of military and veteran students. *Journal of the First-Year Experience & Students in Transition*, *29*(1), 83–98.

Wills, S. (2013). *Insight management: A new profession*. Insight Management Academy.

Wilson, S. (2014). *A design for life: An hour with Alain de Botton*. Delloite Insights. Retrieved from https://www2.deloitte.com/insights/us/en/deloitte-review/issue-14/dr14-design-for-life.html

Wishart, J. (2020). *How to Manage and Coordinate Successful Cross-Functional Teams*. Retrieved from https://www.rhythmsystems.com/blog/dos-and-donts-of-coordinating-cross-functional-teams

Witt, U. (2007). Firms as realizations of entrepreneurial visions. *Journal of Management Studies*, *44*(7), 1125–1140. doi:10.1111/j.1467-6486.2007.00731.x

Wood, M. S. (2005). Determinants of shared leadership in management teams. *International Journal of Leadership Studies*, *1*(1), 64–85.

World Economic Forum. (2017). *Annual Meeting 2017*. http://www3.weforum.org/docs/WEF_AM17_Overview.pdf

Wright, A. (2019). Embodied organizational routines: Explicating a practice understanding. *Journal of Management Inquiry*, *28*(2), 153–165. doi:10.1177/1056492617713717

WTO. (2018). *World trade report 2018*. https://www.wto.org/english/res_e/publications_e/world_trade_report18_e.pdf

X. (1926). The management aspect of the comptroller's work. *Harvard Business Review*, *5*(1), 21-26.

Xu, N., Chiu, C., & Treadway, D. C. (2019). Tensions between diversity and shared leadership: The role of team political skill. *Small Group Research*, *50*(4), 507–538. doi:10.1177/1046496419840432

Yaari, M. E. (1965). Uncertain Lifetime, Life Insurance, and the Theory of the Consumer. *The Review of Economic Studies*, *32*(2), 137–150. doi:10.2307/2296058

Yangzom, C., & Singh, J. S. K. (2019). Ecologically Conscious Buying Behaviour of Organic Products: A Quantitative Study in Thimpu, Bhutan. *Malaysian Journal Of Consumer and Family Economics*, *22*(1), 92–113.

Yanik, B. (2017). An Ethnographic Approach to Education: What Are You Doing in This Village? *Journal of Education and Practice*, *8*(26), 113–118.

Yarimoglu, E., & Binboga, G. (2019). Understanding sustainable consumption in an emerging country: The antecedents and consequences of the ecologically conscious consumer behavior model. *Business Strategy and the Environment*, *28*(4), 642–651. doi:10.1002/bse.2270

Yeoh, P.-L. (2009). Earning the doctoral degree: An example of relationship marketing. *Advances in International Marketing*, *8*(19), 109–117.

Yeomans, L. (2007). Effective Internal Communication. *Journal of Communication Management (London)*, *11*(1), 90–91. doi:10.1108/13632540710726012

Yik, L., & Chin, J. F. (2019). Application of 5S and Visual Management to improve shipment preparation of finished goods. *IOP Conference Series. Materials Science and Engineering*, *530*, 012039. Advance online publication. doi:10.1088/1757-899X/530/1/012039

Yin, R. K. (2017). *Case study research and applications: Design and methods*. Sage Publications.

Yukl, G. (2010). *Leadership in organizations* (7th ed.). Prentice Hall.

Yukl, G. (2012). Effective Leadership Behavior: What We Know and What Questions Need More Attention. *The Academy of Management Perspectives*, *26*(4), 66–85. doi:10.5465/amp.2012.0088

Yukl, G., & Mahsud, R. (2010). Why flexible and adaptive leadership is essential. *Consulting Psychology Journal*, *62*(2), 81–93. doi:10.1037/a0019835

Yunus, M., & Jolis, A. (2007). *Banker to the Poor: Micro-lending and the Battle Against World Poverty*. Public Affairs.

Zamyatin, Y. (2016). *We*. McAllister Editions.

Zeglat, D. (2017). The Impact of Employee Motivation on Organizational Commitment. *European Journal of International Management*, *9*(15), 134–145.

Zhang, X., Qian, J., Wang, B., Jin, Z., Wang, J., & Wang, Y. (2017). Leaders' Behaviors Matter: The Role of Delegation in Promoting Employees' Feedback-Seeking Behavior. *Frontiers in Psychology*, *8*, 1–10. doi:10.3389/fpsyg.2017.00920 PMID:28638357

Zheng, L., Miao, M., & Gan, Y. (2020). Perceived control buffers the effects of the COVID-19 pandemic on general health and life satisfaction: The mediating role of psychological distance. *Applied Psychology. Health and Well-Being*, *12*(4), 1095–1114. doi:10.1111/aphw.12232 PMID:32955170

Zhou, S., & Yang, P. (2020). Risk management in distributed wind energy implementing Analytic Hierarchy Process. *Renewable Energy: An International Journal*, *150*, 616–623.

Zhou, W., Vredenburg, D., & Rogoff, E. G. (2015). Informational diversity and entrepreneurial team performance: Moderating effect of shared leadership. *The International Entrepreneurship and Management Journal*, *11*(1), 39–55. doi:10.100711365-013-0274-3

Zsolnai, L. (2017). *Ecologically Conscious Leadership*. Academic Press.

About the Contributors

Ross Jackson has a doctorate degree in applied management and decision sciences from Walden University, and a Master's in applied economics and a Bachelor of Business Administration from Ohio University. He is an Assistant Professor of Business at Wittenberg University in Springfield, Ohio. He is also a founding partner of Jacoulet, a consulting firm focused on analytics-based strategy development. He has over twenty years of experience as a Defense Analyst with the Department of the Air Force. He is the author or coauthor of several articles including: The Spectacle of Analysis: Analytics as Organizational Propaganda, (Forest Hills, New York: The Institute of General Semantics, 2016) and Following Instructions: Results and Implications from a Comparative Analysis of Air Force Instruction Corpora for Acquisition, Logistics, and Personnel, (Cincinnati, Ohio: INFORMS, 2018). His current research interests include linguistic and existential facets of the military-industrial complex and the intersectionality among analysis, data visualization and détournement. Dr. Jackson is an Associate Editor for the International Journal of Responsible Leadership and Ethical Decision-Making.

Amanda M. Reboulet has a master's degree in Operations Research from the Air Force Institute of Technology (2017), Wright-Patterson Air Force Base, OH and a master's in Business Administration (2010), a Bachelor of Science in Business (2008) and a Bachelor of Arts in French (2008) from Wright State University, Dayton, OH. She is a founding partner of Jacoulet, a consulting firm focused on analytics-based strategy development. Ms. Reboulet's current research interests include accession planning, marketing analytics, and the integration of analytic solutions with business decision-making.

* * *

Fernando Luís Almeida has a Ph.D. in Computer Science Engineering from the Faculty of Engineering of University of Porto (FEUP). He also holds an MSc in Innovation and Entrepreneurship and in Informatics Engineering from FEUP. He has around 10 years of teaching experience at higher education levels in the field of computer science and management. He has also worked for 15 years in several positions as a software engineer and project manager for large organizations and research centers like Critical Software, CICA/SEF, INESC TEC, and ISR Porto. He is a founder member of the International Association of Innovation Professionals and he is involved in the development of the US TAG group for ISO 56000 (Innovation Management). His current research areas include innovation policies, entrepreneurship, software development, and decision support systems.

Kate Andrews teaches in the area of research including both quantitative and qualitative methodologies. She also provides mentorship for doctoral students working on their DBA projects. She has been teaching for over 20 years, and has been the recipient of the prestigious Faculty of the Year accolade from a large university. In addition, Dr. Andrews spent 18 years as an engineering program manager and 10 years as an organizational consultant. Her research areas of interest include job satisfaction, leadership, and training and development. Dr. Andrews has expertise in all areas of organizational behavior including executive coaching, leadership development, performance management, and group dynamics in working in teams. Her experience in the United States includes professor in statistics, research, systems, counseling, communication, motivation, and leadership. Dr. Andrews has developed numerous university graduate courses. She spent 2 years in Israel working for the government and then 8 years in Romania where she conducted a research project with teenage girls who were orphaned, and they needed to learn to function independently. Through the humanitarian organization she founded, she served as a consultant with the Roma population on writing business plans and grants. Additionally, Dr. Andrews created an APA Learning Center for a large university and speaks nationally on doctoral research, APA, and graduate level writing. She edits doctoral projects for format and coherence with university standards. In addition to teaching, she currently works as a leadership consultant and research director.

Manpreet Arora is an Assistant Professor of Management in the School of Commerce and Management Studies, Central University of Himachal Pradesh Dharamshala, India. With around eighteen years of teaching experience she has varied interest areas. A Gold medalist at undergraduate and postgraduate levels, she obtained her Ph.d in International Trade from Himachal Pradesh University, Shimla. Her areas of research interest include Accounting and Finance, Strategic Management, Entrepreneurial Leadership, Qualitative Research and Communication Skills and Microfinance. She has been guiding research at the doctoral level and has worked in the area of Microfinance. As an active seminarian, she has attended more than hundred seminars/ conferences, and has visited several universities and colleges to deliver invited talks on Finance, Strategic Management, Business Communication, Interpersonal skills, Entrepreneurship and Skill Development. She is a motivational speaker and conducts workshops on communication and motivation. Having published more than 20 papers in various journals of national and international repute, she has also worked as content developer of MHRD e-PG Pathshala Project. She has written twenty book chapters in national as well as international books/ handbooks. With four edited books in her credit she is a persistent researcher in the field of Management. She is an active social worker also and is working towards the protecting the rights of women.

Ian Corrie is a Principal Lecturer of Transformative Learning & Healthcare Leadership at the Institute of Health. Learning, Education & Development Research Centre. He is also an Honorary Colonel in the British Army.

Eduardo Espinheira is a Human Manager, Change Igniter, Instructor, Speaker, and Management Consultant with a track record of happier customers. He leverages organizations to become more predictable and achieve operational excellence through people engagement, change management along with standards or best-practices adoption. He is an M3.0 facilitator, holds a PMP Certification and academic degrees in Computer Engineering and Business Management. He is the creator of the Management Bug & Fix concepts and author of the Machiavellian PM Character.

Silvia Fernandes is Assistant Professor at the Faculty of Economics of the University of Algarve. She holds a PhD from this university and is member of the Cinturs (Research Centre for Tourism, Sustainability and Well-being). She lectures Information Technology, Innovation Economics and Entrepreneurship in undergraduate and master courses. She has several publications in books, journals, and communications in national/international conferences in themes such as: information systems, tourism development, innovation, emergent technologies, etc.

Punam Gupta, an expert in linguistics, has taught English speaking and writing to a generation of undergraduate students. She has also written a number of books on English grammar. She has conducted highly acclaimed workshops on value education and gender sensitization programmes over the years. A successful parent, her son is an alumni of Harvard University, and is a doctor who practices functional medicine.

Catherine Hayes is Professor of Health Professions Pedagogy and Scholarship at the University of Sunderland and Tenth Anniversary Visiting Professor of Higher Education Pedagogic Practice at the University of Cumbria, UK. She is a National Teaching Fellow and Principal Fellow of the UK Higher Education Academy.

Dinesh Kumar is Associate Professor at Jagran Lakecity University, Bhopal. He has taught at leading business schools in India and abroad, and presented papers internationally. He has published extensively. He has written four major books on marketing by international publishers. He is the author of Marketing Channels (2012) and Consumer Behavior (2015), both published by Oxford University Press. His book The Connected Consumer (2016) has been published by Business Expert Press, New York. His last book is Rural Marketing, published by Sage in 2018. At present he is working on another book, "Marketing in the Digital Era" which goes beyond digital marketing techniques to show how marketing can gain from going digital, and how.

Paula Martins is assistant professor at the Faculty of Science and Technology, University of Algarve. She holds a PhD from IST (Lisbon) and is member of the Cinturs (Research Centre for Tourism, Sustainability and Well-being). She lectures Computer systems in undergraduate and master courses. She has several publications in books, journals, and communications in national/international conferences in themes related with computer systems, process management, process improvement, etc.

Auslyn Nieto has extensive experience in vocational rehabilitation counseling, and was nominated for the National Distinguished Service Award for Medical and Vocational Rehabilitation (Library of Congress Number: 86.51240). After laudatory achievements as owner of a leading private rehabilitation firm in Southern California, Dr. Nieto wrote successful grants at nonprofit agencies while managing a federally funded employment and training program for mature individuals, and concurrently taught bilingual classes in healthy lifestyle changes through improved eating habits for the Kidshape Foundation. In addition to governmental and nonprofit service, Dr. Nieto facilitates online classes and chairs dissertation committees at a leading for-profit university, a corollary of her academic proclivities both in the U.S. and South America. Dr. Nieto's academic history includes an undergraduate degree in French and Spanish from Fordham University, an advanced degree in vocational rehabilitation counseling from New York University, and a doctorate in higher educational administration from Capella University. Her most recent research findings on doctoral mentoring were published in the Journal of Psychological Issues In Organizational Culture in 2016. As corporate education director, Dr. Nieto develops curricula on nutrition and wellness in coordination with industry leaders. Her most recent accomplishment is the attainment of certification in Evidence-Based Optimal Nutrition: A Quest for Proof from the Harvard School of Public Health.

Pinaki Nandan Pattnaik is Head of the Centre for Management Studies at Nalsar University of Law in Hyderabad, India. He holds a PhD from National Law University in Odisha, India, and he holds two MBA degrees: one from University of Saskatchewan in Saskatoon, Canada, and the other from Maastricht School of Management in the Netherlands. His research interests are in the area of understanding the impact of law in the success and failure of university spinoffs in particular and businesses in general. He also has a keen interest in the area of intellectual property law, its efficiency and impact on businesses, and the spirit of entrepreneurship.

Eugene Petrie possesses superb technical expertise in information technology, with experience facilitating technology initiatives and processes resulting in project improvements. He excels in planning, implementing, and leveraging emerging technologies, and is dedicated to managing resources responsibly through engagement and best practices in areas of management, organizational behavior, research and evaluation, e-business, critical thinking, and problem solving.

Toby Rowland is a Brigadier in the British Army and is currently leading the Defence Medical Academy which is based in Staffordshire, UK.

Roshan Lal Sharma is a Professor in the Department of English, Central University of Himachal Pradesh, Dharamshala, Himachal Pradesh (India). He has been a Fulbright Senior Research Fellow at the University of Wisconsin-Madison (USA) besides being an Honorary Fellow at the Institute for Research in the Humanities (IRH) at UW-Madison during 2007-08. He has authored Raja Rao's Shorter Fiction (Rawat, 2009), Walt Whitman – A Critical Evaluation (Vrinda, 2000); co-authored Som P. Ranchan: Dialogue Epic in Indian English Poetry (Pencraft International, 2012); and co-edited Mapping Diaspora Identities: India and Beyond (2017), He has co-edited Communication in Contemporary Scenario (Anamika 2017), Communication, Entrepreneurship and Finance: Renegotiating Diverse Perspectives (2018), and Envisioning Effective Management Communication (2019), Communication Perspectives in Modern Businesses (Anamika, 2020). He has more than sixty published papers and book chapters to his credit on mystical poetry, Indian Writing in English, comparative literature, literary and cultural theory, folk theatre, and diverse dimensions of communication. He is a member of the editorial board of Review of International American Studies (RIAS), a peer-reviewed international journal. As a bi-lingual translator, he has translated Som P. Ranchan's folk ballad Shirgul Parmar: Ek Adhunik Lokgatha (2008) into Hindi. Two of his translated stories from Hindi to English namely Mridula Garg's "The Girl who Weighed Three Kilos" and Manjul Bhagat's "Rubble" were published by Sahitya Akademi, New Delhi in Vignettes (2018).As a bilingual poet, he has published The Unsaid and Other Poems (2018) and Mount Karol and Other Poems (2008), along with Shabd-Shabd Anugoonj (2017) and Lahar Lahar Bahav Aur Anya Kavitayen (2008) in Hindi.

Monica Shrivastava is an experienced Associate Professor with a demonstrated history of working in the education management industry. She is Skilled in Lecturing, Educational Technology, Instructional Design, and Curriculum Development. Strong education professional with a Doctor of Philosophy - PhD focused in Human Resources Management/Personnel Administration. Interest areas include Change Management, Human Resource, Organizational Development and Database Management.

Mahendra Kumar Shukla is an Assistant Professor in the area of Marketing Analytics at Department of Management Studies of NALSAR University of Law. He holds a PhD from Xavier University Bhubaneswar, India. His research interests are in the area of Sustainability, Marketing, Consumer behavior, marketing channels and product management.

Index

P

Q

R

S

T

V

W

www.ingramcontent.com/pod-product-compliance
Lightning Source LLC
LaVergne TN
LVHW062155300926
849161LV00010B/2675